Beyond The
RAINBOW

May His
Miracles in your
Life be many!
In His Love,

Move we

Alexander-Af...

Beyond The
RAINBOW

Mara Lee Alexander-Azlin

WINEPRESS WP PUBLISHING

Printed in the United States of America

Packaged by WinePress Publishing, PO Box 428, Enumclaw, WA 98022. The views expressed or implied in this work do not necessarily reflect those of WinePress Publishing. Ultimate design, content, and editorial accuracy of this work are the responsibilities of the author.

Unless otherwise noted all scriptures are taken from the Holy Bible, Revised Standard Version. Copyright © 1946, 1952, 1971 by the Division of Christian Education of the National Council of the Churches of Christ in the U.S.A. Used by permission.

A Parting Gift, Copyright © 1982, by
Frances Sharkey, M. D. Reprinted
by permission of the author.
All rights reserved by the author.

ISBN 1-57921-257-3
Library of Congress Catalog Card Number: 99-67519

To the glory of the only God,
who does not watch us from a distance,
but shapes our lives with loving hands,
and weaves them together in wondrous ways.

Acknowledgments

Some people leave "hug prints" on your heart,
and you are never the same.

Special thanks to the thousands of donors and volunteers who gave unselfishly to find a donor for Uriah; because of your efforts, many others have a chance to live.

This book would not have been possible without the encouragement of Trinky Brisco, Margot Johnson, Julie Maly, Stephanie McHargue, and Linda Bryson.

With deep gratitude, the tireless work and support of the Correctional Peace Officers Foundation is noted.

Expert reporting done by Palo Verde Valley Times, The Press-Enterprise, The Fontana Herald News, the San Bernardino County Sun, and the Inland Valley Daily Bulletin brought attention to Uriah's plight. By their gracious permission, excerpts from their fine articles enrich this book.

Coverage by television stations KECY, KCBS, KABC, KTVN, and Mountain Area Productions is gratefully acknowledged.

Information aired on radio KJMB and KLRD was, and is, greatly appreciated.

Thanks are also due CPO Family, The Hemoglobe, The Peacekeeper, Chuckawalla Chatter, Zion Lutheran Times, and Frances Sharkey, M.D., for permission to reprint excerpts from their publications.

The expertise and amiable aid of Tammy Hopf and the WinePress Publishing team were invaluable.

But most of all, this book could not have been written without God's gift of a special little boy: Uriah.

Contents

Roped to the Stirrup
(July 1982–Aug. 1983)

"How are you going to? . . . Never mind."

TWO WEEKS BEFORE THE BABY WAS DUE, I FELL ON MY PARENTS' patio, chasing a dog that had knocked over two-year-old Shiloh. I didn't want to land on the baby, so I fell on my right side. Immediate pain shot up my leg. Unable to stand, I yelled for help. I was a little heavier than when Don carried me over the threshold, but my tall, dark, handsome hero gently toted me into the house and laid me on the couch. Nana brought ice for my ankle, which was already swelling.

I winced. "Thanks, Mom."

"That's a good sign," she observed, an uncharacteristic frown furrowing her brow. "Usually, if it swells it isn't broken."

"I hope you're right."

After half an hour, it hurt worse. Don called the emergency room.

Though Don drove carefully, the slightest bump caused agony. I tried to focus on something other than pain. *I'm worried about the baby. It hasn't moved.*

A doctor opened the door, still giving instructions to the nurse for the previous patient. He rushed over and moved my ankle a little. "It's only a sprain. Keep ice on it, and take it easy for a few days." He swept out the door.

For three days I lay on the couch, watching Shiloh and four-year-old Heather play. Nana and my sister Debbie came to help with chores. Debbie was almost my twin: I was born on her first birthday. Her long, dark hair, framing hazel eyes, was like my own. Sometimes people didn't realize there were two of us until they saw us together.

I gazed at the red and purple that mottled my ankle. *If it's only sprained, it won't make it worse if I walk on it,* I thought. *The baby's due in a couple weeks, and I'll have to walk then.* I pulled myself to my feet and inched toward the kitchen, but grinding bones convinced me to make a sudden U-turn. I made an appointment with our doctor.

"I'm sending you for an X-ray."

"Won't it be dangerous for the baby?"

"It won't hurt the baby because it's due in a couple of weeks."

When I returned, the doctor sighed. He removed his glasses and rubbed his eyes. "The X-ray shows your ankle is broken in two places. Normally, I'd put your leg in a cast and tell you to stay in bed for six weeks, but I know that's not possible." He scribbled something on my invoice. "I'm instructing them to give you a walking cast, but stay off it as long as you can. And after the baby comes, keep your leg up as much as possible." He paused at the door and shook his head. "Good luck!"

In the cast room, the middle-aged man chuckled after he encased my leg in plaster up to my knee and fastened a blue sandal around my foot. "This ought to be some trick," he said, nodding toward my bulging middle.

Friends and strangers looked askance at the cast and my stomach protruding between my crutches. "How are you going to? . . . Never mind," they said. I wondered too: *How will I deliver a baby with my leg in a cast?*

After three weeks, when contractions began, I was able to hobble pretty well. The nurse seemed unconcerned by my crutches. "We need you to walk to advance your labor."

I must look ludicrous swinging up and down the halls on crutches. I don't think this will have the effect the nurses hope. I wonder how it feels for the baby!

The contractions stopped.

🌿 🌿 🌿

During the Sunday morning service, July 25, at Rialto Community Baptist Church, contractions started. Don checked his watch every time I squeezed his arm until they were five minutes apart. We dropped Heather and Shiloh off at Debbie's house, and the fun began.

It didn't take me long to realize the only thing harder than having a baby was doing it with my leg in a cast. Lying in a position to ease my labor pains made my leg throb. A position that soothed the pain in my leg made the contractions unbearable. The baby didn't like the belt wrapped around my middle to monitor activity and kicked it. The pens on the paper strip scribbled from side to side as if measuring major earthquakes.

Labor coach Don stood and stretched. "I'm going to get a snack from the vending machines in the basement."

"Don't be gone long," I panted.

The nurse entered and frowned at the baby's artwork on the paper strip. "I'll have to break the amniotic bag and attach heartbeat sensors to the baby."

When young Dr. Sully came to check my progress, his dark eyes widened in surprise. Things were happening rapidly. By the time Don got off the elevator, I was rolling into the delivery room.

A resourceful nurse tied my cast to the stirrup with a piece of twine. A few good pushes and our third child greeted the world with tears of surprise.

"It's a boy."

A boy? Don peered through the tiny square window in the door. Eager for him to share the unexpected wonder, I yelled, "It's a boy! It's a boy!"

Don was no longer doomed to spend his life surrounded by women; he would have an ally. A bright future of baseball, fishing, and tinkering on an offspring's first car was certainly his. Possibly times three!

We had a bargain; I chose the name for girls and he chose the name for boys. Don had saved up names for a baby boy for years. He named the baby and then named him some more; this would be his last chance. Uriah Elijah Jeremiah Israel Alexander was a big name for a tiny baby.

I nursed Uriah that first evening, half watching the news. He was beautiful: blue eyes; blond hair; eight pounds, two ounces. *He's so strong! He's already trying to hold his head up.*

"Here's a currently breaking news story," the newscaster droned. "There's a riot at Chino prison tonight. . . ."

My attention was suddenly riveted to the screen. *That's where Don is working!* A chilling numbness entered my heart. *What will happen to the children and me if Don is killed in the line of duty as a correctional officer?*

A few hours later he phoned: "I'm OK."

Aunt Debbie, Nana, and the girls greeted us at home. The girls giggled and bounced into Don's arms. They smiled and stroked the baby's tiny arm. "This is Uriah," I said.

A puzzled look clouded Shiloh's blue eyes. "You-riah? Or Me-riah?" she asked.

I giggled. "She's probably worried that if it's her-riah, she'll have to take care of him."

I gazed happily at the little ones gathered around me and then up into Don's loving eyes. *We're a complete family now: two beautiful daughters and a son.* The future seemed to stretch out like an endless strand of sunny, summer afternoons. *These are the good old days,* I told myself. *I'm going to hold onto this feeling as long as possible.*

Debbie and I worked back-to-back shifts as computer aides at Cucamonga Junior High School. She babysat our children while I worked, and I babysat while she worked. Debbie took summer school, leaving me free to care for baby Uriah and play with the girls until September. Uriah grew quickly and soon was off the charts for normal height and weight. Heather's saucy, brown eyes sparkled when she fluttered her long, dark lashes and put on bossy airs, playing dress-up with Shiloh. They clomped around the living room in my old gowns and shoes, their long tresses pulled high in ponytails, faces aglow with excitement . . . and makeup. While Uriah napped, they raced tricycles around the backyard. The sound of squeaky wheels and laughter filled the air. On hot afternoons, Shiloh's dimpled smile flashed as she splashed Heather in the wading pool. Sometimes Uriah joined them for a few minutes. He slapped the water and squealed with glee while I held his waist so he wouldn't topple.

In the evening, the girls sat on the counter and "helped" me make dinner while Uriah tried to scoot around on the carpet. When they heard the front door open and the screen door slam, they scrambled toward the front room, whooping, "Daddy! Daddy!" Often a tickle-and-pillow fight started. First slight, dark Heather and then sturdy, fair Shiloh attempted to tickle Daddy without being caught. The living room erupted in a pandemonium of delighted shrieks, sailing pillows, and flailing arms and legs. Uriah watched from a safe corner, kicking and cooing with excitement, his bright eyes shining. Eventually Don meandered into the kitchen on all fours, the exultant girls clinging to his back. His dark eyes sparkled as he puffed, "What's for dinner, honey?"

On Halloween evening, the children and I attended the All Saints party at church, dressed as Bible characters. Uriah was wrapped in blankets inside a large, wicker basket with a lid. As baby Moses and his mother, we won first place!

I frowned at the raised red bumps on Uriah's stomach when I changed his diaper. Five months old is awfully young to have chickenpox. And the rash moved from place to place.

"It's caused by an immune-system problem," Dr. Sully said. "His immune system is attacking itself. He isn't contagious. It'll go away without treatment."

It disappeared after a few weeks.

Uriah started walking at seven months, and I scrambled to install childproof gadgets to prevent inquisitive little fingers from finding trouble. He toddled after the girls, eager to be included in their fun. But if he was excluded from their activities—such as their bubbly baths when they competed to form their foaming locks into the highest, most exquisite hairdo—Uriah's curiosity sent him tinkering in every unexplored corner of the apartment. When he discovered the pots and pans, he smiled up at me with enchantment. He beat them with a wooden spoon and banged the lids together like cymbals, delighted with his ability to cause clamor despite his diminutive size.

As the summer of 1983 began to wane, Uriah's medical problems grew. He was treated repeatedly for an ear infection that developed in June but never went away. Dr. Sully rechecked his ear on August 8, August 18, and August 23. On August 25, he ate poison berries a child left on our front walkway and was given ipecac syrup in the emergency room. On September 5, another doctor diagnosed him with a possible hernia. On September 6, we were informed Uriah had a heart murmur by yet another doctor.

The week of September 23, the whole family was ill with the flu. It began Saturday with Uriah throwing up in the store. The following Friday afternoon, weary from work, I returned home with the children in our dusty, green station wagon after dropping off Debbie. It was hot, and Don snapped, "It's about time."

"I got here as soon as I could," I defended myself.

"I'm sorry, honey," Don said, slipping his arm around my shoulders. "I've been under pressure at work lately. I just want to go camping and relax."

"That's a great idea! But I need to take Uriah for his appointment to recheck his ear infection first." *It doesn't seem to be bothering him anymore. Maybe I should reschedule the appointment.* But a small, still voice reminded me of my worries about Uriah. "It won't take long, and then we can go," I promised.

There's nothing definitely wrong. Uriah's seen so many doctors lately. I'm sure one of them would have noticed if anything was drastically wrong. I remembered the many times I'd checked on Uriah in the middle of the night during the past few weeks. When I tiptoed into his room, lit by faint light from the hall, sometimes his lips looked blue. In the half-light I couldn't be certain, so I'd snap on the light, but he always looked fine by then. *Did I imagine it?*

Uriah flapped, kicked hard, and hollered in protest when Dr. Sully looked in his ears. It always took both of us to hold him.

Dr. Sully smiled. "That ear infection finally healed."

He turned to go. I blurted out what I thought I'd seen. He stopped, turned toward me, and listened patiently. "I feel foolish," I said, "but I want to be sure."

"I think he's fine; look how hard he fought when we looked in his ears!" he chuckled. "But if it will make you feel better, I can send you for a blood test just to check that everything's all right." He strode from the room, pulled a lab form from a cubbyhole at the nurses' station, and turned to me. "The results won't be back until Monday. OK?"

"That's fine." *Then I can put to rest my fears about Uriah's health.*

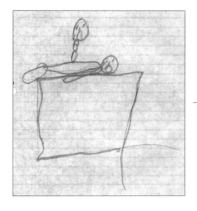

One

Into the Shadow
(Sept. 1983)

God, it's reassuring to know
You won't allow anything to happen
that we can't handle together.

W HEN THE LITTLE, RED NUMBER FLASHING ON THE SCREEN matched the one I held in my hand, I carried baby Uriah back into the lab's "drawing room." The middle-aged black man, on the other side of the table that was crowded with needles and tubes, accepted Uriah's paperwork and organized it. "Arnold Bridges," declared the name tag clipped to his shirt. He knew exactly how to deal with my tough little customer and managed to draw the sample quickly and without much protest.

It was five o'clock on Friday, and I knew the results wouldn't be available until Monday, but as I tried to gather up Uriah and his green-and-white gingham diaper bag, Mr. Bridges swirled the vial of blood and observed its contents thoughtfully. "This kid's been sick, hasn't he?" he asked.

"Yes," I replied. "We all had the flu earlier this week."

He continued looking at the vial a moment longer, then in slow, measured tones stated, "Listen, if you'll wait, I'll run this test right now."

I was surprised. *He's probably tired and has a million things to do, like everyone else. But it will spare me worrying all weekend.* I smiled and replied, "Great!"

Mr. Bridges disappeared into the lab's back room, and I shuffled into the waiting room and began to feed Uriah. I held him close, and he gave a shuddering sigh of contentment as the memory of the needle prick faded into comfort. In chairs across from us, a young mother cuddled a small child and read her a book. The peaceful moment was broken abruptly by Mr. Bridges' raised voice, as he strode from the drawing room. "Don't go anywhere!" he barked at me. "Your kid's real sick. What doctor did you come from?"

Stunned, I managed to stammer, "Dr. Sully . . . in family practice."

Mr. Bridges again instructed me sternly, "Don't leave!" and hurried off to call him.

As I turned my attention from Bridges' swiftly disappearing figure to my young son's innocent gaze, my glance swept across the young woman sitting opposite me. She clutched her daughter, staring at me with such wide-eyed disbelief and horror that I felt I had to say something to break the tension. *Does her expression mirror my own?*

"It always makes you feel so good when they tell you that," I feebly tried to joke, attempting to soothe the look on her face and quell my own rising panic. I tried to smile, but tears welled up in my eyes as I turned away and held my precious baby a little closer. Desperately I tried to pray, but the only words I could find were, *Oh, God! Help! Oh, God! Oh, God!* I was glad He knew me well enough to know what I meant, even if I didn't.

Mr. Bridges emerged moments later. "Go back to Dr. Sully's office," he commanded, "and don't make any stops along the way."

Any stops? I wondered. *How could I stop when I'm terrified for my child?*

Jumping in the elevator and racing down the endless corridor to Dr. Sully's cubicle, my dazed mind reasoned, *Surely it can't be too bad. He looks OK.* Three men in white coats descended on us as we arrived. Dr. Sully briskly introduced the other doctors. "They're going to help me admit Uriah to the hospital."

My mind silently screamed, *He's bad enough to go into the hospital? This is a nightmare! Oh, God! No! Not the dream!*

A nagging fear had been gnawing at the back of my mind for some time. A few weeks earlier, a recurrent dream began shadowing my heart. Unalterable and unavoidable, it started with a group of faceless doctors robed in white who said, "I'm sorry. There's nothing we can do."

My mouth fell open in mute shock as they turned and walked away into oblivion. When I looked down at Uriah in my arms, he was silent, motionless, and blue—his eyes closed in a deeper repose than mere sleep.

Before I could clasp him tightly in my arms, my precious son was gone. Instead I stood holding a crumpled note—tears streaming down my cheeks—in a silent, black void lit from above by a single shaft of light. The paper crackled as I opened it, and my husband's angry scrawl within shouted, "I can't go on like this. You'd be better off without me anyway."

Instantly I was outdoors. A breeze gently caressed my cheek and tousled my hair. The smell of freshly mown grass permeated the air. The growing, green carpet beneath my feet stretched away to the empty horizon, broken only by a mound of dirt like a silent, lonely sentinel near a casket in the ground. Standing on the edge, contemplating the meaning of the hard, black coffin below, I became aware that small hands were tightly clasping mine. My daughters, Shiloh and Heather, peered up at me with frightened, tear-stained faces.

Trying to shut out the indelible images, in emotional, uncomprehending pain, I screamed toward the tempestuous heavens, "God, where are You? Why don't You stop this awful dream?"

The proximity of the quiet, calm reply startled me. It was as if God asked my heart, *"Will you still love Me if this happens?"*

"What?" I gasped, trying to grasp the question. "I don't want this to happen," I responded with stout honesty. I paused, remembering the words of the Lord's Prayer: "Thy will be done."

"But I want Your will to be done," I whispered.

A picture of Peter sinking to his waist in the sea, desperately reaching out to Jesus flashed through my mind. Without God there is no hope. I hesitated, took a deep breath, and made a leap of faith. "God, I will trust You no matter what. As Peter said, 'Lord, to whom else can we go?'"

Then I would awaken, the pillow wet with tears.

꧁ꙮ ꧁ꙮ ꧁ꙮ

Now, as I faced the white-robed doctors in the uncompromising light of day, I felt adrift in that nightmarish dream, but all my senses insisted I was conscious. A doctor swept Uriah from my arms and carried him off to an adjoining room to "check him out." Dr. Sully busied himself with the phone and the voluminous paperwork that needed to be completed. Dr. Brown led me to another room to fill out forms.

As my terrified baby wailed in the next room, I tried to silence my jangling nerves and focus my bewildered mind on the questions Dr. Brown posed: "Any wounds or bleeding lately? Any history of anemia or bruising? Has he fallen and hurt himself?" The questions ricocheted off my heart, and I mechanically answered. *They're checking to see if Uriah's been abused! That's not the problem. But what is?*

Dr. Brown listened mutely as I listed all our trips to Kaiser in the past two weeks and poured out every detail I could think of that might be of help. As I finished, the door opened and the doctor who examined Uriah dropped him, still sobbing, in my lap. "He's in great condition—at least on the outside."

He left the door slightly ajar, and sounds of shuffling papers and muffled conversation drifted in. Dr. Brown watched me sympathetically as I tried to console Uriah. "Doctor," I pleaded, "I know it's too early to tell conclusively, but what are they looking for? What might be wrong with him?"

"There are a number of things that could be causing his condition, such as dietary deficiencies or illness, but we're also trying to rule out leukemia."

Leukemia! The ill-fated couple in *Love Story* sprang to my mind. *She died!* Adrenaline gushed. *My baby's going to die!* "Is there anything they can do?" I asked.

"The treatment for leukemia has advanced quickly in the past few years, and there are a lot of new treatments." While that was encouraging, it didn't stop the panic and fear I felt rising inside.

"Don't forget," he reminded me, "we won't be sure what the problem is until tests are done."

Fumbling my way into the outer office, I sat in a chair to wait. "Uriah will be in the hospital for at least this weekend," Dr. Sully informed me. "His blood count is extremely low, and he needs blood."

I cringed. AIDS was in the news. "What are the chances he might get AIDS from the transfusion?"

Dr. Sully turned and regarded me seriously. "The chances are slim he will get AIDS, but if he doesn't get a transfusion, he will die."

Praying for Uriah's survival and protection, I signed the papers giving permission. *Don needs to know what's happening. I'm making life-and-death decisions, and I don't want to make them alone.* "Can I call my husband?" Dr. Sully grabbed the phone, opened a line, and held out the receiver.

I didn't want to alarm Don. I felt self-conscious talking in front of the doctors. *I'll just calmly let him know Uriah's sick and going into the hospital.* But when he answered the phone, all my resolve crumbled into nothingness, and I began to weep. I managed to faintly murmur, "Honey, they're putting Uriah in the hospital, and I need you. Can you come?"

The doctors probably heard every word in that tiny room, but they were turned away, shuffling papers. After a momentary, stunned silence, Don promised, "I'll be there as soon as I get someone to watch the girls."

Oh, God, how are the girls going to take all this? Dark-haired, dark-eyed Heather was five, and fair-haired, blue-eyed Shiloh was only three.

As I sat rocking Uriah to sleep, Don dashed in. The relief of seeing him, though white and tense, caused me to break into tears again. The lines of worry on his face eased when he saw Uriah peacefully asleep in my arms. He gave me a kiss, and his deep voice rumbled softly, "What's wrong with him?"

"They aren't sure yet," I whispered, "but he needs blood, so they're putting him in the hospital. They need to do tests to make sure it's not leukemia."

His jaw tightened grimly, but before he could reply, the doctors handed him a packet of papers and directed him to the admitting office. I held Uriah close as Dr. Sully led us through a maze of corridors to a place where whimsical animal pictures hung on the walls. *I wish I could wake up and find this is only another nightmare.* At the end of the hall, we entered the bustling pediatric ward filled with nurses who flitted in and out of many doorways, executing endless tasks.

Uriah's room wasn't ready, so we were hustled into a room off the main corridor that contained a shiny, metal table and a host of sterile medical paraphernalia.

The nurses tried to thread a "butterfly"—a needle with two green plastic wings to immobilize it—into a tiny vein in Uriah's arm for an intravenous line, but to no avail. One after another, faces taut with concentration and tension, they attempted to evince their skill while Uriah screamed and thrashed, trying to escape their grasp. They apologized after several fruitless efforts. "Let's get Sanmarco. Don't worry," they told me, "she'll get it started."

Oh, God, please let them get it started.

A strawberry blonde, middle-aged woman entered the room. Her long white coat identified her as Dr. Sanmarco. The nurse moved over for her, a respected authority, to step in. She spoke to Uriah in reassuring tones with an accent and smile, but Uriah refused to be consoled. She found the vein, drew the blood, taped the needle to his arm, and secured his arm to an arm board in practiced, rapid succession. She gave orders concerning him, then swiftly departed to tend other patients. My silent thanks winged heavenward.

There was no room in the pediatric wing that night. A nurse guided Uriah's IV pole back along the rainbow-balloon hallway, down hospital-white corridors, up to the fourth floor. We passed through a tiny room (which acted as an airlock against germs) into a sterile, white room with a large, stainless-steel crib that looked like a cage because it was completely enclosed by bars—*to keep children from climbing out, I suppose.*

Uriah sagged against me, exhausted. The nurse showed me how to slide the side of the crib open so I could lay him down. She observed my anxious gaze and softly advised, "If you leave, we'll have to tie him down so he won't pull the IV out of his arm."

Visions of my son's small body tied in a cage while he screamed in helpless rage were intolerable. I couldn't leave him.

Don hurried into the room, gazed at Uriah's tiny, sleeping form, and retreated into the airlock room. Perspiration beaded on his forehead, and his hand shook as he mopped his brow, so he quickly thrust it deep into his pocket. I told him what the nurse said about restraining Uriah. "Can I stay?"

He nodded mutely. "I'll go get you something to eat." He looked relieved to have a reason to escape.

Still numb with shock, I searched my jumbled mind. *God, help me think! What should I be doing? People need to be told. Who should I call first? My mother. She's the easiest to talk to; she understands me best.*

I dialed incorrectly the first two times, then heard my father's carefree greeting.

"Is Nana there, Boompa?"

He called to her, and she came to the phone, cheerful and unaware. I paused, troubled. It was as if a sword of sorrow had been plunged through my heart, and now I had to take that same sword of knowledge and thrust it through my mother's heart. There was no way to spare her.

My voice all but left me. I could barely hear myself telling her what was happening. I had only theories to give her.

Nana offered to call my three sisters and my employer to request emergency leave. "Is there anything else I can do to help?"

"Just pray. And let people know Uriah needs blood. They can donate in his name, if they want to."

Don returned. I asked, "Do you want to call your mother?"

He shook his head and stared at the floor. "I've got to go get the girls. I'll be by the phone."

Dr. Sully told us Uriah's blood count was dangerously low: 2.75. (Normal is 4.6–6.2.)[1] Later Nana told me, "A nurse friend said it's a wonder Uriah didn't die." That night Uriah's transfusion seeped into him a few drops at a time while the nurse checked for signs of a rash, blood-pressure change, or other indications he might be rejecting the new blood. He got three pints of blood that night. Each time two nurses checked that the blood type and medical-record number matched those on the plastic bracelet he wore, and he cried, presumably fearing another needle prick. His IV infiltrated (came out of the vein) several times and had to be restarted in a new location. His tiny, twenty-pound frame made it hard to find new, usable veins.

All of our children had special blankets when they were toddlers. Uriah now invented a new use for his multi-colored quilt: a security system. When he lay down to sleep, he insisted every part of his body be covered with his security blanket—especially his hands and arms. It didn't prevent someone sticking a needle in him, but it assured him he would be awake before they did. His blanket was a barrier that could not be breached without his knowledge, thus in a small way, giving him control over the pain, which was now a permanent part of his life.

Our "living quarters" that fall weekend contained the crib; a rocking chair; and a long, thin, wood-tone table on wheels with a top that slid open to reveal a cubbyhole and mirror. A television sat high on one wall, and cabinets covered most of the west wall. When I mentioned I wanted to stay with Uriah, the nurse brought a blue foam mat, some sheets, and a blanket for me.

I held Uriah a lot that evening, for his benefit and mine. He clung to me as a drowning man to a fragment of wood, suddenly stripped of his simple, secure world. *He needs the reassurance I'm still here, as much as I need the reassurance he is.* I held him up to our solitary window, and he pressed his face against the glass and crowed with delight at the interesting world four stories below. He babbled and pointed down at the tiny cars and people and later the streetlights that shone out across the city like fallen stars.

The phone calls from relatives and friends faded, and Uriah lay sleeping in his crib.

God, what if Uriah had no appointment today? What if we'd gone camping instead? What if Arnold Bridges hadn't run the blood test immediately? If You hadn't carefully choreographed everything, Uriah would have died on our camping trip. The horror of awakening to find him dead would have destroyed me—and You knew that. It's reassuring to know You won't allow anything to happen that we can't handle together. Uriah's illness is difficult, God, but You must have created my family with all we need to get through this, or else You wouldn't have allowed it to happen, would You?

I arranged a makeshift bed close to Uriah's. Throughout the night when the nurses came to check on him, I sat and watched, ready to reassure him if he awakened.

We slept as late as the phone would allow. Uriah gazed mournfully at his IV and the needle in his arm, but he smiled and pointed to the window when I picked him up.

Don and the girls came by with breakfast. Children weren't allowed in Uriah's room, so Don lifted them up to wave to him through the tiny window in the door. When they became restless and started to look through the contents of cupboards, Don drove them to Aunt Debbie's house.

There was a tap on the door. *Dr. Sanmarco is here on Saturday?* She swished into the room in a long, pale lavender physician's coat and smiled at Uriah through the crib bars. She turned to me and explained in her strong accent, punctuated with many hand motions, "We need to draw bone marrow from Uriah's hip to determine his problem. This involves inserting a hollow tube, which looks like a big needle, into his hipbone and suctioning out a little of the liquid bone marrow inside." She handed me a consent form and a pen. There was no other way to find out what was wrong. I signed.

Don returned just before they began the procedure. I explained what they were going to do. Within minutes, the nurse shooed us out, and the doctors arrived. We waited in the little airlock room, but a couple of screams from Uriah sent Don scrambling from the room. "I'm going for a walk," he stated gruffly and fled.

Perhaps I should go with him. I hesitated. *All I want to do is comfort my child.* Tears stung my eyes as I gazed out a tiny window at people passing far below—people unaware of the anguish we were enduring. *God, it isn't fair! Why do we have to suffer so much? We've been faithful to You.*

"*The rain falls on the just and the unjust. Jesus suffered too.*"

You know everything. I can't hide that I'm angry with You, God. But You also know I don't want to be. Please change me.

The agony seemed hours, but the doctors and nurses came out minutes later, straightening jackets and smoothing back frazzled hair. *At least he's strong enough they had to struggle to hold him down.* I rushed to his side, but the only sign that anything had happened was a small patch of disinfectant-stained skin covered by gauze.

"It'll be sore for a few days," the nurse advised.

Uriah's tears subsided quickly once I cuddled him. He was all smiles when his daddy walked in minutes later.

Don's voice shook with emotion: "I never want to be here again when they do things like that to Uriah. I feel so angry, and there's nothing I can do. It makes me crazy!"

"It would be easier for me if I could be with Uriah and comfort him. At least that's something I could do," I replied.

When the nurse checked on Uriah, I ventured, "Will I always have to leave when a bone-marrow biopsy is done?"

"Some parents stay with their children."

I vowed silently, *Uriah won't suffer through a bone marrow again without someone to hold his hand and calm him. I'll have to do it, because Don can't.* "When will we know the results?"

"Probably at your appointment in pediatrics on Monday morning."

Two

Silent Screaming
(Oct. 1983)

It's a lottery you don't want to win.

D ON MET ME IN URIAH'S ROOM BEFORE OUR APPOINTMENT
Monday. The receptionist at the front desk handed us
an invoice. "Go to the purple module."

The purple sign, labeled "Oncology," stuck out above a
closed door. We pushed open the heavy door and peered
inside. Behind it, a short hallway ended in a waiting room.
A nurse leaned out of a hallway to our left, "Do you have
an appointment?"

"We're Don and Mara Alexander," I said. "Dr. Sanmarco
asked us to meet her here at nine o'clock."

Margarita the nurse smiled and motioned us to the waiting room. "Dr. Sanmarco will see you soon."

The typical, large, hospital waiting room walls were as
white as the couch that hunched against the back wall. A
round table with child-sized chairs sat on the left side of
the room near a television high atop a corner cupboard.
There the similarities ended. A toy box sat against the wall
under the television, and a group of IV poles stood on the
right side of the room near easy chairs and a motorized

recliner. There were already people with small children scattered around the room, waiting.

We sat down, staring dumbly at the cartoon on the television. My heart was in my throat, and I braced myself for the diagnosis. *It must be leukemia. It seems the only explanation for all the symptoms Uriah's experienced.*

Dr. Sanmarco entered and checked with her nurses. She gave them instructions and swept into the waiting room, scanning patients and making mental notes about their treatment. She smiled at us kindly, "As soon as the other doctors arrive, we'll be ready for you."

Maybe everything's fine after all.

Soon Dr. Brown and a short, swarthy doctor arrived. Dr. Sanmarco motioned us into her office. It wasn't large. There was barely room for her desk, which faced the door, and two chairs sitting against the opposite wall. Behind the desk, floor-to-ceiling bookshelves were filled with texts about pediatric oncology and medicine. A colorful collection of masks decorated one wall, and a beautiful picture of a mother and child filled another. I was struck by the subtle difference in the color of this room: it was an extremely pale violet. *It's a much nicer room to be in than the waiting room—except for the reason we're here.*

Moving behind the two physicians, who sat in folding chairs at the left side of her desk, she made her way to her chair and settled into it. She motioned us toward the empty chairs. Don and I sat in the narrow space, finding some comfort in our closeness to one another. We clasped hands and awaited the verdict. Were we doomed to lose our son?

Dr. Sanmarco said, "This is Dr. Haghighat, another pediatric oncologist." He nodded to us and adjusted his glasses.

"Do you remember Dr. Brown?" Dr. Sanmarco asked. We nodded.

"Dr. Haghighat and I are the only doctors who work here in the pediatric oncology/hematology department at Kaiser Hospital, Fontana." She opened the folder of medical records that lay in front of her. "Do you know what's wrong with Uriah?"

"We . . . aren't sure," I stammered.

"Have you heard of leukemia?"

My heart sank. We nodded silently. She and Dr. Haghighat exchanged a glance. "The bone-marrow test is positive," she announced firmly. "Your son has leukemia."

Don continued to stare hard at the front of the desk, and I tried to focus on what Dr. Sanmarco was saying. I expected a flood of emotion to engulf me, but I felt only empty numbness. She paused, as if expecting a reaction, but we gave none.

"There are seven kinds of childhood leukemia. Uriah has the most common type, which responds best to treatment. Each kind of leukemia affects a different type of white blood cell. Uriah's T cells have been affected by acute lymphoblastic leukemia, a form of acute lymphocytic leukemia, called ALL for short. Leukemia is common, affecting one child in ten thousand. Only accidents claim more children's lives."

One out of ten thousand. It's a lottery you don't want to win.

"Many new medications were discovered in the past decade, which can be used to combat leukemia. Earlier there was little that could be done, but now 90 percent of children diagnosed with leukemia achieve remission—that is, the absence of any cancerous cells in the bone marrow. But there are two places leukemia resists chemotherapy: the brain and the testicles. Girls' odds of survival are better than boys' because they have only one place leukemia can hide. Age is also a factor. The best survival rates occur in children diagnosed between the ages of three and ten."

He's too young. How can tiny Uriah defeat a monster like cancer? Strong people in the prime of life are destroyed by it in a matter of weeks. He won't be with us long. Please, God, let him make it to Christmas. I want him to experience celebrating Jesus' birth at least once in what might be a short life. "Has any child younger than Uriah been diagnosed here?" I ventured.

To my surprise, Dr. Sanmarco said, "Yes, a baby diagnosed at six months old is being treated here."

I hesitated, fearing the answer, but asked, "How are they doing?"

Her smile was like sunshine in the midst of a hurricane. "So far, so good." It wasn't much, but it was the brightest glimmer of hope we had been given.

"Several treatments are being studied for effectiveness against leukemia," she continued. "You can choose to have Uriah participate in a protocol—a study—or we can treat Uriah with the chemotherapy we think best for him."

"Which would be better?"

The doctors shook their heads. Dr. Haghighat added, "If you choose not to participate in a study, it's probable we will give him a regimen similar to a protocol."

We're being asked to make a decision that could determine if our child lives or dies, but no one can give us information to make the right choice. We have to make our best guess. That's all anyone can do. It reminds me of a television game show. We have our choice of door number one, two, or three. Behind one of them is our beautiful living child; behind the other two, a little grave. What's maddening is the possibility that the little grave could lie behind them all.

"Regardless of the treatment chosen," Dr. Sanmarco added, "Uriah will always have a low white blood-cell count.

Since white blood cells are our body's defense against infection or illness, you need to keep him away from anyone ill and restrict his contact with others."

His very life depends on how well we keep him from getting sick.

"That means avoiding contact with the general public," Dr. Haghighat stated.

No movie theaters, grocery stores, public parks, or Little League? No Sunday school or church? The more I thought about it, the longer the list got.

Dr. Sanmarco rose. "You can talk privately here and decide." The other doctors filed out. "It's all right if you want to cry," Dr. Sanmarco added. She set a box of thin, scratchy hospital tissue on her desk and went out, closing the door softly.

Neither of us felt like crying. I had cried enough that long weekend, and what she told us was no worse than I expected. Don had progressed through the stages of grief to anger, and he sat with his fists clenched in mute, helpless rage. I wished that I knew how to help him. *At least his anger isn't directed toward me,* I thought. *But it's turned inward, like a deadly shard moving toward his heart. It can cause destruction if it's not removed.*

We sat in that cramped office, the weight of our son's life or death hanging on our shoulders. *How can someone cope in this situation without Christ?* The only one who could know the right decision to make was God. Only He could see the future and the infinite possibilities that could occur with our choices. Trying to get that information from Him was, in my mind, the hard part, since I'm not a prophetess. But God is a loving God. I believed He wouldn't allow us to miss the right decision. I knew that, in the past, as long as I'd been seeking His will, He had always found a way to give me the information I needed to make the right decision. So it wasn't a question of Don's and my making the right decision, but of our seeking God's will in prayer and doing what we believed He wanted us to do, realizing that it was perfectly within God's power to heal Uriah—if that was His will.

I remembered my friend who had wondered how a Christian could cope: "I would think it would be worse being a Christian. Don't you feel God has abandoned you or that He doesn't exist?"

I pondered the distinction between our viewpoints. Throughout the Bible God's people lived through devastating circumstances; the rain falls on the just and the unjust. The difference is we have a God who works all things together for good to those who love Him (see Rom. 8:28). Just as Uriah's blanket didn't stop the needle pricks, so being followers of Christ doesn't shield us from all harm. However, we know Someone who loves us is guiding our future, with full knowledge of what lies ahead and how much we can bear. Those who don't have God in their life must feel completely alone and out of control.

OK, God. I'm taking You at Your Word. You promised to turn bad things to good for those who love You. I can't understand how You could use something so bad for good. It seems to me it would take a miracle. But that's not too hard for You, is it? I've always wanted to see a miracle, but I wish we didn't need one. I'm sure glad You're in control, because from where I sit, things are a confusing mess. I want to do Your will, but I don't know what that is, so I'm trusting You to show me. I'm listening for Your will and watching for Your miracles. Thanks, God, for taking care of us.

It felt much better to drop my cares into God's hands and watch what He would do. Like a child in the passenger's seat, watching the scenery pass, I could sit at ease (instead of trying to drive myself when I didn't even know where we were going), knowing my Father was safely guiding us toward the right destination.

"What do you think we should do?" I whispered to Don.

"I don't know," Don murmured with a shrug of wide shoulders.

"If it's going to be the same treatment either way, and the results from a study might help someone else, we might as well participate. That way some good might come out of all this."

"Yeah, I guess so."

Don walked me to Uriah's room. "I'm sorry to leave you here alone. I just can't stand hospitals. The way they smell . . . the white walls . . ." His face twisted with disgust, unable to form words that would carry the depth of his feeling.

"That's all right," I reassured him. "If you can take care of the girls at home, I will be able to stay with Uriah, and you know how important that is to me."

He smiled as if relieved, grateful I understood and accepted his shortcoming without reproach. He bent to kiss me, then gave Uriah a quick squeeze and tousled his blond hair.

"I'll call you as soon as I know what's going on," I said as he walked to the door. He smiled, nodding. He peek-a-booed Uriah through the window in the door once, then waved and walked away.

Late that night, sitting in Uriah's little hospital room while he slept, I tried to read and understand the papers Dr. Sanmarco had given us. The medical terminology was difficult to understand, but it was imperative that I know what our son's treatment was going to be and what complications could arise.

Generally, whenever I needed to think clearly, I wrote.
So I started a list:

1. **Call Pastor "Al" Albeck.**
   In May 1983, Don and I attended a Marriage Encounter weekend. The communication skills we learned that weekend were probably responsible for the survival of our marriage. Seventy-five percent of marriages break up when a child is diagnosed with a potentially fatal disease. When a child dies, even fewer marriages survive.[1]
   But God also sent us there for another reason. That weekend, the lead pastor was "Al" Albeck. "Some people consider me unconventional because I do things not practiced often today," he'd said, "such as anointing a sick person with oil for healing, as the Bible suggests in James 5:13–16."
   I had mentally filed that information away, just in case I might ever know someone who needed help. Less than a year later, my only son was in need of healing. The Mansells from Marriage Encounter tracked down Pastor Al's number for us, and I was able to make an appointment within a few days.

2. **Acute Lymphoblastic Leukemia.**
   Intermediate prognosis: a 40–70 percent chance of survival. His young age and the fact he was a boy were not in his favor.
   There were three parts to the oncology treatment program. First the rigorous induction phase to get the patient into remission. Next the consolidation phase to try to destroy any hidden cancer cells so remission would continue. Last the maintenance phase in which

lower doses of chemotherapy were used to maintain the remission. These phases were expected take three years.

Three years! He hasn't even lived that long yet! At least if he survives the treatment, he'll be able to start kindergarten like a normal child.

The medical terminology intensified as various chemotherapy treatments and their side effects were described. In the induction phase, Uriah would receive intravenous vincristine, which could cause hair loss (*No more golden curls*); oral prednisone; daunomycin, which might cause heart damage (*Uh-oh!*); and intramuscular L-asparaginase, which on rare occasion caused a severe allergic reaction and death. *Oh, great! The disease is fatal, and the treatment is potentially fatal!*

The consolidation phase required daily oral 6-mercaptopurine, weekly injections of methotrexate into the spinal fluid, and radiation to the brain, which could cause brain damage. *This is supposed to help him?* He might also receive intravenous cyclophosphamide and cytosine arabinoside for six weeks, possibly causing urinary bleeding and sterilization. *My baby will be systematically poisoned! God, how can he survive this?*

The two years of maintenance treatment that would follow promised to be nearly as risky—that is, if the remission was sustained. If the protocol treatment didn't work, the doctor would offer recommendations of other available treatments that might produce a remission. *The worst of all: there's no guarantee it will work.*

It was a staggering amount of information. Just knowing what complications to watch for could save his life! Realization burst upon me. *I will have to become more than just his mother; I'll have to be his nurse and health advocate.* What a responsibility! *Will I have to quit my job so I can care for him? And will I be equal to such a task? I had to leave the room in high school during a disaster film because I almost fainted. If the sight of blood makes me faint, how will I cope with Uriah's bleeding or painful treatments?*

Later I read the list of medicines and side effects to Don. When I'd finished reading, he was silent.

"I know the treatments seem impossible," I said, "but Uriah will die if we don't do something. Should we investigate the cures in Mexico?"

"I don't know. I've heard about too many children dying while using that," he said and then paused. "I wish God would just heal him!"

"We both know He could do that, but God can use doctors to heal too," I said. "Look, why don't we do both?"

"Huh?"

"Let's ask God to heal Uriah and have Pastor Albeck anoint him with oil, but have the doctors begin him on a chemotherapy protocol. If God wants Uriah to be healed, he will be, regardless of the chemotherapy. If it's God's will that Uriah join Him in heaven, then nothing we can do will change that."

"That makes sense. Let's do it."

As the phone clicked into its cradle, I thought about King Hezekiah in 2 Kings 20. Isaiah the prophet was sent to tell the king he would die. Hezekiah turned his face to the wall and prayed, "Remember, O Lord, how I have walked before you faithfully and with wholehearted devotion and have done what is good in your eyes. And Hezekiah wept bitterly" (v. 3).

Immediately the Lord sent Isaiah back to Hezekiah to declare he would live fifteen more years. Hezekiah asked for a sign the Lord would heal him. Isaiah told him to choose: the sign could be the sundial shadow lengthening ten steps or going back ten steps. Hezekiah chose to have time go back, and God made it so. We didn't doubt God could heal Uriah, but until He gave a clear sign that He intended to, we would use every means to preserve Uriah's life.

On Tuesday, September 27, Don arrived early with the girls, signed the papers, and brought the girls for an appointment with Dr. Sully. The doctors had assured us Uriah's leukemia wasn't hereditary and odds were against Shiloh or Heather developing it, but I knew I'd feel better if blood tests ruled it out. After all, if it hadn't been for Uriah's blood test, we wouldn't have discovered his leukemia until too late.

When Don returned to tell me the blood tests for both girls were fine, he signed consent forms for Uriah to receive a spinal tap (lumbar puncture) and an infusion of methotrexate into his spinal fluid (intrathecal methotrexate). Then he hugged Uriah, kissed me, and asked, "Are you OK?" He looked into my eyes, as if searching for any sign I needed to escape.

"This will be better for me and Uriah," I assured him. He paused, looking as if he felt guilty leaving us.

The nurse bustled in, donned gloves, and began arranging metal instruments and swabs on a shiny tray. "I'm sorry, but the children will have to leave."

Don swallowed hard. "It's time for us to go." He gave me a peck on the lips and rushed Heather and Shiloh out of the room.

This time I stayed. Dr. Sanmarco remembered Uriah was a fighter. She turned to me while she pulled on her gloves. "Can you help the nurse immobilize him?"

If he jerks while the needle is in his spine, there could be terrible complications. I pinned his arms down and put my face near his, talking him gently through it. Though he cried, he seemed calmer than he sounded during the first bone marrow. And I was definitely much calmer!

Afterward Dr. Sanmarco said, "He has to remain lying down for a half hour so he won't get a severe headache." I caressed his arms and told him a story. As soon as the time was up, I held him in my lap.

When I was in labor with Heather, I had a spinal tap, and it hurt more than having her. I wonder if it's possible to teach Lamaze to a child so young?

Wednesday I learned that Uriah's appointments would always be in the morning because of the tests that had to be done. Before a patient could be treated, the doctors had to make certain their blood levels were high enough, and they weren't ill or suffering serious side effects. Usually the first thing they did was draw a blood sample from the child and send the parent to the lab with it so a CBC (blood count) could be done.

Uriah would be susceptible to infections because of chemotherapy, even after he attained remission. He might need blood transfusions often to keep his hemoglobin (red blood) count up, because chemotherapy suppresses the production of good cells as well as bad. He would undergo another bone-marrow test and spinal tap in two weeks to determine if the chemotherapy was having any effect.

I'm glad we have an appointment with Pastor Albeck. Uriah will be anointed with oil before they check the bone marrow for cancer. Wouldn't it be wonderful if all the cancer was gone?

Time crept forward until Friday, September 30, dawned. While Dr. Haghighat examined Uriah, he informed me in his strong middle-eastern accent, "You're going home for the weekend after Uriah gets his L-asparaginase." His expression remained serious as he added, "But you must stay

42

thirty minutes after the injection to be sure he doesn't have an allergic reaction."

Going home! I hadn't been certain Uriah would ever return home, and I definitely didn't expect it so soon. It would be so good to have my whole family around me and to sleep in my own bed. Our family life had changed so much! Sometimes it seemed we would never all be together again. *Things will never be the same, but it'll be nice to be a family at least.*

I called Don. "I'm on my way," he chortled.

I packed Uriah's things and took down the cards I had taped over the blank walls. Uriah looked relieved to see my preparations, but he pulled his blanket over his head when the nurse brought a shot for him just as lunch was being served. I wrapped him in my arms, expecting a struggle, but he carefully held his arm still while the nurse inserted the needle. He screamed and cried, but he seemed to know it would hurt worse if he moved.

With the shot over, Uriah's attention turned to his lunch. He was watching a cartoon about a giant who ate pumpkins, and he grabbed the sliced carrots with pudgy fingers and gobbled them down. When a search of his plate revealed no more "pumpkins," he looked at me with pleading eyes: "Mo?" I took the little plastic bowl he'd handed me, and he picked up a chunk of chicken in each hand and crammed both pieces into his mouth. *At least the medicine doesn't seem to affect his appetite.*

"Could he have more carrots?" I asked the nurse.

"Sure, but watch him closely for any sign of an allergic reaction, such as hives, swelling, or wheezing. If there's anything, notify me by intercom immediately."

I nodded my head. "I understand how serious a reaction can be."

Between feeding Uriah bites of mashed potato, I lifted his hospital shirt to check his stomach and back—a common location for rashes to start. The second time I checked, there was the slightest hint of red splotches on his side. I rang the buzzer for the nurse, though it didn't look serious.

"Yes?" she quickly answered.

My heart was afraid. "Uriah has a light mark on one side. It's probably nothing, maybe from my holding him for the shot, but I'd feel better if you'd check it."

She raced into the room and scanned the marks that had already risen into a rash. Her mouth set in a grim line, she sprang from the room to call Dr. Haghighat. She was gone only seconds, but by then Uriah's rash had spread to his arms and legs, and his face began to swell. His eyebrows stuck out a half-inch from his face, his eyes seemed to recede into his skull, and his lips protruded horribly until he no longer looked human, but more like some twisted gargoyle. I was terrified by the rapidity and severity of the changes in this child who no longer resembled my son. He was sobbing with discomfort and fear. I held him close, consoling him softly. I tried not to show it, but I'm sure he sensed my terror. His breathing became labored and noisy as his throat began to swell closed. *He's going to die!*

It couldn't have been more than a minute since the nurse had contacted Dr. Haghighat, but he shot into the room. He assessed Uriah's condition in a single glance and ordered the nurse to bring him some items. He didn't try to take Uriah from me or ask me to leave, which was a relief.

If Uriah's going to die, I want to be holding and comforting him. What will I tell Don if he dies? The shock will be so great . . . if he comes to bring his son home and finds him gone . . .

The doctor gave Uriah shots of adrenaline and Benadryl. He had always seemed in a hurry before, but now he sat and watched as I paced and tried to soothe Uriah and control my own powerful emotions. The terrible transformation slowed, then halted. With grateful relief, I heard his breathing ease as the swelling began to reverse until, once again, I held the small child I recognized and loved. His tear-stained face was peaceful as he slipped into sleep. His breathing became normal, except for an occasional shuddering sigh as he relaxed. *He'll be all right.*

Dr. Haghighat stood, nodded his head. A satisfied sparkle brightened his dark gray eyes.

Well, we won't be going home now, I surmised. *Uriah just had a close brush with death.*

Dr. Haghighat handed me some papers. "He'll be fine now. But if anything concerns you after you get home, just follow these directions to reach me or Dr. Sanmarco after hours. We'll see you at the clinic in a few days."

He acts as if nothing out of the ordinary happened.

"Will Uriah be unable to participate in the study since he is allergic to L-asparaginase?" I asked.

In a well-practiced clinical tone he answered. "Another form of the same drug is given to children sensitive to L-asparaginase." As rapidly as he came, he was gone.

Life suddenly seemed full of instantaneous, erratic changes. Dr. Haghighat seemed to take it in stride, almost as matter of fact. *So these situations must be commonplace. If he's grown accustomed to this, so can I.*

The nurse brought release papers—complete with detailed information on caring for Uriah at home—for me to sign. He was to be on a normal diet but wasn't allowed vigorous activity because a low platelet count made him susceptible to bleeding. If bleeding started, I would have to bring him to the hospital immediately. He would be taking the oral medication prednisone for the first time.

Uriah's next appointment is only days away, but will we be able to take care of him? What if I go into his room and find him dead?

Don and the girls trooped into Uriah's room and flung their arms around us.

Everything's in Your hands, God. I get used to the illusion I'm in control of things, but You really are. And if You can't take care of us, who can?

Three

Ripples of Reaction
(Oct. 1983–Dec. 1984)

So often the living are more desperate than the dying.

U RIAH'S FRIEND, TONY, LIVED IN THE HOUSE NEXT TO OUR APART-
ment. When we arrived home, I went to talk to Tony's
mom. "Uriah has leukemia. The kids won't be able to come
inside our house because Uriah's immune system is depressed.
His illness isn't communicable—your children can't catch it
from us. But Uriah could get very sick from just a cold."

Tears filled her eyes as she hugged me and cried. "But
he can't die," she insisted. "Tony's only a little older than
Uriah. He's Tony's friend!"

Then I realized we might lose friends. Being friends
with a family whose child is seriously ill is a constant reminder to the parents that it could happen to their own.
An unpreventable disease, whose cause is unknown and
is the number-one killer of children, brings a parent face
to face with the lack of power we really possess to protect
our children.

Our relationship with many people changed. Some
kept a greater distance to protect themselves and their
children from the emotional effects of our possible

impending tragedy. The more familiar their children were with ours, the more trauma they would suffer if Uriah died. It's uncomfortable and difficult for parents to explain death to their children.

Some we never saw again. *I can't find fault with them. They're just trying to protect the ones they love. I have to live with this situation, but if I were in their place, how would I respond?* I let them slip away without comment. If the children noticed the absence of their friends, I simply said, "They must be very busy."

The girls played outside with friends because of the threat of chickenpox; it's fatal for children with leukemia. Nothing contagious could be tracked in. Our house had to become a haven for our son if he was going to survive.

The apartment developed a leak, and water ran down behind the wall in our bedroom, soaking the carpet. Don and I slept on a mat in the living room and kept the bedroom door closed because of the sickening mildew smell that permeated the air. Several times the landlord tried to fix the leak, without success.

My thoughts returned to the dream. *The first part has come true; Uriah's terribly ill. Don seems depressed. I don't want the second part to become reality too.* I hid his gun in the garage.

The feeling of strain I hid from the children was never far from the surface. Caring for Uriah wasn't hard, but the tricks my mind played were unmerciful. I watched everything with new fear and suspicion—and I knew it. *Is he getting paler? What if something goes wrong while I sleep and he dies?* I crept into his room and listened to his breathing many times. Sometimes I couldn't hear it, and I'd snap the light on in panic, afraid to find him as blue and motionless as he had been in my dream.

I cried in the shower. This was the only place I could let it out. It would be too scary for the children and too hard on Don if they saw me weep.

Sometimes when I held Uriah, I thought, *This could be the last time*. Once, coming home from work, I passed a local mortuary and made a mental note: *I need to order a coffin for Uriah.* I stared at the red traffic signal. *That's crazy! He isn't dead yet; he's sitting in the car with us. How could I have imagined he was?*

I scribbled my tumultuous feelings down in an old notebook:

> First the examination, then the diagnosis. Then began the silent screaming, as if I was deep-water drowning, helpless free-falling. And the only ones who can hear me are those who are themselves silently screaming. We all lean together to help each other stand against forces we cannot see or fight, so we do not utterly fall.
>
> It's so hard to hold that small, sobbing frame still for injections, bone marrows, and spinal taps when those uncomprehending, innocent eyes look pleadingly into mine. It's agony to leave such a tiny person alone in a cage-like crib at the hospital when he must stay and I must go.
>
> There are times quiet anguish breaks the surface and tears cascade. Then two tiny arms enclose me, a tiny hand pats my arm and little, blue eyes console me. So often the living are more desperate than the dying!

We tried to keep life normal. If Uriah was going to live a normal life someday, he needed to be treated like the girls.

Uriah returned from the hospital with ragged hair because of chemotherapy. I was amazed how quickly it fell. Going to the hairstylist when he was older was a red-letter day for Uriah. It meant he could decide how his hair would look. Normally, like Fuzzy-Wuzzy the bear, he had no choice because he had no hair.

We were glad to have Uriah home, but it was a short stay. He had a fever when he arrived for his appointment Wednesday, October 5. He was isolated in a treatment room to prevent the spread of infection. It was difficult to think of a cold as life-threatening, but children on chemotherapy can't fight infection, and common illnesses can rapidly turn serious. More insidious, sick children can't receive chemotherapy because it depresses their immune system. The longer they go without treatment, the less likely their survival.

Uriah was admitted to the hospital immediately, much to my surprise—it seemed such a slight infection. Unprepared, I hadn't brought the things he would need or toys to amuse him in the tiny treatment room. "I'll be right back," I promised and rushed home to get his pillow, blanket, and other necessities. After that, I kept a bag—full of items for a hospital stay—stashed in the car.

Uriah's cold kept him in the hospital for two weeks. I stayed with him during the day and hurried home after he was asleep to read bedtime stories to the girls and tuck them in. I was wearing out. My weight dropped to 113 pounds. *Well, at least I don't have to worry about being overweight. Don isn't making the endless treks to the hospital, but caring for the girls and trying to keep a tight wrap on his emotions must be equally difficult.*

We were grateful for the ample support of family and friends. I received a phone call from my sister-in-law, Marilyn. "I don't know how you can do it. If it happened to me, I couldn't cope."

"Well, I don't have a choice. If you had to, I'm sure you could."

Just three weeks later, Grandma Ruth called. "Marilyn and Jack's baby, Lindsay, has an inoperable brain tumor."

God, why did You allow them to be plunged into this world of chemotherapy, radiation, and the shadow of death? Sometimes I guess You allow us to get in a difficult situation to demonstrate how tough You've made us. You'll lead us through it just as You led the children of Israel through the wilderness.

Jack asked the doctors, "What will Lindsay's life be like if she manages to survive?"

"She'll be severely physically and mentally handicapped, if she survives."

Marilyn and Jack stopped her treatments and tried to enjoy her fragile life before she faded away, an exquisite bud, unable to bloom.

Marilyn spoke softly when I called. "Lindsay's illness affects Jack and I differently. I feel as if I'm whirling down rapids on a raft, with water rushing over the edges, carrying things away. I can grasp a few things and keep them from being swept away, but I can't worry about the rest; I have to hang on. I just let them go and hope it will be all right.

"Jack says its like he's defending a castle under attack with the walls crumbling away. It's impossible to defend, and he can't stop the destruction."

Both were feeling helpless, but Marilyn was not feeling as frustrated or blameworthy as Jack. Perhaps men's role as protector and family leader makes them feel their impotence more keenly when they discover how helpless they are against such a foe.

Some churches teach that faith will heal all illness. I didn't realize how discreetly destructive this was until I saw how it affected Marilyn and her family. "If you have enough faith, your loved ones will be made well" may seem like a harmless statement, but it also means that unrestored health is caused by a lack of faith. If a child dies, it's because their family didn't have enough faith. Paul had a strong faith, yet God didn't remove his thorn in the flesh (see 2 Cor. 12:7–10). No one could have done more for Lindsay than Marilyn and Jack did. What they endured is impossible to imagine, but they made Lindsay's short time on earth as full as possible for an infant. She passed away quietly, one of the littlest saints. But her loss etched a shadow on Marilyn's heart, and for years she said it ached when she saw Uriah. All I could do was pray.

November 14, 1983

Dear Central School District Staff:

. . . Mara Alexander's 15-month-old son, Uriah, has recently been diagnosed as having leukemia. . . . Uriah is receiving chemotherapy, but this treatment means that he must receive regular blood transfusions.

We have contacted the Blood Bank of San Bernardino County to set up a Blood Reserve Fund to be used by Uriah and other Central School District family members who may face a similar need in the future. Won't you give the gift of life?

Sincerely,

Andrew E. Carlmark
Interim Director of Personnel

Following that letter, there was an outpouring of cards from those who were moved by the tragedy that had befallen us. As I decorated the white walls of Uriah's hospital room with splashes of colorful cards, I prayed:

God, it's awful that Uriah is ill, but because of it people understand how blessed they are to have healthy children and have worked together to create a blood fund for the school district. . . . You're already doing it, aren't You, God? Taking bad and putting it to good use, like You promised in Romans 8:28. If I just look, I'll see good come of anything we have to endure. Even if I can't see it, God, I know You have a good purpose for everything You allow.

Uriah was hospitalized every week or two with various illnesses. He got chemotherapy in the clinic when he was well. One of the first people I met in the waiting room was a thirteen-year-old puppeteer with a four-foot furry monkey.

When he saw me with a small child, worried and uncertain, he reached out to me. It was so different from the aloof behavior I expected from students. "I use my puppets to make kids forget why they're here." He made the whimsical creature cavort with a life of its own. Uriah giggled until tears of joy trickled down his ruddy cheeks.

"What's his diagnosis and prognosis?" he asked. He listened to my halting answer. "He'll probably be fine," he reassured me. "I've been coming here for years, and I've got two kinds of leukemia. The medicine for one makes the other one worse."

To know this young man had endured years of treatment and yet remained hopeful, intelligent, kind, and unafraid kindled hope in me. He provided me with basic information, such as the location of the lab, the closest bathroom, where to get food, and what time the doctors came. I resolved to follow his example and pass on information to newcomers.

I saw him only a few more times. After six months, I summoned the courage to ask the nurse about him. She turned back to her paperwork. "He died," she murmured. *The clinic won't be as bright without him and his puppets. It's up to those of us left to encourage others as he did.*

Parents in the waiting room compared notes on their children, but instead of their achievements, we talked about their illness, treatment, and prognosis. It didn't take long until it became a waiting room filled with friends who understood our problems and challenges because cancer was part of their lives too. It gave us a forum to discuss problems, ideas, and solutions. Often phone numbers were exchanged and lifelong friendships formed.

Before Thanksgiving, the Mariposas sent us a gift certificate to a grocery store. The Mariposas was a nonprofit support group started by the mothers of two Kaiser pediatric oncology patients who died before Uriah was diagnosed. The annual Mariposas events were a Christmas party and a summer barbecue picnic.

❧ ❧ ❧

One day Don returned from a trip to the butcher shop, looking dazed. "What odds did the doctors say Uriah had?"

"What?" I asked, wondering what it had to do with a butcher shop.

He avoided my eyes. "There's a sign at the butcher shop. It says only 10 percent of children with leukemia survive."

"Maybe the sign was old," I reasoned. "The doctors gave Uriah an intermediate chance, about 60 percent. Maybe it was for all kinds of leukemia. He has the most curable kind, you know."

That seemed to reassure him. Later I read the small sign on the donation container on the butcher shop's counter. It was about ALL, the kind of leukemia Uriah had: "90 percent of children diagnosed with acute lymphocytic leukemia are in remission after one year; 50 percent after five years, and only 10 percent after ten years."

Could it be true? It's time to start reading. I checked out library books about leukemia, cancer, death, and dying. The information made me feel better; I knew what to expect. *I hope Don doesn't think I'm being morbid.* "Honey, these books explain so much—"

"I don't want to talk about it," he shoved the screen door out of his way, letting it slam behind him.

I kept it to myself.

Thanksgiving Day we savored the company of family and friends as never before. We hadn't been certain Uriah would even live that long. *God, spending time together as a family is a gift too many take for granted. Someday all I may have to look back on are the memories I make today. At the end of our days together, I want to be able to look back without regret.*

A short time later, with Christmas 1983 just around the corner, all was not well. The Department of Housing and Urban Development sent us a letter December 5. Our apartment building was being repossessed. We had sixty to ninety days to vacate the premises, even though we had paid our rent on time. The car broke down, the motorcycle broke down, and there was no money for the children's presents. Don and I were still sleeping on the living-room floor.

One night while Don was working, Uriah woke up, screaming in pain from an ear infection. I didn't even have a way to get him to the doctor! I paced back and forth with him in front of the aquarium, and we both cried. *God, why do we have to suffer so much when others seem to have no problems, especially those who don't even care about You?* My thoughts turned to Job and Joseph. God had a reason for allowing their misfortunes and turned their sorrows to great joy. *Even if I don't understand now, God, You already know I'll agree with Your reasons when You explain them someday. Deep in the night, I'll try to remember things look better in morning light.*

As soon as Don arrived home, I rushed Uriah to the clinic. This time I wasn't surprised when they admitted him, or by his two week stay in the hospital. The release form instructions were explicit: "Keep Uriah away from people who have colds or are sick in any way."

※ ※ ※

That Christmas, Nana ordered handmade Cabbage Patch dolls that looked like each of her grandchildren. The children loved those dolls, but I wondered what I would do with Uriah's if he died. Uriah's illness had changed the way I looked at everything.

※ ※ ※

Don and I lay on the mattress one night, watching the fish swimming to and fro in the aquarium. "I need you to hide my gun," he confessed. "I've been thinking about suicide."

"Haven't you noticed? It's been gone for a while." He gazed at me in surprise. I told him of my dream. "You've got to get counseling for the stress," I pleaded. "You get angry so easily now and yell at the kids for little things. Before Uriah got sick, they used to run to see you when you got home. Now they drift into their rooms and don't make a sound."

His eyes filled with tears, and he nodded. Dr. Sully counseled Don and prescribed medication to help him with clinical depression—an emotional downward spiral so severe that the only way to recover is to break the body's chemical imbalance with medication. Though not immediate, there was improvement. It didn't take long for the children to notice. It was nice to see him playing with them again. *They need him and he needs them.*

With the purchase of our first home and Uriah's concurrent remission, it was time for me to return to work in early January 1984. Debbie's first baby was due in February. She decided to continue our job-sharing arrangement, though it meant subjecting her family to the same isolation my family faced.

At work, my mind was completely involved with my job. I relaxed more at work than when I slept because there was no room in my crowded mind to worry about Uriah's illness. Strange as it sounds, I left work more refreshed than when I arrived. Work became my relaxation—and I got paid too!

My coworkers were sympathetic and often asked about Uriah. At first I told them how he was, whether it was good or bad news. But some people were terribly uncomfortable and fidgety if my answer was anything less than "Fine!"

"How's Uriah?" one woman asked.

"He's kind of sick after his last chemo. We're hoping they don't have to put him in the hospital."

"So how's Uriah?" she repeated.

"Well, his platelets and white count are low. He's fighting an infection, but as long as he doesn't run a fever, he can stay home. If he gets sick, he won't be able to have his chemo, and the cancer might come back."

"So how's Uriah?"

I gazed at her uncertainly a moment. "He's fine," I murmured.

"Oh, good!" she smiled, finally satisfied. She turned and went on her way, leaving me to gaze after her in amazement. *She needs the illusion, not the reality. Some want the real answer, and some can only handle "Fine!"*

I discovered even a few parents at the clinic were unable to deal with what was happening to their child. They dropped them off for treatment, returning to pick them up when it was over. Medical staff encouraged parents to stay with their child, but doctors and nurses recognized that not all parents thrown into this situation were equal to it. The children seemed to understand this and attempted to protect their parents, doing everything in their power to relay that "Fine!" message to them.

I watched the girls for signs of having trouble coping with Uriah's illness. Once Shiloh awakened in tears from a nightmare. I held her close in the light and consoled her. She snuggled up to me and shared her dream: "Me and Uriah were playing, and he rolled under the bed. He called me, and I crawled under the bed. He rolled through a crack in the wall." With tears in her eyes, she looked up at me. "I tried and tried to reach him, but I just couldn't pull him out."

We checked on Uriah, made sure the wall was solid, and shared a glass of milk. I tucked her in and kissed her little head. "Call if you need me. I'm just a few steps away." *It isn't right for someone so small to have to go through so much. She's afraid of losing him.*

The new house was wonderful. Uriah and the girls romped with the dogs in the large backyard. Uriah was tall for eighteen months, with blond, curly hair, blue eyes, and a quick smile. He loved his cowboy boots and dog. Heather and Shiloh loved to hold and feed Debbie's baby, Joel, a 1984 leap-year baby. But Uriah and Joel became inseparable best buddies.

They were all playing together in the family room one afternoon. "Heather and Shiloh," I called, "we need to go to the doctor for your checkup." Uriah's ever-present smile disappeared. He turned to each of the girls in turn, giving them a heartfelt hug with an expression of utmost sympathy. With a jolt, I understood. *Uriah thinks everyone suffers the same things he does at the hospital: bone marrows, spinal taps, and needles.*

❦ ❦ ❦

We couldn't attend church because of the risk of infection. We had church at home for a while, but we missed the fellowship. Then I remembered the church I attended when I was growing up: the pastor's office at Immanuel Lutheran in Chino had a large window with a view of the church. "Sure," Pastor Wolff chuckled. "Consider my office your box seat every Sunday." *Thank You, God! Church is even more important now that life is so complicated.*

In May 1984 we passed a milestone: Uriah graduated to maintenance chemotherapy. We began to hope.

One summer morning we went to the City of Hope in Duarte for HLA (human leukocyte antigen) testing. Sometimes chemotherapy doesn't work, and doctors try to replace the cancerous bone marrow with healthy tissue from a sibling. The blood type is irrelevant, but it has to be an exact tissue match.

I had my blood drawn first while the girls watched. I hate needles, but I spoke evenly and kept a straight face as a young woman pushed the needle into my vein. "You'll feel a little pinch when she puts the needle in, but then it'll be over. And if your blood matches Uriah's, you can help him if he gets sicker." She removed the needle, and I turned to the girls. "Who wants to get it over next?" I asked. They shook their heads and crossed their arms.

The phlebotomist smiled: "I was impressed!"

On August 15, Debbie drove us to the apartments Kaiser provided near Hollywood for the week and a half of Uriah's radiation treatments. Jean Exline, the resident manager of the apartments, smiled and welcomed us. "We don't usually have people come with children. Most people are older, but another mother and her baby are coming later this week."

After dinner, I leafed through a brochure from a support group called Candlelighters:

Our Dear Sweet Aaron,

When your hand slipped from ours into Jesus' hand Monday night, we knew your struggle was over for eternity. God is the only one who could possibly love you as much as us, and we know you won't be lonesome waiting for us all to be together again. . . .

God is so generous in giving you to us for five and a half years. Though the last two were challenging, they increased our daily appreciation of each other. Each day together was a precious gift and allowed us to do and say things we might otherwise postpone. Every smile, hug, and "I love you" took on a special meaning—we crammed a lifetime of love into a few years. We are grateful there was nothing left unsaid.

We love you for eternity.

Mommy, Poppa, and Sissie[1]

The next morning I settled the girls in chairs at Kaiser to play while I took Uriah to check in. The receptionist was a smiling woman of quick wittiness whose name was Rose. *She must be a special person to work in such a place. The people she sees every day are fighting for their lives against a deadly disease, some without any real hope of recovery. She makes it look so simple to keep a sense of humor and positive attitude here. It can't be easy, but it's necessary for the well-being of those who work here—and for those who want to survive cancer.*

Uriah was terrified of the machinery and of the dark room where radiation was administered. The technicians, both in their mid-twenties, showed us pictures of children who had come for treatment before. "Uriah, you're the youngest we've had yet!" The young woman smiled and hung a Polaroid snapshot of him on the side of the file cabinet with the others.

Her coworker cleared his throat. "Uriah needs to remain motionless during his treatments, but no one can stay in the room with him. So he'll get a tranquilizer forty-five minutes before his treatments."

While Uriah slept, the technicians taped his head in position, painstakingly lining up red laser lights so they crossed at the exact location radiation was to be administered. Then, leaving him lying on the table of the huge machine in the darkness, they closed the heavy door and observed a desktop of dials and controls, flipping a few switches. Then they pushed aside the thick door, and I retrieved Uriah. He appeared unchanged by the invisible treatment, the effects of which were felt, not seen.

That night I dreamed of Nana's house. Uriah sat before me, and on the other side of him was an evil character. Not that he looked evil; it was a feeling that filled the air and made my skin crawl. He sneered at me, grinning with contempt. Pointing to Uriah, he hissed, "I'm going to take your son away, and there's nothing you can do about it."

I was filled with rage. I wanted to shout that he had no power over my son because Uriah was a child of God, but when I opened my mouth, I was unable to speak. The devil who faced me roared with laughter at my helplessness.

All I have to do is to speak the Lord's name, and he'll flee. I began the Lord's Prayer, and though there was no sound to the first word, *Our,* when I mouthed the word *Father,* my voice returned, and I found I was sitting on the couch in the apartment. I fervently prayed the entire prayer. The feeling of malice lingered, though the evil creature had fled. I raced to the bedroom. Uriah slept, undisturbed. I flopped down on the couch and continued to pray. *God, the dream was so vivid, so real. I'm afraid it might return.*

If God chooses to take Uriah home, will I feel God let me down? At the worst, Uriah will live in heaven without pain, fear, or worry. I wish Uriah was older so I could hear him say he believes in God and accepts Jesus' gift of salvation. All I can do is leave him in the hands of a loving God, who is wise and powerful enough to do what is best—for all.

❧ ❧ ❧

The young woman with short, brown hair and striking, deep brown eyes looked exhausted and tense when she arrived at the Kaiser apartments with her three-week-old baby. Jean, the manager, introduced us. After the young woman left for her apartment, Jean confided, "She has an inoperable brain tumor."

My mouth dropped open, and I gazed toward her receding figure. *How would it feel if I knew I would never see my child grow up, get married, or go to school? Unless it happens to me, I could never really know that feeling. I expect to watch my children experience those events, yet my life could be cut short without warning.*

When we know we're dying, we can't ignore our mortality. If we look directly into the face of death, it gives us an opportunity to change our priorities and our lives.

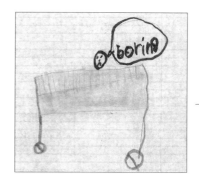

Whistling in the Dark
(1985)

*Only You could know the gift was vibrant life
and not the shadow of death the world sees.*

T HAT YEAR WE SPENT NEARLY AS MUCH TIME APART AS TOGETHER. Now that Heather skipped from kindergarten to second grade and Shiloh was in kindergarten, we had trouble with the chickenpox. Since chickenpox is fatal for children with leukemia, Dr. Sanmarco and Dr. Haghighat advised us to have the girls live elsewhere for three weeks after each exposure because it's contagious the day before there are any symptoms.

Their teachers and the school nurse were careful to inform us if anyone caught chickenpox. Once it got started, there seemed to be a new outbreak of chickenpox every two weeks.

Being separated was hard on us all. When the girls couldn't come home, they lived at Nana's or Debbie's, and I divided my time between home and the girls. When they stayed with Debbie, I took them roller skating in nearby neighborhoods where we looked for the best slopes.

"When can we come home?" Heather asked.

"That depends on how many more kids catch chickenpox," I said.

"How come Uriah doesn't have to leave home?"

"He went last time—"

"He always gets his way." She skated away, her jaw set.

At times we overcompensated, and she would get more than anyone. But there was no way we could give back what was being taken from her: a normal childhood. Shiloh was the quiet one; I worried about her most. Heather made sure she got her share, but Shiloh waited patiently for whatever we could give. She was the one to go to if we needed a hug. For a five-year old, she had a lot of empathy.

If someone was sad, Shiloh's big, blue eyes were sober, but after she hugged them, her dimpled smile would flash because they felt better.

Uriah was quick to laugh, loved games, and looked like any normal three-year old. When he wasn't at the hospital, it was hard to imagine he was so ill. His energy and intelligence seemed unaffected by his treatments, except by Cytoxan, which made him sleep and stop eating, but he took it only once a month. He never complained about being ill, though he realized he was different. We answered his questions about his leukemia honestly. As Christians, it was easier to talk to him about death because we had answers from the Bible.

Joel, Debbie's one-year-old son, went with us for Uriah's appointments, which were no longer twice a week but only once a month. Those who needed treatment most were seen first at the clinic, and often there were emergencies. So it was hard to know how long we would wait for the doctor to see us. I learned a repertoire of instant games, such as "I Spy" and "Twenty Questions." Aunt Debbie taught me "Arthur Bunny" stories she invented about a rabbit whose many adventures included a trip to the hospital. Whenever the boys did something new, Arthur Bunny did it too.

"The Game Bag" was a large sports bag loaded with little cars, travel games, and card games. When we had that bag, no child in the waiting room would be bored because they played with our toys. UNO was Uriah's favorite game. I never *let* him win, but I was rarely the victor.

My scribbles in the old notebook graduated to regular journal entries. Writing made it easier for me to let go of my anxieties. It seemed I could forget about my troubles once they were written down:

Saturday, April 20
    Janet and Andy came to supper. Our macaw, Sarge, and their macaw, Rosie, are in the same cage for the night.

Sunday, April 21
    Uriah got up early and tried to give the birds a treat. One of the macaws bit him. I took him to the emergency room. Thank God his finger wasn't broken.

Monday, April 22
    Uriah's finger's infected. The doctors prescribed antibiotics and a soap soak.

Saturday, April 27
    Don made breakfast and let me sleep in. Janet and Andy came over for a yard sale and supper. Uriah's still running a fever; I'm worried.

Sunday, April 28
    Uriah's still running a fever and has a slight rash on his arms. Janet and Andy stayed to supper again.

Monday, April 29

The doctors said the antibiotic isn't causing the fever or rash but to stop giving it to him. He has a slight throat infection and is still running a fever, 102. Shiloh and Heather's classes have chickenpox. Debbie stayed for supper.

Tuesday, April 30

For our anniversary Don sent a flower arrangement to school. I got him an aquarium. Uriah is staying at Debbie's because the girls were exposed to the chickenpox.

Wednesday, May 1

Uriah's fever is finally gone. Don said the carburetor in our car is defective and has to be replaced.

Thursday, May 2

I forgot to have Don take Debbie's car to work last night, so he met me this morning at Debbie's where I was watching Uriah and Joel. I handed him a piece of strawberry pie. "Would you drive to Cucamonga to trade cars with Debbie? She has the car seats."

"This is a mess," he said. He just sat staring for a long time with his strawberry pie in his lap.

"Either go get the car, or just go home and I can call Debbie." He still sat staring. I tried to hug him to make him feel better, but he jumped and spilled pie all over. I cleaned it up while he went back to staring.

At last he said, "Call Debbie," put his gun on top of the armoire, and left.

He called later. "I feel better. Can you find out if Nana would let Heather and Shiloh stay with her so Uriah could come home?"

I talked to Nana after I picked up Heather. "I'm busy Wednesday and Thursday nights, but I'll watch them anyway if that's what you want. Are you OK?"

"I think so." *I'm a basket case.*

After I told him what she said, Don said, "Just leave things the way they are."

Wednesday, May 22

Uriah came home tonight. Heather stayed in her room. Nana can't watch her until next week. Uriah's so happy to be home, but Heather doesn't want to go to Nana's.

Thursday, May 23

The pain and numbness in my head are increasing. I hope it's just stress. I've been so tired lately. I hope having Uriah home will help.

Friday, June 21

Debbie and Jeff left on vacation.

Tuesday, June 25

We helped Andy and Janet pack all day. They spent the night and plan to leave at daybreak tomorrow to move to Washington. They've been so supportive. We're going to miss them terribly.

Thursday, June 27

Nana and Boompa need a housesitter. I told her the kids and I would do it.

Friday, June 28

We spent the night at Nana's. They will leave early tomorrow. I called the doctor about Uriah. His stomach is bothering him.

Saturday, June 29

The kids fought over the computer, just like home. Uriah's worse.

Sunday, June 30
I didn't give Uriah his medicine because he's so pale. I'm worried about him. We're going to the doctor tomorrow.

Monday, July 1
Uriah didn't get a treatment because his white count is too low.

Wednesday, July 3
Nana and Boompa got home around noon.

Thursday, July 4
We stayed at Nana's house for dinner. The kids lit sparklers and watched fireworks. Nana's worried about Uriah because he looks pale and blue-lipped. He ran a high temperature tonight.

Friday, July 5
Uriah's in the hospital. We're on the fourth floor with the terminal and aged patients in serious condition because there's no room in the pediatric ward. Just as everyone seems to line up at the grocery-store checkout at the same time, it seems all the clinic kids get sick at once. Uriah's running a fever of 104 and being fed intravenously. "There's a possibility Uriah's relapsed," Dr. Haghighat said. "We need to do a bone marrow."

The shadow of relapse again. We're always at risk of losing Uriah.

In the next room was Steven, a twelve-year old who had acute lymphocytic leukemia, like Uriah. His mother and I had spoken a few times at the clinic. She carried a notebook and made detailed notes about any condition or medication pertaining to her son. "Gee, that's a good idea," I said.

"I started it when I realized we parents are responsible to make sure our children get the treatments they need to survive." Steven had survived four relapses and was now fighting an infection they couldn't identify. After the third day of an extreme fever, which refused to break, they put him on ice sheets.

The day Uriah was released, I saw Steven's mother. "I'm glad you're going home," she murmured. "I don't think I'll be taking Steven home this time. He gave up a few weeks ago. He's tired of the pain and wants to die so he won't hurt anymore. He's even made funeral plans."

I was horrified. "I hope . . . things turn out OK. I'll pray." I escaped into Uriah's room, held him, and cried. *God, I hope I never hear Uriah say that. I can't imagine how it would feel to know my child was dying and there was nothing I could do.*

"How would it feel to know your Son was dying and you could stop it, but the whole world would die if you didn't let Him suffer and die?"

Forgive me, God. Sometimes it's so easy to forget that You lost Your Son too. Please be with them, and if possible, give this mother back her son.

I never saw either of them again.

Uriah's bone marrow is normal, but he's on a liquid diet. He can't eat anything with sugar or milk in it—and his birthday is in two days. I bought a loaf of round Hawaiian bread and put candles on top. It looks a little like a cake. We had a few friends over and played lots of games. Heather gave him a book she wrote.

In August, both the motorcycle and car broke down again, but good things were happening too. We went to the Mariposas picnic in August and ate hot dogs and hamburgers, played baseball, watched a clown show, and talked with all our friends from the clinic—some we hadn't seen in months. But the respites we received were few, and the crises frequent.

Thursday, August 15
Uriah's white count has been low for two weeks. He's off all chemotherapy.

Tuesday, September 3
This morning I was awakened from the dream of a storm by Uriah's soft pleading, "Eat, eat." Prednisone makes him so hungry. I stumbled to the kitchen and fixed him a bowl of Cheerios.

At his appointment, Uriah bled too fast when his blood was drawn. Dr. Haghighat said, "Uriah hasn't recovered his blood count. He'll have to have a bone marrow." The ghost of relapse resurrected.

Uriah fought harder than usual. Bone-marrow tests are painful enough when they're routine and we're prepared, but when it's unexpected, it's twice as hard to bear.

"The slides are good," Dr. Haghighat said.

Good for staining, or free from disease? Uriah fell asleep in my lap while I applied pressure to his punctured hip.

I was surprised when Don walked in with a big bag of Kentucky Fried Chicken just after noon. Though Uriah was sound asleep, the smell of his favorite food sent him half-stumbling, half-scrambling to the table. *I'm proud of Don. He hates coming to the hospital.*

As we stood talking, Dr. Haghighat entered. "Uriah has 11–15 percent suspicious cells in his bone marrow. A relapse is 25 percent." He paused. "I'll stain more slides to be sure. Go ahead and eat." But all appetite had left us.

I cried. *It means we'll have to start all over, and we were nearly through!* Don shifted his weight and looked toward the door. *Why did this have to happen when Don was doing so well? He won't come back to the hospital again.*

"It's probably going to take a while. Do you want to go home?" I asked.

"No. I came to have lunch with you." He turned to Uriah: "Hey, sport. How about a game of UNO?"

I watched him deal out our hands. Only a week ago I asked Dr. Sanmarco if the blood tests done at the City of Hope showed the girls could be bone-marrow donors. She studied Shiloh's profile but soon replied, "No, no. There's nothing here. They're just too different." At the time I was relieved because I didn't have to decide if we should risk a transplant, but now I felt trapped because our options had narrowed. *God closed that door. He will provide what is needed; He always has.*

After a few hands of UNO, Dr. Haghighat motioned for Don and me to join him in the corridor. "There are definitely quite a few bad cells. We're taking Uriah off all his medications except one, and he won't get a treatment today. . . ."

But he'll relapse for sure and we don't want that!

". . . We need to find out if he will relapse or recover. Bring him back for a spinal tap and bone marrow next week."

Tuesday, September 10

Uriah's blood levels had improved, so he was slated for more tests September 17. If Uriah relapses while he's on chemotherapy, his long-term survival won't be possible; it will just be a matter of time before his leukemia kills him. An incredible, invisible weight seems to hang over my head. The only way to cope with it is to put it into God's hands. That's where it really is. Life needs to continue, even if our hearts want to stand still.

Heather and Shiloh started school: bilingual third- and first-grade classes, respectively. Events remained intriguing. We were told Shiloh might be dyslexic, and our car burned.

Tuesday, September 17
There were still suspicious cells in Uriah's bone marrow, but his blood levels had improved. He got his treatment and is due back in a month.

In the midst of all that was happening, feeling as if we were stumbling through a hurricane that threatened to tear us apart, Don and I realized we needed to spend time together. Otherwise how could we hope to survive the turmoil? Keeping our family together and strong by nurturing our relationship was the best thing we could do for all of us. Friday, October 11, the children stayed with Grandma Ruth and Grandpa Fred while Don and I went on a motorcycle vacation to Sequoia National Park.

Wednesday, November 13
When I got to work, Debbie whispered, "Ann Weinberger's son was murdered. It appears he saw something someone didn't want him to. Oh, and Mr. Natoli's wife had a baby November 11, Shiloh's birthday!"

I congratulated Mr. Natoli, collected two disk drives, and headed out the office door. On the way to class, I had a discipline problem with three female students, and we went to see Bruce Hemlock, the counselor. Near the end of the discussion, I set my hand on the table. One of the girls noticed. "Guy, look at her hand shaking."

"I've got nerves."

Bruce said, "I think you need to understand that Mrs. Alexander has been through a lot and is under a lot of pressure. . . ."

I started to cry. *They probably think it's divorce or something.* "My son has leukemia, and we don't know if he will live or die."

"Well, my grandpa died from leukemia," quipped one of the girls with a so-what attitude.

It made me angry. "But you didn't need someone to give you a bad time when he did, did you?"

As I got up to leave, one of the girls said, "Well, we're Christians."

"You know, it doesn't help to know you could be Christians and behave like this."

I went to the bathroom. *I've got to pull myself together.*

When I got to the computer lab, Mrs. Weinberger's class was there with a substitute. "Everything's OK," he said.

I sat down and tried to think. What's wrong with me? Why am I having so much trouble? It isn't Uriah's treatment. He's had so many treatments before, and it never affected me this much. Then it dawned on me: Ann's son died. What she must be going through! And I'll probably go through it too before Uriah turns eleven. My heart ached for her and her son and for me and mine.

That rhetoric about the grandfather bothers me. Once a next-door neighbor discounted what I was going through by saying, "Well, so? My aunt died from cancer."

There's so much difference between watching someone sicken and die from a distance—maybe a few visits—and actually living with someone who's dying: fighting to help them stay alive, giving them medication, holding them down and trying to console them during painful treatments and hospital stays. You funnel so much energy into them. It's a constant fight, and the outcome is uncertain at best. For some, the outcome is certain—and fatal. Yet the fight goes on because time can be won.

We received a Christmas card from Dr. Sully who moved to Inglewood in 1984: "Hope everything is going well. I still keep your card in my office. Merry Xmas!"

I gave him that card before he moved! "If you hadn't sent me for the blood test, I know Uriah would have died. And you made a call at our house. House calls in the '80s? Unheard of." *It must mean a lot to him.*

Tuesday, December 17
Don and I purchased wood for a playhouse with a swing set. The kids and I painted its two stories blue and white. This is a very rich Christmas and we are thankful.

Tuesday, December 24
Uriah ran a fever but didn't hurt anywhere. Dr. Haghighat sent him for a chest X-ray. Uriah cried the entire time, and the technician said the X-rays might not be good. We took them to pediatrics, but Dr. Haghighat had to leave, and our case was given to another doctor. "The X-rays are so bad I couldn't tell anything from them," Dr. Quanson said. "Bring him back if he has trouble breathing or starts to turn blue."
Oh, great! It's going to be a relaxing Christmas Eve.
"Bring him back at nine tomorrow morning," he finished.
Christmas Day will be interrupted too.
At 3:00 A.M. when I crawled into bed, Uriah complained his ears hurt. *At least it's an ear infection instead of pneumonia.*

Wednesday, December 25
Everyone gathered at Nana's and started to open presents, but Uriah and I had to go. As I packed Uriah in the car, Leah jumped in too. "I'm coming!"
I beamed at her. *Thanks, God! It's nice not to be alone when the whole world is celebrating.*

Another year come and gone, and we're all still together.

The Gift

At first,
You're silently screaming,
Helpless free-falling without hope.
Dazed and numb, you try to cope.
It's like being flung off a cliff and waiting for God to catch you.
Trusting He will, but fearing He won't.

You can
Scream forever in angry agony,
Or laugh and enjoy the happy times
That are still there if you look for them.
Laughter creates wonderful memories
That will strengthen you in the days to come.

So now,
More alive and aware than before,
Time that would have slipped away
Is experienced to the fullest.
Senses keened by the realization
Of how fleeting life is for all.

Such a strange gift.
How much we would have missed.
How nonchalant and uninvolved our lives.
Only You could know the gift was vibrant life,
And not the shadow of death the world sees.
We thank You, Master of Blessings in Disguise.

Five

A Ray of Hope
(1986)

*Faith doesn't ensure survival, but it makes it easier
for the child and family to function.*

Thursday, January 23, 1986

I ATTENDED A MEETING TO START A SUPPORT GROUP AT KAISER and met Diana Miller. "My thirteen-year-old daughter Jenny had bone cancer, and they removed part of her leg," she told me. "She's already talking about getting a prosthesis and rejoining marching band. Sometimes I feel guilty because Jenny comforts me instead of the other way 'round. When we were told Jenny's leg would have to be amputated, I felt miserable for her until Jenny said, 'Mom, please don't worry about it. I've already given it to the Lord.'"

Tuesday, March 18

Today we met Brandon, a four-year-old hemophiliac. He's very articulate and polite. A real cute character. Bleeding is his problem because he's low on platelets. They found out two weeks ago when they took him for a school checkup. Brandon wears a helmet to protect his head. He can't play outside. His father, an athlete, is taking it hard.

Brandon and Uriah were both shy and wouldn't talk at first but finally played together. During Uriah's treatment, they had to stick Uriah twice, and he screamed. Brandon was there for painless tests, but he screamed just like Uriah.

Monday, March 31

We took a four-day vacation last week. It was nice to be able to drive away from the problems for a while. We went up to Creston, near San Luis Obispo, to see my youngest sister Joanna, her husband Mark, and my newest niece Megan—one and a half weeks old. The kids loved roller-coaster Highway 58 on the way there; so did Don!

Mark took the kids down to the pond and showed them tadpoles and three little snakes—all very frightened. Then they hiked up in the hills and gathered bouquets for Joanna and put wildflowers in their hair.

In San Francisco, Leah and Bob took us to the old fort, Lombard Street, and their favorite spot in the park on a Sunday, when skaters and bikers take over the parkways.

Don's been working a lot of overtime to pay for the car, but when he's off, he's been helping fix up the house. We're trying to get ready for the eventual move.

Tuesday, April 15

Uriah went for his treatment, but his white count was too low.

When Debbie came to pick me up after work, we took Heather to dance, Shiloh to gymnastics, got chocolate milk for the kids at the dairy, picked up Heather, grabbed some take-out burgers, and went to pick up Shiloh. She met me at the door, crying with a wet paper towel on her arm. "I fell off the beam and broke my arm," she sobbed.

"She fell off the beam and hit her arm," the instructor said, "but I think it just popped out of joint and back in." *There's no discoloration. It'll be better in a few hours.* It seemed better—except when she had to do things she didn't want to.

Wednesday, April 16

At the park before school, Shiloh wouldn't play. Shiloh's always so melodramatic, I didn't believe her. Boy, do I feel guilty.

The shoulder X-ray showed a fracture two inches below the shoulder. "From now on I'll listen to you," I told Shiloh. "After all, you're the one who's in there."

Tuesday, April 22

Instead of getting a treatment, Uriah's in the hospital. He's running a fever and has no disease-fighting white cells.

Wednesday, April 23

The girls and I went to visit Uriah. We went home for dinner; I returned afterward until 7:30 P.M. I met Jenny and her family in the waiting room.

Thursday, April 24

Don, Joel, and I went to see Uriah. The IV had infiltrated during the night, and his hand and wrist were swollen to three times their normal size. "It doesn't hurt," he said. The swelling dissipated on its own, but it looked awful.

Don's sergeant's wife will be Uriah's nurse this afternoon.

Saturday, April 26

Grandma Ruth visited Uriah. She brought toys and played cards and games with him. Then she came home with me for dinner.

Monday, April 28

When we returned from Shiloh's appointment for her broken arm, Uriah's bags were on the couch. Uriah's home from the hospital!

"His blood count's low," Don said. "He has to be kept away from people."

"No church Sunday," I sighed.

Monday, May 5

Uriah's blood count is better, and he started oral chemotherapy.

Monday, May 12

Shiloh got her sling off.

Wednesday, May 14

While Uriah got Cytoxan, I met a nice lady with an eight-year-old son. She's from Apple Valley and a crafter with four kids. Her son has ATV—chronically low platelets but not hemophilia. Debbie and the kids came to pick us up at the clinic.

Thursday, May 15

Uriah and Joel were playing with his rolling horse before I went to work. Uriah fell, started to cry, and grabbed at his diaper. When I took off his diaper, I saw a gash in his penis. *How could this have happened?* I discovered the fly button of his overalls had a sharp protrusion from its center. *It looks like he needs stitches—if they can do that.*

Dr. Haghighat sent us to the acute care clinic. I had to carry Uriah because he was in such pain. The nurse said, "Dr. Eastman will see Uriah."

It couldn't be Mark Eastman from high school, could it? It was.

He examined Uriah. "It needs stitches, but I think it would be better to use staples because of the location. I'm going to confer with another doctor, but that's what I'm recommending."

The words conjured up visions of a desktop stapler. *No, it has to be a specialized medical device.* Uriah tried to hold still, and it was soon over. I got to work just before the end of my shift.

Monday, May 19

They removed Uriah's staples—painlessly. I wrote to the overall manufacturer, but they never replied. I was so busy and embarrassed, I let it go.

Wednesday, May 21

Don called at 6:30 A.M. "I'm working overtime, honey."

He called again at 9:30. "There's an outbreak of rubella here. I'm getting tested before I come home."

"Uriah's never been immunized. If you're susceptible, you won't be able to come home!"

"I know."

An hour later the phone interrupted my prayers. "I had my immunizations when I was a kid," Don said, "so I can't carry it home."

"Thank God! Having the children live elsewhere is one thing, but if it keeps you away, I couldn't stand it."

Tuesday, June 10

Uriah's blood count was too low for a treatment. "He's off all medications until you come back next Wednesday," Dr. Haghighat said.

At least he's not in the hospital.

Wednesday, June 18

Uriah couldn't get his treatment again. His blood count was even lower. The doctors sent him for a chest X-ray to see if he had an infection.

Saturday, June 21

Heather's dance program, "Alice in Wonderland," was held in a big auditorium. She and her classmates did a tap dance as unicorns.

Wednesday, June 25

Dr. Haghighat scanned Uriah's file. "We're considering taking Uriah off his treatments in September—providing he stays in remission."

"Really? You mean, he would be all done? Wow, that would be great!"

We could move to Oregon so Don could finally get a promotion! There's so much to do! We could move on!

Monday, July 7

The kids were fighting so much, I was glad to send them to summer school while I worked.

Monday, July 21

Debbie substituted for me so I could take Uriah for his treatment. His blood count was low, but they treated him anyway. "Bathe him nightly and wash his hands often," Dr. Haghighat said.

Saturday, July 26

Joanna and Joel came to celebrate Uriah's birthday with a whipped-cream-strawberry-cake, slip-n-slide, Care-Bear party.

Friday, August 1

Last day of summer school. Uriah's ill.

Saturday, August 2

Uriah ran a 102-degree fever last night. I took him to see Dr. Haghighat. Later at home, Heather and Uriah argued over the computer. She yanked him off the chair, and he gashed his head. Two more stitches from Dr. Eastman.

Tuesday, August 12

A headache kept me up all night and still pounded my head when I awoke. Uriah threw up as soon as he woke up. I made him an appointment for 3:00.

Saturday, August 16

None of our class officers arranged our ten-year class reunion, so who jumped into the breach? Joan Weiss, my good friend.

When Don and I attended, we chatted with Irene Keller and her husband Dave. They have a daughter named Heather too. We made plans to visit them in San Bernardino.

Tuesday, August 19

At Uriah's appointment, I met Shannon's mom. Shannon goes to school in our district, and her mom's interested in working in a computer lab. She'll be at the clinic tomorrow, so I'm bringing information and programs for her. Uriah's OK and got a shot.

Wednesday, August 20

I dropped Debbie off at an appointment this morning, planning to pick her up later after I took Uriah for his shot. But Uriah got Cytoxan, which takes all day to drip in. Don came to the rescue. He picked up the car, brought us food, and picked up Debbie.

Uriah's veins kept bursting, and Janette, the nurse, had to restart his IV five times. "I'm glad you're patient and don't leave Uriah alone," Janette said. "When all the parents leave at once to get lunch and things go wrong, like infiltrations, it's hard for me to keep up."

She finished rechecking the volume of the Cytoxan being pumped through the machine into Uriah and flicked a few air bubbles out of the tube. "Next month is probably Uriah's last treatment, but he'll have to go through a bone marrow, spinal tap, and testicular biopsy."

Wednesday, August 27

We went to the Mariposas picnic, and Dr. Sanmarco commented, "It's time to take Uriah off treatments."

If Uriah no longer needs treatments, I could get a career instead of just a job. I wonder how many of my college credits are still valid?

Saturday, August 30

We finished the insulation and nailed down boards on our roof. I thought we'd start shingling, but Don said, "We've worked hard enough. Let's go camping before school starts."

"It'll be good to get a break before work starts again," I sighed.

Monday, September 15

Red-letter day! Dr. Sanmarco smiled after examining Uriah. "He looks great. No more chemotherapy for Uriah."

Uriah grinned and hugged Dr. Sanmarco. I threw my arms around them both. The elation of hearing those words—words I never thought Uriah would live to hear—made me giddy. "What do I do with his medicine?"

Dr. Sanmarco blinked at the ridiculous question. "Throw it away! He'll have to have a spinal tap and bone marrow, and we'll schedule him for a testicular biopsy."

"We planned to celebrate with our family at Disneyland. Uriah's never been there. Can we go?"

"Sure!" She looked pleased to be able to relay good news instead of a diagnosis of disaster.

Saturday, September 20

Grandma Ruth joined us at the fair to watch Heather's dance competition. Heather beamed.

Tuesday, September 23

We visited the anesthesiologist to make arrangements for Uriah's biopsy. It would be awful if Uriah survived leukemia but not anesthesia.

Wednesday, September 24

Don and I went with Uriah for his biopsy. A man in hospital scrubs came to take him to surgery.

"Aw," said Uriah. "I wanted to finish beating you at UNO."

"Wanna go for a ride?" asked the masked man.

Uriah smiled. "Sure. I'll beat you later," he promised us.

We waited a virtual eternity until Dr. Wang, in green scrubs, called us into the hall. "He's in recovery. Everything looks fine, but we won't be certain until the doctors examine the biopsy."

What a relief! We've completed the last hurdle!

Tuesday, October 21

When I picked Uriah up from Debbie's house, he looked feverish. I put my hand to his burning forehead. *It's a high one.* I called home. "Don, can you take Heather to dance so I can take Shiloh and Uriah to the hospital?"

They drew Uriah's blood and admitted him. "We're afraid he might not be able to fight infection," Dr. Sanmarco said. "His blood counts are low."

I thought we were through with all of this!
I called everyone and canceled our Disneyland celebration trip. Uriah complained so much about his head hurting, I spent the night at the hospital.

Saturday, October 25
Poor Uriah. All his veins are nearly used up. They just keep blowing out. The doctors finally put an IV in his foot.

Sunday, October 26
Uriah's still running a fever. I sure hope his foot holds out.

Monday, October 27
Dr. Sanmarco examined Uriah and sighed. "I can't get any blood out of him because his veins are so bad. He's still sick, but I'm sending him home. He'll be all right, and we need the space for kids who are in worse shape."

Saturday, November 15
We finally made it to Disneyland with Debbie, Jeff, Joel, Nana, and Boompa. I stifled the habit of isolating Uriah. We have so much to relearn about normal life and a lot to be thankful for. Uriah will start school like "a real boy." All the doors that have been closed for so long are open again! The girls can socialize. Little League and all the "little-boy things" are possible again for Uriah and Don.

Uriah will still have monthly checkups, but those will become farther and farther apart until they stop altogether. If he relapses, we'll have to start over, but we'll leave that in God's hands.

Friday, December 12

My friend Beth Collins wrote: "How are you all doing? I was so glad to hear about Uriah's progress. It's wonderful! I'll bet the girls are very happy too. You were so strong under all the pressure; it must be your reward."

God, the only strength they're seeing is Yours, as You support me. I've watched too many people lose their children to think a parent's strength means a child will live. Coping well doesn't ensure survival, but it makes it easier for the child and family to function. Just like faith. God, thank You so much for delivering us from this trial. I'll try not to forget what I've learned. Please show me how to use it for Your good purposes.

Six

Life Amid Death
(Jan.–Oct. 1987)

*If you live life paralyzed by the fear of what might happen,
will you really have lived at all?*

I MAY NEVER HAVE TO GET ANOTHER SHOT!" GRINNED URIAH. The beginning of a new year and a normal life. It was wonderful not to give Uriah countless medications. He had blood drawn at his monthly checkups, and that was it.

We didn't have a lot to dread on our visits. We'd survived, and I felt like a senior member with knowledge that could benefit others just entering the nightmare we were leaving. I passed helpful information on to newcomers. When they saw Uriah had survived years of chemotherapy and had remained bright and unaffected, they saw hope— hope that their own child, whose life seemed to teeter on the brink, might live.

Though joyous in our new freedom, the possibility of relapse lurked just below the surface of my thoughts. It stirred to the top whenever he went for a checkup and quickly submerged again when the tests came back fine. This was the acid test of whether the chemotherapy had done its work well enough. If even a single cancer cell survived the barrage of medications and radiation, it would multiply until Uriah's bones were again filled with cancer. *No good can come of worrying. The best thing to do is enjoy each day to its fullest and not waste a moment.*

❦ ❦ ❦

In early January, I attended the first Saturday meeting of the Mom's Day Off Support Group (MOMs) at Sizzler. Margot, Cathy, Diana, Darlene, Gayle, and I had met at the clinic before, but now we really got to know each other and our children's conditions and experiences.

We discovered we were all Christians and planned to pray before each meeting. Margot put together a flier we could distribute to other moms (and dads). "Our group is being formed to reach out to one another when there is a need: someone to talk to, someone who knows what it's like in our special situations, sitter needs, or just someone to be there and listen."

❦ ❦ ❦

My grandfather died January 15. He was elderly and his death expected, but it came as a shock. A few weeks later, my grandmother died. She was unaware of Grandpa's demise, but people who have been married so long seem to pass away near the same time, as if the rupture of an invisible bond makes the survivor aware they're alone, and unwilling to continue asunder.

January 26

Janet:

We're hoping to go to Crescent City during Don's vacation in April. We thought we might drop by, if possible.

Don heard rumors they're accelerating the building of the Crescent City prison. I'm beginning to feel we may actually move . . .

On February 23 I went to the hospital to pick up Heather's medicine for an earache, and I visited the MOMs whose children had been admitted: Gayle and her son Eric; and Cathy and her son Robbie. Cathy was with Eric in the CT scan room because Gayle had gone to get her daughter from school. "The brain surgeon doesn't have any hope for Eric," she said.

Gayle was the single parent of a young daughter and Eric, a toddler with an inoperable brain tumor. Dealing with her son's diagnosis wasn't easy. As a single parent, she had to keep working in addition to caring for Eric.

Robbie had ALL, like Uriah. After a couple relapses, leukemia doesn't respond to chemotherapy; the cancer builds an immunity to it. Robbie had just suffered his seventh relapse. The doctors didn't have hope, but Cathy's faith did.

March 22

A letter from Irene:

> We're being tested thoroughly. I must rely on the knowledge that God will not give more than I can bear. At times I just want to give up, but I am a fighter.
>
> Mom is on chemotherapy. She has active cancer, and they think it's in the lung. She's doing very well though.
>
> Dave was hurt on the job a month ago. He was knocked off a scaffold and fell about 15 feet to the concrete, landing on his forehead. He should have not even been alive, but there was no neurological damage. Praise God! A broken bone in the hand and toe and some

stretched ligaments in his knee. So we're OK, but it hasn't been easy.

So please pray for me for strength to keep going.

No wallowing in self-pity. All around me people are dealing courageously with horrible misfortunes.

On March 28, Vickie, the mother of a daughter and Kenny—a month-old infant with cancer—joined our MOMs group. Kenny was so young the odds weren't good. We prayed and fasted as Robbie and Eric struggled for their lives.

One day while I waited for the girls to get out of school, I watched the boys play in the nearly deserted park. A woman walked the jogging path, and a man sat in the shade of a tree far across the park. Two Mormon missionaries rode their bikes up and approached the man. *Oh, please, God, don't let him be influenced. And if he's a Christian, send Your Holy Spirit so his testimony might reach them.*

Next they approached the woman. She sat and talked with them. I continued to pray, surprised the man remained. He watched the missionaries a moment, then folded his hands and bowed his head in prayer. *Thank God! He's a Christian.*

Finally they approached me. I gave my testimony and tried to show them the difference between their teachings and the Bible. In frustration, they left. *Thanks, God, for giving me these words, and if possible, use them to help these young men see the truth. They remind me of Saul in zealousness, but just as he was, they are misguided. What a force they could be for You if they would see Jesus' light like he did!*

Departing for home with the girls, I paused on the road by the jogging path before pulling into traffic. The young woman who had spoken with the missionaries raced up to the car out of breath. "Excuse me," she puffed, "I just have to know: Are you a Christian?"

"You bet!"

"Thank God!" She jogged away, smiling.

Those missionaries came to distribute their doctrine, but they were set up by God Himself. He used three Christians, two praying while one witnessed, to reach out to them. Sometimes we know fellow Christians because we feel the Holy Spirit dwelling in them. I'll meet that woman in heaven someday.

I felt a glow of satisfaction. *God was able to use me for His work!* How could I doubt the existence of God when He was working all around and through me in a million little situations? It's beyond reason to think it's coincidence and not the act of an incredibly intelligent, loving God. I can't see or understand all His plans; there are things I'll never understand until I ask Him face to face. But He is a loving God who turns all things to good—even tragedies.

We planned to move to Crescent City as soon as the house sold and the prison opened. "I'm concerned about how Uriah will take the change," I said. "If he relapses after we move, the closest treatment facility is hundreds of miles away."

"We've put our lives on hold as long as we can," Don said.

Kenny didn't respond to chemotherapy and was hospitalized. Cathy and Robbie were on the fourth floor too. After Uriah's appointment April 22, I stopped to visit them. Cathy was just returning to Robbie's room. "I'm so glad the Lord placed Robbie in the hospital so I could be with

Vickie," she said. "Kenny got worse and passed away today. I was there with Vickie when he died, and it was peaceful. She would have been alone if God hadn't sent us here. But Robbie's work is done now, so he can go home."

She expected the Lord to heal Robbie. But as she spoke those words, I had an unshakable feeling the Lord would indeed heal Robbie, but it was not his earthly home he would return to. *Has she unknowingly prophesied her son's death? I must be mistaken.* I struggled to find something to say. "I'm . . . glad you were able to be here. Please give my condolences to Vickie."

"The MOMs ought to send some food over to help out."

"I can send a pot of spaghetti later this week. Is Thursday all right?" I asked.

"Yeah, that'll be great. Hopefully we won't be here much longer so I can help."

Tears forced themselves out of my eyes as I hugged Cathy. *I hope she thinks they're only for Vickie and Kenny.* I fled from the hospital, struggling to bury my feelings under mountains of rationality. *I must be getting really paranoid, God. I'm just imagining things and becoming a pessimist, aren't I? Please, God, heal Robbie, heal Eric. The world could really learn a lot about Your power and love from the miraculous healing of these women's sons, couldn't it?*

On April 29th I received some startling information.

"Joanna was attacked by a dog this morning and will have reconstructive surgery at 6:00 P.M.," Nana said.

"You go. I'll watch the kids," Don told me.

I hugged his neck in mute gratitude.

Nana, Boompa, and I got there at 10:30 P.M. when Joanna had just come out of recovery. She was in pain but better than we feared.

"It was the neighbor's dog. I'm so thankful I wasn't holding baby James. . . ."

Oh, God, we're thankful she'll live.

It took her a long time to heal and even longer to recover from her fear of dogs. Today she and her family own two dogs, a tribute to her courage.

I returned home and learned Robbie had passed away. It was only a week after my conversation with Cathy. *God, it doesn't seem fair Robbie was taken when he and Cathy have done so much to help others.* But I was thinking in human terms, not seeing from God's viewpoint.

Robbie's face beamed from the cover of the service folder.

Our hope is in Jesus Christ and being with Him one day as Robbie is now, and we know that we will see Robbie again. We want you all to know that we are not going to mourn for Robbie. His life has touched so many others. The love and courage he had has given us love and the courage to go on. We wish to celebrate his life, his death, and his resurrection to be with Jesus. Please celebrate with us today—and forever.

I was afraid Cathy's love for the Lord and her bold witness would change with the loss of Robbie, but she remained involved and supportive. Her faithfulness and bravery gave us a blueprint to follow. We could see by her example how to respond if the Lord called our children to Him before we were ready.

Being involved in MOMs encouraged me to seek out information about cancer and cures. I clipped articles about autologous transplants (in which a patient's bone marrow is removed, purged, and returned), the necessity of research on animals, dangers of the Mexican ten-herb tonic, and the donation of organs after death.

Ann Landers mentioned Compassionate Friends, a support group for families who lose a child. Another article acquainted me with the Make-A-Wish Foundation, which grants one wish to a child with a deadly disease. Uriah's four-year-old wish was very modest but could only be arranged by a group like Make-A-Wish: he wanted to ride in a police car.

"It will take time to arrange," Betty Strong said, but she called back after only a couple days. "Would he like a police helicopter ride and tour of the police station?" With great expectation, Uriah counted off the days until July 16.

Don, Joel, Uriah, and I arrived at Fontana Police Station with cameras loaded and adrenaline flowing. Officers Gibson and Delair gave the boys bags full of goodies, introduced us to McGruff P. C. the police car and to Chief of Police Ben Abernathy, and led us on a tour through the police station. Uriah and Joel got to ride in the front of a police car to the Sheriff's Aviation Division where we were given a helicopter ride above our house.

We were warmly received at Fire Station No. 2, and Don and the boys took a ride in the big extension-ladder truck. Uriah was dressed in a firefighter's outfit, and Captain Maghsadi helped him climb the ladder and squirt the fire hose.

Then we met more policemen at Chuck E. Cheese's for lunch. When the pizza was ready, Uriah said the prayer. On our way home, before we turned into our driveway, both boys were sound asleep, but smiling.

🌿❀ 🌿❀ 🌿❀

Sharon Repp was hired as the computer literacy teacher at work. *She's so much younger than I am. I guess a lot of life has passed me by while I've been fighting for Uriah's life.* She was a Christian, and I confided in her about the difficulties we faced with Uriah.

Marilyn Turner was Nana's close friend and librarian at the junior high school. As her secret pal, I had a wonderful time planning surprises for her.

Nana and Boompa planned to tour Europe for most of the summer. Nana said, "I told Anita Tams I really hate to be gone when her daughter Terri is getting married, but we need to get away." She looked at me. "What do you think? Is it OK if we go?"

I knew she was afraid something would happen to Uriah while she was gone. "Mom, everything's fine right now. You can't put your life on hold forever because of what might happen."

July 25
    Terri's romantic wedding was at 11:00, the MOMs meeting was at 1:00, and Uriah's birthday party was at 5:00.

The next day, news of Marilyn Turner's sudden death from a stroke reached me. Then Margot called to say Eric had died. *He's suffered so long; his death is a release—but such a tragedy.*

God, I've fasted and prayed so earnestly. It's bitter to accept Your decision that Eric should be taken. It doesn't seem right one so young and innocent should die without having a chance to live. I know sometimes Your answer is no, but why did it have to be no now? And what will Marilyn's family do without her? I know Your love and wisdom is far greater than mine, but can You give me a clue?

In August, I stopped at a yard sale. I usually didn't even glance at the inevitable stacks of worn texts, but God was at work. As I walked past a blanket strewn with bric-a-brac, a small, green book caught my eye. On the cover were sky-blue letters: *A Parting Gift* by Frances Sharkey, M.D. On the book's back cover, a middle-aged, female doctor beamed down at a baby. "A book dealing with an acceptance of death and a young leukemia patient." I picked it up and realized my expression was being watched with guarded interest.

"That's a good book," the gray-haired man said from a lawn chair under the shade tree.

"My brother died of leukemia several years ago," the woman added, old sorrow tightening the lines of care on her face.

"Oh, I'm sorry," I murmured. "It's hard to lose someone to cancer. Sons of two of my friends passed away last April: one from leukemia and one from a brain tumor. My son has leukemia . . . at least he did. He's been in remission for three years and stopped taking chemotherapy last September."

"It's wonderful they can do so much more now," she said. "Back then, there wasn't much they could do." She handed me my change and looked into my eyes. "Good luck," she wished.

Even though she's a stranger, sharing our experiences creates a bond between us and leaves me feeling validated and stronger.

Later I squeezed the book into the bookshelf. "I'll read it when I get a chance." As summer waned, it remained forgotten.

❧ ❧ ❧

Our friends Janet and Andy moved back to California and became our next-door neighbors. Andy and Don even worked at the same prison.

The night before kindergarten began for Uriah, he laid out his clothes. His green-blue eyes sparkled as I tucked him in. "I'm going to play with the blocks and paint tomorrow! And I want to take a turn on the tricycles! Shiloh said they have tricycles."

I smiled. *At last he'll be able to interact with other children in a normal environment. Uriah's experiences are so different from most children's. His idea of a visit to the doctor would shock his peers! I hope those events blend into the forgetfulness of youth and that he replaces his painful past with new life.*

On September 12, I was late for MOMs, as usual. "Vickie! Cathy! How are you? I'm so glad you came."

"Vickie's expecting!" Cathy announced.

I hugged Vickie. "Congratulations!"

"I got a letter from Diana and Jennifer in northern California," Margot said. "They really like their new home. And look at this!" She showed us a Make-A-Wish newsletter. "Almost all our children are in it! Uriah's police-car ride; Jason's Gold's Gym membership; Jennifer's Apple computer; and the trip to Disney World for Christopher, Darlene's son. Even Eric is remembered."

September 30, I talked with Uriah's teacher. "Uriah's only problem in school is a slight speech impediment, but we expect it to disappear by second or third grade," Mrs. Soderlund, said. "There's another little boy in my class who has leukemia."

"Another? That's against the odds!"

Uriah and R. J. became good friends; they had a lot in common. Lena (his mother) and I became friends too.

"I'm really lucky I have family that live nearby," I said. "I don't know how I'd cope if my sister Debbie didn't help me so much. Do you have family nearby?"

Lena looked away at the floor. "Well, some of my relatives blame me for R. J.'s leukemia."

"What? How could you be responsible—"

"I don't know. They don't understand that leukemia just happens. They seem to think I didn't keep him clean enough, so he got sick."

Puzzled, I glanced around Lena's spotless kitchen. How could she have kept it cleaner? That has nothing to do with leukemia anyway. "What about a church family?"

"Let me tell you about church," her face twisted in pain. "We went to a church, hoping to find some peace or spiritual strength in the middle of all the bad things that were happening, but after we went just a few times, the pastor got up in the middle of church and told us we had to prove our faith by taking R. J. off chemotherapy and not taking him to the doctor anymore. I was so mad—and embarrassed! We just got up and walked out. We stay away from churches now. I'm a Christian, but I don't need that."

How could they do that? Don't they see they're driving people away from You, God? Especially when they need Your help so much. "Lena, that's awful. Not all Christians are like that. I'm a Christian, and we had Uriah anointed with oil for healing, and the people at church pray for us all the time. There are other Christians in the MOMs support group that I belong to, and their kids are on chemotherapy too."

"You mean they think it's OK for Uriah to be on chemotherapy?"

"They know God can use doctors to heal. Would you like to come to a MOMs meeting or church sometime?"

"Yeah! Sure! Sounds great!"

Lena called me the following week. "You know, I can't believe it. R. J. survived his cancer, but now he's really sick. They say the chemotherapy damaged his kidneys and maybe his liver. After all we went through, he might die from the treatment!"

After a couple months, R. J. improved.

In early October, Shiloh caught the chickenpox. *Uriah's off chemotherapy, maybe everything will be all right—please, God!*

"We usually recommend children be protected for a year after their chemotherapy," Dr. Sanmarco said.

"It's been just that long!" *Thanks, God! You take care of things we don't even know about. It's perfect timing—would God use anything less? The kids will miss trick-or-treating, but Uriah won't ever have to worry about chickenpox again.*

ॐ ॐ ॐ

On October 13, 1987, we received a packet from the University of Minnesota's Hematology-Oncology Division:

Dear Mr. and Mrs. Alexander:

The Children's Cancer Study Group . . . [is] studying childhood leukemia and factors that may contribute to the development of this cancer.

. . . The results of this study may help us determine whether a reduction or change in certain environmental factors could contribute to a decrease in the occurrence of childhood leukemia.

Your participation in this very important study will be greatly appreciated.

Don and I filled out the extensive questionnaire. *Our participation might spare others the suffering we've endured. I only wish we could do more.*

Seven

Return to the Valley
(Nov.–Dec. 1987)

Was he going to die some night like this,
tied to the sides of the crib so he wouldn't pull his IV out?
—Frances Sharkey, M.D.

I N THE WEE HOURS OF LATE NOVEMBER, I WAS UNABLE TO SLEEP. *A Parting Gift,* the book I'd bought at the summer yard sale, came to mind. I turned over and tried to sleep, but the thought of the book wouldn't go away. With a sigh, I fumbled for the book on the shelf.

Just a little bit of reading, and I can drift off again. But the more I read, the more awake I became with a growing sense of uneasiness. *This book echoes our experiences far too much.* I read about Mark, a three-year old:

> I looked at the miserable child tied to the sides of the crib. Did his parents know how he slept every night? Was he going to die some night like this, tied to the sides of the crib so he wouldn't pull his IV out?[1]

When I read of David, I was riveted by the similarities. He was diagnosed with acute lymphocytic leukemia at two and a half. His treatments, the way he held still for shots, and his positive outlook on life mirrored Uriah's own. He began kindergarten, as Uriah had, with warnings from the doctor to keep him home when other children were ill, especially with the chickenpox. The questions David's teacher asked were the ones Uriah's teacher asked. David had three years of chemotherapy. His mother and doctor had embraced when he no longer had to have it, just as Dr. Sanmarco and I had a little over a year ago. Later he and his siblings contracted chickenpox. *This is creepy. I have to find out what happens next.* A couple paragraphs later, David had a testicular relapse.

In a male, leukemia cells hide from chemotherapy in the brain or testicles. David and Uriah received chemotherapy into the spinal fluid and radiation to kill leukemia cells in the brain, but only chemotherapy was used to destroy it in the testicles.

"What if we had irradiated his testes at the start of the disease, the way we did his brain? Would that have prevented the relapse?" Dr. Sharkey asked a speaker at a hospital conference.

"We don't do that," the speaker answered. "When the boy grows up, how could you justify having sterilized him?"

"But my patient may never grow up now."

"We can't predict which child is going to relapse. Would you sterilize all boys who would never relapse to save one who might?"[2]

Things haven't changed in the five years since this book was written! Don and I weren't given the option of having Uriah's testes irradiated. We signed countless papers saying we understood he might be sterile because of his treatment.

What difference would one more make—especially if it could
save his life? He could always adopt children, but if he never
grows up, he won't experience parenthood anyway.

David was dying. Dr. Sharkey wrote, "It seems to me
that children hate being in the hospital and would be much
more at peace in their own homes."[3]

David's mother took him home. A new treatment was
found, and David returned to the hospital but withdrew
during the four-day treatment and refused to eat. The doctor told David he was dying, but David already knew. He
hadn't said anything because he was trying to protect those
who loved him. The doctor sent him home as she had promised, though she didn't expect him to live the night.

Once home, David improved immediately. His parents
put his bed in the dining room so he could be near them and
see what was happening in the house and neighborhood. He
ate, drank, and even went outside—feats he was too weak to
accomplish at the hospital. Dr. Sharkey made a house call,
thinking the last treatment had worked, but she wrote, "What
was different wasn't his pathetically wasted body but his spirit.
He was comfortable and no longer fearful."[4]

One Saturday he seemed better and got out of bed. His
mother was so encouraged, she went to the store. His father was pouring him a glass of juice when he died without
a sound. His brother picked up David's kitten and curled it
up next to David. That's how his mother found them when
she returned.

I was crying so hard I couldn't see the page. *Oh, God,*
what does this mean? I pushed away the answer. *This won't*
happen to Uriah. I'm being silly. Years of worry have made me
paranoid. I hid the experience deep down inside. *I don't want*
to scare Uriah, and I don't want anyone to say I brought it on
by thinking it would happen.

I dried my tears and checked on Uriah. *He's fine. In a few days when he has his regular checkup, the doctors will tell me everything's fine, and I'll see how silly I've been to worry.* I fell into an exhausted sleep.

Sunday, November 29
Debbie, Joel, and Lena's family came to church with us! Our family went to Aunt Marilyn's for Thanksgiving.

Wednesday, December 2, Uriah's appointment arrived with trepidation for me.

"How is everything?" asked Dr. Sanmarco as she began to give Uriah his physical exam.

"Fine." The uneasiness I felt when Dr. Sanmarco checked Uriah's testicles turned to alarm when a look of concern furrowed her brow and escalated into horror when she said, "Wait a minute before you go to the lab. I want Dr. Haghighat to look at this."

Dr. Haghighat's normally sedate eyes grew more solemn. "Yes, there's definitely some swelling here."

Uriah didn't know what it meant, but I did. I bit my tongue and fought back bitter tears, afraid of frightening him. *We're going back into the shadowy, isolated world of chemotherapy. Only this time, his chances of survival aren't as great. . . . Stop it! Just wait for the test results. Maybe it's something else. God, please don't let it be true!*

In her office, Dr. Sanmarco told me, "We suspect a testicular relapse."

Before I returned to Uriah, I took a couple deep breaths and tried to calm my pounding heart. "Uriah, I'm sorry, but they're going to have to do a bone marrow and spinal tap today. Tomorrow they need to do a biopsy."

His eyes snapped up to meet mine. "But that means I'll miss school." His blue-green eyes misted over with tears.

He doesn't care about the painful tests. He'll miss school: the world of normal childhood. If the tests come back positive, he won't be able to go anymore.

"They want to admit you."

"No! I want to go home."

That doesn't sound like Uriah.

His volume increased. "Mom, I want to go home and sleep in my bed. Can't we come back tomorrow?"

"What's wrong?" asked Dr. Sanmarco from the doorway.

"He wants to go home tonight," I said.

She entered and laid a hand on his shoulder. "That's OK. You can go home as long as you go to the anesthesiologist first and come back early tomorrow." She turned to me. "At 6:45, all right?"

Uriah nodded his head, satisfied. "Hey, Mom, can we go to Sizzler for lunch?"

I looked at Dr. Sanmarco. She smiled and nodded. That was Uriah.

From the public phone in the hallway outside the big, wide door of the hematology clinic, I could watch Uriah in the treatment room and call people. Margot agreed to call the prayer chains. Lena said she would pray. Debbie volunteered to cover my shift at work and pick up the children after school. "Please don't say anything to anyone else, until we're sure," I asked of her.

Finally I called Lucille, the secretary at Bear Gulch. "Uriah will be out awhile for medical tests. Can you ask Mrs. Soderlund to put together a packet for independent study, and I'll pick it up in a couple days?" It sounded good to me, but it didn't fool her. Years of listening to students' excuses had tuned her ear to know what they weren't telling her.

"Is everything all right?" she asked softly.

"We won't know until the tests come back." Passersby in the hallway avoided my eyes. *The strain of a person trying to maintain control must be showing on my face.* I went to the bathroom, splashed water on my eyes, and dried them. They felt better but remained red. I gazed into the mirror. *Calm down. Nothing's changed. God's still in control.*

The anesthesiologist told Uriah, "You can pretend to be Darth Vader tomorrow and wear a big, black mask."

Uriah grinned. "Wow!"

"Thanks," I said. "You've made this a lot easier—for both of us."

After getting Debbie and Joel home at 5:30 that evening, I was exhausted. But Shiloh had an ear infection.

"I'll watch the kids while you take her," Don offered.

"Thanks, honey." *He seems OK, but he always seems calm for a few days. Then he'll blow up over something trivial if he's really not as calm as he appears.*

Waiting for a doctor to see Shiloh seemed interminable. *I've been at the hospital from nine this morning, and it's almost ten at night. There's still the possibility Uriah's swelling is caused by something else. Maybe he fell or has an infection. Perhaps it's denial, but there's no proof yet, and worrying won't help.* I hoped and prayed.

At the hospital, Thursday, December 3, Uriah and I met a young couple whose baby was having tubes put in his ears. *They seem so nervous and afraid. Virtual ages ago, I thought that was all Uriah needed. It seemed so earthshaking then. Now it seems so trivial.*

Uriah and I played UNO and other games until they came for him. He didn't like the hospital PJs, but he smiled when the nurse took him for a ride. When we had to part, he kissed my hand as I reached out to him.

While I waited, I talked to a man and his wife. "Our daughter's pregnancy was fine until she got toxemia and had a seizure. Now she's in a coma. They're taking the baby c-section and hoping she snaps out of it."

I'll pray for them. And I won't feel sorry for myself.

A murmur ran though the hospital when the lights went black. *I hope Uriah's out of surgery.* A door opened. "Uriah?" a voice asked. I inched toward the darkened doorway. The lights came on.

It was Dr. Wang in green scrubs. This young Asian-American, who spoke without an accent, was a most amazing man. His senses were acute, his reactions quick and precise. Sometimes he came to the ward and played Nintendo with the kids—who were astounded by his high scores. He was held in high esteem by the children, their parents, and his fellow physicians. "Surgery went well," he said. "Uriah's in recovery."

Don stayed home from work with Uriah on Friday, December 4.

That evening at Sizzler, after the kids were done eating, they sat on a plush rug and watched Christmas specials by the decorated tree until we were ready to go.

It was raining so hard we couldn't see our car in the parking lot. We dashed for it, but by the time we got in the car, we were soaked. No one could tell the rain on my face from my tears. *God's crying for us! Uriah's test will be positive. . . . Stop it! That's silly. We won't know until the doctors call with the results! . . . God, I would be very happy to be wrong.*

Saturday, December 5

Crazy day! Prayer meeting 7:30 A.M. at First Lutheran. Delivered the kids to Janet's to make cookies. Picked up Lena for the MOMs meeting that lasted until 4:30. Five o'clock was the popcorn party at Janet's. Lena's family had to leave by 6:30 but didn't go until 7:00.

Debbie and Joel came too. We strung popcorn, made a wall tree, cookies, and fudge. Real good time!

Sunday, December 6
Uriah went to church in PJ bottoms because he's still sore from the biopsy. Choir will meet Mondays at 7:00 P.M. I hope to go. We went to Nana's. Couldn't sleep.

It rained all night and most of Monday morning. At the end of the day, I locked up the computer lab and waited for a teacher to finish printing a project. The phone rang.

"We have a call from Dr. Sanmarco for you," said Mary, the secretary.

My stomach knotted.

"Mrs. Alexander? I'm sorry to have to tell you the results are positive. We need you to bring Uriah to the hospital tomorrow morning."

"All right. We'll be there." *I wish I didn't have to find out at work. I'm afraid I'll break down.* I mechanically finished my tasks.

Mary looked up when I opened the office door. "Mary, I'm not sure when I'll get back to work," I said. "I'll call you when I know."

I picked up Shiloh from school and drove to Valle Vista Elementary School where Nana was cleaning up her classroom after a busy day. She smiled when Shiloh and I walked in. "What a nice surprise—" Her smile faded.

Is it the look on my face? Or some mothering instinct that warned her it's bad news? "Mom, I'm sorry to tell you at work, but I didn't want it to be over the phone. Uriah's leukemia is back."

"What will happen now?" Her eyes searched my face.

"I honestly don't know." She gave me a hug, and I felt better. There's nothing like a hug from your mom, no matter how old you are.

Joan Weiss, Uriah's godmother and my good friend, approached from the corner of the room. Her daughter was Nana's pupil, and she had come to help. *Thanks, God. You sent her so Nana won't be alone when I leave.*

When I picked up Heather, I talked to Uriah's teacher, Mrs. Soderlund. Lena was opening the office door as we headed to the parking lot. "R. J.'s doctors think his leukemia is back in his spleen."

"I'll pray for you. Will you pray for us?"

"What?"

I told her about Uriah. *What a Monday!*

We went with Janet, Andria, and Brian to Baskin-Robbins for a last outing before the isolation began.

Tuesday, December 8
    Uriah and I waited until noon for the doctors to arrive at the clinic. Our room wasn't ready until 1:00 P.M. Nana came in the afternoon, bringing cards and flowers from CJHS. When Don and Heather came, Nana gave Heather birthday presents. Heather watched the nurse try to start an IV in Uriah's arm twice before he had a CT scan, echocardiogram, and X-ray.

Wednesday I stayed with Uriah all day. Nana brought Heather and Shiloh from school. Don went shooting. *Perhaps it will diffuse the anger that may be building in him.*

Dr. Sanmarco entered. "It's time for Uriah's intrathecal methotrexate." In a few motions, a sterile field was set up and a tray of shiny silver tools appeared. Uriah struggled so hard—even though the nurse and I were leaning on him with all our weight—that the doctors had to poke him several times before they could inject the medication into the spinal fluid.

"It's OK, Uriah," I cooed to my sobbing son. "They're all done." Nana's taut expression and red eyes caught my attention across the bed. *I think that was hard on her.* "You know you need to lay down for an hour now. Would you like me to read to you?"

He nodded.

Don and Heather stayed with Uriah that evening while Shiloh and I shopped for Heather's birthday and ordered a cake.

I called a church elder. "Does First Lutheran do laying on of hands for healing?"

On Thursday, Uriah got Cytoxan—an all-day intravenous drip. He started throwing up at four o'clock that afternoon. The medicine administered to help stop the vomiting made him cranky. He lost his equilibrium and fell trying to walk to the bathroom. Don sat with him when I got lunch and rented movies.

I flopped into the chair next to Don. "Dr. Wang is going to put a Hickman catheter in Uriah's chest because his veins are so weak from years of chemotherapy. It's a plastic tube surgically placed in the veins near Uriah's heart. One end will hang out of his chest and be closed by a tiny clamp. A plastic twist cap seals the end when it's not in use. When he needs blood or IV medications, the tube will be used instead of needles.

"There are dangers though. If the clamp and cap are left open or the tube is cut or damaged, he could bleed to death quickly. There's also the risk of serious infection because it's a direct connection to his bloodstream. His tubes will have to be flushed daily with heparin (an anticoagulant), to keep his body from clotting off the end inside, so I'll have to learn how to do that."

Uriah was placed on independent study December 11 [for his school work] for three weeks. Heather's and Shiloh's teachers agreed to watch for problem behavior caused by the upheaval. *So far they seem fine, but I worry about them getting depressed.*

Uriah threw up, but they took him to surgery anyway. After a couple hours, the attendant behind the desk called out, "Uriah?"

I picked up the phone she indicated. "Hello?" The lights flickered out. "Uriah's out of surgery and doing well."

The power was out for half an hour. I dialed the prison. "May I please speak with Don Alexander?"

"I'm sorry. He's gone home for the day."

He was too upset to work. I called Nana. "Uriah's surgery went fine."

"I didn't know he was having surgery!"

"I'm sorry, Mom. I thought I told you. There's just too much going on, I guess."

Saturday, December 12

Debbie played with Uriah so I could throw Heather's birthday party. Lena and her boys came, and Joan and her girls too. The unicorn cake was beautiful, but the sticky hands were the life of the party! I brought Uriah party favors and a piece of cake, but he shrugged his shoulders. "Most of the fun is being able to play with everyone," he sighed.

Monday, December 14

After work Susan sent a Christmas tree, and Sharon Repp sent dinner. Mrs. Soderlund gave me work for Uriah, including a hospital journal and get-well notes from his classmates.

For an hour and a half, the nurses showed me how to care for Uriah's catheter and change the dressing. "He'll always wear elastic netting around his chest to hold the bandages and tube out of the way. There will always be a bandage over his catheter site to prevent infection."

I practiced flushing his catheter while they watched. It took two hours to fill the twelve prescriptions they gave me. Finally, at nine o'clock that night, Uriah and I pulled out of the parking lot. *We're all going to be home!*

Tuesday, December 15, I showed Debbie the emergency procedure to be used if Uriah's catheter was punctured. "Anyone who watches Uriah when I'm gone needs to learn this. It needs to be flushed, using alcohol swabs, betadine swabs, a syringe and needle, and a sterile cap. Uriah has to carry a surgical clamp with him everywhere. I made two of these emergency packs out of bright red, 110 camera cases. One will go with Uriah all the time. The other I'll give to the school nurse."

I took Uriah to the Mariposas Christmas party. *Isn't that little Nicholas from Community Baptist Church in Rialto? God, it amazes me how our path becomes intertwined with others. Too often people come to understand our situation from personal experience. It's like You make our paths cross earlier so it's easier for us to talk. I wish Nicholas was still healthy. I know Your plans are better, but it's so hard to understand them now. At least Nicholas' parents have You in their lives.*

On Wednesday, December 16, Dr. Sanmarco informed me, "Uriah will receive radiation at Sunset Kaiser again. They need to irradiate his testes this time, and that will make him sterile. . . ."

So what?

". . . We need you to sign this waiver."

All I want is for him to survive long enough for it to be a problem.

The next day Uriah's radiation treatment was at 2:45. We stepped off the elevator into a lobby that was unchanged. *Even Rose, the receptionist, is here, friendly and efficient as ever.* She couldn't possibly remember us after the thousands of patients she's helped since our last visit. I handed her Uriah's medical card. "Hi, Rose! How are you?"

Her eyes widened in surprised recognition. She looked beyond me. "Well, Uriah. My goodness, look how you've grown! What have you been feeding that boy? . . . But I didn't want to see you here again. How are you?"

Uriah smiled a toothy grin and leaned against me in mute shyness.

"Unfortunately his leukemia is back, so we're here for more treatment," I said.

"Well, let's hope this does it."

The doctor fitted Uriah with a lead shield so only the right spot would get radiation. The machine fit right down on top of Uriah, but he didn't have to be tranquilized this time. A technician made Uriah an elephant balloon from a surgical glove.

On the way home, there was a traffic jam. We were on the road four hours.

Friday we left early for Uriah's radiation treatment to avoid traffic. We got donuts, drove to the observatory, and looked out at the mountains of home.

Later, at work, Mary said, "There's a bag for Uriah in the teachers' lounge."

I felt like Santa as I swung the bulging bag of gifts from coworkers over my shoulder. Tears of gratitude blurred my eyes.

Saturday, December 19

Uriah couldn't go to the Christmas celebration at Aunt Marilyn's because of the risk of infection. He and I stayed home. A visit from Debbie, Joanna, and Joel livened things up. They each opened a gift, and Uriah opened his bagful from the junior high.

"What's that noise?" Debbie asked.

Janet, Andria, and Brian waved at us from the front yard and dumped three ice chests of snow on our lawn. They crafted a smiling snowman and tied Janet's red scarf around its neck while Uriah observed!

Pastor Dannenburg and elders Tom Katanski, Dale, and Rick laid hands on Uriah, anointed him with oil, and prayed for his healing.

Sunday, December 20

Once again, we sat in the sound room during church. During Sunday school Christmas rehearsal, Margot's son, Jason, chatted with us in the car.

Malena Katanski brought over a huge ham. Janet invited us over for banana splits. *God, Your family is such a comfort to us.*

School was out Monday, December 21, so the girls came to Uriah's appointment. The line was long at the pharmacy. "Can I help you?" the young blonde asked.

"A box of syringes, please."

"I'm sorry. We're out."

"You don't have even a few? I'm out, I need to flush my son's catheter, and I have to be in LA for his radiation treatment in two hours."

"Wait a minute." She disappeared into the back and returned, bearing a box of syringes. "Good luck. I hope you make it."

"Thanks," I smiled. By the grace of God and the use of diamond [carpool] lanes, we did.

Tuesday, Shiloh came with us to LA so we could use the diamond lanes. That night a small red splotch grew on

Uriah's stomach under the stocking net. I cut a hole in the net so it wouldn't press on the sore.

On Wednesday, two days before Christmas, Dr. Haghighat said, "He's running a fever," as he examined the white, red-rimmed, quarter-sized spot on Uriah's stomach. "I need to put him in the hospital. Hopefully he'll go home by Christmas."

Dr. Sanmarco sent a little Rudolph with a huge balloon to Uriah's room.

A man tapped on Uriah's door after dark. "Would you like to talk to Santa at the North Pole on my radio?" The radio operator pulled a teddy bear from a big bag.

Uriah giggled as the scratchy voice of Santa said, "I thought an early Christmas present might cheer you up. Get well!"

Uriah's fever is up. I'll stay until it goes down.

At 6:15 A.M. Christmas Eve, I went home, showered, packed fudge for the nurses, got Uriah's empty stocking, and returned to the hospital. Uriah's fever was down, but the spot was larger and red streaks reached toward his heart. Dr. Haghighat frowned. "I want to transfuse granulocytes (white blood cells), but it might be days before they're available because tomorrow's Christmas."

"Uriah's Uncle Jeff is a granulocyte donor," I blurted out.

"The blood bank will call him if they want to use him," Dr. Haghighat said.

Jeff is an apheresis (white blood) donor who doesn't carry the cytomegalovirus (CMV) in his blood that 54 percent of adults have.[5] Those with normal immune systems have no symptoms from CMV, but infants and people with weak immune systems, like Uriah's, can become very ill or die if they receive it in a transfusion. Jeff was often called to donate CMV seronegative blood for them. I called Jeff.

"Where do I go?" he asked.

"Just wait. If the blood bank calls you, it's for Uriah."

One minute later the blood bank called Jeff: "Can you come in and donate for a five-year-old boy?"

"Is it for Uriah Alexander?"

"How did you know?"

"He's my nephew."

Jeff would be on the machine five to six hours.

"You're still here?" the nurse asked that night.

I nodded.

"We need to move Uriah to a new room."

They're afraid he won't make it.

Dr. Wang peered under the netting at the red, tender skin around Uriah's catheter. "It may be infected."

Uriah's nurse and I played Santa at 11:00 P.M.

Friday, December 25 (Christmas Day)

Debbie dropped me off at the hospital and took the girls to the celebration at Nana's. Uriah opened his presents but didn't want to play with them. He slept in a high fever. He got granulocytes last night. *God, I'm so afraid we'll lose him now.* I picked up Uriah's Christmas Bible, and it fell open to Jesus healing the centurion's servant.

At 8:00 P.M. Uriah sat up, ate, and played, but the blister continued to grow. I spent the night.

After a feverish night, Uriah refused to eat or drink Saturday morning. We played cards for a while and took a nap. At 3:00 P.M., there was a tap on the door. "It's Santa and an elf," said my sister Leah.

Uncle Bob walked in with a big bag of gifts from Nana's. "Ho, ho, ho, and all that, right?"

Uriah tore the colored paper from the biggest box.

"Isn't that cool?" asked Bob. "Look at the blades on this helicopter. Here, you help me put it together."

Later Bob asked, "If you could have anything for Christmas what would it be?"

"A stuffed Odie," Uriah said.

"I thought Garfield was the one who's always stuffing himself."

They got up to leave, and Bob handed me a videotape. "Oh, no! Not home movies!" he said with mock horror.

"Make sure you watch the part where Bob slips in 'dog mess' while catching the football," Leah snickered.

Bob tossed a piece of popcorn at her. "I did that on purpose."

"We'll be back tomorrow," they promised.

It's the best gift they could have given me. I feel like I didn't miss Christmas completely.

Jeff visited. Don and Shiloh couldn't come in because of their colds but waved to us through the windows. Heather stayed and played games with us until 11:30 P.M., when Uriah's granulocytes finished.

Sunday, December 27

When I arrived at 6:04 A.M., they were giving Uriah more granulocytes. He ate little breakfast and slept while I penned a poem:

Christmas Eve at the Hospital

'Twas the night before Christmas, when all through the house,
Lay dishes, dirty clothes, and crumbs for the mouse.
The stockings were hung by the chimney with care,
In hopes that St. Nicholas soon would be there.
Most of the kids were all snug in their beds,
While visions of Christmas morn danced in their heads;
But one's in the hospital; this child on my lap.
This year Santa's deliveries will not be a snap!

With concern his small hand pointed out from the chair,
"There's no chimney! How will Santa know we are here?"
"Why Santa knows plenty! There's no need to dread!
We'll leave him some juice and a letter," I said.
His smile was so trusting, with no lingering doubt.
Then I said a prayer that it all would work out.
Then what to all wondering eyes will appear?
Not a classy, red sleigh with those fancy reindeer;
It will only be me in my white minitruck,
Making a delivery if I have any luck.

More rapid than beagles I drove down the lane,
Recalling which presents were marked with his name:
The blue car and race track, the jacket and pants,
The new bank and Bible, the bug house for ants.
I parked in the driveway, grabbed my purse off the floor,
Then dashed away, dashed away, dashed through the door.
As dry leaves that before the wild hurricane fly,
All his presents I threw in a bag that would tie.
Then off to the hospital I practically flew,
With the truck full of toys, and stocking stuff too.
And then, eyes a-twinkling, I turned off the road,
Eager to deliver my wonderful load.
I pulled in the parking lot and was turning around,
Found a place and parked it, then jumped out with a bound.

I was bundled up warmly, from my head to my foot;
But this Santa bore no trace of ashes or soot!
The bundle of toys I flung up on my back;
How the nurses all smiled when they saw me and my pack!
Their eyes how they twinkled! Their laughter how merry!
For they knew Santa's visit was quite necessary;
Not to be home on this most special of nights,
Makes a child fear they'll miss all of Christmas' delights.

I love helping Santa; it's really great fun,
Making all ready before the first rays of sun.
That look of sweet rapture, of the greatest delight,
That fills children's eyes at Yule treasures first sight.
Not wanting to keep all the fun to myself,
I got help from a nurse, who agreed to play elf.

I feared he would wake, but the nod of his head,
Soon gave me to know I had nothing to dread.
We spoke not a word, but went straight to our work,
We filled up his stocking, then turned with a jerk;
He stirred and he yawned, then rubbed his wee nose,
But he didn't awake from his dreamy repose.
We stacked up his gifts and a little toy whistle,
Then softly crept out like the down of a thistle.
And I heard the nurse say, as she turned out his light,
"Merry Christmas to all, and to all a good night!"

Leah and Bob tapped on our door again at noon. Bob asked, "Hey, Uriah, what would you eat if you could have anything in the whole world?"

Uriah smiled weakly and looked longingly across the street. "An In-And-Out cheeseburger!"

When Uriah had an In-And-Out burger in one hand and crazy-eights cards in the other, Bob said, in mock surprise, "What's this?" He pulled a stuffed Odie from his coat pocket. "Leah, did you put this in my pocket?"

She shook her head. "Not me."

"What's that, Odie?" Bob questioned. "He says he belongs to you." Bob handed him to Uriah.

Uriah giggled and hugged the fluffy toy.

"We'll drop by tomorrow before we leave for home," Bob promised.

Their visits made such a difference. Uriah's finally fallen into a natural sleep. I know he'll make it now.

Wednesday, December 30
Uriah felt better and the redness was gone. Nana brought a lead-crystal turtle to hang in his window. "You get better faster if there's a rainbow in your room."

Thursday, December 31
"Uriah can go home," Dr. Haghighat said. The wound looked strange—a brownish-purple piece of tissue sticks out in the middle, and it seems deeper. Dr. Wang prescribed medicine that dries out dead tissue to help it heal. They never said what caused the lesion, but one nurse confided, "If it leaves a round, hollow scar, it may have been the bite of a brown recluse spider."

The children were playing hide-and-seek the day the red mark appeared. There will be no spiders after I get home.

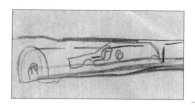

Eight

The Rainbow
(1988)

*It's not really gone . . . as soon as we're
past the clouds, we'll see it again.*

Tuesday, January 5, 1988

URIAH STARTED RADIATION TREATMENTS IN LA AGAIN. JOEL came so we could use the diamond lane. A technician inflated two gloves like balloons and made them into punk rockers with Mohawks for the boys.

Thursday, January 7

Another rainy LA treatment day. Rainbows shimmered in the sky on the way home until the sun went down. Once we went under a bank of dark clouds and Uriah fretted. "Where did the rainbow go?"

"It's not really gone. We just can't see it because of the clouds. As soon as we're past the clouds, we'll see it again."

"Kind of like me if I die, huh?"

I blinked away the tears that welled up. *Out of the mouths of babes . . .*

When it reappeared, we were both happy.

Monday, January 11
Last radiation treatment. No more LA! Hooray!

Monday, January 25
I ran out of prednisone Sunday, and Uriah missed two doses. Dr. Sanmarco didn't yell at me, but it probably would have been easier if she did. I punished myself all day.

Saturday, February 6
Don, the kids, and I went to the mountains for a walk and a picnic. Andy asked us to watch Andria and Brian, so we took them too. Past Barton Flats, we found a tiny parking lot where we ate snacks and built snowmen and snow dogs. The kids built a snow fort and had a big snowball fight with Don.

Monday, February 8
At the clinic, a woman I met last month was having trouble with her son's school. "Do you push Uriah to do school work?"

"It depends on your priorities. I encourage Uriah to keep up with his schoolwork, but I try to remember some things are more important. After all, we don't know how long our children will be with us." Sudden shock and fear filled her eyes and seemed to draw a curtain between us.

Good job. You're supposed to comfort people, not hurt them! God, I messed up again. Please, help her be OK.

It was nearly noon when Uriah got his spinal tap.

Tuesday, Feburary 9
The doctor told me my headaches are probably tension because migraines run in families. Shiloh's teacher called. "She's having trouble. The counselor can see her Friday."

We picked up Debbie, Jeff, and Joel and entered the church where the concert would be held. *Uriah's loved Don Francisco's music ever since Uncle Bob gave him that tape.* With lyrics like "Praise the Lord! Hallelu! I don't care what the devil's gonna do," it was no wonder. When Uriah learned he had relapsed the last time, he got angry. "I know who did this to me. The devil did this. But he's not gonna win because God is stronger, and I believe in God!"

With a kind smile, Pastor Holly took us to a little sound room that held two stools and a chair.

"Do you know if Don Francisco will play, 'I Don't Care What the Devil's Gonna Do'?" I asked.

"I'll find out."

A dark-haired girl named Dena knocked on the window. "Jesus loves you," she said to Uriah. "My cousin has cancer too."

Uriah smiled and waved.

The lights dimmed, and Uriah clambered onto the high stool with his face pressed to the glass. He clapped with excitement when Don stepped into view. Uriah absorbed the opening tune.

"I'd like to dedicate the next song to a special young man named Uriah Alexander," said Don Francisco, nodding toward us. Uriah's beaming face seemed to make the little room glow, as Don belted out, "Praise the Lord! Hallelu! . . ." After the song, worn from his chemotherapy that day, Uriah lay on our blanket, humming to the familiar tunes and clapping for his favorites.

Following the concert, Dena asked, "Can I pray for Uriah?"

He shyly held back.

"I'll pray for you at home," she promised.

Uriah gave her a hug.

Pastor Holly appeared. "Would Uriah like to meet Don Francisco?"

Uriah's smile blazed.

Don Francisco and Pastor Holly laid hands on Uriah and prayed.

Saturday, February 13
Cherrie Buffum, an old friend from the air force, wrote:

"I'll be honest with you, I feel awkward because I don't know what to write. I mean, I'm concerned about Uriah, but I don't want to just ask about him, and yet— I don't want you to think I'm ignoring you all either. If I say something I shouldn't, please forgive me and let me know."

God, I didn't realize it was so perplexing. Everyone must feel like that.

Monday, February 15
We helped Nana and Boompa move into their cabin near Lake Arrowhead. It's a kid's dream house with winding stairways and secret passages. One cupboard opens into a hidden room under the stairs.

Tuesday, February 16
We're in the next phase of the treatment, and I'll miss work. We just finished eight days of Ara-C; now he'll get twelve days of an L-asparginase substitute, Erwinia.

"I want to sit up," Uriah said when it was time for his spinal tap and intrathecal methotrexate.

"We need you to lay down," Dr. Sanmarco said. Uriah lay down, but after twenty minutes, Dr. Sanmarco couldn't get the needle into his spine. "OK, sit up," she conceded. But that didn't work either. Uriah lay down on his side again, trying not to sob. At last, the needle penetrated its mark and the syringe was emptied of its yellow poison. *I feel like a basket case. Uriah probably feels like a pincushion!*

Wednesday, February 17
Uriah handed nurses Val and Margarita and Dr. Sanmarco flowers and cards. *Yesterday was hard for them.*

Sunday, February 21
After church, the girls stayed with Aunt Debbie so I could take Uriah for his shot. We had trouble finding someone to give it to him, so it took a long time.
Aunt Debbie met us in her driveway, "Don't come in! Joel has a fever of 101."
The girls clambered in, and we drove home. *What will I do about a sitter if Don can't watch Uriah tomorrow?*

"Can you watch Uriah?" I asked Don after Uriah's treatment Monday.
"Can't you get someone else?"
"What about Auntie Joan?" Uriah suggested.
"Sure. Bring him over," she said.
Heather got an A+ on her history test and received honor roll and citizenship awards.
Don made supper while Heather and I fed and watered the guinea pigs. "Would you like half a roll of peppermint Lifesavers?" I asked.
She turned toward me with a quizzical expression. "Why are you treating me so nice, like a princess?"
"Because you're acting like one."

Tuesday, February 23
It was only 11:00 A.M. when Uriah and I got back from his treatment. Debbie was still sick, but Joel was better. "I'll watch Uriah play outside at my house so you can go to work," she offered.

Uriah fell asleep early, so the girls and I played Monopoly and watched *The Neverending Story.*

Heather woke with a fever Wednesday, February 24. At the hospital, Uriah's temperature was normal when they drew his blood sample, but when I got back from the lab, they were taking his temperature again with a glass thermometer: 100.7. "We can't treat him today, but we'll take some blood cultures," Dr. Haghighat said. "You must send Heather somewhere else."

"Heather can stay here," Debbie said. "Joel and I are getting better."

"You're sending me away?" Heather asked.

God, this is awful. Heather's feeling unloved because I'm sending her away. I paused. *I better call Val at the clinic; I forgot to ask something.* "Should I stop giving Uriah Thioguanine?"

Silence.

"Mara, he was supposed to take it for only eight days."

I gave him six doses too many! My heart began to pound. *What have I done?*

"I'm surprised he tolerated it. It usually makes them very sick."

I guess that explains why his stomach didn't feel good. "Val, what will this do to him?"

"Right now the doctors are busy. I'll get back to you."

I cried as I drove Heather to Debbie's. *God, how could I make such a stupid mistake? Especially when it's important?*

Debbie hugged me. "God will take care of it."

At home the phone was ringing when I opened the door. "You need to bring Uriah back right away," Margarita stressed. "His white count's really low, and he's going to get really sick."

"OK," I said and hung up. Sobs wracked me. *She acts like I was careless, and it's my fault. And it is! The instructions are on the bottle. I just blew it.*

Don tried to console me. "I'm taking a few days off work."

I called Debbie. "I can bring Heather home."

"I want to stay here," Heather said.

And I thought she was upset because I sent her away! I hung up the phone, and it rang in my hand. *God, You must have made Margot call. Thanks.*

Janet dropped by. "I've never seen you this upset. What's different?"

"It's my fault he's in the hospital. What if I wiped out his bone marrow completely? Then . . . then . . ." I cried, unspeakable words caught in my throat. She wrapped her arms around my shoulders and cried with me.

I called Bear Gulch. "Lucille, Don will be late picking up Shiloh."

"What's wrong?"

She always knows. I can't admit what I've done. "Uriah's in the hospital with a fever."

I pushed aside the heavy clinic door, laden with Uriah's hospital bag. Tears had washed away my makeup. Val, on the phone, pointed Uriah and me to room 5. Margarita wandered in and chatted with me. Val gave me a hug. "Here's a copy of Uriah's protocol so you can follow his treatment."

Dr. Haghighat studied my face compassionately. "Uriah's on many, many medications. Every person reacts differently to them. Any of them could have caused this problem."

I nodded my head silently. *It's nice of him to say that, but we both know what caused it. This mustn't ever happen again!*

Thursday, February 25, Don was sick in bed. Heather was running a fever, so after work Shiloh and I picked her up.

Shiloh went to the hospital with me at six o'clock, the aroma of warm, chocolate-chip cookies wafting from our parcel. Sounds of mirth echoed down the hallway. Shiloh gaped. "Is that Uriah laughing?"

We scurried in. Uriah was cackling and playing UNO with Patti, a student nurse. Shiloh, Uriah, and I were building with Legos when the loudspeaker crackled: "Visiting hours are now over."

While Shiloh was in school Friday, February 26, I visited Uriah. Dr. Sanmarco came in wearing a mask because she didn't feel well. "Uriah's count is so low he needs a transfusion."

Later I picked up Shiloh. "Can I go see Uriah?" she asked.

"Sorry, honey. Dr. Sanmarco said no visitors."

Red blood hung from Uriah's IV pole when I arrived. He did homework and we played games until the nurse changed his catheter dressing.

Saturday, February 27
    I was so tired after I read to the girls the night before, I just fell into bed. I got up early, and Don and I talked. I think he's worried because he's never seen me really upset. At least he knows I'm human—and he's not mad at me.

Nelda was hanging a bag of white cells for Uriah when I got to the hospital. "Uriah will get white cells for five days," Dr. Haghighat said. "His count is low, only 300, so you need to wear a gown and mask in his room."

Please, God, don't let it drop any lower. Normal adult white cells number between 4,300 to 10,000. On chemotherapy, Uriah's count hovers near 3,000.

Pastor Dannenburg visited and prayed with us.

Sunday, February 28

Don took time off of work so I could be with Uriah when he got blood. "I remember him when he was a baby," his nurse said. "What happened with his medication?"

"I made a mistake." Everyone knows! I wonder if any of them think I did it on purpose. I have a road map now; I'll read the complete label on every bottle before giving medicine to Uriah and carry a pad to write down what the doctors tell me. I just wish all the crazy things going on in my life would slow down.

Monday, February 29

Uriah's count is only 200.

Tuesday, March 1, I was bathing Uriah when Dr. Sanmarco came to examine him. "All his counts are low," she sighed.

"How's his white count?"

She looked at me over the top of her glasses. "How much lower can it go?" she asked.

Lena called at 11:30 P.M., worried Uriah was near death. I reassured her but stayed up late worrying. *What if I've given him such an overdose of chemotherapy, I wiped out his bone marrow? He'll die for sure.*

After the girls were at school Wednesday, I went to the hospital. "Uriah's going to have a spinal tap. Can you break the news to him?" Barbara asked. He cried but did Lamaze and tried to hold still.

"He'll need to have a peripheral blood draw later to rule out a catheter infection," Barbara said.

Uriah grabbed my arm.

"I'm not going to work," I promised.

The fellow who came to draw blood stuck the needle in Uriah's arm and jabbed it around. Uriah screamed in pain.

"I think I'm deaf in my left ear!" he said and shifted the needle. "I just can't find the vein with these stupid gloves on!"

My consternation grew. *Well, you're not going to do it without them!*

Dr. Sanmarco rushed in when she heard Uriah scream again. "What's wrong?"

The phlebotomist released Uriah's arm and stood up. A look of confusion muddled his face. "I'm just having trouble finding a good vein."

Dr. Sanmarco shot him a withering scowl and strode out. She stalked back in wearing a sterile gown and mask and waved the useless technician away with disdain. Uriah used Lamaze and didn't yell; someone he knew was in control. The sample was drawn quickly, and minutes later he fell asleep.

That's how I feel sometimes, God, like I'm screaming in pain and fear because of the things we're going through. But when I remember Someone I know and trust is in control, I can stop screaming—at least until I get distracted and take my eyes off You. Please help me remember You're always here, and You'll make the bad times as quick and painless as possible and turn all the bad into good.

Debbie jumped in when I picked her up from work. "You forgot. The girls get out early today. Lucille said she'd keep an eye on them."

The girls sat in the grass, like forgotten baggage. "I'm sorry," I said. "Can I make it up to you with a treat?"

Their eyes shone. They picked a snack, and I got colored paperclips for Uriah.

That night he made colorful paperclip chains and hung them from wall to wall. But he didn't eat.

Thursday, March 3
    "Uriah's blood count is up to 600!" the nurse said.
"My stomach and head hurt," he complained.

Friday, March 4
    Uriah threw up. The doctor's put him on a liquid
diet and a different antibiotic. His head and stomach
were hurting too much to play games.

Saturday, March 5
    Uriah's count improved and his fever went down.

The next day Don waited in the parking lot until the
girls and I got to church. "We can sit in the pew with the
'regular' members."
    Debbie, Joel, and Jeff sat with us. "I'll take the girls to
Nana's cabin," Debbie offered.
    "Yeah!" the girls whispered.
    "Uriah's on a regular diet," the nurse said. "And you
don't have to gown up anymore."
    Thanks, God.

Monday, March 7. "Uriah, I'm here!" I called. He remained motionless. "Uriah?" I touched his shoulder, but
he didn't respond.
    "I gave him something for nausea," explained Georgie,
his nurse. "His catheter's infected."
    After supper I returned to see Uriah. I pushed through
his door and froze in fear. *His room's empty!* I felt numb. I
ran back into the hall.
    "Oh, he's just been moved to room 6," said a nurse.
    Could it all end that quickly, Lord?

There was less redness around Uriah's catheter Tuesday, but there was drainage. Dr. Sanmarco said, "It looks better."

That afternoon I sat in Dr. Whitmore's office. *I always feel sorry for doctors who get our family as patients. We don't fit the average patient profile. We must be difficult for a new doctor to deal with because a death is probable.*

"I want you and Don to talk about Uriah's death," he said. "It's important that you and your husband discuss it. Both of you need to deal with the possibility of your son's death."

He really thinks it's important. Will Don talk to me about it?

I clattered into the living room. "Don, Dr. Whitmore said we need to talk about the possibility of Uriah's death."

"I need to talk to you too. I'd like to go into business with Andy, buying houses in foreclosure, fixing them up, and selling them."

"No," I said. Don's face hardened in anger, and he marched to the front door. I tried to explain, "I can't take any more stress. Can't you just wait until Uriah is better?"

"I can't place my life on hold forever!" he snapped.

"You haven't done a lot during the fourteen months Uriah's been off chemotherapy."

"It helps having a friend."

"I must admit, you've done a lot since Andy got here. But I'd be really resentful if you start fixing up someone else's house when ours is still in a shambles."

"The reason the house isn't fixed up is because we don't have enough money," he defended. "I hoped to earn it with this job."

"That sounds logical, but I can't face seeing even less of you, or the extra stress."

He swept out the front door and slammed it.

At 7:45 P.M., I got to Uriah. I stayed late so I could spend time with him, but I felt bad because the girls wouldn't get their time.

Don was in Uriah's room when I got there in the morning Thursday, March 10. "Uriah's doing well. He might go home this weekend," Dr. Haghighat told him.

After work Friday, Uriah's bags and blankets were on the couch. *He's home!* Don had picked him up at 3:00. We celebrated with pizza at Andy and Janet's.

I called the nurse. "Did you flush Uriah's catheter tubes?" "Yes. It got done."

Saturday, March 12

There was a birthday party for Joel at Nana's cabin. *Most people worry about missing their children after they grow up and move away. I worry about missing Uriah if he never does.*

That night, instead of flowing smoothly when I flushed Uriah's catheter, it pushed back. *I sure hope it's not clogged.*

Sunday, March 13

As we sat in our isolation room at church, people smiled and waved to Uriah.

Uriah's catheter was easier to flush.

Wednesday, March 16, I soaked Uriah's tubes in betadine solution, and Dr. Haghighat examined him. "The small port seemed sluggish," I told Val, as she tried to draw blood through it. She couldn't.

"You should have called right away," Dr. Haghighat scolded.

Val put a chemical in his tubes to dissolve the clot. "I can get blood now, but there's still some pressure when I flush it."

"Soak it fifteen minutes more, and send him for a cathetergram," Dr. Haghighat said.

"You haven't had one of those yet, have you, Uriah?" Val asked. "It's just X-rays of your catheter; it doesn't hurt." Uriah bobbed his blond head in relief.

A sound like a machine-gun burst rattled the walls around Uriah as he lay on the table in a dark, cold room while a doctor flushed his tubes and rapid, multiple X-rays were taken. The doctor's face told me something was wrong. "Uriah has a sheath—a little blood clot—hanging off the end of his catheter."

Back at the clinic, Dr. Haghighat's face was grave. "We must give him stronger medicine to dissolve the clot. He needs to be in acute care because of possible serious bleeding caused by the anticoagulant."

Uriah had his own nurse because of the risk involved. I took the day off.

Janet and Joseline were Uriah's nurses. "It looks like you're having an awful time with all these people to play cards with," I teased.

Uriah smiled and giggled. "I haven't lost yet!"

Don called, and I explained the situation. "Well, that's just great!" he said. "The neighbors have been playing loud music, the dogs are barking, and now this!" He slammed the phone down.

I called him later. "Could you watch Heather and Shiloh so I can stay at the hospital tonight?"

"I've had too much."

Stress? "Have you taken your medicine?"

"What? No, no. I mean booze."

He was sick when I got home, and I was unsympathetic. *I want to return to the hospital at midnight, because they're planning to draw blood from Uriah's arm, but I'm not sure about leaving the girls with Don.* I packed, took out the trash, showered, made the girls lunches, and stuck a note on the fridge: "Don't forget to wear green."

"I can take care of the girls and get them to school tomorrow," Don said.

I hope so.

On St. Patrick's Day Georgie gave Uriah a leprechaun mask and green shamrock glasses. He wore them through the halls in his wheelchair, giggling and waving on his way to a cathetergram.

When the nurse and I helped Uriah climb onto the table, Don came in. We waited outside while X-ray machine shots rattled the door. Then all was still—for too long. The nurse peeked out. "Mom, Dad, come in, please." She blocked the way and whispered, "Uriah's catheter was obstructed and has blown. The doctors are on their way. I think he's a little scared."

Don spun away and stalked off. *Why do these things always happen when he comes to the hospital?*

I rushed to Uriah. "So, you've been having adventures, huh? What did you do, break their machine?"

"Nah, my catheter popped right there," he said with a nervous giggle, pointing to the white tubing projecting from his chest with a silver surgeon's clamp firmly clipped above the puncture. "The doctor was flushing it, and all of a sudden there was water spraying all over!"

Uriah became the center of hubbub. Dr. Wang, Dr. Haghighat, Dr. Sanmarco, technicians, and nurses thronged to the scene. The doctor who blew the tubing was nowhere to be seen. *How could he have broken it? He shouldn't have pushed so hard! . . . And I shouldn't have given Uriah an overdose. We all make mistakes.*

Dr. Wang repaired the catheter in the pediatric ward. "Don't use the catheter until two."

"We'll give Uriah medicine for a day," Dr. Haghighat said, "and then do a cathetergram. If the clot isn't gone, he'll get medicine a second day and another cathetergram. But if the clot doesn't dissolve by then, we'll have to pull the catheter."

When they remove a catheter, they literally just pull it out. He'd have to have shots until another catheter could be implanted.

"Hey, Mom, look!" Uriah grinned. "No IV! I can go to the bathroom by myself."

His medicine finished at 8:00 P.M. I brushed his teeth with a sponge toothbrush used to prevent bleeding, read to him, and kissed him good night. Janette and Joseline were there. *He's in good hands. I sure need a good night's sleep.*

At the hospital on Friday, March 18, Dr. Sanmarco sighed, "Uriah's cathetergram looks the same. I guess we'll pull it today."

Uriah's head jerked up and we exchanged a look. "We were told he'd get another day of medicine first," I said.

"Who said we would give more medicine?" she demanded.

"Dr. Haghighat."

She left to consult with him and Dr. Wang. *I can't go to work and leave Uriah to face this alone.* Hours later, Dr. Sanmarco entered. "We'll give the medicine one more try."

The staccato sounds rolled from the X-ray room three times Saturday. Uriah grinned and the nurse smiled. "It's gone."

"Thank God!"

"He can go home," Dr. Sanmarco said sternly, "but I want you to come by the clinic to discuss how we can make sure Uriah gets the right medicine at the right time."

She thinks this was my fault. This time it wasn't me.

At the end of April, when Uriah was placed on a different protocol, I was given a road map of the treatment and information about the drugs used. *At least my mistake showed them this information should always be given.*

Tuesday, May 3
"Are you coming to the information meeting about Camp Ronald McDonald For Good Times?" Val asked.
Send Uriah away? What if he doesn't get the proper care? What if his catheter is damaged?
The two young hosts explained the camp was staffed by nurses and medical technicians, and campers received their regular chemotherapy. Two camp counselors for each group of six children slept in the cabin with them. Any child whose doctor would permit it, was allowed to attend—even those who were terminal. We saw wonderful pictures and heard such glowing testimonies from kids who'd attended, that I signed up Uriah.

One morning I awoke in such pain, I couldn't get out of bed. It hurt to breathe. The doctor gazed at the test results. "It might be your gallbladder." *What if I become unable to continue to care for Uriah?* The pain was tolerable by the end of the day. *Thanks, God, for restoring my health. I'm sorry I took it for granted.*

Don applied at different prisons, including Blythe, for a promotion to sergeant. *We'll be separated until the house sells, and it can't be sold until the repairs are made.* I worked every spare minute to fix it.

Don wrote a journal entry:

Stress Factors

1. Neighbors—Loud music (i.e., guitar w/ amp, stereo, and full drum set). No recourse—they don't care. Sheriff unable to help. Two years.

2. Neighbors—Drug dealers. Sheriff unable to solve problem. Buyers/addicts make it unsafe for kids to ride bikes in the street. Can't feel safe in front yard. One year, nine months.

3. Promotion—Wife wants to stay here in valley or nearby area. I need to get away from the smog. (I'm allergic to it.) I can receive a permanent promotion at Blythe, but this means three or four months away from home and family; Mara must quit her job and make a three-hour drive to Kaiser Fontana for Uriah's treatment every week. Six hours on the road and treatment time. I'll have to make up her lost pay with three overtimes each month on top of the three I need each month now.

4. My temper—When I'm home, I can't go outside. The sight of my neighbors makes me angry. At first it's slow to build, and then for the slightest reason I explode. I don't want to relapse to the point of when Uriah got sick and I needed meds to help me deal with stress.

    It's affecting my work. Worst of all, it affects the way I deal with my family. They're caught with no way out. I can see the kids are worried about being around me. They don't want to be yelled at or get in trouble for just being in the same room with me. Shiloh can tell when I'm upset, and she'll give me a hug and leave the room. Then I just feel worse. I end up being a bad father and husband.

5. Uriah—I haven't learned to deal with his illness. I can't go to the hospital when he gets his treatment because it drives me crazy! I lose my temper and say things that hurt others around me, others with children who may die.

At Uriah's third appointment, the only other family in the waiting room kept far from us. The nurses ignored the eight-year-old boy's wracking cough, and Don was outraged. He said loudly, "I thought they were supposed to stay in a treatment room if they were sick so they won't get other kids sick."

The other couple was silent, but their faces were taut with anxiety. I wished I could pull the words back. Condemnation seemed to hang in the air. Sharon Marsh, leader of the Mariposas, said evenly from the hallway, "His condition isn't contagious, but if it will make you feel better, we'll put him in a room." The silent family shuffled out of sight.

I slipped out to Sharon. "I'm really sorry . . ."

"I understand. Their son is terminal. He's not expected to survive this month."

The words pounded into my heart like nails.

Oh, God, we're all so human. We make unintentional mistakes that hurt others and can carry unseen wounds of guilt for decades. It's hard to forgive others, but it's even harder to forgive ourselves. Jesus showed us how important it was to forgive others, but since He was sinless, He couldn't demonstrate how to forgive ourselves. But I guess if You can forgive me, then I have to forgive myself and do the best I can. I'll be perfect in heaven someday, but You'll have to upgrade me a lot!

Don's journal continued:

Uriah has a heart catheter in his chest. It's been there for months now. I still can't change his tube caps or chest dressing.

Mara writes books on the subject of death and dying, and I can't talk to her about it. This hurts her, and I feel bad, but I can't deal with the subject matter.

When Uriah finished his first three years of chemotherapy, I realized I had considered him dead. In my mind he was already dead. When he relapsed and there was doubt about whether he'd live, I broke down at work crying, twice.

Since November '87, I've started drinking more than normal just to help me cope with life, sometimes heavily. I've considered suicide several times. I put more and more responsibility onto Mara because I can't deal with it, and it's not fair. It makes me feel guilty and adds to my stress.

I've been trying to be a better Christian. Mara's one, and she's able to deal with our life situation much better than I am. My Christian friends tell me to let God deal with my problems and let go, but I don't know how or can't.

Lately I've been able to find comfort in reading my books or sleeping. When I'm asleep, I can usually hide from life. This is bad. I need help because right now I just want out.

The children and I didn't see things the way Don did. The kid's drew pictures of Don helping them with their bikes and having a pillow fight on their Father's Day cards that year.

I wrote:

I'm sitting here looking at the most beautiful flower arrangement. All to say you love us, even though we keep you awake and make you angry. Sometimes I think we feel we've messed things up, and you hate us a little. When you do something beautiful like this, it makes me feel secure and loved. You even made dinner and let me take a nap.

You gotta take care of yourself because you're irreplaceable. You're a great daddy and husband. Thank you for being my sweetheart.

Thursday, June 2

A group from the clinic attended a Sesame Street production at the LA Coliseum.

These children deserve the delights of a normal childhood. It's sad many simple pleasures must be denied for their health, when they might not live to enjoy them in the future. As caretakers, our goal is to make their lives worth living in the midst of pain and illness.

It was risky for Margot's son, Jason, to travel in an airplane full of people and dive off the cliffs in Hawaii. But he and his parents will enjoy those memories forever instead of just recollections of darkened hospital rooms, medication, and pain. It's better to live boldly with joy than to timidly hide in fear of what might happen. What if at the end of life, we had never ventured to truly live? As Jason said, "What's the worst thing that could happen? I might die?"

Tuesday, July 19

Uriah and I labeled his bags, tossed them on the huge pile of baggage, and checked in boxes of medication at the nurses' table in the midst of a grassy area teeming with people. The buses pulled up, and eager campers streamed aboard. I waved goodbye as he pulled out of sight. *He's gone!* An unexpected spasm of emptiness filled me. *Is this how I would feel if he died?* Tears dripped off my chin. *I'm never dropping him off alone again.*

While Uriah was gone our family played at a water park, fished, picnicked, went out to eat, and saw a movie in a theater like a normal family. We mailed Uriah a care package for his birthday. He was all smiles and bounce when we picked him up. "When can I go again?"

Thursday, August 11, I fumbled for the jangling phone after midnight. "I'm fine," Don said.

"What?" I was instantly awake.

"Coming home from work, I hit a black dog on the freeway. There was no moon. The bike made a shower of sparks when I laid it down, but I just kept rolling," he said calmly. "The nurse says I look like I've been ship-wrecked because my pants are just shreds. I just need you to bring me some pants."

Thanks, God.

Friday, September 9
Debbie summed up my birthday: "Empty-nest syndrome and turning thirty in the same week! Hope you have a happy birthday anyhow!"

"Uriah can start first grade even though he's on chemotherapy. Some people home school their children, and others just keep in close touch with the school," Dr. Sanmarco said. "He's had the chickenpox, but some children get them twice."

Uriah's teacher, Mrs. Alexander, looked nervous as she took the emergency clamp I handed her. She peeked at the tubes under Uriah's chest netting.

"He'll tell you if there's something he can't do," I said. "As long as he doesn't get them wet or play contact sports, he'll be fine. If any children have chickenpox, could you call me?"

"Sure."

That night, Uriah packed ample supplies into his backpack and chattered about all the things he would do at school. His enthusiasm spread to the girls, though they insisted, "We just want to see our friends."

It probably seems odd to them that someone would want to go to school. For Uriah, it's defiance against cancer and the odds—a small victory in the battle to keep his leukemia from robbing him of his childhood.

In October, we had dinner with the Zdunich family who moved in across the street. Their daughter Geneice was Heather's age, and they were Christians. *It's an answer to prayer. Without them the neighborhood would be spiritually desolate when we leave.*

Don started work in Blythe on November 7. We hadn't sold the house, but the kids and I would have to move during Christmas break. *God, You're going to have to help us if You want us to go because I can't make it happen. Please show us what You want us to do.*

Don came home on weekends to help us work on the house. The MOMs group held a bake sale November 19 to benefit the Mariposas Christmas party. On Thanksgiving we stuffed ourselves at Nana's cabin.

Saturday, December 3
    The Ronald McDonald Christmas party at a mansion near Hollywood included face painting, haircuts by hairdressers of stars, lunch, makeovers by makeup artists, stars' autographs, personalized cartoons, shows, lots of food, and of course, a visit with Santa. Uriah returned with so many presents, he had to carry his photo with Santa in his mouth.

Monday, December 5
    Heather attended Mile High Pines Camp with her sixth-grade class. They gave her a pine disk necklace with a rainbow for her birthday, December 8.

The MOMs Christmas party was December 17; the Alexander family Christmas was December 18; I baked cookies for the Mariposas Christmas party, December 20; Heather's birthday party was December 22; Uriah's treatment was December 23; and the Sunday-school program was December 24.

In the midst of that busy week, God quietly and unexpectedly answered my prayer. Who has time to buy a house just before Christmas? And yet on December 22, God granted us a buyer. *So often, God, You answer in a way I don't expect, without fanfare. I know You'll remove all the remaining obstacles. We'll be moving to Blythe in the new year.*

Nine

Life on the Edge
(1989)

*Instead of feeling cheated by his illness,
he used initiative and determination to
turn his dreams into reality.*

IN MID-JANUARY WE MOVED TO BLYTHE, IN SPITE OF URIAH'S three hospitalizations that month. Andy and Janet helped us pack, drive to Blythe, and unload. Boxes were stacked upon boxes, and the couches had to be placed on end because there was no room. But we were in!

"I hate moving," I said to Don. "Promise me we will move only once more—to Oregon."

Heather wrote to a friend:

Today is Saturday. It is the first day I have been in my new house. *Boxes are everywhere!* I hate it!

Are you having fun back there at Bear Gulch? I am not having fun here. My sister's bed is set up, but not mine.

My brother is the kid my mom likes best. Maybe because he has cancer. He is a big brat. He's always saying to anybody who makes him mad or sad, "I know

you hate me." I try not to hate him, but he's always trying to make me hate him.

Outside my house right now the sky is purple and
the wind is blowing. There is a sandstorm.

Write back (W/B)

Friends Always,
Heather

One night I noticed our cat looking at something on a
box we hadn't unpacked. "Heather, would you see what
the cat's looking at?"

She peered over the cat's shoulder, screamed, and flew
across the room into the easy chair. I leaned over and gazed
at the box a moment before I could see the scorpion. I
grabbed a book and smashed it. Scorpions outside the house
is one thing, but inside?

A couple days later, another ran across the living-room
floor, blending so well with the carpet that Don couldn't
see it though he was standing nearly on it. I smashed it
with his boot.

"I'm ready to move back to Fontana!" I announced.

Don sealed all the pipe openings instead.

Shiloh brought a hamster cage in from outside. That
night, her bloodcurdling scream brought us pelting into
the room she shared with Heather. The tiny scorpion that
crawled onto her forehead didn't sting her and was still on
her pillow until Don crushed it. Everyone inspected things
they brought into the house after that.

One evening a tarantula strolled across our backyard.
It was easy to catch in a bucket. After the kids had a look,
I released it in the desert. I was fascinated by the large,
shiny, purple-and-orange tarantula hawks that zoomed
over our yard.

The first Sunday we drove to the Spanish-style Lutheran church on Chanslorway, no one was in the parking lot. A young, bearded man in a white robe was picking up trash that had blown into the church courtyard.

"When do services start?" I asked.

He smiled and extended his hand. "I'm Lonn Maly, the principal of the Lutheran school. I'm just filling in for Pastor, who's out of town today. The service starts in half an hour. Are you new to the area?"

"Yes. We just moved to Blythe. We'll be back for the service."

He waved to Don and the kids. "See you then."

The schoolchildren sang during the contemporary, upbeat service. The congregation seemed friendly. *Thanks, God, for putting this good church home here.*

Pastor Hoemann came to our house the following week and welcomed us. We explained Uriah's condition. "We'll be there regularly," I said. "We probably need to be fed more than anyone."

Every morning the dogs and I walked Heather to the bus stop for Blythe Middle School where she joined the tiny combined junior and senior high school band. I drove Shiloh and Uriah to Appleby Elementary. Shiloh was in fourth grade, and Uriah was in first grade. When Uriah was in class, I was a parent volunteer. When he couldn't attend because of the risk of infection, I helped him with classwork in the teachers' work room, and I cleaned and repaired the school's computers.

At Uriah's first speech class, Mr. Johnson got Uriah to speak clearly by using conversational play with words. They were both talking to Mr. Johnson's shoes at one point—and laughing a lot—while Uriah learned.

Monday, March 13

Margot sent me her testimony notes:

I started having double vision and numbness from my feet on up. Diagnosis: multiple sclerosis. Six weeks after my diagnosis, our fourteen-year-old son Jason was diagnosed with leukemia. I just didn't understand how all of this could be happening to us. But even though there were tears, I turned Jason over to the Lord for care because I knew I was not the one in control. The Lord used the doctors and chemotherapy to put Jason into remission.

Jason developed a digestive problem and couldn't keep food or drink down for the next five weeks. Pastor Dannenburg and the elders came to the hospital with our family, anointed Jason with oil, and we prayed. Two days later Jason was eating normally and was home by Sunday. Jason was in the hospital forty days. It makes me think of Jesus in the wilderness forty days being tested by Satan.

At the end of March, Don became the radio liaison coordinator, preparing an operational procedure manual. In mid-April, he traveled to Las Gatos and Galt for special SERT (Special Emergency Response Team) training. His probationary period ended May 7, and the following day, he was working as an acting lieutenant. *He's finally moving up in his career.*

The trips Uriah and I took for his treatments became routine. Before the sun was up, I packed the truck with the game bag, food, and his overnight bag. Uriah usually tipped the seat back and slept during the four-hour drive. Sometimes he needed a shot at nine o'clock in the morning and another at nine that same night, which meant we weren't home until after one o'clock the next morning. After ten o'clock, the truck drivers parked off the road, their rigs outlined with parking lights, like odd-shaped Christmas trees. *I'm like one of them, ferrying my precious cargo back and forth, trying to meet my deadline for delivery. I wonder if they recognize my car because I drive so much?*

Wednesday, May 10
   Don received a memorandum from Captain Roberts: "Due to your daily professional appearance and demeanor, you have been selected to be a member of the CVSP committee to give input to the department's uniform advisory committee."

Heather played beautifully at the band concert May 24. The next morning, she flew from Ontario, California, to visit Leah and Bob in San Francisco. It was hard to watch her fly away. It reminded me of Uriah's trip to camp. *At least this time Shiloh and Uriah are with me. Please keep her safe, God.*

The hot June weather made our electricity bill skyrocket. Uriah developed an allergic rash wherever sunlight touched his skin. "It's because he's on prednisone," said Dr. Haghighat. "Keep him out of the sun."

"I'm concerned about Uriah's progress, especially his reading skills," Miss Lees said. "He should go to summer school so he won't be held back."

"Summer school sounds fun," Uriah said. "I don't want to stay in first grade, so I'll work really hard."

Jason, Margot's son, graduated from high school. He missed a lot of school because of treatments or illness, but with determination, he not only got good grades but also held a job at the same time. Instead of feeling cheated by his illness, Jason used initiative and resolution to turn his dreams into reality.

I explained Uriah's health to Mrs. Bates and Mrs. Gefre Monday, June 19, before their summer-school special-education class started. "Would it be possible for me to be a parent volunteer?"

"We already have an aide, Mrs. Phelps," Mrs. Bates said, "but if you'd like to stay, you can."

They had three class centers: nutrition, reading, and home economics, followed by a trip to the school's swimming pool. "The class is full, but they just keep sending more students," Mrs. Gefre said after class. "I suppose we'll have to put them in larger groups, but we won't be able to give them the individual help they need."

Mrs. Bates and Mrs. Phelps nodded.

"Do you have access to computers?" I asked. "I taught junior-high students basic programming for seven years before we moved to Blythe. I could teach simple programming as an additional center, if that would help."

The trio exchanged surprised glances. "Some of them have trouble reading. Do you think they can do it?" asked Mrs. Bates.

"Some of the programs are only a line or two long, and Uriah's done them."

"Let's give it a try."

The children wrote programs, learned graphics, printed their pictures, and used a word-processing program to write stories about summer school.

"Dr. Haghighat said you can go in the pool, as long as I change your dressing immediately afterward," I told Uriah when it was time to swim. He bounced with glee.

One day the instructors brought the children to the high dive. "You can jump in from up there if you want to." The seventh- and eighth-grade students balked at the drop from the end of the board. Uriah turned to me. "Mom, can I go?"

Just like Jason's dive off the cliffs in Hawaii? "Sure, Uriah." *He might never get another chance.* "Jump feet first and hold your tubes against your chest."

He clambered up the steps while the older students' mouths hung open in disbelief. "What's he doing?" they whispered. "He won't jump; he'll chicken out."

Uriah stepped to the end of the board, paused a moment, then sprang into air, shattering the water with a loud splash. He emerged from the depths, laughing, and paddled back to the side. "That was fun! Can I go again?"

"Yeah, but you'll have to wait in line," I said.

All the older boys had queued up. Upstaged by a first grader! Uriah went as often as he could that day and every day.

When we missed class for Uriah's treatment, the students made cards for him. Adolfo drew a picture of a boy jumping off the high dive, which made Uriah chuckle.

It's heartwarming to see the comradeship grow between Uriah and a class so much older. I think they sense he has real courage. They've seen his catheter, and I think they're a little awed by how nonchalantly he treats it, as if everyone had one.

Monday, July 17

The last day of summer school, the students cast ballots for the achievement award for citizenship. Uriah looked up in surprise when his name was called, and he grinned from ear to ear as he went up to get the medallion on a red, white, and blue ribbon: a symbol his peers accepted him as a fellow and not just an onlooker in life.

Tuesday, July 25

Uriah's seven. It's hard to believe we were afraid he wouldn't have his second birthday.

One Sunday in August, Lonn Maly chatted with me after church. "Is there a reason the children don't go to school at Zion?"

"We'd prefer to send them here, but we can't afford to."

"Come in during the week, and let's see what we can do."

Monday I tapped at the wood door inscribed "Principal."

"Come on in," he said, opening the door. Shelves filled with texts and files lined the walls. "Have a seat," he said, pointing to a chair. He pushed aside the paperwork he'd been working on. "Did you know there's a scholarship program available for members of Zion?"

"You don't understand," I looked at the floor. "We couldn't pay anything. I could teach a computer course and take care of the computers if that would help." I ventured a sideways glance. *That sounds ridiculous!*

"All right, . . ."

My mouth dropped open.

". . . bring in your lesson plans, and I'll show you where the computers are."

It took a moment before I recovered enough to take the papers he held out to me. His blue eyes twinkled at my astonishment.

This is wonderful! The smaller class size at Zion means Uriah will be able to attend more school with less risk. He might be able to catch up since there will be increased individual instruction.

"I want to stay in public school," Heather said. "I've worked so hard to fit in!"

"We'll make a contract with you," Don said. "If you stay out of trouble and make good grades, you can stay." Heather qualified for Mrs. Steadman's Gifted and Talented Education (GATE) class, for Algebra $1/2$, and for high school band.

Though I became Sunday-school director, there was another ministry the Lord placed on my heart. After a lot of prayer, I tapped on Lonn's door again. "Could I start a choir and drama group for Zion's students?" I asked.

"Are you sure you want to do this?" he asked. "I know you take Uriah out of town for treatments once a month, and this will take a lot of time."

"Unless there's someone else who wants to do it, I'd like to try."

He smiled. "What's your plan?"

Tuesday, during the first Sonshine Players and Singers practice, lots of kindergartners wanted to run through the aisles.

"Need a hand?" asked Mary Watts, a faithful Sunday-school teacher.

"How about two?" said Carolyn Baschal, mother of Uriah's classmate Sabrenia.

"Sure! You're lifesavers," I puffed.

Wednesday, September 6

There was much sadness at the passing of a teacher at Zion Lutheran from skin cancer. The weekly school newspaper, *The Zion Times* reported: "Today we say farewell to our friend and teacher, Mrs. Nancy Owens. In our hearts we know she has moved to a far, far better place. God blessed Mrs. Owens during her short life and truly blessed each of us who knew her, worked with her, and learned from her. . . . Rest peacefully with our Jesus, Mrs. Owens."[1]

Margot wrote:

Things have been hectic. Jason has a two-tube catheter and is home now doing OK. Dr. Sanmarco saw Dr. Falk in LA Wednesday to see if Kaiser will do an "outside-the-family marrow transplant" for three patients. Jason is one of them. God's in charge. Hope is better than no hope. And God's will is still best. I'm in a waiting, holding pattern, and I know God's grace is on us.

Jason's only hope of long-term survival was a bone-marrow transplant. His brother, James, didn't match Jason's tissue type. With odds of one in twenty thousand, they hoped to find someone outside the family who did. And it was a race against time.

Thursday, September 28

The Sonshine Singers chattered nervously as they lined up to go into morning chapel, but their faces shone as they sang "Children of the Lord," carrying glittering spiritual armor of heavy cardboard. The next week they giggled as they donned costumes of butterflies, kangaroos, an octopus, two crocodiles, and a fuzzy-wuzzy bear for "The Butterfly Song."

"My teacher's neat!" said Uriah and bounced into the car. Julie Maly, Lonn's wife, was so youthful, tiny, and possessed such unquenchable energy, she could easily be mistaken for a student. Her cheerful, positive attitude was like sunshine the moment you stepped into her first- and second-grade room.

Her laughing, dark eyes grew serious when she heard my explanation of Uriah's leukemia. She bent to look at his tubes. "Is it OK if I touch them?" she asked Uriah.

"Sure," he said, pulling them from the elastic net that held them to his chest.

She examined the caps and clamps. "How does it work?"

Uriah assumed an air of authority. "See, they put the medicine in here, so I don't have to get a shot. And these keep the blood from leaking out."

She gently handed them back to Uriah. "I just want to be sure I know what to do in case anything happens." She handed extra homework to Uriah. "I need you to do this at home to improve your reading and math skills. You're keeping up well with the class."

Uriah grinned.

Julie turned to me. "Do you have any questions for me, Mom?"

No wonder he likes her; she talks to him, not about him. Her expectations of intelligent, responsible behavior are self-fulfilling.

Uriah's classmates appeared to be ordinary second graders, but they were special people who didn't ostracize him when he was bald but accepted him as he was.

※ ※ ※

The Colorado River Country Fall Fair provided the opportunity for local school children to place their best work on display in the Learning Fair. Shiloh got a ribbon for historical fiction. Uriah got one for nonfiction:

When I Had Cancer

Hi! My name is Uriah and I have cancer. It's kind of fun and kind of boring. You can go to camp and sometimes you don't have to get a shot. Sitting around half of the day with an IV is boring.

When you are in the hospital with an IV it is kind of fun because you can play and you can watch TV you can ask your mom if she could bring the cards.

Hardly words I would have chosen, but Uriah had a unique point of view.

Uriah was at the clinic on Halloween getting his Cytosar shots. Val was dressed as a baseball player, and Georgia as a

157

pumpkin. "Gee," said Uriah staring at the floor. "I forgot my costume."

In a moment, Val and Georgia appeared with a scrubs shirt and mask. Uriah was all smiles.

$$\mathcal{H}_{\circlearrowright} \quad \mathcal{H}_{\circlearrowright} \quad \mathcal{H}_{\circlearrowright}$$

Sunday, November 12, The Sonshine Players performed (for chapel and church) the comedy *Who Said Animals Are Dumb?* by Martha Bolton. The nervous cat, rabbit, and tiger actresses were startled when everyone laughed in church, but it was the sound of success, and they continued with zeal.

Two hundred miles from home, Uriah was admitted to the hospital for illness. *Talk about a family divided. I don't want to leave Uriah alone, but what about Don and the girls?* I called Don. "Uriah's in the hospital. Should I leave him alone and come home?"

"No. I don't want him left alone."

"But what about the girls? How will they get to school?"

"Heather can ride the bus to school. Is there someone who could give Shiloh a ride?"

Uriah's dark-haired, freckled friend, A. J., attended Zion Lutheran. His parents lived a block from us. "What about Linda and Freddy?"

Don called, and they picked her up for school.

Once a week, I went home to wash clothes and catch up on things, especially spending time with the girls and Don. The next morning, I'd drive back to Fontana.

Uriah's class made cards and Mrs. Maly sent them in a giant card: "We sure do miss you, Uriah! Keep working on getting well, and I'll try to keep all under control until you return. I love you! Mrs. Maly."

Many of the cards were games and involved bad cells being zapped by good cells. Others drew rainbows.

❧ ❧ ❧

Don had a four-day weekend for Thanksgiving, so we stayed at Nana's cabin and visited Uriah. I overheard a nurse in the hallway: ". . . I don't know if she's possessed, but there's no way anyone can make their body do those things."

That's someone who needs to know Jesus. I'm not qualified to help her. I called Pastor Dannenberg at First Lutheran in Fontana. "She needs someone to share scriptures with her."

"Yes, she does."

"Will you go see her?"

Silence. "I perceive that perhaps God has not raised up the person who needs to talk to her yet."

Does he think God wants me to go? Driving to Nana's cabin, listening to Bryan Duncan's song, "Whistlin' in the Dark," I prayed for guidance. *God, I'm not qualified to help her.*

"*The disciples weren't qualified either; they were just fishermen.*"

But You chose them because You created them specially for that purpose.

"*I made you too.*"

OK, God, unless You tell me otherwise, I'm going to do my best. Just stop me if I'm wrong, and give me the words You want me to say.

I prayed a lot that night; I was going into battle with an unseen enemy. Don prayed for me while I searched my Bible for passages to help the afflicted girl. *Uriah's being released tomorrow. This is my last chance to reach her.*

During visiting hours, I entered the room she shared with three other patients. A middle-aged woman with worried eyes held her hand; a man by her side gazed at them. "Would you mind if I visited with her and read a few scriptures?" I asked. *God's Word won't return void, even if I do everything else wrong.* They nodded mutely. I turned to her. "Is that OK with you?"

Wary, she studied my face. She dropped her eyes and nodded.

"Are you a Christian?" I asked.

"Yes," she murmured.

"Let's pray." We clasped hands. "God, bless the Word we will share, give understanding to our hearts, and send Your Holy Spirit to fill us. Protect us with Your presence and be among us as You promised: 'Wherever two or three are gathered in My name, I will be there in their midst.' Amen."

I read scriptures of God's strength over darkness and of people cleansed from demons by Jesus, in His name. "Tell me about your faith," I asked.

"I met these people who said they were Christians. They could do amazing things with power they said was from God. They asked me to join them, so I did. But I saw that they used their powers to hurt others. That's not right. I was afraid, so I told them I wanted to quit. They told me if tried to leave . . ." Tears choked her. "They're using their power to hurt me," she whispered, "or kill me."

"That doesn't sound like the loving God I know. Some members of Calvary Chapel were involved in Satanism before God set them free. They'll know how to help you get away from this group. Just look in the phone book and call them."

"I'll call them. I'm so tired. I just want out."

We prayed again for her protection and release from evil. *My life is full of light and goodness compared to the sinister darkness she struggles with. I've whistled into that darkness. I hope it helped.*

Tuesday, December 14
    Uriah and Shiloh performed in Zion School's annual
Christmas play. Uriah was a robot in a cardboard-box
costume with a light-up nose. Two days later he was
admitted with a catheter infection.

We lived in the last mobile home on the edge of the
desert. One December night, Don noticed a car cruising
up. When the driver spied Don watching, he sped away.
"They'll be back later," Don stated.

After nine-thirty, the car crept down the road with all
lights extinguished. "Stay inside," Don said. "I must have
made an inmate enemy." He slipped out, unseen. He
waited, service revolver drawn in the shadows. The car
glided up the driveway. Stealthy footfalls approached our
front gate.

"Peace officer! Freeze!" bellowed Don as he aimed his
gun at the unknown.

"Don't shoot! Don't shoot!" Freddy Mendez shrieked.
Bags hung limply from his raised arms.

"It's just us!" Linda shouted from the car.

Don lowered his weapon and chuckled.

"We knew it was a lean Christmas for you," Freddy
babbled. "We decided to play Santa."

"Well, thanks a lot. But you should have said something so I didn't scare you. How would I explain it to the
kids if I shot Santa?" Don laughed.

Freddy shook his head. "Believe me, I'll never try to
sneak up on you again—and I'll warn any other Santa to
call first!"

"The look on Freddy's face!" Don chortled when he told
me.

Friday, December 22

Uriah wasn't feeling bad and appreciated seeing Santa when he gave gifts to the sick children at the hospital.

God, I'm amazed that people spend their few spare hours at Christmas doing such things. Thanks for showing me good still exists in this world.

Sunday, December 24

"Take him home," Dr. Haghighat said. "But call immediately if he gets worse." We celebrated Christmas at Nana's cabin.

Ten

Darkness Is Falling
(Jan.–Mar. 1990)

I cry, "Darkness is falling . . ."
He says, "Darkness is falling through . . ."
—Bryan Duncan

Wednesday, January 31, 1990

FIFTH-GRADE SHILOH WON SECOND PLACE IN THE SPELLING bee at Zion and would be an alternate for the Riverside County Spelling Bee in February.

Blythe Middle School Bulletin, Friday, February 9, 1990:

CONGRATULATIONS!!! To HEATHER ALEXANDER, a seventh grader who is the Spelling Bee Champion of the District!!!

My life hummed with activity. Carolyn Baschal and I planned to have a booth at the street fair in February. I collected equipment and parent volunteers to create a better nursery program at Zion. I made props for the Sonshine Singers.

But things weren't going well. Don wrote:

Hi, Honey,

Got another invite to play cards, same number. Where ya been? I'll be back around 9 or 10 P.M.

Daddy

It sounds innocent, but I'm suspicious. . . . I'm just being silly.
"Gone shooting with friends," Don's next note said. When it got dark, I worried. At ten I called Tim, but he didn't know anything about a shooting trip, nor did any of Don's other friends.

At one o'clock in the morning, I met him at the door. "After we went shooting, we went to Silly Al's for a drink and pizza."

"But you said you'd never go there because that's where officers go to cheat on their wives."

He shrugged his shoulders. "That's just where the guys wanted to go."

"Who did you go with?"

"Oh, people you don't know."

Please God, let me be wrong.

Don said, "The guys are getting together for a stag party."

"Where can I reach you in case of an emergency?" I asked.

"John's having the party at his place."

I waited for an hour and called the number he gave me. Laughter, music, and party sounds echoed over the phone. "Is Don Alexander there?"

"He went to the store to pick up a few things. Do you want me to have him call you when he gets back?"

"No, don't bother, because he won't be calling me from there. He'll be calling from somewhere else."

Don called a few minutes later. "What's up?" he asked, silence like death surrounded his words.

It's not even a pay phone. "I told John not to have you call me."

"Why not?"

"I know you're not really at John's."

"No, I had to get some things from the store—"

"Don, you're not at the party! You're with the person you're having an affair with."

Silence. "I'll be home in a few minutes."

Oh, God, what do I do now? Why doesn't he just tell me the truth? Was I spending too much time working for You? Wasn't I good enough? How could he do this to the children?

An hour later he drove up.

February 19

    Uriah couldn't be treated today because he was exposed to chickenpox a week and a half ago. Margo called me at the hospital to tell me her fears. Jason is in the hospital, very ill. When we visited him, he was doing better; the tubes were out of his lungs and stomach.

A few nights later Don left another note:

Mara

I'm at the Courtesy Cafe (corner of Lovekin and Hobsonway). One of our officers is transferring out on Saturday, so a few of us are meeting there. I wanted you to come but didn't want to miss the get together. It's 4:45 P.M. now. I'll be back in a couple hours.

Daddy

He won't be home when he said he will. He's probably not where he says he is.

After eight-thirty, he called. "I've had too much to drink, and I need you to pick me up."

My voice was icy. "I'm putting the kids to bed. As soon as I'm done reading to them, I'll come and get you."

"Yeah, OK."

Why does he sound nervous?

I tucked the kids in and told Heather where I was going, but not why. When I entered the dimly lit bar, I recognized prison employees. *It really is a prison personnel gathering. Maybe I misjudged him.* They stared back at me as if I were a horse about to be shot. *They know!*

I spotted Don on a stool at the end of the bar and made my way to him. "Are you ready to go?" *I want out of here, away from their stares.*

"Yeah, well, I just ordered a sandwich."

A small, trim blonde woman sat around the corner of the bar from Don. "Don't be rude, Alex. Introduce us."

"Mara, this is the officer who's transferring out."

God, I can't believe this is happening! No wonder they're looking at me that way. It's her!

"I'm so glad to meet you," she gushed, patting the stool between Don and her. "Have a seat."

"I don't have time for this." I turned to Don, irritated: "My children are home alone."

Don's sandwich arrived, and he crammed it in his mouth. She laughed. "I've never seen anybody eat a sandwich that quick before, sergeant." A man sitting next to her put his arm around her and pulled her close.

I must really be getting paranoid. She can't be the one. But I know there's someone by the way they're looking at me.

Don gulped the last of his sandwich, and we threaded our way to the door. He started to the car but turned back. "I forgot something."

The woman and her date came out and climbed into a big truck parked next to "the Beast," which we had borrowed from Freddie and Linda Mendez. The old, off-road vehicle took a lot of strength to shift, a lot of skill to start, and made lots of noise, but we were grateful for it since our car didn't work. Don drifted back toward the Beast without going into the bar.

It's too bad a rock hit the windshield and put a crack in it when Don was driving. We'll have to replace it before we return the Beast.

The big truck's engine started. Don paced around the Beast, scowling. *Something strange is going on here. All I know is, the children are home alone and I need to get back.*

"I just want to walk around in the desert for a while," Don said when we got home.

I didn't stop him. *He's drunk and there's no moon. I hope he doesn't get bit by a snake or lose his way.* After an hour, I begged him to come in.

Friday, February 23
    I took Don's boots to be fixed. Uriah couldn't walk far because he wasn't feeling well, so we sat on the curbside for four hours while the windshield on the Beast was replaced.

After the kids were asleep and Heather was at her first babysitting job, I settled on the couch. Don cleared his throat. "I need to talk to you about something."

My eyes snapped to his face. He was staring at the floor, digging for words.

Oh, God, here it comes!

"I want to leave you because I'm not happy," he said.

"Why?"

"I don't know why. I just can't explain it."

"Why can't you stay and try to work things out if there isn't anyone else?"

"I've never been much of a family man—"

"Malarkey!"

"There is someone else."

My suspicions had been right. "What did I do wrong?"

"Nothing."

"I know who it is."

His eyes leaped up from the floor, disbelief on his face. "Who?"

"It was the blonde at the bar."

His eyes returned to the floor. "Yeah," he murmured.

"She wants to meet you."

"Why? What's it to her who I am?"

He shrugged. "I'm going to spend the night with her because she's leaving for Corcoran tomorrow."

"It's your life. Do what you want."

"I'll call her from the gas station." A little later the truck squealed to a halt next to the mobile home.

"What's wrong with you?" I hissed. "You're going to wake up the kids."

"She was with someone else."

I stared at him.

"A friend! She told me not to come over. She couldn't talk. I let her know I told you about her. I'll talk to her at work tomorrow."

※ ※ ※

I tapped at Pastor's open office door. He pushed back from his desk and smiled. "Mara! Come on in."

"Pastor, do you have a minute?" The pain on my face made his smile fade, and concern filled his eyes.

"Sure."

"Don's having an affair. He wants to throw everything away . . ."

"I know things may seem pretty bleak, but this is probably just a phase. If he's willing to come in for counseling, I think there's a good chance you can work through this."

"He said he would."

$\approx$ $\approx$ $\approx$

At home, Don smiled. "I talked to her. She said she wants to get to know me better, and she's dumping the other guy. I need a picture of myself to mail her. I'm going to marry her, so we need to talk about how to divide things."

I sure hope this doesn't kill Uriah. I had dreamt Don was dead, but I never dreamed this. I'd braced myself for years for the loss of a loved one, but I thought it was Uriah I might lose, not Don. *God, help me to cope! I have no way to deal with this.*

Thirteen years of marriage, gone in an instant. It's like investing everything in a business that goes bankrupt. *I feel like I'm walking away with nothing. And I worry that what I've invested in the children will be lost too. I don't want to lose their love. I feel like he's playing up to them, or is it just that he is happy?*

"You can have custody of the children," Don said, "except every other weekend. You can drive them up to Corcoran, stay overnight, and bring them back."

It's so simple when Mommy and Daddy live together. My children's world would be shattered, and I couldn't do anything to stop it.

"Tell anyone you like," he said.

I don't want to tell anyone; it might work its way back to the children before we can tell them, but I need prayer desperately. Tell the children? When? How?

Uriah's illness meant we'd have to move back near Fontana. *I guess I'll ask Nana if we can live at the cabin for a while until I find a job and a place to live.*

I'd often wondered how it would feel to have my "other half" ripped away if he suddenly died, but I did not think he would tear himself away. *I'm half a person, wondering what I'll do now. The cold, slow ache of loneliness is already beginning to creep upon me.*

Monday, February 26
    Shiloh came with me for Uriah's treatment. Because he was exposed to chickenpox, we had to stay in the spinal-tap room all day while he got his Cytoxan. They poked Uriah four times to do the spinal tap, but he used Lamaze so well, he hardly cried.

After I put the children to bed, Don and I talked.

"I love you both," he said, "but I'm not happy here with you, so I want to get to know her better. Pastor thinks I have hypoglycemia and put me on a no sugar, no white-flour diet, with lots of vitamins—and no alcohol."

I need to make sure he takes his medications and stays on his diet. Pastor thinks he won't be interested in her when his depression ends.

Don proudly poured all the alcohol down the drain. "She called while you were gone, and I talked to her boys. They seem nice. I asked if Heather wanted to talk to her, but she said no."

"The kids and I will move to Nana's cabin after the kids finish school this year," I said.

He clutched the edge of the sink. "I need a drink—real bad."

February 27

"Mom, I can't go to school," Shiloh said. "I feel like I'm going to throw up."

"It's just nerves, honey. You can stay home today, but tomorrow you have to go back. Heather, are you going to ride the bus home or walk to Zion?"

Heather scowled and left for school.

Yesterday I went through guilt. Today I'm going through despair. I cleaned and washed clothes. It hurts most today, so far. I cried. I'm cutting my time into sections. I can't face this week or even today, so I'll concentrate on just getting through the next half hour. At least I'm not down to five minutes yet!

I felt despair drain away as I drove to my appointment with Pastor. Acceptance is coming. It's good to feel peace returning. I feel exhausted and wrung out, like after a fever breaks, but I know the Lord's in control and it'll all work out.

Don said, "I bought romantic greeting cards for her today." From the desk, I got one he hadn't mailed to me. *He may as well send it to her.* I told him, "It's a good thing you didn't send me this one. It says, 'In your hands . . . my future!' Promise you won't tell me the things you're doing for her. And don't call her when I'm here. It just hurts too much."

He handed me his knife. "Lock this up so I don't hurt myself."

I had a terrible urge to use it on myself. I locked it in the gun cabinet. *Maybe this suicide stuff is an attempt to get me to back off. Pastor said as long as Don has her, he won't do anything. And soon he'll snap out of it.*

"I want to go see her every other Monday, Tuesday, and Wednesday," Don said. "I'll wait for you and Uriah to get home from his treatment and then go. Shiloh and Heather can stay with Freddy and Linda on Mondays if I can't get back in time."

This is really affecting me. I forgot the syringes for Uriah, and we don't have enough.

We went to church to have our family portrait taken. "I want my picture taken separately," Don told the photographer.

Wednesday, February 28

Shiloh and I were sitting on the back porch, working on her project for the barbecue, when Don drove up. "I got a letter of instruction for something I didn't do! I'm going to appeal it. Anyhow, I thought today was a bad day to do overtime."

He tried to call her, but she wasn't home.

I feel him shutting me out of his life now. It hurts, but I don't cry so often now. I feel loneliness wash over me sometimes, like ocean breakers. I think I've lost him for good, even though people say he'll be back. What kind of an emotional pretzel will I be by then? Will I be able to take him back?

I had always thought affairs were over when the wife found out. *I'm expected to sit calmly by while he carries on his affair and then resume our marriage if he decides he wants to be bothered. There must have been something I could do to prevent this. It's hard to believe we all mean so little to him, or she could mean so much so quickly.*

Thursday, March 1

It just hurts too much. I want to run away and hide. We can't even stay together for the children. Even though it could be so serious for Uriah, he can't stay. It seems so selfish: the only unhappiness that matters is his own. I feel deserted, abandoned. The fabric of my life is coming apart, and all I can do is watch it unravel.

The death of a dream is so hard. Everything we ever hoped or dreamed together is dying: our old age together, taking the kids to the Grand Canyon, moving to Oregon. . . .

I need to make new dreams; otherwise I have no hope, and all I have to look forward to is pain, loneliness, and uncertainty. At least God's in control. I must remember that.

"Mom, I'm getting more headaches and they're hurting worse," Heather said. "And now my knee hurts when I walk."

Uriah threw up in school. "My head's been hurting all day," he said.

I peered at the slender glass tube. *He isn't running a fever, but I should take both of them to the doctor.*

Saturday, March 3
"Uriah's fine." the doctor declared. "Heather has vision problems—20-40 and 20-50—and a disease in her knee. Here's an excuse for any activity that hurts her."

I need to explain things to the children. They can see something is wrong. I don't want them to think Uriah's getting worse. I called them to the table. When I finished, they were silent. "How do you feel about this? Please tell me if you're worried about anything. Daddy still loves you; he just doesn't love me."

"I don't mind Daddy getting married again, but I don't want you to," said Heather.

"Why not?"

"I've heard enough horror stories about the wicked step-father from my friends."

"What if she turns out to be the wicked stepmother?"

"I'll just go outside and play basketball."

"I want to talk to her on the phone," said Shiloh.

"I wouldn't know what to say," said Uriah.

"Are you scared or looking forward to things?" I asked.

"Why are we doing this?" Shiloh asked.

"Daddy's doing this. I wanted things to stay the way they were," I said.

"I don't like it," said Uriah.

"I don't care if you remarry," said Shiloh.

"I'd like you to get married before I grow up and get married," said Uriah.

"What will happen to you after we move out?" asked Shiloh. "Maybe I could stay with you until I get married."

"That's fine with me, but don't worry. I won't be lonely. I'll have friends, things to do, and visits from you kids. But after you move out, I might remarry so I won't live alone."

❧   ❧   ❧

I put deep-heating rub on Don's sore shoulder. "I want to go to Corcoran and see her Sunday after work," he said.

He'll be away from home a lot. I guess we need to get used to it. Uriah's going to need a positive father-figure in his life. I'll see if Uriah can go to A. J.'s house on Tuesdays.

Sunday, March 4, I told Don, "I think Uriah's having mood swings. I explained to the kids what's happening. Heather said she doesn't want me to remarry, but Uriah said he would like me to marry again—"

"That hurts!" Don exploded.

My mouth gaped. *I didn't think he would care.*

He turned to the window. "I want to go shooting with the kids today. I need you to get balloons and cardboard."

"Shiloh and I need to work on her project—and finish it."

"I need to find out if this relationship will work," he said gazing outside.

"What?"

"I was just thinking out loud. She made an appointment for me to have a tour of the prison Tuesday."

It sounds so settled it hurts.

"I need to learn to flush Uriah's tubes."

He doesn't want me in town when the children are up there with him. I'll probably come the first weekend, until I can make myself let go.

"When her baby gets his shots, I could come down here to visit and sleep on the couch."

"She won't go for that. Then again, she may feel if he doesn't care enough about me to stay faithful, forget it."

"I'll probably stay with her mom or at a motel while I'm up there because it's too soon for another man to move in. It would be too sudden a change for her kids."

I'm surprised you would show such sensitivity. Especially since you didn't shown any for our children when it came to sudden changes.

How does she view it? Maybe she doesn't think she's destroying a good marriage. Perhaps she thinks it was tottering already.

He said he hasn't been happy for years. Yet he seemed so happy since we moved here. He says he doesn't know why he left me. Maybe he's afraid to tell me the real reason.

"If you have jury duty Monday, I'll take Uriah for his treatment," Don said.

"Why can you do all this stuff now? Was I that bad?" I asked.

He gave me a cold look and turned back to the window. "Her mother doesn't like her husband, and she sounds like a really nice person."

"What if she doesn't like you?"

How could she like someone who dumped a wife and three kids to carry on an affair with a married woman who has three kids?

At the hospital March 5, Uriah's counts were low, but they treated him anyway. Heidi, the psychologist, gave me advice about Don and me. "Mention it to the doctors. Stay in counseling and involve Uriah in Big Brothers."

When we got home at 5:00 P.M., Don helped us unpack the truck, and I helped him put his gear in. "I'll call the kids tomorrow," he said.

I watched him drive away. I turned and climbed the stairs alone. "Shiloh, can I help you with your project?"

"Mom, I got a progress report," said Heather.

I took the slip. "Your child is getting a D in Algebra because work has not been completed." *Just one more worry on a lousy Monday.*

Tanya, our Doberman, got up at every sound, expecting to see Don return home. I didn't sleep.

Tuesday, March 6 was a hard day.

I just feel so numb. God, I miss Don so much.

Heather King stopped me in the parking lot when I picked up Shiloh from school. "Darren and I were hoping you and Don would come to dinner sometime this week."

"I'll . . . talk to Don about it. Thanks." *Just seeing two people so happy together hurts. I have to play charades of the hardest kind. He's off having a blast, destroying everything we worked so hard to make. I'm hurting, the kids are hurting. When did he change? Why did he change?*

I feel so broken. Pain follows me everywhere with no sign of slackening. Is this really what my life is destined to be? Oh,

God, give me a right attitude toward Don and this woman. Give me the right attitude for my life, and please help me deal with this pain that consumes my whole being. God, help me to see the good in this; right now it is so hidden from me.

I rushed home with the kids and started supper. We played a few games, but when Don hadn't called by 8:20, I called him. Her five-year-old son answered. "Alex!" he called.

She picked up the phone, "Hello?"

"The kids would like to talk to their dad, if that's all right."

"Alex, phone."

He talked to Uriah, Shiloh, and finally Heather.

I keep fighting the urge to tell friends. As if more people agreeing with me could make him see sense. Am I seeking vengeance against him by trying to make them upset with him too? Or is it simply a way to ease my pain? He'll never come back.

I went running at 5:30 A.M. Wednesday, March 7 after prayers. *Everything familiar hurts. I even hate my volunteer work.*

I told Pastor about the disastrous phone call. "You shouldn't tell anyone else because there might be healing. Running in the morning is great. It's better than putting your hand through a door," he joked.

"That's not my way," I murmured.

"If you move out, you and Don shouldn't be reunited."

That's the first time he's mentioned it might not work out. "I'm not sure about that, but after I have a job and friends, it will be too late. I still love him."

"But," Pastor said, "every day causes a little more of that love to die."

Prednisone made Uriah so hungry he tried to eat my purse strap on the way home.

After I read to the kids and tucked them in, I heard a terrible racket. Somebody driving like an idiot pulled up beside our house. In fear, I peeked out the window. *Don's home early.* He stomped into the house and slammed the door with all his might.

"The children are asleep!" I protested. "Why are you home?"

"I came home early because of the long drive and a double shift." He slumped in the easy chair, scowling. "It turns out her kids don't know. The eldest resents me, the youngest loves me, and the baby's too young to understand. She was worried her husband might come home early, so I had to leave. The youngest son's in counseling. She wants the change to be gradual, so June sounds good to her too. She's thinking about moving out here then."

"Whatever."

"She's worried her husband will get an early discharge, and he'll be staying there for the next four months, so I won't get to see her at all."

This woman's using him. She's going to drag this out as long as possible, until he's all used up like an old, empty sack, and then she'll throw him away. Is she heartless?

He began pacing and muttering with agitation.

"You either calm down or leave," I said. *If he behaves like this, we'd be better off without him.*

He dialed the phone. "Pick up! Pick up!" He slammed the receiver down. "If he's done anything to her . . ." he muttered. Fifteen minutes later he said, "Wait a minute; this is a wrong number. How could she have written down the wrong number?"

She's playing him for a fool, for every emotion she can possibly pull out of him. I locked the gun cabinet. *He's acting irrational. He says he's made up his mind to marry her. Tomorrow will probably be bad, but tonight my emotional yo-yo is still. This has got to stop.*

Thursday, March 8

It's time to let go. He's looking for reasons to hate me now. They won't be hard to find. I must learn to hold my tongue; peaceful coexistence by avoidance. Whatever his life will be, he's got to make or break it on his own.

It was after 7:00 P.M. on Friday, March 9 when the kids and I got home because we stopped to buy shoes they needed. I thought Don would be at work, but he was home. "Well, I'm glad you're home at last," he snapped. "I miss my kids. I was worried they got hurt or you ran off with them, but your stuff was still here, so I figure you're just going to keep the kids away late every day so I can't see them."

That stung. *What did you expect?* I put my hurt and anger to work. After half an hour, Don came into the bedroom where I was hanging clothes. "I'm sorry for the way I'm acting," I told him. "But it's hard to suddenly be without love."

"Look, I'm sorry," he said. "I meant to hurt you because I was angry and worried. It felt good when I saw you were hurting; but after a while I knew it wasn't right."

Margot called. "Jason had a 90 percent relapse—or involvement at least. They won't do a bone-marrow transplant if he isn't in remission. They're trying him on the usual treatment one last time."

When I sat down in the living room, Don said, "I think I need to tell T. Ray. I don't care if the prison people know, but I don't want anyone else to know yet."

"You won't be upset if I hire a lawyer to make sure we get what we need, will you? I know I won't be thinking clearly."

"Sure, that's fine."

"And Uriah will need a man he can talk to. Is it OK if I ask Freddy if Uriah can come over on Tuesdays?"

He nodded. "Freddy's good."

He sat up late, shooting at rabbits. *I don't know when and if she's going to drop him, but I don't want to find him dead. The ammo gets locked up.*

"I'm just confused," Don said Sunday morning. "Sometimes I want to stay here at home, sometimes I want to be with her, and most of the time I just don't know."

"But I thought you were so happy up there!"

"Not really."

"But you sounded like you were in heaven."

"You called at one of the good times. A lot of the time, I just sat around."

Later he yelled while he ironed his shirt. "The car's fixed but runs crappy. The mechanic told me we should get rid of it. Bad luck has always followed me. It's an Alexander curse."

"Did you think you could lose your bad luck if you left us?"

"That's not it. I expected the bad luck to follow me."

In anger I quipped, "What kind of a chance will I have with a sick kid like Uriah?" I was horrified when I realized Uriah was sitting on the couch with a look of shock and dismay on his face. I turned toward him, anxious to ease the pain I had caused. Don grabbed my wrist and dragged me toward the bedroom. I fought back until he let go. We knelt as one beside Uriah, trying to console him.

"I'm not leaving you," Don soothed.

"But you're not staying," I said.

"I'm not through talking yet!"

"I had to say something. Uriah was starting to hope you weren't going to see her anymore."

The unspoken hope flickered out on Uriah's face. "I'm OK," he sighed.

In the bedroom, I told Don all the angry things I felt about being left alone to raise teenagers and a sick child. "Every other weekend does not a parent make!"

That night my eyes were red from crying. *Thanks, God, for forgiving my mistakes. I just hope I can forgive myself. Don acted like he forgave me. Please let Uriah be OK.*

Carolyn and Sabrenia came with us for Uriah's appointment on Monday, March 12. We planned to go to the snow afterward. "We're giving Uriah vincristine, but his platelets have been low for two weeks, and his white count has dipped," Dr. Haghighat said. "We need to do a bone marrow."

I'm not worried. He had Cytoxan the week before last, and they treated him last week despite the low count. It's just a check.

I called Don. "They did a bone marrow. Please don't leave to visit your mistress until we know the results."

"It's time for her to chase me for a while."

Val was working across the hall in the regular pediatric clinic, so I sneaked over see her. "Have Uriah stop by and say hi before you go," she said.

In Uriah's treatment room, I explained to Heidi, the psychologist, how things were going with Don. *Why is she staying so long?*

"Dr. Haghighat wants to talk to you."

Oh, God, no!

Heidi slipped into Dr. Haghighat's office behind me.

No, no, no! Maybe she just wants to be sure I tell Dr. Haghighat about Don.

Dr. Haghighat swung around in his chair to face us. I dropped into a chair.

He sighed and opened the six-inch-thick medical folder before him. "Poor Uriah," he lamented.

"How bad is it?" I whispered.

Eleven

Starting Over
(Mar. 1990)

Joy is something from the inside:
a gift from the Lord that has little to do
with what's happening around you.

A MARROW RELAPSE: 90 PERCENT LEUKEMIA CELLS. *And he's on chemotherapy.* I read the fine print in the paperwork I signed. *His chances are poor. He needs to gain remission with deadly doses of chemotherapy, and we must find a donor or use a transplant of his own cleansed marrow.* "Could the things going on in our private life have caused Uriah's relapse?" I asked Dr. Haghighat.

"What happened couldn't have triggered it."

I'm not so sure.

I went to the pediatric waiting room. "Carolyn, Uriah's relapsed."

She searched my eyes. "You're OK?"

"Yeah. But it's gonna take some time to get him settled."

"I'll take Sabrenia for a walk."

She's got to explain to Sabrenia. Sabrenia and Uriah are so close. They've even joked about marriage someday.

I sat down beside Uriah. "Sorry, dude."

"Relapse, huh? Now we can't go to the snow. Do I have to go in the hospital?"

"Yep."

"Bummer."

The answering machine came on when I called home. *I hope Don didn't change his mind and leave.* After Uriah's spinal tap, Don answered the phone.

At 5:00 P.M., as I wheeled Uriah to the pediatric wing, we saw Carolyn and Sabrenia. "I'm sorry about all this. We should be able to go soon."

"I'm sorry, but your visitors will have to leave," said the nurse preparing Uriah's Daunomycin.

They followed me to the waiting area where I called Nana. When I returned, Dr. Sanmarco was waiting. "How are you doing?"

"I'm OK. I've got to drive my friend back to Blythe and pick up Don and the girls tonight."

She scrutinized my face. "Be careful driving back . . . and don't worry about Don. Just take care of yourself and your little ones right now."

I smiled at her concern. "I will. Thanks."

Now that Uriah's sick, I don't have time or energy to waste on Don and his mistress. It all needs to be focused on Uriah and the girls. We need to move back here now so Uriah can get his treatments and the girls won't be left with friends while he visits his mistress.

Uriah handed me the phone. "It's Grandma Ruth."

"How much has Don told you?" I asked.

"Just that Uriah's relapsed."

"You need to call him back and ask him what else he needs to tell you."

Later she called back. "I'm very disappointed."

"I'd like to talk to you more about it later. I thought you might have some advice."

I hugged Uriah. "I'll be back soon with Daddy, Heather, and Shiloh."

He nodded and rolled over for a nap.

I unlocked the truck for Carolyn and Sabrenia. "I'm sorry you came all this way, Sabrenia, and we can't take you to see snow for the first time. Maybe we can try again another time."

We drove through dry Calimesa toward the desert. Fat white flakes began to float earthward. "It never snows here!" I chortled. Within minutes, a white blanket covered the ground. I pulled off the freeway onto a side street for a quick snowball fight. Carolyn and Sabrenia rolled up a little, smiling snowman. *Thanks, God. You know our hearts even if we forget to pray. You've raised our spirits and reminded us You know what we're going through. You're still in control.*

"I'll cancel all your projects for this week and see if Mary Watts will help me do the Kite Day project," Carolyn said.

At 12:30 A.M. I dropped my keys on the counter at home. "Don," I said, "the kids and I will have to move to Nana's cabin."

"Why?" he shouted.

"Uriah's going to need lots of treatments. Why should I stay out here? For you? You need to call her and tell her what's going on."

After he told her, she said, "I don't think you should come. Your wife is going to need you."

Nice of her to decide that now.

"I'm sleeping on the couch!" Don snapped.

Tuesday, March 13, at 4:00 A.M. I packed the truck. When we arrived at eight, Uriah was eating and drawing. "Hi, Uriah," I said. "The girls can't come in, but look!" They waved from outside the locked, sliding-glass door.

Uriah got radioactive intravenous medication. The nurse posted a radioactive warning sign on his door. "His urine has to be collected in these containers for twenty-four hours. You need to wear gloves."

I turned to Uriah. "Don't start swinging from the walls or anything like that."

"I'm saving that sign for my door at home," he said.

Uriah lay on the table with sensors attached to his chest and back and watched his heart beat on a tiny monitor. The muga scan monitored his heart activity so any damage from Daunomycin could be identified. "He's very close to his threshold for that medication," Dr. Haghighat said. "We can give him only three doses."

Pushing Uriah's wheelchair back to pediatrics, we saw Nana in the waiting area. "You have a lot of people waiting to talk to you," she said.

She looks like she's been crying.

Pastor and Don awaited in Uriah's room. Pastor had cards from Uriah's class.

My dear Uriah,

You just get out of that hospital *right now* and get back to Zion. You have work to do! Ha ha!

Don't worry, I know that your job right now is to get that body strong again. So put your trust in Jesus, and let Him do His work at fixing you up again. I love you so much—you're always in my heart. The children are thinking of you, and we're praying too.

Sending you smiles and all good things,

Mrs. Maly

"I'll leave so Nana can come in," Don offered. Pastor followed him out.

Joan called before Nana came in. "Your mom had a teaching evaluation today. It must have been really hard with everything that's going on."

Nana listened silently while I told her of Don's mistress. "You're welcome to stay at the cabin," she said.

Pastor tapped at the door. "I've got to get back to Blythe, but I'd like to pray with you first."

We clasped hands and asked God's blessings.

"Thanks for making such a long trip, just for us," I said.

He smiled. "I had to come to bring the cards."

Nana rose. "I have to go too."

"We need to go talk," I told Don.

Uriah opened the steaming shrimp dinner Don brought from Sizzler. I gave him a hug. "I don't know if we'll make it back before you go to sleep."

Waiting for our food in a little diner, I felt happiness rise inside me. *Such a strange sensation under the circumstances. It bubbles up inside despite all the destruction taking place around me, like Paul singing in prison.* "You know," I told Don, "I can tell joy is something from the inside: a gift from the Lord that has little to do with what's happening around me. My son's in the hospital dying, and you've left me for another woman, but I feel so happy right now."

He gave me a dark look.

He's wondering why I'm happy and he isn't, after all he's done to try to find happiness. He's only made himself more miserable. I feel sorry for him, but he isn't my problem anymore. "Heidi suggested the girls stay with you—or with friends, if you have to visit your mistress—in Blythe for a week or two, until things calm down, but I want them with me and settled into a new pattern as soon as possible."

"The girls and I will stay here until Friday; then we'll go home," Don muttered. "Then they can stay with friends if I leave and attend school until the next Friday."

"Then I'll come home, pack their things, and move to Nana's cabin," I added. *Everything's so uncertain. I'm afraid of what Don will do if she dumps him, and I don't know how Uriah will do. The doctors have made plans only through Friday.*

❦   ❦   ❦

Mark, Joanna, and their children were staying at the cabin on vacation. Joanna hugged me. "How's Uriah doing? How are you and Don . . . doing?"

"Our marriage is breaking up over another woman, and Uriah's sick, but we're OK. We're not fighting or hostile. Is it OK if we stay here too?"

"Sure. We're gone most of the day."

Don tried to call his mistress, but she wasn't home.

Our conversation with Joanna and Mark flagged. We escaped to our rooms.

❦   ❦   ❦

At 6:00 A.M. I said my prayers and got ready to go. Joanna was holding baby James in the kitchen. He rubbed his big blue eyes and beamed an angelic smile. Meagan came upstairs to give us each a hug and a shy smile.

"Can I stay with Joanna and Mark today?" Shiloh asked. "I love to play with James and Meagan!"

"Sure, honey," I said.

188

Don called his mistress. "She's busy." He called back after a half hour. "She only had a couple minutes, so we couldn't talk."

Maybe this whole situation is one she doesn't want to get involved in.

Don and Heather drove me to the hospital. Uriah had a cardiogram. "It's good so far," Dr. Bhatt said. They gave Uriah Erwinia and took his blood pressure every fifteen minutes. Except for being hungry all the time—and ornery—Uriah seemed the same as ever.

Uriah drew pictures of animals and stapled them together to make coloring books. "I'm going to sell them for twenty-five cents to make money for the church."

Such a businessman.

"Will I be like the man in the family when Daddy is gone?"

"Not really. Except for opening jars I can't." I ruffled his hair. "I will have to be the mommy and the daddy."

I set up the Nintendo in his room. Renee, the child-development specialist, or the "play lady," as Uriah called her, poked her head in the door. "Do you want to play games for a while today?"

"Sure!" he beamed.

Later Dr. Haghighat nodded after examining Uriah. "We might release him from the hospital Friday, but not from the area."

❧ ❧ ❧

I went to church with Margot and prayed with Elder Tom Keely and Pastor Dannenburg. *God, how silly of me! I've been carrying the weight of deciding what Don's and my relationship should be, instead of leaving it to You. Please show me what You want me to do.*

Julie Maly sent an announcement to the parents of Uriah's classmates:

> . . . [M]y heart hurts to tell you this, but our precious Uriah is very sick, and we all *need* to pray for him every day. He is no longer in remission of "lymphoblastic leukemia." The children's reactions are varied with different questions and concerns. . . . I'm sure questions will come up at home also, and I need your help as you encourage them to talk about their feelings, etc., as they bring it up. (And, dear parents, . . . praise God and thank Him this week for your healthy child.)
> God Bless You!
>
> Mrs. Maly

Don took me to lunch Thursday, March 15: "I want to see her, but for two months she won't see me because her husband will be home, discharged from the Marine Corps. Until he starts working for CDC, she's afraid he'll take off with the boys. She's going to take the boys on vacation for five days at her mom's cabin. I hope I can see her then."

That night Don went to the kitchen looking for a drink. I confronted him. "You're not supposed to have alcohol."

"I'm worried about myself. I enjoyed hurting myself with the fireplace poker this afternoon."

"I have to keep the girls with me for their protection."

"That's good. I'm going for a walk."

"That's fine, but you should put on shoes and a coat at least."

He went for a walk in the snow in his socks and shorts. I put on boots and a coat and walked outside. *I'm being an enabler.* I went in and loaded the dishwasher. He seemed calmer when he returned.

Don called me at the hospital the next day: "I talked to her. She said 'I couldn't take you away from your wife when she needs you so much. You should try to make your marriage work during the next two months.' She dumped me!"

Anger blazed in my heart. *The kids and I are going to be fine; I don't need him. It's an excuse to salve her guilt and make herself a martyr. How dare she walk in, crumble our lives into little pieces, and waltz out? She's ill.*

Don continued, "I burned her picture in the fireplace. I won't be doing anything that involves her anymore. I was already having serious second thoughts, and I would have dumped her in a little while."

"Unfortunately you're the only one who could know if you would have done it, since she dumped you first," I said. "Her timing is impeccable in this game of ruining lives."

❦ ❦ ❦

Dr. Sanmarco examined Uriah. "He should be able to go home for the weekend, as long as his count is OK."

Don took me to lunch. "Can we get back together?"

God, I've already reorganized my life and prepared to go on alone. It would be easier to go on alone rather than struggle to resuscitate our relationship. But Grandma Ruth said Uriah needs a father right now. And she's right.

"When and if she calls back, I won't be tempted," Don promised.

I wonder. I think I can risk going through all this again for Uriah's sake. "I won't walk away from you now, but if this happens again, this marriage will end."

When I got back from lunch, Uriah's IV was unhooked. I picked up the doctor's written instructions: "Contact with immediate family members only." We took Uriah to the cabin and had the truck nearly packed when Nana and Boompa drove up. They waved to Uriah in the truck.

"Don and I are going to try to work it out," I whispered to Nana.

She seemed distant. "No one can make that decision for you."

Sunday, March 18

At church we sat in the microphone room so we could be isolated from the rest of the congregation. Pastor gave us communion in our little room. After the service, concerned friends crowded the door, asking, "How's Uriah?"

We moved Uriah to the car. He smiled and answered their questions through closed windows. I held a brief Sunday-school teachers meeting. Don talked to Freddy and Linda and fielded questions Uriah couldn't answer about his health. The fellowship of friends embraced us, like the warmth of a crackling fire on a frosty eve.

In preparation for a grueling week of Uriah's treatments, we packed the car and truck and set off that afternoon. Don and the girls went to Nana's cabin, but Uriah couldn't be near Meagan and James, so he and I went to Sharon Repp's. At 9:00 P.M. she opened the door. "Oh, hi! We just got back from church. I thought you'd need to stay here someday because Gary suggested it without my saying anything. Sometimes God sets things up without our realizing it."

God, she has everything I wish I had—a clean, beautiful house, a loving husband, a good career. Jealousy? I guess so. Put that at the top of the list of things I want You to change about me. I'm sorry I was ungrateful. You've given me some wonderful gifts: children, friends, good health, and most of all Your Son.

Monday, March 19

At the clinic Uriah's medicine hadn't come. "I didn't know I was supposed to call," Barbara said. He got Daunomycin but not Erwinia. We left at noon with a road map of his chemotherapy.

Later I filmed as Don and the kids tossed snowballs and sledded down the steep hillside. Don and the girls went to Andy and Janet's for dinner, so Uriah and I built a snow fort. Then we toasted ourselves by the fireplace and roasted marshmallows.

Tuesday, March 20

"Don't knock down Uriah's snow fort," I said.

"Why not?" Heather asked.

"It could be the last one he ever gets to build."

She shot me a cynical stare. "He's not that sick."

"Your brother is dying, Heather. He needs a bone-marrow transplant or he will die."

After breakfast, the kids and I built more snow forts. Later Heather's and Shiloh's melted, but Uriah's remained standing.

Don got up late. "You're just wasting the whole day away!"

"We're all waiting for you," I said. He stopped scolding but seemed angry.

We sat as far apart as possible in Dr. Sanmarco's tiny office. "At the end of this week, Uriah's name will be entered in the registry to find a bone-marrow donor," Dr. Sanmarco said. "Dr. Falk will be contacted to determine who will perform the transplant, and Uriah will have a bone-marrow test to see if he's in remission. Once he's in remission, some of Uriah's bone marrow can be harvested for an autologous transplant, in case no donor is found."

Neither of us could take the girls to the spelling bee Wednesday in Riverside. We drove the girls to Debbie's house.

"I could take another day off work. . . ." Don said.

"It's too late. Debbie took a day off work so she could bring the girls to the spelling bee." *It seems so long since they won the first spelling bee. So much has happened.*

At the cabin I was putting Don's uniforms in the dryer when the phone rang. "Mara, I got information about a group called Life-Savers that searches for bone-marrow donors," Joan Weiss said.

"Thanks. It helps so much. I didn't know where to look."

Don frowned. "I don't want to go, and you aren't helping me get ready." He stomped from the room. "I'm going to be late!" he yelled.

I hung up his uniforms and the phone rang. "Has Lena called yet?" Janet asked. Don scrutinized tiny wrinkles on some of his uniforms. He jerked them off the hangers and tossed them to the floor.

"No. Listen, Don's trying to leave, and I need to get off the phone. He's upset."

I folded his uniforms into a bag.

"I don't want to go," he said.

"We both know you have to."

I walked him to the truck. He got in and drove away in silence.

The phone rang. "Is there anything we can do to help?" Lena asked.

"We're just relying on God to show us what to do. How's your new baby, Jessica?"

"We're all doing well. R. J.'s recovered. We're still going to church! I'm teaching R. J. and Jason how to pray—and trying to learn how myself!"

Oh, God, she's been through so much, but she's still trying. I can too. Thanks so much for this encouragement. You give me hope.

During Uriah's appointment, I tapped on Dr. Haghighat's door. "Do you think you could give me a doctor's excuse for Don? They're threatening to dock his pay for taking last week off."

"Sure." He pulled out a pad and wrote. "Bring Uriah back Friday for more Erwinia."

No one was at Debbie's house when I went to pick up the girls, so I opened the packet Joan gave me. The Life-Savers Foundation information described founder Dr. Brutoco's search for a donor when his wife had leukemia. He found one, and she had a successful transplant. He began the nonprofit Life-Savers Foundation in 1988 to test donors for the federally funded National Marrow Donor Program (NMDP). It kept a confidential, computerized registry to match donors with people who needed a transplant. The NMDP coordinated transplants and research at thirty-two transplant centers and sixty-three donor centers but had no funding for donor testing.

The odds of finding a match were 1 in 20,000, and the registry contained 80,000 donors. Life-Savers had tested 55,000 and its goal was 250,000, so anyone who needed a donor would find one. To hold a donor drive, I needed to contact organizations to solicit funds for testing, such as churches and public-service groups. I also needed volunteers to set up the test area and to clean up afterward.

Debbie and the girls pulled into the driveway. Both girls wore medallions and carried certificates. "How did you do?" I asked.

"Not very well," Heather murmured. "I only came in thirteenth."

"What do you mean, not very well? That's great!"

I hugged Debbie. "Thanks, Deb. Well, back to Blythe we go."

Don submitted a memo at work:

On 12March90 my son suffered a massive (90 percent) leukemia relapse in his bone marrow. If the doctors are able to get his leukemia back into remission, he will require a bone-marrow transplant. If a bone-marrow donor can be found, he will have a 20 percent chance of survival, along with a four-week to four-month hospital stay.

Until this happens, he will be receiving intensive and experimental chemotherapy. Among the many other side-effects, his immunities will be reduced, requiring frequent hospitalization.

So long as his mother remains healthy, she will be able to take him for treatments. If she so much as gets a cold, she will not be allowed near him. For this reason, I am requesting to be able to use the 288.75 hours of combined vacation and CTO time I have built up, on a short-notice basis. Due to my son's having had leukemia since Sept. 1983, I have little or no sick leave built up.

Thursday, March 16

Heather, Shiloh, and Uriah went to school the next day with a camera to take pictures of their friends. The girls can stay up at Arrowhead on weekdays and come home on weekends, and Don can come to Arrowhead on his days off so we can be a family four days a week.

But what about Uriah? I talked to his teacher after school: "Julie, I'd like Uriah to stay enrolled here. If you give me his work, I can tutor him at home so he keeps up with the class."

"Sounds like a good idea to me. Let me check with Mr. Maly." She picked up the intercom and asked him. She smiled and nodded. "I'll get work for him right now."

I tried to get the laundry and dishes done before picking up Heather from confirmation. After we ate, the kids and I set out for Arrowhead.

Friday, March 23

I had a migraine when the kids and I started the drive back to Blythe at 6:30 P.M. I stopped a few times to run around the truck and slapped my face to stay awake, but we made it.

Saturday, March 24

When the kids and I ran errands, we saw Heather's classmate Darlyne Hansen working at a bake sale for Mrs. Steadman's GATE class. Darlyne came home with us.

Tim and Lori Ray dropped by. Heather spent the night at Darlyne's.

Sunday, March 25

Heather was acolyte at church this morning. We stayed afterward to practice the Easter play written by Carolyn. We got home before Don and packed, but it was 6:00 P.M. before we were done. "Why do we always have to leave so late?" Don snarled.

Heavy traffic made it hard for me to follow his truck with the car. Halfway there, he pulled off the freeway and stopped at a gas station. "What's up?" I ventured.

"If you'd follow close enough, things would sure be easier!"

I retreated to the car in anger. That night I dreamed he was with his mistress.

I dropped Heather off at school and took Uriah to his appointment Monday, March 26. He took the spinal tap hard. While he was trying to recover, Barbara gave him a shot in the leg. He cried. "Why couldn't she *wait* just a minute?"

"Calm down, it's all over now. Here, let me deal a game of UNO." He won. "Now you deal. I'll be right back," I said and made my way to the nurses' desk. "Barbara, didn't you say Uriah's catheter was hard to draw from?"

She soaked his lumens with special medicine. "They're fine."

"Now we need to pick up the girls from school," I told Uriah as I unlocked the truck. I slipped behind the wheel and gasped.

"What's wrong, Mom?"

"Oh, my chest hurts a bit." We sat in the parking lot until it nearly stopped. I called Don. "I'm sorry we'll be late, but my chest was hurting."

"Take Uriah to the clinic, and go see a doctor."

"I don't want to do that. Do you really think I should?"

"Yes!"

❧ ❧ ❧

"I'll send you for an EKG," the doctor told me, "but I think it's just an anxiety attack."

"You've got a strong heart. It ought to keep pumping for a long time," said the technician. I returned to the clinic for Uriah.

"Is everything all right?" the nurses and doctors asked.

I nodded.

"Get some rest," they said.

Easy to say, hard to do.

I called home. *No answer? I hope he isn't coming.* I sat in the car a moment, wondering what to do. A rap on the window made me jump. Don towered above me. *Is he upset with me?*

I rolled down the window. "I'll follow you to the cabin." He climbed back into his car and sped away. When we arrived, he scowled and stomped into the cabin.

I'm angry, frustrated, and tired. Sometimes I feel like this won't work out.

Uriah

I will not be afraid

Twelve

Now or Never
(Apr.–July 1990)

*Suddenly I discover You've been working
all along in a way I didn't expect.*

Sunday, April 8, 1990

THIS IS THE DAY HEATHER STARTS TAKING RESPONSIBILITY for her own spiritual life. She stood with the other confirmands in white robes at the front of the church and declared what her faith meant to her. Then she knelt and received her first communion.

God, I always knew Heather understood what the Bible was about, but I wasn't sure if she felt it in her heart. I worried she thought she could wait because she was young. Once, driving home, I told her, "None of us know how long we have to live. We could even be killed on the way home today. So it's best not to wait."

The final decision was hers, no matter how much I wished I could make it for her. *Thank You for guiding her. Now that she's witnessed to her faith in You, I know we'll be together in Your kingdom someday.*

I called the Life-Savers Foundation. "There are 90,000 people in the registry now," Bob Weekly said. "You'll need to organize fund-raisers to pay for donor testing."

Monday, April 9

Don wrote a report for Sgt. R. Ryan:

My son . . . is being treated at Kaiser Hosp. Fontana, and is now back in remission. The next step is to find a bone-marrow donor. . . . If a donor can be found, he will then have a 20 percent chance of surviving the transplant. The recovery will take three to six months and requires Uriah to stay in a sterilized room. Until the bone marrow starts to produce enough blood, he will receive blood transfusions.

Uriah's condition is stable at this time but may change quickly. The chances of another relapse increases with time, and each relapse is harder to treat, and the subsequent remission is shorter and harder to maintain.

At this moment I have used all my sick leave. So long as my wife is healthy, I won't need to use very much time off. Should she catch a cold, I will have to take her place in the care and treatment of Uriah. This is due to his low white count while in this stage of chemotherapy (200 as opposed to a normal count of 6,000 to 7,000).

Any assistance you can obtain will be appreciated.

Respectfully submitted,
Sgt. D. F. Alexander

Mrs. Maly sent this note home with her students:

HAPPY EASTER!

Thought you needed to know . . . . Uriah is completely *in* remission now. (And God is so GOOD!!) Uriah's next step is the bone marrow, and we'll know more after Easter break.

With a warm heart,
Mrs. Maly

Thursday, April 19

Uriah's on interim chemotherapy until the end of this week.

I'm concerned stress may be pushing Heather over the edge. On March 25 she wrote "My stuffed cat really purred. Darlyne said there was something strange about me, like I'm half alien or an illusion. If she could see the things Mother Unicorn has seen or been through, she may confirm her own words."

April 11: "The unicorns were up and around in the middle of the day. That's unusual, especially at the cabin."

April 12: "I would have seen the unicorns still out if I had opened the closet door fast enough. The door was closed, and they were running around. When I got to the door, they knocked and I knew it was them. When I opened it, they were gone."

It might be just a fantasy—an escape from the strain we've been under. What do I do now? Should I take her to the psychologist? *God, help me know what to do.*

Jan Cipkala-Gaffin, outpatient coordinator at Children's Hospital of Los Angeles, was the contact for the NMDP. I called her April 24. "I'm trying to find out if Uriah's HLA typing has been placed in the registry for a donor search."

"We've received no information about him."

What! "Who is supposed to send the request for a search?"

"His doctor."

"Hopefully you'll receive the information soon. We're interested in holding a bone-marrow drive to locate a donor for him."

"Before you expend a lot of energy and time, why don't you find out if a compatible donor already exists?"

"That's good advice. Thanks."

Monday, April 23

When we returned after the weekend, I found Nana's note. "The TV turned itself on three times last night; we don't know why."

That made me nervous. We couldn't get the door from the garage to the house open, so I crawled through the doggie door and opened the garage.

In the morning, I took Shiloh to the book fair and took a check to Heather's school so she and Don could go to Disneyland with the school band. The trip will do them both good.

On Friday, April 27, I called the clinic. "Has the search for Uriah's donor been started?"

Silence. "There's been no progress," Margarita said.

"When can we talk to the doctors about this?"

"Just a minute. I'll find out."

Uriah's been in remission for two and a half weeks. I hope something's been done.

"They said to come in at 2:30."

Sitting in Dr. Sanmarco's office, Don stiffened in taut frustration. "You haven't even sent the paperwork yet?" he asked, incredulous.

I had to stay with Uriah for his treatment, but I followed Don into the bustling hospital hallway. He turned to me, blinking back tears. "I'm going to drop the girls off at Janet's for a while. . . . I . . . I need some time alone."

That evening, when we were all gathered back at the cabin, I gave Don a hug. "How are you?"

He shrugged.

"Listen, let's move back to Blythe," I said. "Uriah's treatments will take a lot of time, but if we're going to be a family, we need to be together.

He nodded.

Uriah was in the hospital Monday, May 1, for his treatment of Daunomycin and Ara-C. Dr. Haghighat removed the stethoscope from Uriah's chest. "A transplant costs a lot of money."

Approval for funding must be holding them up. But if they wait too long, it'll be too late.

I called Debbie DeForge, whose son had an autologous transplant. "Hi, Debbie. I was hoping you could give me some information about the transplant process."

"How's Uriah doing?" she asked.

I described his treatment.

"Oh, no. That's the one they put Garrett on when he relapsed. He didn't stay in remission through the twenty-eight days without chemotherapy."

"I'm not comfortable with it. It's been three weeks since his last chemo. I guess that answers my question; we don't have much time to find a donor."

Tuesday, May 2

Our application for financial aid from the Leukemia Society of America was approved. They reimbursed us for some transportation and pharmaceutical costs.

Monday, May 14

We received a letter from Linda Pietz, whose son, Jordan, was being treated at the clinic for leukemia:

My family and I are fasting on Wednesday for Uriah, Jordan, and Jason, and also to tear down the strongholds that exist in that clinic. If you would like to join us in prayer that day, it would be great. Don't feel you have to, but as the Lord leads.

I am mad now. I'm tired of the fear and all that has gone on down there. Forgive my preaching.

Yours in Christ,
Linda Pietz

On May 16, Jan Cipkala-Gaffin told me "I still haven't received any information."

"What would we need to get things going?" I asked.

"We need to have Uriah HLA tested again, have his HLA records faxed to us, and have Dr. Haghighat send records summarizing Uriah's diagnosis, treatment, and current condition."

"Well, I guess I'll be the squeaky wheel until it happens." I called Dr. Haghighat.

May 17, Dr. Haghighat dictated a letter. May 18, a secretary called me for authorization for it to be sent to Dr. Lenarsky. I was overjoyed. *Perhaps at last we'll see some progress in our quest for a bone-marrow transplant.*

May 18

Dear Mara,

Yesterday I had some real good prayer time with the Lord. I think I am going to continue to fast each Wednesday for the clinic, the personnel, and patients. The Lord impressed upon my heart Matt. 16:19.

Yours in Christ,
Linda

May 22, Don and I faxed Uriah's medical history and HLA typing to Dr. Lenarsky and Janet Cipkala-Gaffin. *Any day now it might be too late.*

Wednesday, May 30, Uriah and I went to Children's Hospital in Los Angeles for his HLA typing. The doctor checked Uriah's spleen, ears, and eyes and explained the bone-marrow transplant procedure. Jan drew two vials of Uriah's blood. "Would you like to see where Uriah will stay while he recuperates from the transplant?"

I nodded. We followed her through a maze of hallways to a private area. Gloves reached through a wall into each separate cubicle so parents could interact with their child without infecting them with a touch. Uriah peered through the glass. A little girl played on her bed. "Uriah can bring anything he wants with him, but after the transplant no new things can be brought in. No physical, skin-to-skin contact will take place until after the white blood count has risen high enough to prevent infection."

This looks good. I hope we get a chance to use it.

A giant letter of rainbow colors was sent by Uriah's class June 4:

> Hey we miss you and it was so great, radical, and awesome to have you back with us those days. You sure do know how to shine for Jesus! Just having you around is like our own special RAINBOW! We love you gobs!

June 6, we received a copy of the billing Children's Hospital of Los Angeles sent to Kaiser for the HLA typing: $883.00. June 8 another letter said our insurance had been billed $820.40.

Becky (whose son Brett had leukemia), Linda, Margot, and I prayed for Jason; he seemed to be slipping away—20

percent relapse, 60 percent, then 100 percent. Jordan Pietz went on maintenance. Jason went into the hospital. "I'm going to die on Sunday," he said.

Uriah was admitted with an eye infection. *God, I'm glad we're here to support Margot, but it hurts because I've seen that those who support are the next to mourn. I can see the wisdom in that. Observing from a position of support allows us to learn, so it'll be easier to bear when it's our turn. Yet we're never ready for it to be our turn, and we hope it will pass us by.*

I went to buy Uriah a gift and saw Nancy at the store. "We're next door to Jason," I told her.

"I've been meaning to visit him," she said.

God, it must be important for her to see him before he dies or You wouldn't have arranged our meeting. "Don't wait. Go today." It took a moment for my words to penetrate, then her eyes widened. She visited Jason that evening.

Late Saturday night, Uriah looked up at me. "Just tell me when it happens."

He knows Jason's in the next room dying. He dozed, but an unspoken prayer seemed to hang in the air.

Parents stood outside their children's doors, perhaps drawn there by the strange, anxious anticipation that seemed to fill the air. I talked to Sami's dad as he stood in the doorway of her hospital room.

A nurse approached me. "It's time."

I drove to get Margot and James from home so they could join Tom at Jason's bedside before he departed Sunday, June 24, at 12:05 A.M.

Sunday, just like Jason said it would be. I woke Uriah. "Jason's gone to heaven."

He opened his eyes, nodded, and fell into a deep sleep, at last. The watch was over.

Goodbye, Jason. We're sure gonna miss your smile. I'll be glad to see you again someday.

Jeremy was admitted to the hospital. "I'm going to die," he told the nurses.

"You'll be all right. It's just an infection," they said. But later they moved him to the fourth floor.

Uriah improved and we left Thursday, the morning after Jason's memorial service. Kathy's words long ago echoed in my mind: "His work is done. Now he can go home."

Don's right elbow was injured in a scuffle with an inmate June 27. It took three officers to control that inmate. Now Don has to wear a Velcro support on his arm.

Thursday, June 28

The notice from Children's Hospital stated, "We will continue to bill your insurance for sixty days; after that, the balance will be your responsibility." We had an authorization for outside medical care that covered bone-marrow collection, transplantation, and office visits. "The invoice has been approved for payment," Olga at Kaiser said, "but sometimes it's a lengthy process. Send me the bill."

The next billing jolted me: $5,921.60 for a matched unrelated donor (MUD) search and additional DR typing for fourteen potential donors. If it saves Uriah's life, it's worth it.

Monday, July 2

Margarita called from the clinic. "Uriah needs gamma globulin. He was exposed to the chickenpox while he was in the hospital."

Jeremy died from the chickenpox. The typical symptoms were lacking because it attacked internally, causing liver and lung damage. It was tragic; Jeremy was in remission. He had survived cancer.

Jeremy knew. Jason even knew which day. Kids know if they're dying, whether we tell them or not. Trying to protect them by silence may not be best. It may make them afraid to talk about it because they fear it's taboo. Or they may feel they've been lied to. Not every child wants to know, but I should be sensitive to what Uriah wants and respect what he says about what he's going through. He's the one who feels it all.

Uriah got chemotherapy and was released even though he was on antibiotics. *It's seven weeks since he's had any chemotherapy. They're worried too.*

Wednesday, July 4

Uriah's sunny disposition dissipated. "I hate Shiloh and Heather!" he screamed. Bruises multiplied on his arms and legs. *He's low on platelets.*

We celebrated with friends at the Sunday-school party with watermelon, water balloons, and games, and watched fireworks.

Thursday we picnicked and splashed in the river with the Kelms and friends.

Friday, July 6

Uriah got chemotherapy. Dr. Haghighat frowned. "His platelets are only 179,000. If they drop any lower, we'll have to do tests on Monday."

I'm almost certain of what they'll find.

Saturday, July 7

I called Ruth Sheppardson, a volunteer for the American Cancer Society in Blythe, and explained Uriah's plight. "Is there a gasoline reimbursement available through the American Cancer Society?"

"Our funds are limited, but I'll send the application if you meet me at the ACS table in front of Kmart."

She was the picture-perfect grandma with white hair and a quick smile. Uriah peered at her from behind me with a shy smile. "I'm sure glad to meet you," she said, holding out a toy car. "I've heard good things about you. Did you know you're the youngest person to get benefits? Most of them are old people like me."

We've utilized only a couple support groups because of ignorance of the help available. Until recently, we didn't know about Candlelighters, For Kid's Sake outings for children, or the National Cancer Institute's free information and coloring books for kids with cancer. People should be given this information when their child is diagnosed. The MOMs group could distribute it at the clinic.

Sunday Uriah was angry and tearful at church. "What's wrong?" friends asked me.

"He may have relapsed," I whispered.

"We'll pray."

At home, I answered a knock at the door. "Linda, Freddy! It's good to see you! I wanted to ask if A. J. could spend the afternoon."

Uriah trotted into the living room. "A. J.! Come on, you gotta see my Chameleon game."

Linda watched them retreat out of earshot. "I heard a rumor Uriah might be out of remission."

"I'm afraid he is. They'll probably do tests tomorrow."

"If you need anything, just call."

"Thanks. I will. And thanks for letting A. J. stay; it might be a long time before we're back in town again."

Nana called. "I want to come by the clinic during Uriah's appointment to make sure he's in remission before we leave for Europe."

I saw another clinic mom in the pharmacy July 9. "Ten children have died in the past two months," she murmured.

It must be really hard for the staff to deal with so many deaths, I thought as I retraced my steps to the clinic.

When Dr. Sanmarco walked into the treatment room with test results, I braced myself. "Everything looks fine," she said.

I was astounded. "His tests came back OK?" Relief flooded through me.

"Yes." She smiled. "He can't have his chemotherapy because he's been exposed to the chickenpox, but he's OK."

Nana took us to Sizzler for lunch, and we followed her home for a planned rendezvous with Don and the girls.

"Everything's OK then?" Don asked.

I nodded.

"I've got to see the doctor about my arm," he said and gave me a kiss. "I'll be back in a little while."

As he drove away, Debbie phoned. "Did they reach you?" she asked urgently.

"Who?" My heart pounded.

"Margarita called for Dr. Haghighat."

"No. Thanks, Deb. Bye." I dialed the hospital with shaky hands.

"There are some suspicious cells in the peripheral of the slide," Dr. Haghighat murmured. "You need to bring him tomorrow morning for a bone marrow."

I hung up the phone limply. *Oh, God, what a cruel reversal!* I turned from the phone without words. Nana's worry lines deepened. Uriah's smile dissipated.

When Don returned, Uriah chirped, "Let's go to Sizzler!"

Don shot me a puzzled glance. His face grew sober as he read my expression. "I thought the blood test was good."

"So did I, until they called."

❧ ❧ ❧

Tuesday, July 10. Dr. Sanmarco repeatedly forced back the plunger on the empty syringe embedded in Uriah's hip, but the bone marrow refused to flow. *I don't need to wait for the results. It must be packed with leukemia.*

"She couldn't get any out," Uriah said. "That isn't good."

"You know they'll have to admit you."

"Yeah."

He seems OK.

Dr. Sanmarco called me into her office and closed the door. "He's relapsed."

"Yes, I know. What happens now?"

"Just enjoy the time you have left with him."

What! I tried to keep my voice even. "What about the bone-marrow transplant?"

"There's not much chance of that happening. Don't get him upset by telling him he's relapsed. Just take him home and enjoy him."

Uriah wants the bone-marrow transplant—slight though the chance seems now. Of the original fourteen possible donors, one was disqualified and another didn't match. *We're running out of time.* "He already knows he relapsed."

"How?"

"He's spent years watching his friends progress or die. He just knew, and we talked about it." *I couldn't keep him from knowing even if I lied.*

As Dr. Sanmarco and I walked toward Uriah's treatment room, Nana and Ann Weinberger came in. I didn't need to tell Nana. Her expression told me she knew without a word. I hugged her and cried.

Dr. Sanmarco hesitated. "Do you want me to tell him?"

"Sure."

"Uriah, you relapsed again."

"I know." He shuffled his UNO cards. "Hey, Mom, how about a game of cards?"

"OK. Deal. I'll be back in a minute." Nana and Ann turned questioning eyes to me in the hall. "I'll call as soon as I know what they're going to do," I promised. *I'm glad Nana's with a friend. She's got a difficult choice to make about her trip.*

Dr. Sanmarco changed her mind several times about Uriah's treatment, but he ended up in the hospital after a spinal tap.

I tried to call everyone who should know. *It's time to begin the bone-marrow drives. It's now or never.*

Don and the girls returned to Blythe to care for the animals and pack for an extended stay.

❦ ❦ ❦

On July 11 Debbie stayed with Uriah while Nana and I went to breakfast. "Anita Tams died of a heart attack," Nana said, brushing away a tear. "The funeral's tomorrow."

God, Anita was her best friend. So many bad things are happening to Nana, please take care of her. "Can I go with you? How are Terri and Barb?" We cried for their loss—and our loss—of their mother.

"She sure was feisty," I smiled. We chuckled as we remembered the antics of the gray-haired widow who boldly raised two Christian daughters in a turbulent world while she laughed at the time to come. *She's reunited with Walt, at last.*

Nana watched my eyes. "If it's all right, we've decided to go on our trip."

"I think it's a good idea. You can't keep your life on hold. Things can always happen. He should be OK until you get back."

Don called from Blythe. "My arms are tingly and numb," he puffed. "I can't catch my breath."

"It sounds like a panic attack. If you think it's a heart attack, have one of the girls call 911. Otherwise, just stay calm and rest. Call me in an hour."

The phone rang, unanswered, when I called back after an hour. I worried until he walked through the door with Tanya, Uriah's dog.

"I didn't know how long Uriah might have," Don whispered.

We played with Uriah until 7:00 P.M. At the cabin Don seemed distant, distracted, and uncommunicative.

Thursday, July 12. "The truck's making funny noises," Don said. "I can't go stay with Uriah—I'm not doing well enough."

I left early to spend time with Uriah before the funeral. "Oh, boy!" he shouted when I gave him a Metroid Nintendo game for his birthday.

That ought to keep him busy while I'm gone.

My car refused to start. I called Debbie.

"I'll be right over to pick you up," she said.

The first line of an ancient hymn rumbled out the door as we walked into the old church where Anita had brought us for vacation Bible school. It was so crowded; many people couldn't even get into the church, let alone sit. Anita looked beautiful, as though she would awaken at any moment with her radiant smile. I cried as I sang the second verse: "Jesus loves me, this I know . . ."

I was late to meet Joan at the hospital. Uriah showed me the birthday outfit she gave him. "Hey, Mom," he said, "I'm being released." Joan played a few games of UNO with us and helped us pack.

July 14, before we left the cabin for Blythe, Don took pictures of Uriah and the girls to use on fliers asking for help locating a donor.

Carolyn called. "You've got to hear what Sabrenia told me."

"God and Jesus are in my heart, right?" Sabrenia said. "So if Uriah goes to be with them, he'll always be in my heart!"

Out of the mouths of babes . . .

The skin around Uriah's catheter was red. The hydrogen peroxide frothed when I changed his dressing that night. *God, he's got a catheter infection. We may not make it to church. I hope it gets better; we don't even have any clean clothes. I really need just one day to catch up.*

Don thrashed and made muffled noises in his sleep. I shook him and called to him. *Another nightmare.* He awakened, shaky and sweaty. *He must be under attack by Satan. He's trying to do what's right, and Satan always puts up a fuss*

if you try to change for the better. God, Don's a Christian. Why are You allowing him to have these nightmares?

One night he awoke in tears. I flipped on the light, hoping to chase away the shadows that hung over his heart. "What was it?"

"The whole family was in my dream. We lived in a beautiful house in an unspoiled land. It was perfect. I had a sword God gave me to defend our home, but I didn't want to use it. Because I didn't, I lost everything—even all of you."

This dream wasn't sent from Lucifer! God, sometimes I think I know what's happening, and suddenly I discover You've been working all along in a way I didn't expect. You've sent a resounding message You want him to understand. "I think God sent that dream. The Word of God is the sword of God. I remember that from a song the children's choir sang. It makes sense. God's telling you to use it or lose it—all."

That week Don stopped at the Bible bookstore and bought a new Bible and a *Strong's Concordance*. He started reading and kept reading.

God, I always wanted Don to be our family's spiritual leader, and it looks like my prayers have been answered. But what a lot we had to go through. I wish more men would take their place as spiritual leaders instead of leaving it to their wives. The church would truly be strong if the men in this nation would take the responsibility God has given them and say, "As for me and my house, we will serve the Lord."

I remembered a sad statistic Pastor Wolff of Immanuel Lutheran once shared during an adult Sunday-school class comprised of mostly women. "It makes a big impact when a father comes to church. If the father in a family attends church regularly, 90 percent of the children will become faithful Christians. When only the mother goes, only 10 percent of the children grow into Christians."

A look of dismay crossed the face of a woman who always brought her three children. "That's so low," she protested. "I'm doing everything I can, and it will have so little effect. It's just not fair."

The only other option is to give up, and zero percent is definitely worse than 10 percent.

"I wish I had known these statistic before I got married," the woman lamented. Many of us had to share her regret.

Men of God are usually formed by extreme situations, created from people I wouldn't expect. *It's a good thing You're in control, God. You see what we can become, not just who we are. Now it seems Don is going to be one of those special men. Not only will it be a blessing to him, it will be wonderful for the whole family.*

❦ ❦ ❦

I called Bob Weekly of Life-Savers. "There's been a change," he apologized. "Life-Savers and the National Marrow Donor Program split two weeks ago because the NMDP is too slow."

"What?"

"There's more than one registry. Each has its own list of donors. The names of donors previously tested will be in both registries, but new recruits will not be in the NMDP registry, only in ours.

"For $300 we will search our registry each week for a donor for Uriah. There are 105,000 donors in our registry now. You need to pay for the search before we can conduct donor recruitment drives."

That's an awful lot of money for us right now, but we will get it somehow if we must.

"You'll need to hold fund-raisers," Bob continued. "We could get some key chains with Uriah's picture that you could sell at Christmas time."

"Bob, we don't have that kind of time. Uriah's relapsed so many times, we need a donor drive long before the end of the year."

He kept talking about Christmas.

Is that the best they can do?

I called Jan. "We wanted to have a bone-marrow drive, but Life-Savers and the NMDP split. Life-Savers says the NMDP won't have all the donor information. Do we have to search each of them separately?"

There were shuffling noises and then an angry man's voice. "This is Dr. Falk. What Life-Savers is planning to do is illegal! All the names of donors *must* be turned over to the NMDP. We have no authorization to work with Life-Savers. They don't do enough to protect donors."

"OK. Do you have a number for the NMDP?"

Linda Abress of the NMDP answered my call. "Can you answer some questions about bone-marrow drives?" I asked.

"Sure."

"Why did the split with Life-Savers occur?"

"Life-Savers has a lawsuit pending against a family that was doing a search. Life-Savers wants exclusive recruitment and is withholding donor information. The family in the lawsuit is trying to regain control of the funds they raised and deposited into Life-Savers for typing."

"The Life-Savers representative said the split was caused because you are too slow in processing donor information. How long does it take?"

"Right now it takes three to five days to create a record. It will get faster, though, because we're changing over to an automated bar code system. We charge fifty to sixty dollars per donor tested, and there are 148,000 donors in our registry."

"How much does it cost to search your registry, and how do you handle funds for donor drives?"

"There's no fee to search our registry, and any funds you raise for donor testing will be put into a special account in Uriah's name."

That's enough to convince me. They're cheaper and have a bigger registry. And they don't have a lawsuit pending against their clients.

I signed a recruitment cooperation agreement on July 23, 1990. Three sets of instructions arrived July 24. Before June, only Life-Savers had done recruitment. Now the NMDP was trying to help desperate families organize drives without them.

I kept careful notes about everything Linda Abress told me. "For fund-raisers you could try a talent show, pancake breakfast, band concert, spaghetti dinner, bingo, yard sales, walk-a-thon, volleyball tourney, or ask businesses to pay for their employees' testing. All contributions are tax deductible.

"Checks should be sent by registered mail to the NMDP twice a week, and careful records must be kept. A week before the test date, cash contributions should be mailed to the NMDP in the form of a cashier's check. No tests will be done that can't be paid for. We need a letter of credit from you that states no donor will be tested without money in hand, and you're willing to accept personal financial responsibility for donor testing up to fifty dollars per person, up to one hundred eighty people, liability not to exceed nine thousand dollars."

That's a lot of money, but it won't matter. We just won't test anyone we can't pay for. "Maybe you should make up a financial liability form for those interested in running a drive to sign," I suggested.

"The labs can test between one hundred thirty and one hundred eighty people at a time. They carry ten or twenty extra tests so people who walk in and want to pay for their test can. The cost of donor testing at a drive is fifty dollars, but it would cost seventy-five dollars if each person were tested separately. The number of donors needs to be estimated two weeks in advance so supplies can be shipped and arrangements for labs can be made. Testing can be done Monday through Thursday."

It'll be harder for people to go on a weekday. "What about Sunday?"

She paused, checking this variation. "Sunday testing is possible, but more difficult because the labs and blood banks, which supply the phlebotomists, are closed. Half an hour before the drive begins, a blood-bank representative will in-service the volunteers who staff the drives."

"What about free testing for apheresis donors?"

"Just a minute," she said. Papers rattled. "Interested persons must first be set up as a normal blood donor and allow thirty days to be set up as an apheresis donor. They need good veins in both arms, good health, and the willingness to spend the hour and a half to two hours it takes to make an apheresis donation."

That doesn't sound easy, but some people might be interested. "Thanks, Linda. I'll be in touch."

I'll need people to help me since I have to take Uriah for his treatments. I need a media organizer to make the public aware of Uriah's plight and request help; a fund-raising organizer to find groups willing to donate money or operate fundraisers; and someone to set up the test drives, find volunteers to staff them, and locations to hold them.

I made a form to calculate the number to be tested at our drives, a contribution record sheet, and a prepaid donors list. I thought I was very clever until I called Linda after a few days.

"We've decided not to use a letter of credit," she said. "The number of tests will be determined by the amount of money in your NMDP account one week before the test. The number of walk-ins will be limited to the ten to twenty extra supplies the lab carries."

I think they're as new to this as me. They keep changing the rules.

I called Theresa Kelm from Zion Lutheran. "I'd like to have a donor drive in Blythe."

"What a good idea."

"Would you be the coordinator for Blythe? We could try Bingo games, yard sales, walk-a-thons, or a pancake breakfast. We could contact churches, the police and fire department, the cable, radio, and newspapers. If we could raise just five thousand dollars, we could test one hundred donors!"

She was enthusiastic. "I'll start contacting people right away."

God must have smiled. Our aspirations were so modest. I was unprepared for the outpouring that would ensue.

Thirteen

Chance for a Lifetime
(Aug. 1990)

Only a stranger can save Uriah.
—Peggy Olson

MY SISTER DEBBIE AND CHRIS OLESON FROM FIRST LUTHERAN Church organized Fontana drives.

"Why don't you do one in Arrowhead?" Janet asked. "I'll organize it."

"Great!" I said.

Using a notebook of a different color for each area, I kept track of fund-raisers, activities, contacts, volunteers, and test days. The notebooks rapidly filled. *It's going to be like a full-time job, making appearances with Uriah, talking to the groups we ask for help, and keeping up with Uriah's medical care. But I have to do it. No matter what the outcome, I'll need to know I did everything I could. God, You gave me this child to care for, and if You want him back, You'll have to take him from me so I know it's Your will.*

I wrote to Ann Landers and philanthropists, asking for help; sent public-service announcements to Christian radio stations; and contacted publishers of newsletters and magazines about our donor drives.

"A good group to contact in Fontana is the Exchange Club," Margot told me. She gave me the name and number of President Michelle Todd. "Is there anything else I can do to help?"

"Margot, you used to work for the Fontana *Herald-News*. Could you get me an interview or tell me how to go about it?"

"I'll see what I can do."

Monday, July 30
Michelle Todd returned my call. "Why don't you join us at our luncheon meeting Wednesday and explain how our donation would be used?"

I dialed Margot. "Margot, they're interested! But I have to make a presentation on Wednesday."

"Great! Let me call the paper back." A few minutes later, Margot called. "They'll send a reporter and photographer to the Exchange Club meeting to do an article about Uriah and his need for a donor."

Oh, God, what a wonderful opportunity You've provided! But what if I blow it? Please give me the right words.

The maitre d' at Marie Calendars ushered Uriah and me into a spacious back room with tables set up in a large U-shape. My heart pounded. *Now all I have to do is get up in front of people I've never met before and explain coherently why we need their aid. Help, God!*

Michelle Todd reached out to shake my hand. "Welcome, Mara and Uriah. I'm glad you could make it. Sit down anywhere you like."

The members arrived in small groups and took their seats. *These are some of the most influential citizens of Fontana!*

Police Chief Stout sat next to us. "What are you up to now?" he teased Lt. Carns, who sat across the table, spin-

ning saucers on their edges. He was fined for his shenani-
gans, as were those who showed up late. In fact, fines were
levied for a multitude of infractions—some fictitious—and
in high spirits, the members bantered before paying them.
We were introduced, roll was taken, and lunch began.

Next the business meeting unfolded. "New business!"
Michelle soon announced. "Our guest, Mara Alexander, has
a matter for your consideration." She gestured me toward
the podium. *Here we go, God!* Butterflies swarmed. I felt
shaky. *Please don't let me trip! So much is hanging on what I
say next. . . .*

"First let me thank you for allowing Uriah and me to be
your guests. . . .

"My husband and I settled in Fontana in 1980, and our
son was born at Kaiser Hospital in 1982. But when Uriah
was only a year old, he was diagnosed with acute lymphoblastic leukemia. Overnight our lives changed. We took our
baby to receive chemotherapy and radiation at Kaiser Hospital. After three years of grueling treatment, he no longer
had to take any medication.

"In 1987, he was granted a wish by the Make-A-Wish
Foundation and treated to an extensive tour of the police
department. . . .

"Unfortunately, his cancer is back, and chemotherapy
will not be able to stop it much longer. But there is a way
my son could be cured: he needs a bone-marrow transplant.

"There is a national registry of unrelated marrow donors,
but there is only a 10 percent chance that one of the donors
in the registry will match my son. The search, begun in May,
has not located a donor, and now we are running out of time;
we must find a donor before the end of September.

"Becoming a donor requires only a simple blood test. If a
donor matches someone in need of a transplant, the actual

donation of bone marrow takes only one afternoon, and the donor usually resumes normal activities the next day.

"I am attempting to organize a bone-marrow recruitment drive in Fontana. The first step is to raise funds and locate people willing to be marrow donors. Next representatives from the National Marrow Donor Program will come to Fontana and facilitate the testing of donors. After the HLA typing, the donor information will be placed in the national registry.

"The valuable data collected will help not only my son, but also the sixteen thousand children and adults across the nation each year who need a bone-marrow transplant. Any help you can give in finding or locating donors will be received with the greatest gratitude. Thank you."

"Thank you. I will contact you later with our decision," said Michelle.

After the meeting, Uriah and I were interviewed by Louise Skura.

August 1, 1990, *The Fontana Herald-News:*

Uriah has hope for donor

By Louise Skura
The Herald-News

Uriah is a soft-spoken eight-year old. The polite, blond boy is all smiles as he eats his ribs, getting barbecue sauce on his mouth.

He is looking forward to going home this weekend to Blythe to play with his Doberman pinscher, Tonya, and to ride his bicycle.

"I go outside and she'll run by my bike," he said.

But this week, like every other week, he has to stay in Fontana, near Kaiser Permanente Medical Center, to undergo chemotherapy, spinal taps, and other treatments someone as spunky as Uriah should not have to go through.

Uriah has acute lymphoblastic leukemia, and it is more serious than it has ever been. Uriah needs a bone-marrow transplant and is looking for an unrelated donor. Like 75 percent of the leukemia patients in his situation, his two sisters cannot help him.

But Mara Alexander, like her son, has faith.

"It's not too late," she said. . . .

At this moment, time is most important. Uriah cannot wait too long.

Although he was diagnosed at an early age, Alexander believes, "in a way, it was a blessing." He has never known another way of life.

But life is meant for living, and Uriah has a plan.

"He wants to be a policeman during the day and a fireman at night so he can sleep in the firehouse and slide down the pole," his mother says, hopefully.

Mara has a plan also. She is organizing a bone-marrow recruiting program and is asking for help.

A simple, but costly, blood test is used to determine bone marrow matches. Each blood test costs about $75. Through the blood test, doctors can determine whether there is a marrow match.

The first marrow donor drive will be from 1 to 7 P.M. Aug. 26 at the First Lutheran Church. . . . Volunteers must be between 18 and 55 years old and in good health.

"The odds could be one in 1,000 or one in a 1,000,000. One in 20,000 is average," said Linda Abress of the National Marrow Donor Program.

The program has more than 168,000 donor volunteers in its registry. Since it was started in July 1986, Abress said the registry has assisted in matching more than 400 marrow transplants.

Volunteers can also help by becoming apheresis donors at the San Bernardino Blood Bank. If requested, the blood bank will take a blood sample to determine a marrow match free of charge. . . .

The most optimistic person, though, is Uriah. "I have faith," he said, "I know I'll be OK."[1]

Thursday, August 2. "I got a memorandum today," Don said. "There's going to be an investigation to evaluate conduct by officers in the scuffle with that inmate June 27. I'm not worried. We did it by the book."

The next day friends with ideas for fund-raisers came to a meeting organized by Theresa Kelm at church. "I can be coordinator for the prison," volunteered Lori Shay.

"Donors will be tested August 26 and September 16," said Theresa. "The early drive may be small because some fund-raisers won't have been held yet, but it'll give us media exposure that will allow us to have a larger second drive. Mid-September is about all the time we have to find a donor."

Jack Morey Jr. and his father, a Scout leader, met with Don and me at a Blythe coffee shop to discuss their plans for fund-raisers by the Boy Scouts.

☙ ☙ ☙

August 8, the *Palo Verde Valley Times* (a picture of Uriah and Tanya, his dog, appeared at the top of the banner article):

There's a rainbow behind the clouds
By Dona James
Times Editor

Uriah Alexander isn't very different than any 8-year-old boy.

He loves dogs, Matchbox cars, likes to play Nintendo and going fishing with his dad. He enjoys school, laughs a lot, and sees the magic in rainbows.

He's only different in one way.

Uriah has Acute Lymphoblastic Leukemia and his only chance for survival is a bone-marrow transplant. The search has begun but, so far, a suitable donor has not been found.

Uriah and his family have been coping with his disease since he was 14 months old.

"He's used to the hospital, the needles, the tests. . . ." says Uriah's father, Don Alexander. "He's been dealing with this all of his life."

Uriah has a catheter inserted into his chest, and this eases some of the discomfort that comes from administering various medications.

"He's gone though a lot for his age," his father said. "He was receiving a bone-marrow test once a week, spinal taps every two weeks, chemotherapy, radiation . . . he's lost his hair three times. That's an awful lot for such a little boy."

"He must have the transplant," Uriah's mother, Mara, said. "At this point his chances are zero. . . ."

"Right now we're looking at maybe two months . . . the end of September," she continued. "That's why finding a donor is so crucial."

But Uriah is open about his illness, and he talks with his mother about death. Being raised in a Christian home, Mara explained that Uriah has confidence that things will be right. "He knows if his body isn't strong enough he'll go to heaven and have a new one," she said. "But he has a lot of hope and faith."

Mara remembers when Uriah became angry and said, "You know what, the devil did this to me. But I'm not worried because I have faith, and God is a whole lot stronger than the devil."

Now he's decided he wants to be a policeman during the day and a fireman at night.

He also wants to get married, have four kids, four dogs, and three cats. "He has plans for his life," Mara said.

Uriah attended second grade at Zion Lutheran School this past year. Don and Mara credit the teachers and the staff at the school for the time and attention given Uriah and the way he loves going to class.

"A child with leukemia suffers through isolation," Mara said. "It's very difficult for a young child."

"But I guess you just have to pack as much into every day as you can," Mara said. "Right now we're just hoping for the best."

Once a match is found it will take approximately two weeks to get a room at the hospital. Don explained that only 12 rooms are available for patients of this type, and there is a long list. And, after the transplant, Uriah will be looking at anywhere from two to four months in a sterilized room. "If we can find a donor and this is successful, Uriah knows he won't have leukemia anymore," Mara said.

A computerized national registry of bone marrow donors is maintained but, besides the small numbers of donors available, there is only a ten percent chance that one of them will match Uriah. Becoming a potential donor requires a simple blood test but carries a charge of $75 per person. A bone marrow donor recruitment drive is being conducted in Blythe to pay for the blood tests and find a donor for Uriah. Donations are being sought and several fundraisers are being planned to raise the needed funds.

Donor testing dates are August 26 and September 16 from 1 to 7 P.M. in the board room of the Palo Verde Valley Community Hospital. Donors, volunteers, and funds are needed. Interested persons should contact Theresa Kelm.

"He knows everyone is looking hard to find the right donor," Mara said. "He is hopeful, but he is also very accepting of what is happening to him.

"We were driving back from the hospital one day and we had to tell him that we really didn't know what his chances were. There was a beautiful rainbow in the sky and Uriah was talking about it. All of a sudden the rainbow disappeared behind a cloud. . . . "Mom, where did the rainbow go?'" he asked me. "We'll keep driving Uriah and pretty soon we'll be past that cloud. Then we'll see the rainbow again."

He said, "Rainbows are a lot like me, aren't they? I may be gone but, after a while, you're going to see me again."

"Rainbows are a promise for him," Mara said. "They're a promise for us too."

"And as we drove I kept thinking to myself, please God, let that rainbow still be there when we get past that cloud."[2]

A front-page photo showed Jack Morey Jr. receiving a $150 check from Blythe Jaycees' President Larry Beynon for testing potential donors. Jack pledged to raise $750 for donor testing as his Eagle Community Service Merit Project.

Another front-page article outlined fund-raisers already planned, which included the following:

Bake sales August 11 and August 18, organized by Carolyn Baschal. A car wash August 11, coordinated by Linda Schlueter. A baseball-game competition September 1 between four Blythe law-enforcement agencies, sponsored by CPOF and coordinated by Lori Shay. A teen dance August 25 at the American Legion Hall, sponsored by Boy Scout Troops 275 and 449.

Warden urges support

Chuckawalla Valley State Prison Public Information Officer Eric Flamer told the *Times*, Tuesday morning, that CVSP is also striving to help in the Alexander family's search for a bone-marrow transplant donor for their eight-year-old son, Uriah. . . .[3]

On August 7, a memo was sent to all CVSP employees from Warden Robert D. Briggs:

On August 3, 1990, our institution received a call from Mrs. L. Shay, representative from the Correctional Peace Officer's Foundation; requesting to have a donation box in place at CVSP for Correctional Sergeant D. Alexander's son. The child is a leukemia patient and is in dire need of a bone-marrow transplant.

Sergeant D. Alexander was one of the initial supervisors on the activation team here, promoting from CIM.

The Foundation is also attempting to set up other fund-raising efforts within the Blythe community, to assist in the needed funds. Donations are being requested from CVSP staff in an effort to obtain the needed monies for Sgt. Alexander's son's transplant. Donations obtained will be utilized for the costs of medical tests to be given to interested donors.

I am authorizing two donation cans to be established. . . . Interested staff members who wish to be tested for a bone-marrow transplant may contact Sgt. Alexander . . . or Correctional Officer Flaharty.

Let us all be supportive to our fellow staff member in his family's time of need. Donate what you can.

Robert D. Briggs, Warden

Support began to pour in. The *Palo Verde Valley Times* and the *White Sheet* printed our announcements, and Warner Cable and Jim Morris of radio station KJMB aired our announcements at no charge. The Chamber of Commerce mailed letters requesting help and collected donation checks at their office.

I wrote a thank-you note to the people of Blythe:

> I can't thank people enough for what they have done. When I tell people about the activities and donations in Blythe, they are astounded. Uriah is both pleased and amazed that there are so many people who care enough to help him. *Thank you* just isn't a big enough word. How can you thank someone for the gift of a lifetime?

August 10, the *Palo Verde Valley Times:*

Community of Blythe united in projects

The entire community of Blythe is coming together to help 8-year-old leukemia patient Uriah Alexander find a bone-marrow transplant.

[Below previously listed activities were a couple new ones:]

•Prizes—The VFW Ladies Auxiliary is selling tickets on a . . . color television set, donated by Mark Myskowski of Kmart. The ladies are also looking for prize donations from other businesses. . . .

•Spaghetti Supper and Bake Sale—The VFW and Ladies Auxiliary will be holding a spaghetti supper and bake sale on August 18. . . .[4]

Check Presentation—Dr. John K. Maltby, Maltby Chiropractic Office, presents check for $750 to Don Alexander, Uriah's father, as Theresa Kelm looks on. In presenting the check, Dr. Maltby has issued a challenge to the entire medical community of Blythe, to match the funds. . . .[5]

More than forty-three different fliers appeared during the course of our search. Most were variations of the simple cut-and-paste job I did with a photo of Uriah. "There's a cure. . . . It's you!" Fliers were posted everywhere, and people mailed them to relatives in other states and cities. People all over the United States sent help and encouragement.

One anonymous, handwritten flier:

Tough Times, Tough Kid

. . . In order to assist Uriah to have future dreams, assistance is needed from everywhere, including Peace Officers. His dream to be one of us is touching.

. . . His only chance for cure is a bone-marrow transplant. . . . So to increase this tough kid's chances, we are conducting a bone-marrow drive. . . .

Uriah has since had another relapse on 7-9-90. Each time he is in remission, it is for a shorter time. We are very short on time now. . . .

Please give a tough kid the *Opportunity to Dream!*

The first fund-raisers were held August 11. Carolyn Baschal, Verda Walliser, and others manned bake-sale and craft tables in front of Sprouse Rietz—despite the sweltering heat—and accepted donations of baked goods and cash. Uriah stayed in the car because of low counts, but he waved and smiled.

At the car wash in the Carl's Jr. parking lot, we joined the line of waiting cars. Organizer Linda Schlueter was trying to get teen volunteers, including Heather, to wash cars while they sprayed each another.

The canisters with pictures of Uriah on them, which Tracy and Harvey Capra placed in local stores, filled rapidly.

Margaret Richt prayed with the staff of the Benny Hinn show that Uriah and I would attend the Orlando, Florida, show for his healing. *I'm touched by this woman's concern for my son, but the trip won't fit into our schedule. The centurion told Jesus He didn't need to come to his house to heal his servant (Matt. 8:8–10). God can heal Uriah where he is . . . if that's His will.*

Maggie Kim, Bone-Marrow Organizer of the Riverside and San Bernardino Blood Bank, volunteered to oversee the bone-marrow drive in Fontana on Sunday, August 26. *She's giving up her day off to help us. What a wonderful friend to find in the midst of such dismal circumstances.*

KLORD Christian radio sponsored a Superfest Concert every summer. "If we could get a booth, we could probably raise a lot of funds," said Debbie. "Superfest IV will be held August 10, 11, and 12. But it costs $275 for a booth space." Undaunted, Debbie contacted KLORD. "Can you give us a break? We're representing a nonprofit charity."

They listened to her explanation. "We'll let you operate the booth for the cost of two adult tickets." But when they arrived, officials waived even that fee.

Sgt. Larry Clark of the Fontana Police Department called. "Chief Stout asked me to find out what Uriah would like to see and do on a tour of the police department."

"Wow!" I said.

"Would he be interested in police dogs, a police motorcycle ride, the shooting range, or where they train?"

"Would he! Uriah would love all of that!" *What a wonderful, unexpected gift! Uriah's Make-A-Wish gift keeps giving.*

Uriah and I went for a tour of the new Fontana Police Department Wednesday, August 15. "It's a lot bigger than the old one," Uriah said in awe.

Mr. Horst, a cheerful, civilian volunteer, led us to Sgt. Clark who showered Uriah with gifts from the police department and Mayor Nat Simon. "Guess what?" Sgt. Clark asked. "I'm your tour guide today."

After an extensive tour, the sergeant led us to the underground garage, and John McMillan glided up on a police motorcycle. Uriah's mouth hung open a second; then he grinned. "My dad has a motorcycle, but it doesn't have the neat lights and siren."

"You want to go for a ride?"

They slowly circled the parking structure three times, lights flashing and siren blaring.

"Thanks. It means so much to him," I said as Uriah climbed down.

John smiled at the ground. "I just hope everything works out all right," he said, his voice husky with emotion.

God, so many people are doing so much for Uriah. Please, God, don't let them be hurt. Let them rejoice with us. It seems selfish to involve them in our pain, but the only alternative is to give up.

At the Rialto Sheriff's Aviation Division, Uriah flew a helicopter with Sgt. Federoff. Then we drove to the San Bernardino Sheriff's Academy and watched the 101st Academy practicing drills in the hot sun and met their mascot, a big dog named Buckis, who was there years before when Don attended the 67th Academy Class. We watched target practice at the shooting range, and the range master let Uriah keep some brass.

The entire class gathered in formation and were officially introduced to Uriah. They presented him with gifts and a signed card. "Thank you!" Uriah shouted to them in academy fashion.

While we ate pizza back at the police station, Rick Lopez, the recruitment officer, shook Uriah's hand. "I hope you'll be contacting me again in several years to become a police officer."

John Koval of the Fontana Police Benefit Association said, "We're planning to donate money for donor testing, and we're encouraging officers to be tested."

We wrote lots of thank-you notes and made a lot of fudge. A special thank-you was sent to the 101st Sheriff's Academy Class:

> Thank you for allowing my son to share a little bit of your day with you. We hope that someday he will be able to be a member of a class like yours, but even if he never can, you have allowed him to reach out and touch a dream that his eight-year-old heart holds dear. Thank you for the gifts, but most of all, thank you for sharing yourselves; the caring you have shown builds the hope in his heart and gives him the strength and courage to fight on toward the life he longs to live.

The article from the interview Joan Weiss arranged appeared in the August 16, *Inland Valley Daily Bulletin:*

8-year-old Uriah looking for the perfect match
By Peggy Olson
Bulletin Staff Writer

> Uriah Alexander's blue eyes dance. He ogles his opponent and flashes a winning smile, confident he once again has outwitted a challenger in a "mean" game of UNO.

He talks of romping with his dog, Tanya. He giggles about the kitten that ate his fish. He appears to be 8 going on 18, a boy waiting to unravel the mysteries of life.

But Uriah's robust good looks are misleading. He has been battling leukemia, a fatal blood disease, since he was 14 months old. His doctor says his treatment options are all but exhausted. His tenuous chance for survival hinges on a bone-marrow transplant.

"We are running out of chemotherapy. A transplant is the only chance he has for maybe surviving," said Dr. Alba Sanmarco, Uriah's pediatric oncologist/hematologist at Kaiser Permanente Hospital in Fontana. "While there are risks, if there is no transplant he is certain to die."

Only a stranger can save Uriah. . . .

Uriah knows the chance of finding an unrelated donor match is about one in 20,000.

If the "miracle match" is found and his transplant is a success, he intends to catapult down a water slide, go bowling, and whoop it up at Knott's Berry Farm.

He has been denied those pleasures because his immune system is depressed, and he is extremely vulnerable to infection after extensive chemotherapy and radiation treatment, said his mother, Mara.

. . . Once when Uriah had a relapse, Mrs. Alexander was obviously depressed. "He turned to me and said: 'It's OK, Mom, I always wanted to see heaven.'"

"He knows if we don't find a donor, he's not going to make it. He knows about God and heaven, and I don't think he is afraid to die."

Although Uriah is currently in remission after a relapse in July, Mrs. Alexander is not optimistic.

"There is no sign (of cancer cells) now," she said. "But we do know it will come back. Remissions get shorter and shorter."

Dr. Sanmarco's prognosis also is bleak. "There is no longer a chance for Uriah to remain in remission for a long time. Then you get to a point where remission isn't possible at all."[6]

In making her appeal, Mrs. Alexander said: "Most of us are touched by cancer at some time in our lives. In most cases there is nothing you can do. In this case, there is. You can cure.

". . . The recruitment drive is not just for Uriah. You may not be able to help my son. But you may help someone else."[7]

Some pain in saving a stranger

There is some pain involved.

But a blood marrow donor—who may save a life—recovers within a day after giving as little as a cup and as much as a "coffee pot full" of marrow.

The smaller amount is needed for a baby, while the larger (about 10 percent of a donor's marrow) is required for adults who will die without a marrow transplant. "Donors recover from the procedure in a day, although there may be some minimal pain and discomfort for about a week," said Dr. Carl Lenarsky, pediatric oncologist and director of bone-marrow transplantation at Children's Hospital of Los Angeles.

Medically, Lenarsky said, the risk for donors is relatively small. "The major risk is general anesthesia."

Bone marrow replenishes itself within a few weeks, according to the National Marrow Donor Program, a network of transplant centers, donor centers, collection centers, and recruitment groups.

Donors, Lenarsky said, are in a unique situation. "You have a healthy person who volunteers to be put under anesthesia for a complete stranger. So these are quite remarkable people."

During the procedure, needles are inserted into the hip bones to remove marrow. The aspirated marrow is then flown to the recipient and given as a blood transfusion.

Marrow transplants, Lenarsky emphasized, are fraught with risks and given to patients with fatal blood diseases as a last resort.

Traditionally, brothers and sisters were sought as donors. But since only about 20 percent of patients have family members with matching marrow, Lenarsky said the medical profession has looked for other options.

"One is utilizing a matched unrelated donor," the doctor said. "Another is to remove the patient's own bone marrow, treat it with chemotherapy, and freeze it. This autologous marrow transplant is possible when there is a minimal amount of leukemia."

A third option, Lenarsky said, is using a parent's marrow in a mismatched transplant.

In any event, Lenarsky said the results are not fantastic. "We are talking about a 30 to 40 percent chance of long-term remission and cure, depending on each individual child."

Still, the doctor said, donors have a unique chance to save a life in exchange for a minimal amount of pain.[8]

Janet Anderson was busy up at Arrowhead. Santa's Village donated 100 free passes for donors. Much support came from Calvary Chapel. Mr. Dennis Auden, hospital administrator of Mountains Community Hospital, let us use the hospital for the donor drive.

Heather's band teacher at the junior high in Arrowhead called me. "I've got leukemia too. Don't let him give up; there's always hope. Here are numbers for some groups who might help." *It's amazing, God, how You've placed so many helpful people in unexpected places.*

But not everyone was eager to help. Janet called a local church and requested help. "He's not a resident of Arrowhead or a member of the church," the priest quipped. "I can't help. I'm just too busy."

"Can't you at least pray?"

"Well, yes," he said, sounding sheepish. "I guess I could."

God, Janet's not a Christian. What if she thought all Christians were like that?

Instantly a scripture was impressed on my heart in reply:

And [Jesus] answered, "It is not fair to take the children's bread and throw it to the dogs." She said, "Yes, Lord, yet even the dogs eat the crumbs that fall from their masters' table." Jesus answered her, "O woman great is your faith! Be it done for you as you desire." (Matt. 15:26–27)

You used them to help each other? Janet and the priest both grew from this! God, only You could turn bad into good, like water into wine.

Joe Lyon, of Mountain Area Productions, which aired Christian programming on a local cable channel, contacted Janet and requested an interview with Uriah, Don, and me. *It's intimidating, but it'll help the drive.* They aired the interview twice.

"Have you noticed the blood-bank stickers they give when people donate blood?" asked Debbie. "It might spread news of our drives if we use a similar idea. I cut white contact paper into little squares and drew a rainbow and smiling clouds that say, 'I helped make a rainbow!' on each."

"What a great idea! It'll let the donors know how much we appreciate them."

August 17, the *Palo Verde Valley Times:*

Keep the love and prayers flowing

Eight-year-old Uriah is back in the hospital in an isolation unit. The community is asked to remember that Uriah needs all the prayers, well wishes, and involvement in the scheduled activities everyone can give, to make his needed bone-marrow transplant a reality.[9]

• Car Wash . . . August 25 . . . sponsored by SADD.

•'50s and '60s Dance . . . August 25 sponsored by the Elks.

• Rummage Sale . . . August 25 . . . sponsored by CPOF and Zion Lutheran Church and School.

• Pizza—Domino's Pizza will offer $1.50 off each pizza . . . and will give $1.00 to Uriah for each coupon redeemed to this cause. . . .[10]

Domino's Pizza Challenge

Domino's Pizza would like to challenge our competitors . . . and any other local restaurant to match our fund-raising amount for one week. The restaurant with the highest amount raised will be treated to pizza (or whatever) for the crew by the restaurant raising the least amount. Call Domino's Pizza to accept this fun and worthwhile challenge. Nobody will really lose helping someone else!

One afternoon Chris, Jason, and Theresa Kelm, along with Shiloh, Heather, Uriah, and I tucked the fliers under windshield wipers in parking lots. We paused at Courtesy Coffee Shop because August's scorching sun made the children dry-mouthed. "I'm going to ask if they have a glass of water the kids can share," Theresa said. She returned with several glasses of donated soda. "Yeah!" the kids shouted.

Kids on chemotherapy love pizza. Heather once made a poster for Jason Johnson: "Warning to all pizza trucks: This is a Predni-Zone." We ordered many pizzas with Domino's flier coupons, and so did others: 600 coupons were redeemed.

Saturday, August 18
At the bake sale, Carolyn Baschal drew clouds, rainbows, and "There's a rainbow behind the clouds" on T-shirts.

At the VFW spaghetti dinner, Uriah had to stay in the car, so he and I played cards. Chuckling, VFW members tapped on the door, "Dinner is served." Uriah posed for pictures, spinning his fork and slurping spaghetti.

Wednesday, August 22
Tommy Li called for an interview.

Leukemia victim, 8, tries to pack full life into time remaining

By Tommy Li
The Sun's Fontana Bureau

At the age of 8, Uriah Alexander knows how to fire a rifle, ride a bicycle, and fish in the Colorado streams.

The blond, blue-green-eyed boy would like to pack as much as he can into a life that may be cut short by leukemia.

"What I like doing now is just playing with people," said Uriah, whose family moved from Fontana to Blythe.

"I like making things. . . . Today, we made a flag."

But tomorrows may be few for Uriah if he doesn't receive a bone-marrow transplant soon.

"If he doesn't get a bone-marrow transplant, he's going to die," said Dr. Alba Sanmarco of Kaiser Permanente Medical Center in Fontana, where the boy is being treated. "If he gets a bone-marrow transplant, he may live. It's hard to tell [his chances]."

Uriah was 14 months old when he was diagnosed at Kaiser with acute lymphocydic [lymphocytic] leukemia, a common type of cancer that strikes children.

Chemotherapy and prescription drugs over the last seven years don't seem to be stopping the disease: Uriah has gone into three relapses. His latest one ended Monday, but doctors believe his remission may last as long as two months.

That is why the child desperately needs the transplant. Family members are unable to help because tissue types don't match.

Although the odds of finding a match outside the family ranges from one in 20,000 to one in a million, the slim outlook hasn't stopped the Alexanders from organizing blood testing days for the public on Aug. 26 at Blythe's Palo Verde Hospital and Fontana's First Lutheran Church.

A Sept. 18 testing date is also scheduled at Mountains Community Hospital in Lake Arrowhead.

"We know that the clock is ticking. We have less than three months," said Uriah's 31-year-old mother, Mara.

"We just have to wait and see what God has planned," Mara Alexander said. "We're really aware of how important today is. So we try to live for today."

Even Uriah has the right attitude.

"He's a very positive child. Always happy and smiling. He's a forgiving child. He's not very angry about it," the mother of three said.

Uriah makes the best use of his time now with his family, playing favorite card games such as UNO. He even has a book of rules for card games in his small bag of items he brings to the hospital.

"It's hard having it (leukemia), that's the one thing. I don't like it," he said softly.

But he's looking forward to the day of his bone-marrow transplant and overcoming the cancer.

"(I'm) going to the water slide . . . Knott's Berry Farm and bowling," Uriah said.

Anyone who would like to sign up or donate money to help pay for the cost of the blood testing can contact Mara Alexander. . . . More information about becoming a donor is available by calling the National Marrow Donor Program.[11]

August 22, the *Palo Verde Valley Times:*

Donor testing dates draw near for Uriah

. . . Uriah Alexander was home in Blythe this past weekend but returned to Fontana on Monday to continue treatments on an out-patient basis. Time is passing quickly for Uriah and his family as they wait to find a donor match for the bone-marrow transplant needed to save Uriah's life.[12]

• Bowl-a-thon . . . September 8. . . .[13]

August 24

My twenty-one-year-old son recently recovered from cancer, and a good friend is now recovering well from a bone-marrow transplant. I pray Uriah may be added to the cancer success stories. The American Cancer Society has become my favorite charity since Jeff's illness.

Sincerely,
Nancy Kettle

P.S. Please don't bother with an acknowledgment—I'm sure you have enough to do.

Someone out there knows how busy and crazy our lives have become.

A mysterious package arrived at Zion Lutheran Church:

Mr. and Mrs. Alexander,

Becky sent me the article in the newspaper about your son. I sincerely hope and pray that you find a donor for him. . . .

I've taken the newspaper clipping to three different churches and each has placed Uriah on a special prayer list, so there are a lot of good Christian people back here praying for him and your whole family.

I hope he likes the clown. If it brings just one little smile and gives just one minute of joy to him, then God has paid me for the time and effort I took to make it for him.

Love and prayers.

A friend in your time of trouble,
Judy Mulvaney

From the box tumbled a brightly colored, rainbow clown with a laughing face, holding a bunch of balloons.

Hi, Uriah!

I'm "Gudbudy Deran Boclown." I came from Illinois to keep you company on days that you aren't feeling so good.

A grandma person heard that you were pretty sick and read an article in the newspaper about you and a rainbow that hid behind a cloud, so she made me like a rainbow. Now you have your own to look at every day.

Always remember what you[r] Mom said about rainbows being a promise from God; He will take care of you!

Lots of people back in Ill., where I came from, are praying that you'll soon be well again.

Uriah kept Boclown on the table by his bed.

August 24

On behalf of the First Funds of Children's Resources Board of directors and staff, please find enclosed a donation . . . to help pay for donor testing in Fontana . . . for Uriah Alexander.

We pray that a bone-marrow match will be found so that he can have the opportunity to live out his dreams and know a full and rewarding life. God bless this brave little man.

With the children at heart,
Peggy Lewis, Executive Director

The Topeleski family of First Lutheran Church in Fontana applied for this donation. *God, so many good people are pulling for us!*

🙰 🙰 🙰

On Saturday, August 25, students Against Drunk Driving sponsored a car wash, and there was a rummage sale at Zion Lutheran Church. Barrels, boxes, and tables overflowed with cast-off sundries sold by Carolyn Baschal and Lori Shay to people who dug through the stacks in search of treasures. We found a few of our own!

That evening it was time to dance. There was an adult '50s and '60s dance at the Elks Lodge, and a teen dance at the American Legion Hall sponsored by Boy Scout Troops 475 and 449.

The car wash brought in $550, the bake sales and rummage sales $1,800, the VFW spaghetti dinner and bake sale $1,600, the Elks dance $200, and the Boy Scout's teen dance $300. From Fontana, the Police Benefit Association donated $150, the Exchange Club donated $150, and Aid Association for Lutherans (branch #2132) donated $150. In addition, hundreds of people sent checks, big and small. Our dream of raising $5,000 to test 100 donors was already doubled! With over $12,000 in our NMDP account, we scheduled 150 tests in Blythe (where people had raised $7,900) and 75 in Fontana (where donations totaled $2,600).

It's about loaves and fishes, isn't it, Lord? If we just let You use us and the insignificant little we have for Your purposes, You can do miracles. God, I'm overwhelmed by the generosity of those around me—and by Your grace. So often we ask for less than You're willing to bless us with. Now, if just one person will match, all our prayers will be answered.

ꗍ   ꗍ   ꗍ

Sunday, August 26 arrived. *The first donor testing day. What better way to start than in prayer at church?*

Kenya Briggs and her photographer from *KECY-TV Channel 9 News* in Yuma found their way to our mobile home and spent forty-five minutes interviewing us.

I followed Don and a masked Uriah, who both wore their rainbow shirts, into Blythe's Palo Verde Hospital before the donor drive. Heather and Shiloh ran to the babysitting area to help in the nursery. "The Alexanders say thank you!" a banner over the door declared.

Becky Worthington, who operated the lab at Palo Verde Hospital, had flawlessly organized the volunteer phlebotomists and numbered stations around the perimeter of the room: (1) donors signed in with Theresa; (2) filled out a health questionnaire and read information about becoming a donor; (3) had a health screening by the Blythe ambulance drivers; (4) completed a donor information bubble sheet; (5) had their blood drawn in a lab tube; (6) had a bar code stuck on the sheet and tube, which were packed by lab personnel; and (7) received juice, cookies, rainbow stickers, and other goodies at the refreshment table from American Cancer Society volunteers.

We mingled with the steady flow of people for an hour. A murmur arose near the door. "There's a reporter here," Theresa smiled.

"Hi, Kenya. Glad you found us."

"It was no problem. This is very well organized," she said, her eyes sweeping the room.

"I figure you probably got enough footage of Uriah already, but we wanted to check with you before we leave for the Fontana drive."

"We're just going to shoot a little here and wrap it up. It'll be on tonight. Be sure to tune in."

"We wouldn't miss it!"

※　　※　　※

I reached out to shake hands with the tall, young man at the sign-in table at First Lutheran Church. "You must be Chris Oleson. I'm Mara. How's it going?"

He nodded. "So far, so good."

"Debbie, these thank-you posters you made for the Fontana Police Department, the 101st Sheriffs Academy Class, and 'All Our Rainbow Makers' are great!"

"Oh, that's not all. You've got to see this!" She held out a notebook entitled, "Notes to Uriah." Inside donors had jotted uplifting messages to Uriah.

Maggie Kim sat at the health screening table.

"It's nice to meet you in person!" I said. I filled out paperwork for my test. Then I glanced down at the long sleeves of my dress. *I can't pull these tight sleeves up! They won't be able to draw my blood.*

"I have an extra white lab coat in my car," Maggie offered.

"Thanks, Maggie!"

❧ ❧ ❧

That night Uriah and I returned home to see ourselves on channel 9. It began with Uriah and the girls playing.

"The charm of a smiling face, the enduring beauty of a rainbow, hope for the future, and faith in God," said Kenya Briggs. "These are the weapons the Alexander family are using to battle the leukemia in their son's body. A battle which eight-year-old Uriah Alexander began waging when he was only fourteen months old."

The camera focused on Uriah's face. "Sometimes it can really be hard on you. Especially when you are going to get a—what are they called?—a bone marrow and spinal tap."

"But medicine and treatments can't help Uriah any longer," Kenya said, "and his only chance for survival hinges on a bone-marrow transplant. A gift his family members have unfortunately found they cannot give."

The scene shifted to donor testing at Palo Verde Hospital. "So today, the people of Blythe are lining up to see if they could be that special donor."

The camera focused on Freddy Mendez having his blood drawn. "He has a big, big meaning in life. His attitude. His will to live."

Kenya Briggs stood in the empty hospital corridor. "The battle to save Uriah is truly a fight against time. Doctors are saying he's in his final remission, and they expect the cancer to reappear in his blood at the end of September. If that happens, Uriah's chance for a bone-marrow transplant and a new life will be lost."

Uriah sat on our couch. "I'm not worried."

"Are you scared of dying?"

Uriah nervously shook his head no, his expression discrediting his denial.

Next the camera focused on Don and me. "We hang onto God pretty much," I said, emotion twisting my face and voice. *Please God, I don't want to cry.* "We know it's going to work out for the best, and we want God's will, which is not always ours. So we're just trusting that God's gonna do what's best for everyone." Tears trickled down my cheeks.

The cat and dog played. The children played. "Uriah and his family have plans for his future," Kenya said. "Someday Uriah wants to be a policeman. He wants to go to Disneyland. He wants to ride a water slide. But today he's waiting for a rainbow."

"I just hope they find somebody," Uriah smiled.

"Reporting from Blythe, I'm Kenya Briggs, for *News 9*."[14]

August 27

President David Lam asked this be sent to you ASAP—so excuse my not sending to our secretary for a more "professional" transmittal! Lions are glad to help.

Jim Lester, Treasurer
The Crestline Lions Club

Donna Parkinson—the teen who met Uriah at the Don Francisco concert in Fontana—called and we prayed.

August 29, the *Palo Verde Valley Times:*

123 test as marrow donors for Uriah

The community of Blythe turned out 123 people volunteering to be tested as a possible donor for a bonemarrow transplant needed to save the life of 8-year-old leukemia victim, Uriah Alexander. Approximately 150 people have signed up for the next testing, scheduled for September 16. . . .

Several members of the medical community have answered a challenge issued by Dr. John Maltby and donated money; the Palo Verde Rod and Gun Club donated $250; approximately $1,000 has been collected through the donation cans.[15]

 Fourteen

Needle in a Haystack
(Sept. 1990)

> Every person who gets tested buys him an opportunity for another chance at life.
>
> —Janet Anderson

Take me out to the ball game

Softball games in honor of Uriah Alexander will be held Saturday, September 1 . . . at Todd Park.

The teams competing will be Chuckawalla Valley State Prison Correctional Officers, California Highway Patrol, Blythe Police Department, Blythe Fire Department, Riverside County Sheriff's Department, US Border Patrol, Veterans of Foreign Wars, and the American Legion. . . .

All proceeds will go toward the bone-marrow drive. . . . Come and enjoy the fun. Let Uriah Alexander see many more rainbows![1]

Uriah wore his rainbow shirt to the ballpark and posed for photos with Jean Smith at the CPOF table where she sold items to support the donor drives.

Carolyn Baschal operated the bake sale and craft table and sold helium balloons with our logo. The table was covered with yellow paper so people could write messages to Uriah.

Theresa Kelm held out white saddle covers with a bright rainbow blazing across clouds that said, "There's a rainbow behind the clouds." "Carrie Stroschein and I made these for the pony rides, but Alan Stroschein fell through a roof and isn't in any shape to give pony rides. We thought we could cut the pads in half and make banners to use at our donor drives."

The Colorado River Country Band and DJ Bill Preston played music in the gazebo. The Blythe police table had a police car and a police dog. Uriah was treated to a ride around the block. Uriah hugged Ruth Sheppardson at the American Cancer Society table.

Ysaias Zamudio, flyweight boxer, showed Uriah how to use the practice equipment he'd set up in the shade of a tree. Uriah posed with Ysaias and his 1990 North American Boxing Federation and Intercontinental title belts. *The value of the heavy, golden emblems on those belts pale in comparison to the worth of Ysaias' kind heart.*

Uriah's picture was taken with each team before he threw out the first ball. The hot, humid, bright blue sky sported huge, fluffy thunderclouds piling up over the river to the east. Every purchase of food or sodas bought Uriah a greater chance of survival.

Theresa and Heather were sitting in the dunk tank together when Uriah missed with his first two balls. Heather turned to Theresa. "There's nothing to worry about. Uriah can't hit the broad side of a barn."

His third toss slammed the target soundly. Heather bobbed to the surface, spluttering.

When the crowd swelled, Uriah had to stay in the protection of the announcement stand and draw winning raffle tickets. Les Warning, who also had cancer, won the grand prize of a television.

The sun was setting when the Blythe Volunteer Fire Department won the tournament. They presented Uriah with the signed ball. One volunteer handed Uriah a fly ball, hit by Mike Scioscia on April 27, 1985: "I was going to give it to my son, but I thought you might enjoy it."

A big party makes a *big* mess. The whole family helped Lori Shay and others clean up. At ten o'clock that night, Don and I stumbled to the car where the children slept. *I think I could sleep for a week.*

Theresa Kelm distributed fliers with our thanks:

> We would like to thank the entire community of Blythe for their participation in the . . . softball tournament. . . . The Blythe Volunteer Fire Department took first place, and Chuckawalla Valley State Prison took second. VFW vs. American Legion: 4-3. . . . $3,000 was donated to the National Marrow Donor Program . . . to pay for the testing of potential marrow donors on September 16. . . .

September 5, the *Palo Verde Valley Times:*

Uriah back in hospital

> . . . As of presstime Uriah Alexander was hospitalized. He was admitted to the hospital and is receiving blood transfusions for a low blood count and antibiotics to combat any premature infections. Approximately 125 people have signed up for the September 16th

bone-marrow donor testing. It is hoped there will be 200 volunteers. . . .

Lori Shay, the CPOF representative for Chuckawalla Valley State Prison, has initiated a statewide drive for donors through CDC. So far, $22,000 has been collected and will be used to test 300 correctional officers and their wives as prospective bone-marrow donors at a convention to be held September 10 in Sparks, Nevada.[2]

Ice-sitting contest planned

. . . The Blythe Jaycees are holding a "Polar Bear Chill-A-Thon Ice-Sitting Contest" and hot-dog sale Saturday. . . .[3]

Mt. Calvary Lutheran Church, Lake Arrowhead, September 1990 newsletter:

Bone-Marrow Donor Needed

Uriah Alexander is an 8-year-old boy with leukemia who needs a bone-marrow transplant. Uriah attended a couple Lenten services last winter at Mt. Calvary. His family was staying on the mountain so that he could receive treatments at Kaiser Hospital. A testing date for donors has been set for September 18 at Mt. Community Hospital.[4]

Friday, September 7

Dr. Haghighat and Dr. Sanmarco worked long, hard hours, and if one went on vacation, the other was on call twenty-four hours a day, and our children waited long for treatments. I asked Kaiser's membership services for an additional doctor in the clinic, that more information be made available for parents, and that a support group for parents be formed.

The *Palo Verde Valley Times*, September 7:

Blood drive set next Friday for Uriah

A blood drive for Uriah Alexander has been scheduled for Friday, September 14, at the Blythe Women's Club. . . .

Eight-year-old Uriah, who is suffering from Acute Lymphoblastic Leukemia, has been hospitalized since Monday night and is receiving blood transfusions. Donating a pint of blood, in Uriah's name, will help to replenish the blood bank for Uriah and other patients in need of blood.[5]

A beautiful college girl from Rancho, California came to the clinic for treatments with her books and studied while she waited for her appointment, but she was never too busy to play a game with Uriah. September 7, while he was sick in the hospital, she sent a white, toy puppy tied to a big, red, heart-shaped balloon. The note said:

Uriah,

I came today and there was no one to play "Nerts" with. Get well soon because I've learned how to play now. See ya. God bless.

Lots of love,
Reema Nasser

Uriah picked up the little dog and bounced the balloon off his hand. "I've got to get back," he said. *Friends make all the difference sometimes, don't they, God?*

257

Don took Uriah to the bowl-a-thon September 8 and photographed Uriah with the CVSP and Palo Verde Hospital teams. There were over $4,000 in pledges!

I contacted Sondra at the City of Hope when I heard they did HLA testing free for those who donated a pint of blood. "You mean anyone willing to drive to Duarte to donate blood can become a donor without cost, any time they choose?"

"An appointment has to be made, and we can test only ten people a day."

"I called because it's too good to be true. Can we publish your phone number for appointments in our articles and fliers?"

"Sure," she laughed.

In early September, Jan and Cindy, who worked with Nana at Valle Vista Elementary School, began a donor drive in Rancho Cucamonga. The *Inland Valley Daily Bulletin* donated a half page for their notice. In the accompanying photo, a boyish smile lit Uriah's face as he knelt by his Doberman, Tanya.

time is running out
for our friend uriah
will you help?
free testing
September 26, 1990
rancho san antonio medical center
Monday through Friday
city of hope
(Must donate one pint of blood)
Please call and make your appointment today.
We need a lot of participation and volunteers
to help this child.
If you can in any way help or have any questions,
please call Jan Marciano or Cindy Galbraith.[6]

God had set up friends in strategic places. People we hadn't seen in years got involved. Years before, as a young teen, I wrote to Gary when he was far from home and going through a tough time. Gary contacted us: "I work in a printing shop, and I'd like to donate some fliers." They were bright and eye catching, and there were so many! *God, You've put together such amazing things already; it doesn't surprise me much. It's astonishing to think such a small kindness so long ago could result in such a priceless gift. Truly, all things are possible with God. How could anyone believe all this could just happen by chance? Either incredible, impossible odds are at work, or there is a God.*

People whose lives had been touched by cancer called. Pat Walker's family had been HLA tested for a relative but weren't entered in the registry. We compared her family's typing to Uriah's. They didn't match. "Please come and get tested for the registry anyway," I said.

Judy Brennan's father, Mr. Small, died from cancer, and the family made a memorial donation to the NMDP in his honor.

Theresa Kelm's stepmother, Sally, contacted Janet. "I live in Arrowhead, and I want to help." And she did.

Tommy Li of the *Sun*, who interviewed Uriah, called. "I'm sending a donation."

We're not just a story to him; he really cares about Uriah. It's amazing how many people care. God, I'm truly grateful.

"I heard a rumor: matching funds for minority testing are available," I told Bonnie Foxcroft of the American Red Cross in Los Angeles. "That would be a dream come true. It would stretch our donor testing dollars much farther."

"Funds are available, with a cap of $25,000 per family," she confirmed. "You'll have to apply for a grant for every test date with Linda Abress of the NMDP, though."

"With pleasure!"

The Correctional Peace Officers Foundation helps families of slain correctional officers, but Office Administrator Charleene Corby said, "We'd rather prevent a death, if possible."

Their donor drives at prisons throughout California and other states were launched at the CCPOA Convention in Reno, Nevada.

September 8

Hi, Don and Mara:

I have been handwriting notes all day to wardens and contact people—writer's cramp. . . . Don, enclosed is your ticket. I'll pick you up in Reno. Take care, my friends, we will make it through this—we will!

Char

September 10

Reno's KTVN camera focused on activities at the donor drive, as the commentator explained, "The inspiration for all of this comes from an eight-year-old boy from California. Uriah has leukemia and needs a bone-marrow transplant to save his life. His father is a correctional officer in California. He's in town for a convention and to help find that much-needed donor."

Don spoke evenly, though what he said was difficult for any parent to say. "The quicker we get the donor, the better, because if he relapses again and they can't get him into remission, he'll die."

More pictures of the donor drive flashed on the screen. "The fact that four hundred California correctional officers are in town, all of them willing bone-marrow donors, gave our local blood service the impetus to start our own pool of potential bone-marrow donors," the commentator added.

"We would like to type a lot of donors in the Reno area and get them in the national registry," a representative of the local blood bank said. "We would also like to obtain fund-raisers or funds from companies and organizations in the area to help underwrite the cost of the tests."

The reporter's blood was drawn as she said, "The bone-marrow banks are all linked by computer. So, even though my blood type might match someone's in New York, they could find that out in a matter of minutes."

"It's extremely important," a representative of the national donor bank said. "Without this network, families would have to go through little, small registries of maybe five, ten, fifteen, or maybe a thousand donors, and it might take the entire time of the life of the child to actually find a match. With the national registry, one phone call accesses two hundred thousand donors."

A man who'd been tested was asked, "So, if you got called up for a bone-marrow match, you'd go?"

"Oh, definitely. Most definitely," he replied. "I have a little boy of my own. I'd love to have somebody to do that for me if I ever needed it. And certainly, I am willing to do that for another officer's child."

"We'll find a match for Uriah," Charleene Corby commented. "That I don't have a doubt about. It's the other children that we will also help."

"Twenty-five years ago, I lost my husband of marrow carcinoma," a middle-aged brunette woman said. Tears brimmed in her eyes. "And I think this is a wonderful program, and I hope to God that I'm the donor. I really would like that."[7]

September 10

The Palo Verde Teachers' Association offers the enclosed check for the furtherance [of] the Uriah Alexander Fund effort. Additionally, we have encouraged our members to make personal donations to the fund. Our good hopes and best wishes are extended to Uriah and your fine efforts.

Respectfully yours,
Gerald Colcun

Enclosed please find a check in the amount of $150 donated by the employees of the California Men's Colony. Be assured Uriah will be in our thoughts and prayers.

Sincerely,
Donna McDaniel, Office Services Supervisor II

How many tests can we afford? Blythe's donations totaled almost $14,000 and Fontana's, $2,370. *Funding is ample, but there aren't enough donor sign-ups.* "We'll test one hundred fifty in Blythe and seventy-five in Fontana," I told Theresa.

"We might try one more drive in Blythe after school begins and everyone's back from vacation," she suggested.

"We can try, but Blythe is small, and some people can't be tested because of health or age. It's possible we've tested most of the eligible people in Blythe."

❧ ❧ ❧

The internal investigation into the scuffle Don and other officers had with an inmate concluded. A Special Service Unit report alleged the inmate turned on officers June 27, and his burns were a result of his struggles with them. No physical abuse by the officers was discovered.

September 12
Diana from MOMs wrote from Ukiah, California:

> If God's willing, I pray that He sends a donor quickly. I know that through this all, God has brought many people forward and has taught them the meaning of love, kindness, concern, and giving. He has also raised up an army of prayer warriors, many of whom you do not even know and probably never will (except in heaven).
>
> I sure don't understand God's ways—but I do know that His ways are much higher than ours, and by knowing that, we can maintain our peace in trusting Him.
>
> Please let Uriah know that he is a very special little boy, and he has a very special place in our hearts.
>
> Diana

Thursday, September 13
I ordered 100 tests for Janet's first drive in Arrowhead September 18.

September 14, *Palo Verde Valley Times:*

Uriah: Blood drive today, golf and dinner this weekend

. . . A blood drive for Uriah has been scheduled for today, September 14, at the Blythe Women's Club. . . . Prospective donors between the ages of 17 and 70 are urged to donate.[8]

Dinner-Dance . . . Saturday, September 15 at the Jaycees Building.

. . . The Los Amigos Club of Blythe will hold a golf tournament . . . Sunday, September 16. . . .[9]

"Can you put together a video about Uriah, showing what a typical day is like for him?" asked Jan Marciano, coordinator of the Cucamonga drive. Don and I compiled footage of Uriah.

Larry Beynon, president of the Blythe Jaycees, called. "I've been contacted by William Pennycuff, who wants to give a motor scooter to Uriah." The children took turns riding the bright, yellow moped.

September 14

Dear Parents:

This is to inform you that a meeting will be held on Thursday, September 20 . . . to discuss available resources within the community as well as formation of support groups. Please try to attend. Thank you.

Sincerely,
Alba Sanmarco, M.D.
Hushang Haghighat, M.D.

A start, at last. Talking to membership services sure worked fast.

September 14

Dear Jan Marciano and Cindy Galbraith:

Earlier this week our students learned about Uriah Alexander's urgent search for a bone-marrow donor. Ever since that time, the faculty and parents of Holy Name of

Mary School have witnessed a little miracle of our own. We are inspired by our students' eager response of determined involvement and thoughtful concern about Uriah's health. On behalf of our faculty, parents, and students, it is my privilege and joy to send to you our donation for such a worthy cause.

Sincerely,
Ms. Sandy Janclaes

Our Brownie Troop was touched by Uriah's desperate need. We hope this donation will help.

Sincerely,
Pat Metoyer, Leader
and 3rd Grade Brownie Troop #356

The Jaycees served us a fine steak dinner in a private upper room on Saturday, September 15. Rod Worthington, the auctioneer, wore his tuxedo—and shorts! Uriah had worn shorts, a dress shirt, and a bright red bow tie. "Hey, we match! Maybe I should go help you," Uriah suggested.

"Sure," chuckled Rod.

Uriah turned to me expectantly. "OK, as long as you stay away from most of the people," I said.

"I'll keep an eye on him," said Barbara Martin of the chamber of commerce, as she winked. "I'll put him to work picking the winning tickets."

The room bustled with people. Those who served food and cleared tables seemed to have as much fun as those who dined. Goodwill was almost palpable, adding zest to the festivities.

Uriah was photographed, a smile on his face and a gleam in his eye, holding the key to the grand prize: a truck. Uriah drew the winning ticket and waved goodbye.

The following day, after church, we went to the second donor drive in Blythe. Heather and Shiloh helped in the nursery. The children drew and wrote notes to Uriah. Uriah joked and talked in his nearly adult fashion with sheriffs, correctional officers, and others who came to save him.

Tracy Sudyka from Zion Church was an elementary-school teacher. "We need to film someone being tested, so others will know how easy it is. Would you let us film you?" I asked her.

"I don't think I'm the best candidate for filming," she said, "but you can follow me through the steps, if you want to."

"Thanks, Tracy." *This should encourage those who are a little hesitant.*

After the last donor was tested, we gathered all the volunteers and took a group photo holding the rainbow banner. Bright smiles shone through weariness. *God, we have so many to thank for so much.*

Dearest Uriah,

Your picture is on our refrigerator and you are in our hearts daily. If we are not found compatible, we pray that God will provide someone else. . . .

Be tough—you are loved!

Jeff and Kathy Schmidt

Hi Uriah,

We still remember you at Bear Gulch School. Keep that smile on your face. You're a neat boy.

Love,
Your school nurse,
Mrs. Nuelle, R.N.

Uriah,

With God's help this can be overcome. Remember He is always with us.

> Sunday-school teacher
> [Immanuel Lutheran, Chino]
> Lillian Vogel

Uriah,

Rick and I hope so much that a donor is found. You are a very brave little boy. Help your mommy be brave.

> Rick and Dyann
> [Nicholas' parents from Rialto
> Community Baptist Church]

Hi Uriah.

Your picture and story moved me to get involved. Thank You, God. Bless you!!

> Love,
> Marcia C

Uriah,

I pray that you will always have hope and joy filled with love. I don't know you, we've never met, but Jesus loves you and so do I. You look a lot like my 7-yr.-old son. I bet you two would have a ball playing. You take care, sweetheart, and I'll keep you in our prayers.

> Love in Him
> God Bless You!
> Patti Hill

When I explained to my 6-year-old boy, Steven, where his father and I were going today and why—he wanted to come and have his blood tested too—even if it hurt.

P.S. It didn't hurt a bit!!

Susan Terberg

Good Luck, Uriah and Family

We are all praying for you and will keep the thoughts high at CIW. Inmates and staff are with you all the way.

Sgt. Cox

Inmates would pull for us? I usually think of them as a force opposing officers. God, I guess I still have a lot to learn.

September 16, the *San Bernardino Sun:*

Fate of 8-year old hangs on transplant from some stranger

By Michel Nolan
Special to The Sun

LAKE ARROWHEAD—". . . In some ways, this situation is like the Lotto," said Uriah's aunt, Janet Anderson, a Lake Arrowhead resident. "Every person who gets tested buys him an opportunity for another chance at life."

But this is a high-stakes game and the clock is ticking. Despite 11th-hour efforts by Uriah's family, no donor has been found.

"Chemotherapy and medication worked to a limited degree in the beginning," Anderson said, "but since then there have been three relapses, each one progressively worse."

He went into remission in August.

"Doctors are afraid he won't be strong enough to survive another relapse," she said. . . .

Donor testing has been scheduled . . . Tuesday at Mountains Community Hospital, Lake Arrowhead.

A fund-raising festival has been scheduled . . . Wednesday at Straw Hat Pizza, Rancho Cucamonga, Mara Alexander said.

Four people passed a preliminary blood test Aug. 26 at the Lutheran Church in Fontana, she said.

Bake sales, pancake breakfasts, and other community fund-raisers in Blythe and Rancho Cucamonga have raised over $18,000 for the bone-marrow transplant fund. . . .

"We're really aware of how important today is," his mother said. "So we try to live for today.

"Uriah has a lot of hope and faith that we will find a donor . . . but he knows that if his body isn't strong enough, he'll go to heaven and have a new one."

A devout Christian family, the Alexanders are accepting of God's will.

But, said Mara Alexander, "There is so much Uriah would like to do. He's not ready to leave yet."[10]

Theresa made thank-you fliers that listed all the contributors. I ordered five hundred thank-you notes from Brisco's. When I finished writing, I had only two left.

Monday, September 17

At 1:00 P.M. Uriah was interviewed by Jim Lampley in Los Angeles at CBS studios. Next we picked up left-over supplies from the Fontana donor drives. At 7:30, we met volunteers for the Cucamonga donor drive at Straw Hat Pizza. We ate pizza, listened to plans, and answered questions. "The video will be completed tomorrow during Uriah's treatment," I promised.

At 9:30, we met Theresa in San Bernardino to get extra supplies from Blythe for the Cucamonga donor drive.

A photo entitled, "Dinner-dance for Uriah pays off," by Robin Richards, appeared in the *Palo Verde Valley Times:*

> . . . Larry Beynon, . . . President of Blythe Jaycees, is presenting Kelm with a check for $9,117.58, raised for eight-year-old leukemia victim Uriah Alexander at a dinner-dance September 15. . . .[11]

Tuesday, September 18

Uriah and I went to help Janet, Andria, and Brian set up for the Arrowhead donor drive, but they had everything in place. The support from volunteers and donors was uplifting. *These people know they're doing something important. Something that could change a life extraordinarily. Your Son gives us a transplant, doesn't He, God? More than just blood or a bone-marrow transplant that extends life, He gives spiritual life to our souls, stillborn by sin. And all we have to do is ask.*

A special notice by CPOF:

> From the bottom of our hearts, the parents and friends of Uriah Alexander say, "Thank you."
>
> Last week, at the Nugget Hotel in Reno, a bone-marrow drive was set into motion by your CPO Foundation in conjunction with the California Correctional Peace Officers Association (CCPOA) Convention. During this two-day blood testing, 301 members and friends participated. . . .

Set for the first week of October, a blood screening will be conducted at the California Correctional Center (CCC) in Susanville. Plans are currently under discussion to conduct major drives at several other institutions. However, you don't need a major drive to see if you are *the one Uriah needs.* Tell them you wish to be tested for a possible match with *Uriah Alexander.* There will be no cost to you; your CPO Foundation is taking care of that.

If that sample matches completely, you will be notified that you are possibly the person that can *save Uriah.*

The *Inland Valley Daily Bulletin* of Ontario, September 18:

Group to hold fund-raiser to help boy with leukemia

By Peggy Olson
Bulletin Staff Writer

Time grows shorter for Uriah Alexander.

After battling leukemia for most of his life, doctors say the 8-year-old former Fontana boy can't survive without a bone-marrow transplant.

"He really doesn't have much time," said his grandmother, Edith Miller. "We don't know from one day to the next if he'll relapse. We just live one day at a time."

Uriah is registered with the National Marrow Donor Program, which maintains a registry of possible donors. But so far, no match has been found. . . .

"Friends of Uriah," a committee of Rancho Cucamonga mothers, has joined the donor search.

The 20-member committee will stage a fund-raiser Wednesday at Straw Hat Pizza, 8710 19th St., Rancho Cucamonga.

Owners Gary and Cathy Burbank have agreed to donate 50 percent of the proceeds from all food and soft drinks sold. . . .

Entertainment will be provided by impersonator Ron Stein in "Memories of Elvis," . . . Freckles the Clown . . . [and] the Teenage Mutant Ninja Turtles. . . .

Uriah will be driven to the fund-raiser by Golden Moments Limo. . . . But the youngster won't mingle with the crowd.

Exhaustive chemotherapy and radiation treatments have left his immune system depressed, according to his mother Mara.

"Now he is extremely vulnerable to infection and has to be isolated from people," she said.

Setting a goal of $15,000, "Friends of Uriah" hopes to raise funds to test at least 300 prospective donors . . . Sept. 26 . . . at Rancho San Antonio Medical Center. . . .

Nearly 1,000 possible donors have been tested through the family's efforts. "Friends of Uriah" has raised about $6,000 in previous fund-raisers, but more funding is crucial for the search that could save Uriah's life, said Jan Marciano, committee chairman.[12]

At the hospital, I videotaped Uriah playing cards, being weighed, hugging Dr. Sanmarco and Dr. Haghighat, having his blood drawn, being hooked up to the IV, and eating pizza for lunch. He wasn't done when the clinic closed. He and Sami were both admitted to finish their treatments. He looked tired and pale from the treatment, sitting in a hospital bed, playing cards and joking with his nurse Georgia while she unhooked his IV and flushed his catheter. "I'll get you a basin if you feel nauseous," she offered.

He giggled. "I would rather throw up in your shoe if you don't hurry and get me unhooked!"

On Wednesday, September 19, two sheriff's motorcycles sat in Larry's driveway, waiting to escort the limo to Straw

Hat Pizza. Uriah, wearing his mask, stroked the gleaming motorcycles. "Could I sit on one?"

Deputies Tomassi and Ammerman helped him onto one of the black, glossy seats and explained the gadgets on the dash. I hovered nearby with a basin. *He's still nauseous from yesterday's treatment.*

We followed the motorcycles to Straw Hat in a shiny, white limousine with dark, tinted windows. There were cheers from the crowd peppered with TV cameras. *I've never seen so many people at our fund-raisers! It awes me to think this is all for Uriah. Some of these people have never met us, yet they are willing to help him live.*

Volunteers in bright orange shirts motioned to the crowd, "Please move back."

God, how will I keep Uriah separate from this crowd?

"When God closes a door, look for a window."

My eyes shot to the roof. "Could you open the sunroof?" I asked the kind driver.

Uriah stood on my lap and popped out of the opening like a jack-in-the-box. Cheers and whistles broke from the crowd. Girls giggled and peered through the wrought-iron fence around the courtyard of Straw Hat where the rainbow banner hung. "Oh, isn't he cute?" A volunteer carried a huge balloon bouquet to Uriah, and the CBS channel 2 film crew moved in for an interview.

Randy Stein, who once played for the Brewers, presented Uriah with an autographed baseball.

Ron Stein, as Elvis, sang Uriah a few lines from the "Wonder of You." After the crowd had gone to get their pizza, Uriah asked, "Can I go listen to Ron sing?" We sneaked to a back door behind the stage where Ron belted out, "You Ain't Nothin' but a Hound Dog. . ."

A murmur ran through the stagehands, "Tell Ron Uriah's here!"

Ron slipped backstage. "Can I dedicate a song to Uriah?" Uriah nodded and was whisked onstage by Ron. After the song he gave Uriah an autographed picture and his white silk scarf.

We were on the CBS late news:

"A young boy from Lake Arrowhead has leukemia and needs your help tonight," Jim Lampley said. "His doctors say he may have only until the end of this month to stop the disease. He's a brave 8-year old and he knows he has just one chance."

They cut to the interview Uriah had in Los Angeles Monday. "I know one thing that's a cure," said Uriah.

"What's that?" asked Jim Lampley.

"A bone-marrow transplant. . . ."

"Are you going to have a bone-marrow transplant?"

"Yeah. At least try to," said Uriah with a giggle and smile.

"Uriah's doctors say his only chance for survival is a bone-marrow transplant," said a voice-over by Jim Lampley.

Freckles the clown made balloon animals at Straw Hat. "Tonight," continued Jim Lampley, "friends and volunteers mounted a large fund-raiser at a pizza parlor in Alta Loma."

The crowded dining room at Straw Hat and volunteers making heart-shaped pizzas appeared. "They need money to pay for tests for potential bone-marrow donors. Cash from pizza sales and video arcade games was donated to the cause."

Posters of Uriah came into focus. "Doctors have been searching for a bone-marrow donor since May, but it's tough to find a match."

I stood in Straw Hat's parking lot surrounded by the crowd. "Uriah's mom is hopeful about a donor," Jim said, "but knows that time is running out."

"It's a real scary thing, you know," I said. "If we can find someone, it will be wonderful, because it will give him a whole new life. If we don't find someone, we're just going to enjoy as much time as we have left."

Uriah popped out of the sunroof and waved at the cheering crowd. "Uriah himself made an appearance tonight in a donated limousine," said Jim. "He couldn't leave the car because the risk of infection is too high, but that didn't dampen his spirits."

Uriah's smiling face at the studio interview filled the screen. "How are you gonna feel the day your mom tells you, 'Uriah, we have a donor, and we're ready to do it'?"

"I'll be glad," beamed Uriah.

"I bet you will," replied Jim. "'Cause what is that going mean?"

"I may not have leukemia," Uriah finished.

Jim Lampley, sitting at the news desk, said, "Again, doctors say they must have a donor for Uriah before the end of this month or it could be too late. If you're interested in being a potential bone-marrow donor, tests will be conducted Wednesday, September 26, at San Antonio Medical Center in Rancho Cucamonga. . . ."

His female co-anchor added, "What a smile on that little boy!"[13]

The *Palo Verde Valley Times* September 19:

Battle for Uriah continues

. . . "There's a rainbow behind the clouds" has become a battle cry in the attempt to find a bone-marrow donor for Uriah. Here's the latest news from the front:

Friday—37 pints of blood were donated in Uriah's name in a collection drive held at the Blythe Women's Club. . . .

Saturday—A sell-out crowd attended a fund-raiser dinner/dance for Uriah held by the Blythe Jaycees. . . .

Sunday—117 residents from Blythe, plus 70 from Fontana, were tested as prospective marrow donors for Uriah.

The Los Amigos Club, . . . held a benefit golf tournament at Blythe Municipal Golf Course . . . [and] will donate $1,000. . . .

Theresa Kelm, the hard-working organizer who has spurred on so much of the community's efforts, reports that Uriah's condition remains in remission. He is still receiving chemotherapy once a week as the search for a donor continues; but for now his blood count is up and he plans to attend school today. . . .[14]

Atascadero, September 19

Hope you find a donor. I hope this donation helps. We're keeping our fingers crossed here at CMC for you.

Donna Miller

Carolyn Baschal's mom, Mary Baschal, worked at First Lutheran Elementary in San Fernando and organized a donor drive there.

Uriah Needs Your Help!

Uriah has leukemia and is running out of time. The family needs our *prayers*, our support with our offerings, and a bone-marrow donor for Uriah. You and I can be the "rainbow behind the clouds. . . ."

The Lord is giving us an opportunity to do *His* work and reach out to those who are suffering or in need. Share from your heart what you can in offering, and keep the

Alexander family in your prayers. . . . A simple blood test can tell if you might be a possible bone-marrow donor. . . . If 10 or more people consent to the testing, medical personnel from Blythe will come here to do the testing. *You can help!*

So many people were tested at the City of Hope that we got a call from them: "Thanks! Lots of people have come to be tested for Uriah."

"I saw this in the Sunday paper," Janet said, handing me a clipped cartoon.

There was little time to plan the Sunday-school picnic September 23, so we had a barbecue, pot luck, and games. The water-balloon toss inevitably ended in a water-balloon fight. One boy splattered Theresa and me with a water balloon. We spoke in a silent glance and sneaked up with an ice chest of water when his back was turned. "Look out!" his friend hollered. Theresa and I ended up wearing the water, much to the delight of the Sunday-school students. Heather threw a water balloon at me, but I ducked and she smacked her friend Noah in the face. Her amazement was memorable. "Didn't know I could still move that quick, did ya?" I said.

Tuesday, September 25

"I'm Father Bob Lark," the man on the phone said. "There's a San Diego invention called reagent, made to fight cancer. It's a free treatment for those who will take it. Judge Press' wife achieved a leukemia remission with it, and 19,500 cases have been treated with it. It's based on oxygen and dispels toxins. It's not on the market because the phone's been tapped, and its creator and his notes disappeared."

"Why?"

"Because what works won't benefit investors. There's a philanthropist in San Bernardino who could get you started on the treatment. It's illegal to administer because it isn't approved by the FDA."

Are the vultures descending on us, or did You send him? I don't believe it, but when and if the doctors give up, what harm could it do?

Wednesday, September 26

The billing from Children's Hospital indicated we were now responsible for $797.00 of the $5,920.00 bill. *It's only a matter of time before we'll be responsible for it all.* They enclosed a form letter from Kaiser stating the claim was denied. "Your account is being reviewed for possible collections."

I called Olga at Kaiser. "Write to them explaining Uriah is a Sunset referral patient, and all bills should be forwarded to them," she said.

I gave the correct address to Rene in patient accounts at Children's Hospital. *I hope this works. Trying to straighten this out on a public telephone in a hospital hallway while Uriah's admitted is not fun.*

Don, Uriah, and I found a back entrance to the donor drive at the new medical center in Cucamonga. The smallest detail had been seen to by scores of volunteers.

Many messages of hope were written:

Dear Uriah,

I love you. I'm praying for you every night.

Mrs. Denise Soderlund
[Uriah's kindergarten teacher at Bear Gulch.]

Hi, Uriah!!

I love you. I hope you are still writing and making beautiful pictures!

Love,
Mrs. Alexander
[Uriah's first-grade teacher]

Hi, Sweetheart!

Hope God finds a donor for you soon! I saw you in the hospital when I visited Jason, and you were giving the nurses a fun time. God bless you, Uriah.

Love,
Nancy Homan

Uriah,

You are a real fighter and we are proud to do anything to help you.

> Your brother and sister in Jesus,
> Jane/James Wright

Uriah,

God has made you so special. Your need has galvanized a whole community and touched all of our hearts. Our purpose in living has a bigger picture because of you. Your admission of faithfulness is indeed inspiring! May God bless your love and faithfulness.

> In His majestic love,
> Sylvia Beres

You have captured the hearts of thousands of people. God bless and good luck.

> Marla Lindsay

Dear Uriah and Mom,

Just thought I'd let you know that our son had leukemia too. It took eight very long years—but just this past August, he was pronounced cured! So the rainbows really do appear! We're praying for you.

> Emily and Steve Topor

Hey Uriah,

Hope I'm the one!

> Love,
> Debbie

That night Marianne Banister sat at the *ABC Channel 7 Eyewitness News* desk.

"A young boy who has leukemia remains hopeful for a life-giving bone-marrow transplant. But now time may be running out. Bob Banfield has this story."

Scenes of donors filling out forms and being tested flashed on the screen. "Most of the four hundred people who gathered at San Antonio Medical Center in Rancho Cucamonga do not personally know the eight-year-old leukemia victim who desperately needs a bone-marrow transplant to save his life," Bob said.

"They have used nearly every kind of chemotherapy there is, and the cancer is just too strong," I said. "So at this point, the only thing that is going to work for him is for them to completely destroy his bone marrow and replace it with healthy bone marrow from a donor."

Donors sat at tables, filling out paperwork. "More testing is scheduled for October 11 at San Antonio Medical Center in Upland," Bob said. "Ongoing testing at City of Hope." The bright colors of a rainbow banner flashed on the screen. "Bob Banfield, *Channel 7 Eyewitness News*, Rancho Cucamonga."[16]

The *San Bernardino Sun*, September 27:

Volunteers brave needles for boy with leukemia
By Tommy Li
Sun Staff Writer

Rich Rojas hates having a needle stuck into his arm for blood tests.

But the Cucamonga Junior High School teacher didn't mind Wednesday. He wanted to find our whether he could help Uriah Alexander, an 8-year-old leukemia patient desperately in need of a bone-marrow transplant.

"I can't stand needles. Last time I gave (blood) was 10 years ago when I got married," said Rojas, 34, of Victorville.

"I have two kids also. I figured if something happened to them, I'd get help."

"It's been wonderful to see all these people come out," said Uriah's mother, Mara, 31.

She and husband, Don, 32, brought Uriah to the hospital Wednesday to thank the volunteers.

. . . Uriah cannot wait long. His remission could end within days, Don Alexander said.

Most recently, Uriah was given experimental medication known as VM26, which doctors hope will prolong the remission.

"We'll find out when the end of September comes whether or not this medication is going to help," Don Alexander said. "Basically, it's not a cure. It's going to buy more time for us."

Results of Wednesday's tests won't be known until late next week.

More testing is scheduled at San Antonio Medical Center in Upland . . . on Oct. 11, said Jan Marciano, organizer of a group called Friends of Uriah. . . .

Despite the odds, Wednesday's volunteers were willing to do what they could to help save Uriah's life.

"I came out because I had a little brother that had leukemia. I was only 15 at the time, and I couldn't help," said Linda Embry, 41, who drove from Buena Park to the Rancho Cucamonga hospital. Her brother died at age 5.

Uriah's kindergarten teacher from Rancho Cucamonga's Bear Gulch Elementary School took a blood test. "I hope that I'll match, that I can help him," said Denise Soderlund. "You never know, you have to try." [17]

The *Inland Valley Daily Bulletin* September 27 photo by Tom Zasadzinski showed volunteers testing donors in the background, while Don, wearing his cowboy hat and a big smile, held smiling Uriah.

Donors give to help little boy live

By Sharon Greengold
Bulletin Staff Writer

. . . People lined up, filled out their addresses and telephone numbers, and patiently waited to have two tablespoons of blood drawn from their arms.

During the six-hour period, blood was drawn from about 400 people and more than 100 people who dropped by without appointments were turned away and scheduled to return Oct. 11.

All of the blood samples are to be sent to a laboratory to be analyzed for compatibility with the blood and bone marrow type of 8-year-old Uriah Alexander.

. . . If a marrow match is found among the vials of blood, the donor of the matching blood will be requested to become a marrow donor. If agreeable, the donor will be placed under general anesthesia and have marrow extracted from the hip bones in the back, according to the National Marrow Donor Program booklet.

. . . Bonnie Muis drove all the way from Phelan to have her blood tested. "We have mutual friends who told us about Uriah at church," she said.

Gary Van Clief and Martin Munday, both of Rancho Cucamonga, waited along with the others for the chance to have their blood tested.

. . . Van Clief said, "I've heard different stories about donating marrow, but you can't compare it to what this little boy is going through."

Munday said: "It makes your own problems seem pretty small compared to this little guy."[18]

A card arrived with a large donation. "Waiting with you, Praying for you, Believing in His power. Your Friends at Zion."

"You can fill up for free at our gas station if funds are tight," the Callans offered.

God, with the help of good people like these, we hope to succeed.

Fifteen

A Thousand Cranes
(Oct. 1990)

*. . . The ancient Japanese legend says the crane
lives for 1,000 years and anyone who folds a
thousand cranes will live a very long time.*
—Palo Verde Valley Times

O N MONDAY, OCTOBER 2, 1990, HEIDI OF SOCIAL SERVICES
informed me, "Mara, Dr. Sanmarco would like to see
you."

Uh-oh, what's up? "I'll be right back," I promised Uriah,
whose IV pumped chemotherapy.

Dr. Sanmarco's face was grim as she motioned me to a
chair. "I was called into my superior's office and given a
complaint you filed against me with membership services."

Complaint?

"I never would have given a donation or given Uriah
that toy if I knew how you felt. I'm going to disband the
Mariposas because of you, and the clinic won't have a support group."

"I went to membership services to request an additional doctor for the clinic because there are so many patients," I said. "I don't know what complaint you're talking

285

about. Can I have a copy of it?" I was appalled by what I read:

> She indicates that the physicians and staff are dependent on her to inform them as to the reason for the visit.

If they didn't know what they were doing, I wouldn't let them treat Uriah!

> She would like the care given by Dr. San Marcos reviewed. Dr. San Marcos has difficulty making a decision as to the treatment to give for her son's care as she has changed treatment many times.

"Dr. Sanmarco, this is not what I told them." *She doesn't believe me.*

> She is concerned she was never given any information regarding her son's illness nor were attempts made to be sensitive to any other concerns she may have had. . . .

Other concerns? I want information made available to parents, that's all.

> She feels patients or family should receive a phone call to invite them to [Mariposas] meetings.

That's ridiculous! I was told the Mariposas is a private support group and its meetings are not open to parents! We need a separate, new support group for parents.

I gazed across the desk. *Dr. Sanmarco thinks I'm a treacherous, egotistical idiot trying to ruin her career and wrest control of the Mariposas for my own purposes. It's a revelation to discover these doctors and nurses can consider me a reason-*

able person for years and suddenly, with the stroke of someone's pen, consider me a despicable miscreant. The damage is done. How can I minimize it? "Dr. Sanmarco, I'll go to membership services and protest this. It's not what I told them."

The woman I had spoken with was on vacation. Someone else had typed the complaint from her notes. *The stress is already unbelievable without this.* I wrote membership services a three-page rebuttal:

> . . . I feel it would be helpful if members approaching membership services for aid were allowed to review their "confidential" worksheets before they are filed so any corrections to content can be made before a misunderstanding occurs. . . .

Many nurses treated me coldly after that. *They must have read and believed that report too.* I lingered near faithful friends and hoped others would recognize the truth someday. I had to keep going; the clock was ticking away the hours of my son's life. Much to their credit, Dr. Haghighat and Dr. Sanmarco continued to care for Uriah.

Larry arranged for Uriah to have a tour of the sheriff's SWAT training building in Los Angeles. The obstacle course ranged up and over buildings, incorporating obstacles that necessitated incredible skill.

Don, Uriah, and I went for a ride in a large helicopter with two pilots and three crewmen. We flew above the city, strapped inside, facing a large, open doorway. When the helicopter banked right, we found ourselves staring at the ground directly below, suspended by the motion of the helicopter and the restraints.

"Whoa!" Uriah giggled.

At a station in the mountains, we ate lunch and talked with the men who were both firemen and sheriffs.

"Gee, maybe I could work with you guys someday!" Uriah said.

Deputy Ascherin asked Uriah questions about his leukemia and explained his job. "Come back to visit after it snows. It really looks cool then."

Uriah nodded. "That'd be neat!"

Uriah couldn't ride in the rescue harness hanging from the helicopter because of his chest catheter, so Don went. Terry jotted on his card, "Here's your lift ticket," he said. "Call for heli-lift after catheter pulled," it said.

Back at the training station, Larry lifted Uriah out of the chopper. *If Uriah lived a normal life, he probably never would have had so many incredible experiences. If his life is short, at least it's been rich and interesting.*

Wednesday, October 3

The *Los Angeles Times* article, "U.S. to Audit Medical Foundation" reported that the Life-Savers Foundation was being audited by order of the US Health Department because of requests from five senators. Families of cancer patients complained that thousands of dollars donated to Life-Savers couldn't be accounted for. Allegedly, volunteers waiting to be tested were turned away, even though money was left from fund-raising. Life-Savers was ordered to release donor information to the NMDP by a federal judge in July.

The October *Courier* newsletter of Rialto Community Baptist Church:

You may have read about the Alexander family in the newspaper. They were faithful members of our church family, but had to join another church, which was able to provide a separate room for their son, Uriah. . . . His only chance for survival is a bone-marrow transplant. . . . Becoming a potential donor requires only a simple blood test . . . call Maggie Kim at the Red Cross Blood Bank.[1]

Each drive seemed to start another. We planned to test thirty to fifty of the LA SWAT team and sheriffs on October 4; seventy-five at First Lutheran in San Fernando on October 4, and three hundred fifty in Cucamonga on October 11. There was a drive in Arrowhead on October 18 and one at Calvary Chapel of Ontario in November.

CPOF planned drives at Susanville, October 1 and 2; YTS Heman Stark School, October 22; CIM, October 23; CIW, October 16; California Men's Colony, October 24; El Paso Robles Boys School, October 23; Atascadero State Hospital, October 23; and one for Pelican Bay.

Friday, October 5
    A nine-by-twelve envelope filled with contributions had this memo:

Best wishes from your friends at the Chicano Correctional Workers Association, CIM Chino Chapter, and California Institution for Men Complex.

Respectfully,
Gabriel Gutierrez
CCWA Chino Chapter President

On a trip to visit my sister Joanna and her husband Mark in Brookings, Oregon, we stopped at the donor drive in San Fernando. Posters hung on fences around the school: "Uriah needs your help!" Uriah couldn't come in, so principal Earl Renolds and his wife came out to meet him. I handed Earl a bag of rainbow-colored candy. "This is to thank the kids for their help."

We dropped by to see Diana from the MOMs group. "Jenny's started college and is doing well," she said. "We'll pray for Uriah."

At Joanna's church October 7, the choir sang "I Believe in Miracles."

"Pastor had a daughter who died from leukemia years ago," Joanna whispered.

It might cause him pain to meet us. We may bring into sharp focus memories time has mercifully softened.

He shook our hands after the service. "It's rather courageous of you to take Uriah out in public."

"We take precautions, but church is absolutely necessary. We trust God to protect Uriah when he's here."

The simple fun we had! Heather, Shiloh, and Uriah rode tiny tricycles around the patio with cousins Meagan and James, their knees sticking out at strange angles. Heather climbed the tree in the backyard. Mark, Joanna, and all the kids played a comical game with a football. We walked along the beach and splashed in the river. The pajamaed children played with balloons in the living room. Before long, even the adults were batting balloons, trying to keep them afloat or bounce them off someone's head! All too soon, it was time to return home.

The two Manx kittens we got from Lori and Tim Ray bounced instead of walked. Fluffy was black and Garfield was an orange tabby. "I love Garfield—the cartoon *and* the kitten," giggled Uriah.

A Parting Gift. Now we have kittens. I hope the similarity ends there.

The *Inland Valley Daily Bulletin*, October 6:

Educators seek donors for stricken child

By Paul Hughes
Bulletin Staff Writer

CHINO—As a former Fontana youngster clings to life, battling the leukemia that has slowed him for seven of his eight years, Chino school district officials are calling on employees to be tested as possible bone-marrow donors.

Uriah Alexander, whose doctors originally said his remission would end in September, responded well to a new series of chemotherapy treatments, said his grandmother, Ruth Alexander. He is still in remission after about five months, she said. Ruth Alexander is a substitute secretary in the Chino Unified School District.

Prospective donors can be tested Thursday during a special drive for Uriah at Rancho San Antonio Medical Center in Rancho Cucamonga. Those who want to be tested are asked to call the center to make an appointment. . . .

Uriah, who has been able to attend school when he feels well, is in good spirits, said his grandmother. "He knows what's coming up and is facing it pretty well," she said. . . .

He was able to take a trip to Northern California to visit an aunt this past week, but was due back Monday, in time for his weekly chemotherapy treatments, Ruth Alexander said.[2]

Monday, October 8

A donation collected at CIM arrived in a manila envelope with the article about Cucamonga's drive taped to the outside. "R. C. West is collecting needed donations for this worthy cause. Don Alexander was assigned to the R. C. West yard prior to promoting to

Chuckawalla. Let's keep up the spirit and help a comrade in need." It was signed by eighty-nine donors.

October 9

Dear Parents:

At our parent meeting on September 20, 1990, some parents expressed a strong interest in forming a Parent Support Group. We are having a follow-up meeting on Wednesday, October 24, 1990 . . . to discuss plans for such a group. . . .

Sincerely,
Heidi Walker, L.C.S.W.
Rene Buonocore,
C.C.L.S. (Child Life Specialist)

Wow! I thought. *There might be hope yet!*

October 10

Enclosed is the Ageless Reflections check . . . for the Uriah Alexander fund, donated by the senior citizens who participate in the Palo Verde nutrition program.

Yours very truly,
Leora Hollingshead
Program Director, Ageless Reflections, Inc.

The first NMDP statement showed we had tested 762; contributions totaled over $51,700; a balance of $21,600 remained. *There's plenty of money to hold drives, but how much time does Uriah have?*

. . . The response you have received by friends and community groups in your area has been marvelous. I am pleased to see that recruitment efforts are continuing. I am especially glad that you have been able to take advantage of the matching family funds the programs received through a grant from the Navy.

Tami Brown and Tanya Moore let me know of their meeting with you. I hope you find it helpful, because of proximity, to work with our western office. I want you to feel free and call . . . if there is anything we can do for you. . . . We are all hoping for the best for Uriah.

Sincerely yours,
Linda Abress

The juxtaposition of two photos in the *Palo Verde Valley Times* made them even more meaningful for me. One, by Robin Richards:

"**Firemen Help**"—Lori Shay receives a check for Uriah Alexander from Blythe Volunteer Fire Department President Dan McIntyre. . . . Although itself largely dependent on the philanthropy of others, the department went ahead to raise funds for the 8-year old.[3]

The other, by Howard Decker, showed a tree in a raised planter:

"**Remembering**"—Members of the Junior Women's Club of Blythe dedicate a memorial at Zion Lutheran School for Nancy Owens. Owens, a club member and teacher at the school, passed away [a] year ago.[4]

I received an enthusiastic call. "My name is Brett. I've been healed by a pastor from the Vineyard. He's been praying for Uriah and would like to meet him."

God, I know You can heal Uriah anytime and anywhere, but I don't want to be like the man in the joke who sat on his roof during the flood and turned away help, saying, "God will save me." When he got to the pearly gates, God asked, "What happened? I sent a boat and a helicopter!" It's entirely possible this is how You will heal Uriah; then again, maybe this will just test his faith.

Janet, Uriah, and I met Brett in a Blue Jay parking lot the next morning. Brett's dark eyes sparkled with excitement. "I'm so glad you agreed to meet with Pastor."

He led us to a huge home in a gated community by Lake Arrowhead. His young, smiling wife led us to a lower floor where a wall of glass exhibited a panoramic view of the lake. The pastor, an ex-pro football player, seemed genuine and spiritual. "Can I lay hands on you and pray for your healing?" he asked Uriah.

Uriah agreed but watched me closely while the pastor prayed, as if uneasy. "I'm sure God has healed Uriah," he said. "I hope you'll join me in a revival of churches."

"I know God can heal Uriah—if He wants to. The Old Testament says a prophet of doom is to be believed, but a prophet of good tidings will be proven a prophet when the thing prophesied comes to pass.[5] I hope you're right. Only time will tell. I'll call and let Brett know how things are going."

Brett's wife handed Uriah a giant Mickey Mouse. "We bought this on a whim, hoping Uriah's favorite cartoon character was Mickey."

Uriah smiled from ear to ear. Mickey was nearly as big as he was.

We climbed in the car and waved goodbye. Uriah turned to me: "Mom, I don't *feel* any different."

At the second donor drive in Cucamonga on October 11, young and old encouraged us:

Hi! My name is Christy. I'm just a kid myself, so I really hope I can help you! My dad's best friend went through the same thing as you—two years ago! We just celebrated two years of remission! In '92 we'll be doing the same for you. Keep happy thoughts.

Christy Mosca

Denny Auden at Mountains Community Hospital in Arrowhead called. "The lab said they're picking up the samples at 5:00 P.M. on October 18, but most of the people are scheduled to be tested between five and seven."

"Thanks for calling. I'll get it taken care of." I called the NMDP.

"We'll make sure they're there from noon until 7:00 P.M.," said Linda Abress.

It's good to be able to leave that problem to them.

Brent Nelson, the brother of my high-school chum Becky Nelson, was a member of the 101st Sheriff's Academy Class. "The 101st Class would like to make Uriah an honorary member and have him attend our graduation Friday, November 2."

"You couldn't give him a better gift!"

"We've also scheduled a run to benefit Uriah's search."

God, You've known all about this since I was in high school, didn't You? You have woven my life together with others in a fantastic design. It's not just random chance. Only You could coordinate all these things.

Monday, October 15
Uriah fell off the motor scooter Sunday and was bleeding from his catheter site. Now he's in the hospital with a staph infection. If it doesn't clear up, they'll have to pull it. Today he went for a cathetergram.

"That doctor didn't unclamp it when she flushed it," Uriah said, "and stuff went spraying all over me."
Dr. Wang repaired it again. Now his small lumen reached to his knees.
I wrote thank-you notes as quickly as I could, and Uriah signed them.
Carlos Castro, a CHP officer, contacted the hospital, trying to get in touch with us. "I have some things my co-workers and I purchased for Uriah."

October 17, 1990

Dear Mrs. Alexander:
Thank you for taking the time to come in and clarify your concerns and requests regarding the Pediatric Department.
I forwarded your letters to the Chief of Service for Pediatrics for his review and action. He asked me to let you know that the physician staffing for Hematology/Oncology is appropriate for the number of patients. . . .
We understand the parents' need for support groups, and this request was made known to our Social Service Department. . . .

Sincerely,
Carolyn Tornero
Area Manager, Membership
Service Department

Wednesday, October 17

Uriah's still in remission, but we haven't found a donor yet. There's been no shortage of prayer and caring for us, but we're on borrowed time. Should we try the autologous transplant using Uriah's bone marrow? The chances of success are only 10 percent because it's Uriah's third remission.

Jan Cipkala-Gaffin had more information. "Five people matched the A and B loci of Uriah's HLA type and have been asked to be tested further, but four have not scheduled an appointment yet. The donor-testing process has a two-week turnaround time. It will take four or five weeks to get everything in place for a nonrelated donor transplant. Two or three weeks is the soonest we could do an autologous transplant."

"What do you think we should do?"

"It would be wise to look into other options and probably not wise to wait."

I called Debbie DeForge about her son's autologous transplant. "How did it go for Garrett?" I asked. "Would you do it again?"

"I wouldn't know any better what to do this time than the last time. Garrett's situation was so much like Uriah's: third remission—radical transplant or experimental medication. The transplant could cut his life shorter if it doesn't work, and he'll have to stay in the hospital. On the other hand, you never know how long he has on medicine, or if they'll ever find an unrelated donor."

"Monday we have an appointment to talk with Dr. Falk," I said.

It's a heavy decision—more a guess than anything. The only one who could possibly know is You, God. We want unrelated donors ruled out before we do an autologous transplant.

"I really don't care either way," said Uriah. "I just need time to think about it."

Joaquin Grijalva, a nine-year-old boy in the San Gabriel valley was on Channel 9. *He needs a bone-marrow transplant too. I wonder if they would want to have a drive? I'll leave my number and wait for them to contact me.*

Contributions and notes continued to arrive:

> The Junior Women's Improvement Club of Blythe is proud to offer our help to your family in this time of need. Use it for your purposes—even gasoline costs. We hope it helps.
>
> Heather King
Social Amenities

> After speaking with you several weeks ago, I decided to go by the City of Hope and donate for Uriah. I was notified that I was not a suitable donor. Hopefully, in the future I might be of some help to someone else. . . . I have two grown sons with families. . . . I would like to think that someone would be of help to them if ever the need arises.
>
> I do hope that a suitable donor is found soon for Uriah. Your family is in my prayers.
>
> Sincerely,
Gail A. Castillo

A *Palo Verde Valley Times* letter to the editor:

> We at Clancy Osborne Realty would like to thank everyone who participated in our recent open house. . . . We owe special thanks to Theresa Kelm. When we asked Theresa if she would be interested in finding volunteers to help with serving of the food for a $500 donation to

Uriah Alexander's family, we expected her to follow through, but . . . the number of people who showed up and their willingness to work was extraordinary. . . .[6]

The receptionist at Sunset Kaiser stood. "Don and Mara Alexander? I'm sorry you had to wait. We have to take care of the patients first."

"That's OK. We're used to waiting."

A handsome man with dark hair and intense eyes reached out to shake our hands. "I'm Dr. Falk. I'm glad you could come." We followed him to his office and he motioned us to a corner group.

He's sitting with us instead of distancing himself behind his desk. What happened to his professional detachment? Isn't he afraid of becoming involved with patients who are likely to die? I like this doctor.

"What would you like to know?" he asked briskly.

I pulled a notebook from my bag. "Can you tell us the difference in the success rates of autologous versus unrelated donor transplants?"

His eyes registered surprise. He regarded us carefully, as if gauging our understanding and emotional strength. "Normally, I'm the first contact people have when a transplant is an option, and generally the parents have no idea what is involved. This is refreshing!

"Very little work has been done with matched unrelated donor [MUD] transplants and auto [autologous] transplants, and any estimate would be a supposition. A SIB [sibling] transplant is best, and a MUD transplant is better because there's no leukemia in the marrow, and graft versus host disease [GVHD] seems to result in a lower relapse rate. In an autologous transplant there is no GVHD.

"I'm least comfortable with an autologous transplant with ALL, but in the future it will probably be done a lot. Eventually all transplants will be autologous but not until something new besides the current treatment is available. Only one out of five autologous transplants is successful, but not in the long run; there is a return of the disease in nearly all cases. Some fall out of remission after years in the clear."

This is great! We have come to a man who has answers— and is willing to share them, even if they're unpleasant.

"There's something worse than not having a transplant," Dr. Falk warned us. "A failed MUD is worse than a failed autologous transplant and worse than chemotherapy. If the donor's marrow is not a close enough match, the white blood cells produced by it will consider Uriah an invader and attack every part of him. It is a tortuous, agonizing, slow death.

"Then there's the possibility the marrow might not engraft—that it might fail to attach and never produce blood cells. If an autologous transplant is done, back-up marrow is harvested in the event the bone marrow is damaged and won't engraft. In a MUD transplant, medication is given to encourage engraftment, but if it's not effective, the patient will die, most likely of multiple infections."

"How many autologous transplants have been performed?"

"Hundreds. Maybe eight hundred; probably not a thousand. If you want an autologous transplant, you should let me know as soon as possible because I will need time to reserve space and schedule Uriah at Children's Hospital; otherwise, it can't be done until after Thanksgiving. If he's free of infection, the transplant could be accomplished in four or five days, with three to four weeks needed for marrow regeneration. There's no guarantee it will work, however."

"Is it possible to store the bone marrow so we can look for a donor until he relapses, and do an autologous transplant at that point?"

"We can't store the bone marrow. He can have only one kind of transplant, and it's very unlikely a donor would be found during the autologous procedure. There might not be sufficient marrow to get enough cells in one draw, but it would be better to draw twice than to risk taking him off chemotherapy—especially in Uriah's case. The best advice is to find an unrelated donor, but not to wait too long to do it."

"Are there any other options?"

"Some people, such as Dana Farber in Boston, are working with monoclonal antibodies, but their success rates seem no better." He sighed. "No one knows the best way to do an autologous transplant. There's no difference in the success rates of treated and untreated marrow transplants."

"Why do they purge bone marrow then?"

"Simply because [bad cells are] there, even though purging takes out good cells too, and it may not engraft after the treatment." He shook his head. "A small number don't reengraft—even in MUD transplants."

It sounds scary. All that effort and Uriah could still die. It's inevitable without a transplant though.

"I don't want you to make a decision right away," he said. "I don't want to hear from you until at least three days have passed. If you choose to proceed with the autologous transplant, Uriah's marrow will be harvested at Kaiser, purged at Children's Hospital, and reinfused into Uriah at Kaiser. If you choose to go with a MUD transplant, it will take four to six weeks from the time you locate the donor until the transplant takes place, and it will be done at Children's Hospital."

I hesitated. *This question seems bold, but we need the advice of someone knowledgeable.* "Dr. Falk, what would you do if Uriah were your son?"

He reflected for a moment. "An autologous transplant wouldn't be possible if Uriah relapses, so I would wait four to six weeks, and if no donor had been found by then, I would proceed with the autologous transplant."

"I'm concerned about the three weeks it will take to get everything in place for an autologous transplant. What if Uriah relapses?"

"Three weeks won't make a difference; if he's that close to a relapse, the autologous transplant wouldn't work anyway."

"Thanks for all your help," I shook his hand. "At least now we can make an informed choice."

We drove home in silence. *God, a failed MUD transplant is the worst way to die. Don't allow us to find a donor if it's the wrong thing to do, and prevent the autologous transplant if it's wrong. I'm going to pursue the transplants wholeheartedly, but I want You to prevent them if it's not Your will that they be done.*

I waited three days to call Dr. Falk. "We would like the autologous transplant done before Thanksgiving, if possible."

He consulted his schedule. "There's lab time available November 14 and November 21. The best course of action is to draw the marrow on November 21, have Uriah spend a great Thanksgiving with family, and return the following Monday to begin the transplant."

The first step for the autologous transplant was a bone-marrow test. Dr. Haghighat drew Uriah's bone marrow. "Call later today for results," he said.

That afternoon Margarita answered the phone. "I'm sorry. Dr. Haghighat was admitted to the hospital with a medical problem. There's no one here who can read the results."

"I hope he feels better," I said. I hung up the phone. *This is an outrage! Only a week ago I got a letter assuring me they have enough personnel.* I called membership services and complained. "My child's life could depend on the results, and another Kaiser doctor is waiting for the results."

Dr. Haghighat called from the hospital the following day. "The marrow is normal."

Someone else should have done this! "Thanks, Dr. Haghighat. I hope you feel better."

The following week, Dr. Olson came to the clinic periodically.

Mrs. Maly made the long trip to visit Uriah in the hospital, bringing papers from school. The children learned the banner symbols for the twelve disciples and designed one for themselves. A huge rainbow blazed across Uriah's. "This doesn't surprise me," Julie said.

October 24, the *Palo Verde Valley Times:*

Students make cranes

Margaret White School fourth grade students folded 1,000 paper cranes for Uriah Alexander, the Blythe boy who is battling leukemia. The students got the idea from the novel, "Sadako and the Thousand Paper Cranes," which is about a Japanese girl who developed leukemia after the atom bomb was dropped in her home town of Hiroshima. In the story Sadako Sasaki started folding cranes because of the ancient Japanese legend which says the crane lives for 1,000 years and anyone who folds a 1,000 cranes will live a very long time.

Fourth grade teachers, Tracee Sudyka and Judy Williams, introduced the novel and the art of origami paper folding to their students who diligently folded cranes in an attempt to lift the spirits of Uriah. . . . Many students spend their recess and lunch times making the origami cranes. Others folded cranes when they got home from school. Some students folded as many as forty cranes a day. The goal to fold 1,000 cranes was met in only four days. . . .[7]

Grandma Ruth brought Uriah a folder from the school where she worked:

Uriah,

My fourth-grade class heard that you would like to get some letters! Here are my students' biographies. We would like to hear from you!

Mrs. Smith's Fourth Grade,
Walnut School, Chino, CA

I read the biographies to Uriah. He sighed, "Mom, can I wait until I feel better?"

I nodded. *Maybe when he's in isolation after his transplant, he can write to them. We've got to find that elusive donor before it's too late.*

October 24

I phoned Don at lunchtime from the hospital. "Children's Hospital has DR typed five more potential donors. It cost $2,100, and Kaiser has paid only $91, but at least they're starting to pay."

"Well, prison administration put a letter of instruction in my file because of that inmate scuffle months ago. It says it's 'not to be considered adverse action,' but it's a black mark against me. I didn't do anything wrong, but there's not much I can do about it. There's just too much going on."

I attended the parent support-group planning meeting that evening.

"There's a video tape that prepares children for bone-marrow and spinal-tap procedures that could be purchased for the clinic," Renee Buonocore said. "If any parents have publications that might make a useful addition to the literature available in the clinic, please bring them in."

"Perhaps we could start a library of donated books," a parent suggested.

"Before we plan anything," said Heidi Walker, "you need to know that none of the doctors or I can lead this support group, and you can't meet at Kaiser without an employee leading it."

"We really want to have meetings at Kaiser," another parent said. The other parents nodded.

"What if we asked the nurses if they would lead the group?" asked Linda Pietz. "There's so much we could do. Like having a speaker every other month, a parent-support phone tree, and maybe one for the teens."

"How about crafts for the kids while they're at the clinic?" asked another.

"Or in the hospital?" added another.

"Or volunteers to give parents at the hospital a break for lunch or give 'survival baskets' to parents of new patients?"

"How about a clinic treasure chest?"

"And who's going to do the Christmas parties and summer picnics after Mariposas disbands?"

A task force to find employees to lead the group was formed. "I'll take this information back to Dr. Sanmarco," Heidi promised, "and we'll set up another meeting after the task force reports."

Thursday, October 25

"How's the typing coming for Uriah?" I asked Jan at Children's Hospital.

"One person was unavailable," she said, "one person didn't match, and there's one new partial match."

Theresa put out a flier:

. . . There is a brand-new partial match in the registry for Uriah.

This Tuesday, October 30, Uriah will be tested to see if he is still in remission and then receive his chemotherapy. His infection in his catheter cleared up Friday. . . .

Just knowing that over a thousand people have been added to the national registry, and that at least three people have already benefited from this drive, and that so many people have been so caring is a comfort to them. *However, the Alexanders are not giving up hopes of finding an unrelated donor.* . . . if he has any degree of relapse, an autologous transplant would no longer be an option, and an unrelated donor would be his only hope!

"I've tried to explain what's happening to Uriah's classmates," Julie Maly said. "Can you write something that would explain it to the children?" She sent my simplified explanation home with her students:

Leukemia

Inside the bones of all people there is a liquid called bone marrow. The bone marrow makes blood cells—white cells, red cells, and platelets. The white cells fight germs, the red cells carry food and oxygen to all parts of your body, the platelets plug up any cuts or scrapes so only a little blood leaks out.

Sometimes something goes wrong with the bone marrow. No one knows why yet. Some of the blood cells stay little and can't do their job. These little cells make more little cells and crowd out the cells that are trying to do their job. This makes the person tired and pale. They also get sick a lot. But no one else can catch the bad cells by being close to that person.

Doctors give people with bad cells medicine that kills the cells that are crowding out the good cells. Some good cells die too, though. Sometimes the person has to stay away from other people because they don't have enough good cells to fight germs.

Sometimes the medicine is enough to make a person with leukemia well again. But sometimes their bone marrow keeps making bad cells even though they take their medicine. When that happens, the person needs new bone marrow.

The new bone marrow needs to be exactly like their old bone marrow, but without any bad cells. The person's brother or sister is usually the best person to get new bone marrow from, but if they don't have the same kind of bone marrow, that won't work. Then the doctors look for someone else with the same bone marrow as the person who is sick. It is very hard to find someone that has the same bone marrow, so the doctors use a computer.

If the doctors find someone with the same kind of bone marrow as the person who is sick, they ask if they can use some. If the person says yes, they put the person to sleep and take some bone marrow out of their bones with a big needle. They take only enough for the sick person and leave lots for the person who gives some away.

If they can't find anyone with the same bone marrow, they can take some bone marrow from the sick person, take out any bad cells they find, and use the cleaned bone marrow for the new bone marrow.

They give the sick person medicine that kills all their old bone marrow. Then they put the new bone marrow in with a needle. It takes a long time for the new bone marrow to grow enough to make all the cells the sick person will need, so they have to stay in the hospital a long, long time. But if the new bone marrow likes living in the sick person, it will grow and grow.

Then that person won't be sick with leukemia anymore, and they won't have to take medicine for it anymore. Then they will be strong and well, just like you and me!

Saturday, October 27

C/O (Chaplain) Z. Turmezei had met Don for only a few minutes in September at the prison, but they discovered they had the same training officer when they worked for the Chino Police Department. "I found out about Uriah only this morning, and my wife and I are praying for his—and your—healing."

God, You've woven such special people into our lives.

The *Chuckawalla Chatter* prison newsletter:

Chicano Correctional Workers Association

On October 28, a Halloween fund-raising party for Uriah Alexander was given at Don Julian's Restaurant. $100.00 was raised from this event. A $25.00 donation was also received from CCWA Tehachapi.[8]

Tuesday, October 30

At the parent support-group task-force meeting, a lot of good ideas were shared: a bereavement group, adult speakers who had cancer as a child, PR to make the community aware of our kids, a direct blood-donor pool, an NMDP speaker, craft Saturdays for all kids, and a December auction of kids' crafts done in the clinic. My heart was heavy. I probably won't be able to be a part of this. If Uriah continues to be treated, I have a reason to come to Fontana; if he dies, my family will need me.

Wednesday, October 31

"Monday we went in for testing," my sister Joanna said. "We were numbers fifty-three and fifty-four at Pelican Bay. Sue went later and she was number 106, so we tested OK, I think."

Sixteen

Thy Will Be Done
(Nov. 1990)

*Faith healed those who waited for the angel
to stir the water of the pool by the Sheep Gate. . . .*

November 1

I APPROACHED THE BOARD OF DIRECTORS REGARDING YOUR HUGE phone bill. Please use the enclosed check toward that bill. Don, Mara, our love and best wishes are with you and the family.

Charleene Corby

"I'm not old enough to donate," teenage Mike Steiger of Rancho Cucamonga told Uriah, "but I read about you in the paper and wondered, would you like to see my baseball-card collection?"

"That sounds like fun!"

Tim showed Uriah his cards and explained the fine points of collecting. "This magazine gives the going price for each card."

"I brought some of mine with me," Uriah said. "How much is this one worth?"

"Let's see. Here it is: nineteen dollars."

"Wow!" Uriah regarded his card with new respect.

"Would you like some duplicate cards I don't want any-more?"

"Sure."

"Here's a couple boxes to keep them in."

Mike wrote to Orel Hershiser about Uriah, hoping the baseball star might donate a signed baseball card to be raffled. A check from Orel Hershiser came in the mail. *I always thought of famous people as being too self-centered and busy to care about ordinary people. Orel proved me wrong. There are decent folk in all walks of life—even the rich and famous!*

On Friday, November 2, Uriah and I were ushered to the front of the auditorium for the 101st Sheriff's Academy Class graduation. "You'll be called up on stage," I said. Uriah gazed back at the people crowded in the huge hall. "I'll go with you if you want me to," I added.

Near the end of the program, Brent Nelson took the microphone. "Over the last eighteen weeks we've had many special guests and dignitaries come to the academy, but one has touched the hearts of all of us in a very special way. Uriah Alexander, although only eight years old, suffers from leukemia and came to us through the Make-A-Wish foundation. Though small in stature, he has the heart of a lion, full of life and the will to live. Uriah, would you please come up here?" The room exploded in applause, and the graduates rose. Uriah motioned me to stay in my seat and marched up the steps, dwarfed by the vast stage but unintimidated.

"It is a . . . privilege for us to present Uriah with a class T-shirt and a plaque, making him an official member of the 101st Class San Bernardino Sheriff's Academy." On the bronze plate at the bottom of the large walnut plaque shone: URIAH ALEXANDER, HONORARY MEMBER 101ST SESSION, SAN BERNARDINO COUNTY SHERIFF'S ACADEMY, NOVEMBER 2, 1990, SECOND TO NONE.

Uriah filed outside with his fellow graduates and stood at attention in his sheriff's shirt and hat until dismissed.

The *Inland Valley Daily Bulletin,* November 5, 1990:

Bone-marrow donor recounts emotional bond with recipient

by Peggy Olsen
Daily Bulletin

> Kirk McVey signed up for the chance of a lifetime.
>
> The opportunity came. His bone marrow was harvested by doctors at the City of Hope Medical Center, flown to Washington State, and transplanted into a young leukemia victim.
>
> . . . The physical side effects, he said, are minimal. "But no one is prepared for the emotional tie you feel for the recipient."
>
> ". . . You're told you can back out at any time if you're not comfortable," McVey said. "I just can't imagine anyone doing that. Once you make that commitment, you couldn't pull the chance from someone."[1]

Young leukemia victim is living "on borrowed time"

By Peggy Olsen
Daily Bulletin

> The clock still ticks.
>
> But 8-year-old leukemia victim Uriah Alexander lives on borrowed time.

Unless a bone-marrow donor surfaces by Nov. 21, Uriah's chance for survival hinges on an autologous transplant—an experimental procedure with only 10 to 20 percent chance of success.

"That means they harvest Uriah's own marrow. It's only been tried eight [hundred] times before," said Mara Alexander, Uriah's mother. "The doctor who does autologous transplants said the chances are much better with an unrelated donor. . . ."

"Time is running out," Alexander said. "He really is living on borrowed time."

If the autologous transplant is necessary, doctors will harvest Uriah's bone marrow on Nov. 21 and complete the transplant after Thanksgiving.

"That's if he is still in complete, 100-percent remission. They can't do it otherwise," said Alexander.

Alexander's fear is that Uriah will suffer a relapse at any moment. "Doctors are getting concerned he's near the end of remission," she said. "They don't say anything to him, but he notices they're nervous. Kids pick up on those things."

One last attempt to find a marrow donor is scheduled Nov. 8 at Calvary Chapel of Ontario. Blood samples will be taken from prospective donors to determine a possible match. Further tests are required if initial tests are positive. Appointments for testing may be made by calling.

Blood samples have been taken from residents of Rancho Cucamonga, Lake Arrowhead, and Blythe who responded to Uriah's plight. In addition, there are about 200,000 prospective donors listed in the National Marrow Donor Program's registry. But there is no match for Uriah.

Nevertheless, Alexander said her son maintains his cheerful disposition.[2]

A CPOF flier mailed November 7 had a photo taken while Uriah was in the hospital. His eyes were black from bruising caused by low platelets. He wore no shirt, and his catheter and IV were visible.

Uriah—Gift of Life

. . . time is of the essence. . . . Below are listed the dates, times, and locations of our next major blood testing program. Our goal is to test 300 each day. . . .We are pleased that the Administration and Staff at Galt are working with the CPO Foundation to help the URIAH FUND FOR LIFE work. Please won't you take the few minutes to help us SAVE URIAH?
Galt Academy
Tuesday, November 13, 1990
Wednesday, November 14, 1990

Donors at Calvary Chapel of Ontario on November 8 wrote amazing things:

This is better than the lottery! I hope I'm the lucky one. God bless you, we love you.

Love,
Robin Sherrill

Hold on to the Lord, for through Him all things are possible. My baby sis at 18 months went through leukemia and she is now 13 years old and very beautiful. I will be praying for you. Love you.

Janera

I wish you could see all the people here just for you. You are a special little man. Maybe someday we'll meet. If not here, I'll see you in heaven. I'll save you a seat when I get there. God bless you, little man. Hang tough.

Love,
Larry, Kristian, and Jacob

The ophthalmologist examined Uriah before the transplant. "Uriah has cataracts in both eyes, but they don't extend into the nerve or retina. There are also unusual changes in the lens—cornea. I wonder if they're caused by the chemotherapy? I want to follow up on them."

"He's going in for a bone-marrow transplant, and I don't know how long he may be in isolation," I said, trying to convey more than I said.

The doctor turned to me. "I'll . . . make a return appointment for four months instead of two."

The *Palo Verde Valley Times:*

No match for Uriah so far

Another testing date is being planned for possible marrow donors in 29 Palms. To date, with all the funds collected, 1,137 people have tested and been put into the national registry of bone-marrow donors.

. . . Three people have found matches through this drive but, so far, there has not been a match for Uriah.

Of the five people that were possible matches for Uriah, only one went for additional testing. The results were negative.

Uriah is back in the hospital now, suffering from a low blood count and an infection caused by his catheter. They had earlier estimated that the chemotherapy administered to him in September would only hold him in remission until the end of November.

Uriah's doctors are now considering the autologous process. . . .[3]

When Uriah got home, he photographed everyone he knew and loved. The crazy photos included church family and friends, nurses, our dogs, cats, and blue-and-gold macaw. *After he goes into his isolation room, nothing can go in until the transplant is all over. Just seeing pictures of all the family and friends praying for him might give him encouragement when his spirits sag.*

We celebrated Shiloh, Andria, and Brian's birthdays with a barbecue at Janet's house. We walked around Lake Gregory, and I videotaped the children as they teased and raced. They squirted each other with the drinking fountain, then raced on, wetter and cooler. The kids chased Janet's dogs and vice versa. Too soon we found ourselves trudging across the empty parking lot to the cares we had left behind.

We weren't the only ones struggling with tragedy in the midst of the holidays. Another family lost their six-year-old daughter, Wendy, in a traffic accident. William worked at the prison with Don. He and his wife Rosa visited us in Blythe.

The school district newsletter:

We would like to express our deepest sympathy to our friend and colleague, Rosa, an instructional aide. We offer this in hopes that it will bring you comfort and peace:

I'll Lend You a Child

"I'll lend you for a little time a child of mine," He said.
"For you to love while he lives, and mourn for when he's dead.
It may be six or seven years or twenty-two or three,

But will you, till I call him back, take care of him for Me?
He'll bring his smiles to gladden you, and should his stay be brief,
   You'll have his lovely memories as solace for your grief.
I cannot promise he will stay, since all from earth return,
But there are lessons taught down there I want this child to learn.
I've looked this wide world over in my search for teachers true,
And from the throngs that crowd life's lanes, I have selected you.
Now will you give him all your love, nor count the labor vain,
   Nor hate Me when I come to call to take him back again?"

I fancied that I heard them say, "Dear Lord, Thy will be done.
For all the joy Thy child shall bring, the risk of grief we'll run.
We'll shelter him with tenderness, we'll love him while we may,
   And for the happiness we've known forever grateful stay.
But should the angels call for him much sooner than we've planned,
   We'll brave the bitter grief that comes and try to understand.

—Author Unknown

Henry Urquizu, head of Social Services at Kaiser, met with the support group's task force November 13. "Heidi and Chris—department administrator at pediatrics—and I are trying to coordinate an *emotional* support-group after the holidays. Each meeting will start with information about a topic open for parent discussion. Part of the meeting can be used for activities. Chris is willing to lead the group."

Linda Pietz asked, "Can we meet at Kaiser to coordinate activities for the children and the support activities the task force talked about?"

"Because of liability, a Kaiser employee has to be present. You'll have to meet off Kaiser grounds if you want to meet before the end of the year. Our focus is on feelings. Perhaps you should form an auxiliary support group."

"More things are necessary for a child's health than just emotional stability."

Henry nodded in agreement. "But you can't interact with the children in the clinic or hospital until you've received training by Renee; the chief of pediatrics' OK for the use of pediatric space; and the OK of all the doctors."

Linda and I exchanged glances. *This is a dead end.*

"Will the emotional support group meet in the clinic?" LaVonne asked.

"It would be better in a conference room. We'll send a letter shortly with meeting information. Call Social Services for information for your flier."

"What about the time for activities?" I asked.

"You can use the last fifteen minutes of the meeting. Speakers can address emotional issues only. If you want to look into new treatments, you'll have to have the speaker come another night after you've contacted medical personnel to be there."

"Can packets of information for parents of newly diagnosed patients be created and passed out?" Linda asked.

"The materials will have to come out of the budget of the department providing them. Social Services might be able to fund a limited number."

"But information is free from sources like the American Cancer Society."

"All information will have to be approved by Dr. Sanmarco."

"What about a bereavement group?"

"That should be part of the auxiliary."

I walked Linda and LaVonne to their cars. "I wonder if the next meeting will be a support-group meeting or a support-group formation meeting? Do you realize it took us five months of meetings to get to this point? What did you think about the meeting?"

"I think it's clear, the answer is *no, no, no,*" Linda said. "Nothing we really want to do is going to be allowed. As far as I'm concerned, it's the death of the support group."

After the next support-group meeting, I had to agree with Linda. Only a few parents attended those meetings because they were for those with problems. Those who were coping well and wanted to help the children weren't interested.

Tuesday, November 13

"Your account with Children's Hospital of Los Angeles has been turned over to a collection agency."

I'm so frustrated. Perhaps the collections people can help sort things out. I called them.

"This kind of thing happens all the time with Kaiser," the gal from Medac said. She was able to get the two parties to cooperate immediately. The next billing showed the balance had been paid.

Friday, November 16

Uriah's pretransplant testing continued with another muga-scan. His heart function had gone from 65 percent to 55 percent—still normal, but the Daunomycin had affected it. Another test in the pulmonary clinic measured his lung capacity and strength.

November 16, the *Palo Verde Valley Times:*

Uriah . . .

A drive spanning from community wide to worldwide has not yet turned up a match for a bone-marrow transplant. Uriah and his parents, Don and Mara Alexander, are still hopeful, but the autologous procedure at this point will have to be conducted in the event that a donor match is not found.[4]

Uriah had hoarded large syringes without needles. One day he filled them all from the water pitcher. When nurse Kathy walked in, he soaked her and giggled. Kathy fled. I heard her voice in the hall, "Barb, you've got to go see Uriah."

Barbara cautiously opened the door, but Uriah's aim was good. She shut the door. "Gee, thanks, Kathy."

Kathy reentered the room prepared, with a plastic bag over her uniform and a plastic shield over her face. Behind her, nurse Bob was armed.

"Hey, you can't shoot me!" Uriah said, pointing to his catheter site.

"There's nothing wrong with your foot," replied Bob, dousing it.

They put a sign on Uriah's door: DANGER: ENTERING URIAH'S ROOM! *They can remember Uriah this way—happy and mischievous—if things don't go well. No one's spoken that thought, but we all know it.*

Monday, November 19
Tomorrow Uriah will go into Kaiser Sunset for his transplant. All the tests are done, except today's bone-marrow test.

Dr. Haghighat sighed after looking at the slides. "I'm sorry. Uriah's in 70 percent relapse."

I cried for a while. *God, I'm so disappointed. But I prayed that You wouldn't let it happen if it shouldn't.*

Uriah's response was typical. "Well, let's go out and get Kentucky Fried Chicken!" So we did.

While I waited for the doctor to admit him, I let people know. "He's supposed to be in for weeks, and they don't think the high-dose methotrexate will reinduce remission."

"We don't have the medicine here," the nurse said while she set up Uriah's IV. "His treatment won't start until Wednesday."

I opened the hospital bag and took out the holy water in a plastic bottle fashioned to look like Mary, the mother of Jesus, which someone had sent us. "N. D. de Lourdes" said the base. I anointed Uriah with it. *Faith healed those who waited for the angel to stir the water of the pool by the Sheep Gate in John 5:2–9. We have faith.*

November 20

I just wanted to inform you that we tested another 160 at the CDC Galt Academy this past Tuesday and Wednesday.

Love and best wishes,
Char

Dr. Haghighat came to Uriah's room Tuesday. "Would you like to take Uriah home for Thanksgiving and return Thursday night or Friday for the treatment?"

"That sounds good, but I need to talk to Don about it first. He's at a doctor's appointment to make sure his cough isn't contagious."

Don and I went to the clinic an hour later. "Don's cough isn't contagious, so we'd like to take Uriah home for Thanksgiving," I told Dr. Sanmarco.

"We should wait longer to start the treatment so you can take him to Knott's Berry Farm on Friday," Dr. Sanmarco said. "He will never be in good condition again after it. Since he can't have a bone-marrow transplant, we should consider just stopping the treatment and making him comfortable, concentrating on quality of life."

Don looked pale and dazed when we left. We stopped at the waiting area by pediatrics. "Don, we need to talk." He stared into the wall, unheeding. I touched his arm. "You've got to snap out of it. It may not be all over yet." He turned to me as if numb, but his eyes showed comprehension once more. "The first thing we need is more information." I tried to call Dr. Falk, Jan Cipkala-Gaffin, and Margo to no avail. I sat down again, frustrated.

My first experience with death sprang to mind. As with most children, it was the death of a beloved pet—a snow white guinea pig with black ears, called Snowflake. She'd been my confidant, sharing my tears and joys, since I was eight. She grew old and so fragile I changed soft rags in the bottom of her cage daily and tempted her to eat fruits and vegetables. A couple days after my junior-high graduation, she was in trouble. I was so upset my father sent me out of my room while he gently lifted her frail body. I sat on the couch in the living room and prayed with all my twelve-year-old heart. *God, I need her. Please, please don't let her die!* The Spirit of God gently touched me. *I'm being selfish. Why should she continue suffering just because I need her? What would be best for her? God, You know.* With an effort of will, I released her into God's hands. *God, do what is right. If she should die, take good care of her until I get there.*

As soon as the words flew from my heart, my father called from the bedroom. "Mara, I'm sorry. I thought she was going to be all right, but she just stopped breathing."

God, You waited to take her until my faith could grow enough to let go and trust You to take care of her. It was no coincidence, and I'll never forget Your mercy.

But is this the same? Are we really at that point yet? Is it time for Uriah to go already?

I turned to Don. "Help me reason it out. Do we want him home for Thanksgiving?"

"Yes."

"I agree. Do we want to go to Knott's Berry Farm on Friday? Joanna and Mark won't be out until after Monday. Are we ready to give up? Or more important, is Uriah ready to give up?"

"No, I don't think so."

"Then brace yourself. We need to go back and let them know we want the treatment started Friday."

We embraced. Then with hands clasped, we rose with renewed purpose.

"But I thought we would just keep Uriah comfortable since a bone-marrow transplant isn't possible," Dr. Sanmarco said.

"I tried to call Dr. Falk," I said, "but we weren't able to get through. We don't want to make a decision until we talk to him. For today, we would like to take Uriah home for Thanksgiving."

"I'll call Dr. Falk tomorrow," Dr. Haghighat said.

"I'll call him too," I said.

"Well, I know he won't say that it's impossible. He will say, 'Let's see,'" said Dr. Sanmarco.

"Well then, let's see!" I said.

Tommy Li of the *Sun* came to the hospital. After he talked to Uriah, he and I met Dr. Sanmarco in the hall. "I don't know what you want me to say," she told me.

November 21, *The Sun:*

Leukemia patient suffers fourth relapse
By Tommy Li

FONTANA—Uriah Alexander, an eight-year-old boy suffering from leukemia, may be facing his last Thanksgiving.

For months, the Blythe boy has been seeking a compatible bone-marrow donor for a transplant that would help him battle the disease.

On Monday, he went into his fourth relapse, according to a diagnosis made at Kaiser Permanente Medical Center in Fontana.

"It's not a real good scenario," said his mother, Mara. "He could have a reaction to the chemotherapy and be gone tomorrow.

"Everything that they do from this point on hasn't been tried a lot of times. It's kind of a last ditch effort."

. . . Because new medication would most likely produce severe side effects, doctors have decided to postpone treating Uriah until after Thanksgiving, Alexander said. . . .

Alexander, 31, who also has two daughters, has been determinedly optimistic since her son was first diagnosed with the cancer at 14 months of age.

"It's never too late until it's all finished. There's still some time. . . . You just have to take it one day at a time."

Uriah's most recent remission lasted four months. . . . Family and friends organized a number of blood testing drives throughout the county to locate a donor, but none was found. The National Marrow Donor Program is investigating two possible matches in the United States and France, Alexander said.

But even if the right donor were found now, Uriah would have to be in remission to undergo the transplant.

On Tuesday, before leaving his room at Kaiser to spend Thanksgiving at his grandmother's home in Lake Arrowhead, Uriah was eager to be with his family.

He was looking forward not to turkey, but to a ham dinner.

"I think just being with the family is special," his mother said. "The thing he's going to need is to remember that people love him."

After having Thanksgiving dinner, Uriah is scheduled to return to Kaiser on Thursday night for testing.

And everyone, including his doctor, will begin hoping for yet another remission, even though they don't know the odds.

"It's hard to tell," said Uriah's doctor, Alba Sanmarco. "There's no answer. Only God knows."[5]

November 21, the *Palo Verde Valley Times:*

Uriah needs your prayers

Eight-year-old Uriah, . . . is out of remission and has relapsed. To date, testing of prospective donors has failed to turn up a match for Uriah, and doctors had scheduled an autologous transplant (removing Uriah's own marrow, cleansing it, and injecting it back into the body) beginning today. The relapse, determined on Monday, rules out this procedure.

. . . Cards and letter may be sent to Kaiser Hospital. "The cards brighten up his room and, other than that, he just needs your prayers," his mother Mara said.[6]

Below the article was a photo by Howard Decker of children coloring cards in a classroom. "**Cards for Uriah—** Students of Mrs. Sudyka's fourth grade class at Margaret White School prepare greeting cards to send to Uriah Alexander, who has to spend Thanksgiving in a hospital room far from home."[7]

Uriah's classmates at Zion also wrote to him.

The *Palo Verde Valley Times:*

Recognize the specialness

Editor:

Often we measure the quality of life by numbers and amounts, the length of life we live, and the amount of things we are able to accumulate during that time. Another way of measuring quality may be seen in what we have accomplished with our life.

I would like to suggest that Uriah Alexander in his short life and even shorter time in Blythe has sparked some tremendous achievements. The people of Blythe need to be highly praised for how they have responded to a call for help. It seems obvious as a community we have risen to this call. But there is more happening in the life of our community than our response. Uriah has blessed all of us with his life. He has helped us as much, if not more, than we have helped him and his family. Uriah has enabled us to see what we are capable of becoming as a community. He has helped us see the heights we can rise to as human beings in our relationships to one another when we care about people as our first priority.

We as a community need to thank Uriah and his family for who we have become together, even if it is only for a moment in time.

Lastly, we do pray for a quality of life that will continue for years for Uriah. We all recognize the significance of every single gift of life in this world, and its specialness to us all. Look what one seven-year-old boy has done for us. If we did not recognize this specialness in life, would we all be working so hard to save one?

George C. Cushman, Pastor
Community United Methodist Church[8]

On Wednesday, November 21 Jan Cipkala-Gaffin reported to me, "There's no new information about the donors we're waiting on, but five more people from England matched on the A and B loci. Dr. Lenarsky would still be willing to do a bone-marrow transplant if they can get Uriah into remission."

Dr. Falk returned my call: "How are you?"

"We're fine."

"I hope you aren't too fine or I'll be worried."

"All I mean is that Uriah is out of the hospital, feeling fine, and we're looking forward to a nice family Thanksgiving tomorrow."

"I talked to Dr. Haghighat. He has some plans to get Uriah back into remission."

"I'm glad you aren't saying it's time to give up, because they were talking about quitting, and we aren't ready to give up."

His voice became strident and angry. "Let me give you some good advice. Try what Hush has and we'll see, but don't rake your kid over hot coals."

I was bewildered. "Is a bone-marrow transplant still possible if they can get him into remission?"

"I wouldn't rule it out, but let's see."

I hung up the phone, humbled.

Dr. Haghighat answered my call to the hospital. "Uriah responded twice before to a Daunomycin induction, and I think it would be worth trying one more time. That way Uriah will be in good condition for Thanksgiving, and if it doesn't work, we can always go to the high-dose methotrexate treatment next. We could start his treatment today, before Thanksgiving."

Thanks, God. I'm glad Dr. Haghighat hasn't given up.

The first few days all went well, but the day Dr. Haghighat was gone, Dr. Sanmarco told me, "Uriah's liver enzymes are high. I don't know whether it's caused by the leukemia or the medication. The only way to tell is to do a bone marrow."

She did the test. "Uriah's in remission. That means it's the medication, and I don't know what we can do for him in that case."

Uriah smiled. "At least I know I'm responding!" he chirped.

When we returned to the clinic after lunch, Dr. Haghighat was in the cubicle where they examined bone-marrow samples, counting leukemia cells one by one. He approached us. "Uriah is still 12 percent relapsed."

Dr. Sanmarco, Dr. Haghighat, and I sat in his office, discussing possible courses of action. *He's taking three things that are hard on the liver: Erwinia (for L-asparginase), Allopurinal, and a sulfa drug to prevent infection. They can't give him the Erwinia shot he's due for. They want to repeat the liver enzyme test in a week. They can continue prednisone and give him one more shot of vincristine.* "No decision needs to be made about taking him off chemotherapy right now," I said. "Let's keep him on prednisone and see what happens when he returns for his shot of vincristine; the liver enzymes might go down."

The enzymes dropped from 1,192 to 364 in one week! He got his shot of vincristine, and I began tapering his prednisone. *He's due for a bone-marrow test in a week. I don't see how it can possibly be good.*

November 29

Victim hopes for a miracle

By Peggy Olsen
Daily Bulletin

Eight-year-old leukemia victim Uriah Alexander is still hoping for the bone-marrow transplant that could save his life. . . .

"The doctors say it's still possible to do the (unrelated donor) transplant if we can find a donor and if we can get him into remission again.

"We know the chances are astronomical. But we just can't sit back and wait. He says he's not ready to give up yet."

A final drive to find a donor is set December 17 from noon to 5 P.M. at First Baptist Church in Montclair. For information and appointments, call Lena Harrell.

. . . A course of chemotherapy that was previously successful is being used in an effort to effect another remission, Mara Alexander said.

"He feels pretty good. But he knows he needs a donor. He says it's the only thing he wants for Christmas."[9]

November 30

. . . Last year at this time, there were approximately 65,000 volunteers in the National Marrow Donor Program Registry. Today there are over 230,000, and the number continues to grow each day. This growth is largely the result of your efforts and those of others who have undertaken community recruitment of marrow donor volunteers.

Sincerely yours,
Bruce Casselton

Fund Name: Uriah Alexander
Contributions: $55,441.78
NMDP Matching Funds: $25,000.00
Total Funds Received: $80,441.78
Costs Incurred: $79,350.00
Funds available for further drives: $1,091.78

DATE	LOCATION	# OF DONORS	COST	CONTRIB.	NMDP MATCH
8/26/90	FONTANA	45	$2,250	45	
8/26/90	BLYTHE	123	$6,150	123	
9/16/90	FONTANA	71	$3,550	71	
9/16/90	BLYTHE	117	$5,850	117	
9/18/90	ARROWHEAD	89	$4,450	89	
9/26/90	RANCHO CUCAMONGA	317	$15,850	158.5	158.5
10/4/90	LOS ANGELES	58	$2,900	29	29
10/4/90	SAN FERNANDO	48	$2,400	24	24
10/11/90	RANCHO CUCAMONGA	271	$13,550	135.5	135.5
10/18/90	ARROWHEAD	60	$3,000	30	30
11/8/90	ONTARIO	170	$8,500	85	85
11/12/90	BLYTHE	18	$900	9	9
12/18/90	TENTATIVE 200		$10,000	171	29
TOTAL	200	1,387	$79,350	1,087	500

God, we've come so much further than I dared dream. There's still a drive to be held and more funds available. Just like loaves and fishes.

Dr. Haghighat handed me a note:

"To whom it may concern: Uriah has terminal leukemia in its final stage."

We used it to arrange a free trip to Knott's Berry Farm for our family and his cousins, Brian and Joel, on November 30. Uriah wore his mask while they fed koi fish, played with animals in the petting zoo, and raced model boats. We screamed on the roller coasters until we were hoarse, went on log rides, and took turns at the shooting gallery. The souvenir Uriah chose was a coonskin cap for keeping his bald head warm.

Kenya Briggs of *KECY Channel 9 News* sent a video copy of the story she did about Uriah to Lori Shay:

11/30/90
Lori,

Please see that Uriah and his family get this tape.
Please wish them my best—my thoughts and hopes are with them.

Kenya Briggs

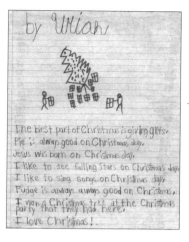

by Uriah

The best part of Christmas is giving gifts.
Pie is always good on Christmas day.
Jesus was born on Christmas day.
I like to see falling stars on Christmas day.
I like to sing songs on Christmas day.
Fudge is always always good on Christmas.
I want a Christmas tree at the Christmas
party that they had here.
I love Christmas!.

Seventeen

All I Want
for Christmas
(Dec. 1990)

Throughout the holiday season,
Uriah has only wished for one thing. . . .

GEORGE KAPLANIS OF THE ARROWHEAD HOLIDAY HILTON OF-
fered to donate two VCRs to help raise funds for Uriah.
"Would you donate them to the clinic?" I asked.

"I'd be glad to, if you can bring me a letter from the
hospital, accepting them," he said.

December 3, 1990

Dear Mr. Kaplanis:
    . . . As you know, our pediatric oncology unit treats
cancer patients ranging from toddlers to teens. . . .

    We were fortunate to have two VCRs for these chil-
dren until recently, when one was stolen from the pediatric unit. Our second is in poor shape due to excessive
use. Two VCRs from the Arrowhead Hilton would be sincerely appreciated. If you have any questions regarding
this matter, please feel free to call me. Happy Holidays!

                                        Renee Buonocore

December 4

A letter to the parent task force from the Mariposas:

"This memo is designed to address the dissolution of the Mariposas Foundation and its disassociation with any parent group now being formed. . . .

"The Mariposas find that . . . their goals are not consistent with the goals of the parent task force, and not wishing to divert interest from such a group, would prefer to cease operating as a support to the families being served here."

Disappointing, but expected.

Butch Hull called December 8: "I'd like to take Uriah for an airplane ride."

Don and Uriah took pictures of our mobile home, the prison, the dam, and the Blythe itaglios. Uriah even flew the plane.

December 10, 1990

. . . The CPO Foundation has been able . . . to set up numerous blood testing facilities across the state in an effort to find a match to save the life of Uriah. As yet, no match has been located for Uriah (we will continue to look), but matches have been found that could save the lives of six or seven other children so afflicted. Our prayers are with each. Our thanks to each one of you that volunteered to be tested, and to those who have so unselfishly given the transplant to save a life. . . .[1]

The employees of GTE adopted us as the family they would play Santa for and sent bags of goodies shortly before Christmas. The kids loved the pogo stick!

Mrs. Maly gave Uriah an award on December 12: "This award is given to Uriah Alexander for a dynamite job in keeping up with schoolwork."

The CCWA of Blythe and Tehachapi sent Christmas cards that contained cash.

Thursday, December 13
      A catastrophic time bank request was made for Don by Lieutenant R. Ryan, because Uriah's time is expected to be short.

First Evangelical Lutheran Church and School in San Fernando sent a check:

We pray that this small showing of our love and concern is of help. Uriah, as well as you two, continue to be in the thoughts and prayers of our students, families, teachers, and church members.

Earl Reynolds

Monday, December 17
      Lena organized a donor drive at First Baptist Church in Montclair, with volunteer phlebotomists from the College of Osteopathic Medicine in Pomona. They tested fifty-five.

When we arrived in Fontana the next day for the Mariposas party, the truck was making bad sounds. "It's the alternator: three hundred sixty-six dollars to fix it," the man at the gas station said.

"One hundred forty dollars for parts and sixty dollars for labor," said the Nissan dealer. "We can do it right away."

"Uriah, we have to get the truck fixed," I said. "We can't stay for the party."

His eyes filled with tears. "But, Mom, this is the last time. I just wanted to see Santa, 'cause this is the last time."

My heart skipped a beat. *Is he giving up?* "What do you mean?"

"Mom, you told me this is the last Mariposas party because they aren't going to do Mariposas anymore."

What a relief!

At the party Meredith's mother told us, "Some reporters have been waiting for you for a long time."

Janet Gilmore of the *Press-Enterprise* asked me a few questions, then interviewed Uriah while the photographer snapped pictures.

I saw Terri, Sami's mom. "Would you watch Uriah at the party so I can get the truck fixed in San Bernardino? I know it's an imposition—"

"No problem!" Terri assured me.

I passed Dr. Haghighat on my way out. "Merry Christmas!"

He smiled. "I have hope."

Hope for Uriah? I paused, uncertain what to say.

"I told the reporter that," he said softly, a twinkle in his eye.

I'm surprised! Dr. Haghighat believes in miracles! He's such a quiet doctor, but he makes every word count. I didn't get a better Christmas present that year than the tiny glow of hope he planted in my heart. *He's not promising everything will work out; he's just letting me know he's hoping with us.*

Wednesday, December 19

Don and I took Uriah for his bone-marrow test. Tracy, a bright three-year old, and her parents were there. She'd relapsed after being off chemotherapy only a month. They were trying to find a donor for her.

Uriah cried during his bone-marrow test. We ate lunch at Sizzler. The weather was cold and windy. It sprinkled. Back at the clinic, the results showed 11–15 percent bad cells.

"Take him everywhere he wants to go and let him do anything he wants," Dr. San Marco said, "because he'll never be in good physical condition again after the high-dose Cytosar." He got a shot of vincristine to slow the relapse, and I got a plan to taper the prednisone and a note for Disneyland and Sea World.

December 21, the *Palo Verde Valley Times:*

Thanks to Blythe

Editor:

I received a call from the *Press-Enterprise* asking about our town's response to the need of Uriah Alexander. I told them that the entire community put on fund-raisers, . . . Over $50,000 was sent to the National Marrow Donor Program for testing, and . . . over 1,500 people will have been added to the national registry. We have received 15 calls from people who said they matched for another person, . . . and the cards, gifts, and financial aid keeps pouring in for the Alexanders.

They asked me why there has been such a tremendous response, . . . and I said the people of Blythe didn't stop to ask, "Why help?" They asked, "How can I help?" But you know, who can explain a miracle? Especially a miracle of love.

Merry Christmas, everyone. You have made Jesus very happy on His birthday! And thank You, God—for working out the details.

Thank you all. Keep it up, Uriah—beat those odds!!!

Theresa Kelm[2]

Boompa got a kit to make tin soldiers, and Uriah helped him make the tiny troopers for hours. Although he received soldiers for his work, the best thing he got was spending time with Boompa. They seemed closer after that day.

In the hospital, the Teenage Mutant Ninja Turtle Donatello brought Uriah a helium balloon and took a photo with him. Outside in the hall, Donatello pulled off his mask. Sweat trickled down Sgt. Clark's face. "I never would have guessed it was you!" I gasped. "Just another of your uniforms, huh?"

He smiled, winked, and became a turtle again.

The week before Christmas, we took Uriah to Disneyland in a wheelchair. He felt good, but he'd lost most of his hair. Uriah went to the petting zoo first and used half his film on "It's a Small World."

Christmas Day:

Boy's wish: the right donor
Many help, but no bone marrow match found

By Janet Gilmore
The Press-Enterprise

Ask 8-year-old Uriah Alexander what gifts he might want for Christmas and you'll get no help. He smiles, looks at you with bright green eyes, and insists that he has no preference for a conventional gift.

And he means it.

Throughout the holiday season, his mother says, Uriah has only wished for one thing: a matching bone-marrow donor.

Uriah has had leukemia since he was 14 months old. He has been in and out of hospitals, in and out of remission, for years. He recently had his fourth, and probably his final, relapse.

But don't get the impression that this is some lonely, solemn little boy. Uriah's bright smile and cheerful manner has carried his parents through tough times and inspired the small town of Blythe to shower him with gifts, encouraging notes, and money to cover costly bone-marrow testings. . . .

Blythe resident Theresa Kelm, the main coordinator of the local fund-raising drive, believes the community responded so dramatically because Blythe is a small, friendly town that rarely gets the opportunity to help a terminally ill child.

Some residents, she said, were just won over by Uriah.

"He has got a dynamic personality," Kelm said. "Uriah's just a sweetheart and just loves people, and they can see that in him."

Practically every building in town contains businesses, organizations, and individuals who have participated in the donor drive, Mara Alexander said.

"I think we've tested just about everyone in the Blythe area who can be tested," she said. "Unfortunately none of them matched."

Uriah's doctor, Hushang Haghighat of Kaiser Permanente Medical Center in Fontana, said identical twins make the best match. Beyond that, it's a long shot.

"It is very unusual to get someone to match," Haghighat said. "A one in 50,000 chance."

Recently, doctors suggested that the Alexanders consider the quality of Uriah's life and weigh whether it's worth it for the boy to keep up his tiring medical battle against the disease.

"We asked Uriah," Mara Alexander recalled, "and he said 'No! I'm not done yet.' He was just angered that we would say that to him."

At times, Alexander says, she wonders whether Uriah's quick, optimistic remarks indicate he isn't dealing with the reality of the situation. But at other times there's little doubt.

Once, she said, he offered her a comforting smile and said, "Mom, I always did want to see heaven."

Uriah is expected to survive through January, perhaps February, she said. Doctors are trying to induce remission through chemotherapy and sustain Uriah in case a matching donor is ever found.

"It's really going to take a miracle at this point," Alexander said. "We do believe in God. We do believe in miracles."

When he has the opportunity, Uriah plays with friends, goes to school, and plays Nintendo. But much of his time has been spent in hospital rooms, undergoing painful spinal taps and chemotherapy.

Uriah said he endures the painful medical treatments because he knows that's the only way the search will continue for a donor. He doesn't readily offer such information; ask him how he's feeling and he smiles and offers a perky: "Fine."

He prefers to keep his mind off depressing thoughts.

"If I think about it," Uriah said during a recent Christmas party at a Fontana church, "I get mad and just lose control, and that's when the leukemia comes back. The best way I get over it is [for others to] leave me alone and after a little while I'll be fine."

Blythe area residents have been inspired by Uriah's hope, and the family's hope, in finding a donor. Those who didn't qualify for testing, because of age or ailments, donated blood and joined with others in sending encouraging notes and participating in fund-raising events.

"The people in Blythe came with everything they had," Alexander said. "It wasn't just someone donating to a cause. People have reached out to Uriah in a very special way."

Residents who meet and talk with Uriah have trouble believing he is so ill, Alexander said, but it's not difficult for her to understand.

"How can you live with despair?" she said. "You can't live without hope."[3]

We went to Marilyn's the Saturday before Christmas. Uriah's mask hung around his neck, but he felt well. He got a flexible, vertical race-car track, and soon Don and everyone's kids were designing impossible loops and racing the cars.

Christmas Day at Nana's cabin with family, everyone opened presents and feasted in defiance of the possibility of Uriah's impending death. Heather got the satin LA Raiders jacket she'd wanted so much. Shiloh and Heather got sterling jewelry with bells. Uriah got baseball cards and paraphernalia. Don folded his new belt in half and snapped it a couple times. With a twinkle in his eye he called, "Heather, help me try out my new belt!" Everyone snickered at the jest.

Debbie gave me a counted cross-stitch of three children building a snowman. The older girl was dark-haired, the younger was blonde, and the little boy wore a coonskin cap.

Boompa modeled the old-fashioned flight goggles Nana gave him.

Inside the pencil case Julie Maly sent was a bookmark. "God bless us, every one." Tiny Tim's words seemed to echo in my heart. *Just having Scrooge care for Tiny Tim was enough, but the whole town of Blythe and other friends are praying for Uriah. I hope it's enough.*

The day after Christmas, Leah and Bob, Grandma Ruth, Don, Heather, Shiloh, Uriah, and I went to the Los Angeles Zoo. *Don's a little irritable. He's apprehensive about Uriah being in public; his mask might not be enough. But it's getting to the point it won't matter anyhow.*

We took the camcorder and filmed the kids popping up among startled groundhogs under plastic bubbles that were landscaped into the display, and we took pictures of them as vampire bats and gazelles at photo spots. At sunset we split up and ran to see favorite animals we'd missed.

Uriah, on Don's shoulders, headed for the exit and waved as he passed the camcorder. Heather modeled Don's hat like a ham when she realized she was being filmed. *We're tired but happy. It's been a good day.*

When we got back to the cabin, Dr. Sanmarco had called. "Something about a donor," Nana said. The *Press-Enterprise* article in Blythe and Riverside had caused a barrage of calls to Theresa and the hospital to find out how to become donors. "We didn't know who to have them call, so we took down their numbers," Dr. Sanmarco said.

"Thanks!" I said. *More people to contact!*

For school, Uriah drew people putting presents under a tree:

> The best part of Christmas is giving gifts.
> Pie is always good on Christmas day.
> Jesus was born on Christmas day.
> I like to see falling stars on Christmas day.
> I like to sing songs on Christmas day.
> Fudge is always good on Christmas.
> I won a Christmas tree at
> the Christmas party that they had here.
> I love Christmas!

December 28, 1990, the *Palo Verde Valley Times:*

Blythe is special

Editor:

It was going to be a pretty bleak Christmas; the worry, grueling schedule, and financial drain had worn us down, and we just weren't in the Christmas mood. But the magic of Christmas—people reaching out to each other in lovingkindness—touched our weary hearts and brought that Christmas spirit to life in us. Someone entered Uriah's name in a drawing for the Christmas tree at the CVSP Spouses Christmas, and he won! Uriah pointed out we couldn't have a real Christmas tree without lights, so we dug out the Christmas boxes and soon our tree was beautiful. But the elves of Blythe weren't through playing Santa yet! Anonymous packages, bags, and Christmas cards with donations for us began to mysteriously appear at Uriah's school and in the homes of close friends. The joy of Christmas in the eyes of a child who still believes in Santa Claus and miracles is such a special gift. We want to say a special heartfelt *thanks!* to all the special elves of Blythe; for once again you have given us a priceless gift that will never fade or tarnish—the memory of a family Christmas that sparkles with the joy and magic of Christmas in spite of adversity. What makes Blythe so special is not its location but the people who live there! Merry Christmas, Blythe! Happy Birthday, Jesus! And God bless us, every one.

Don, Mara, Heather,
Shiloh, and Uriah Alexander[4]

Friday, December 28

I sent the rest of the money in Uriah's bank account to the NMDP.

Uriah went back into the hospital for treatment. Don brought lunch and went to get the truck serviced. Bob and Uriah played Nintendo while Leah and I got food from In-N-Out Burger.

The following day, Renee helped Uriah with a Micro Machines Super City, but he seemed sluggish and had trouble seeing shapes. He lay down to rest before his second dose of Cytosar and Decadron. He was sad and angry. Nothing seemed to please him.

Dr. Sanmarco peeked into the room. "Can I see you a moment, Mrs. Alexander?" She returned to the hallway, and I got up to join her.

"That bothers me," Uriah said.

"His liver enzyme levels are elevated," Dr. Sanmarco told me in the hall. "Eighty over four hundred four yesterday, one hundred ninety-two over five hundred sixty-three today. We're going to repeat the test this afternoon, and if the results are bad, we may have to discontinue the treatment. My thirty years of experience indicate we should not go for broke, and maybe since there is no donor we should just keep him comfortable."

I shifted my weight uncomfortably. "I don't think that will work for him. What will he be put on?"

"I don't know."

"What are normal liver enzymes levels?"

"Thirty over thirty-five is normal, but Uriah's are normally elevated because of chemotherapy. At the highest levels during the Daunomycin induction, they were 1192."

I tried to call Don but got Leah. "Don's gone to buy parts for the truck. Bob and I are taking the girls ice skating and to a movie."

I went back to the room to talk to Uriah. He cried. "I'm so hungry! I don't want to be left alone, but I want you to get me some food."

I went to the vending machines and got him popcorn. "Let's make a list of what I should get you for lunch." Nana and Boompa walked in. "You're an answer to prayer!" I said. *Now someone can stay with Uriah, and I can get his lunch quicker.*

Uriah seemed to perk up, but when Boompa and I got back with lunch, there were tears in Nana's eyes. "He got frustrated when he couldn't get the Nintendo game to work."

"This is bothering me!" he yelled and ripped his hospital bracelet off. He continued to holler until Dr. Sanmarco came in. She tried to tickle him, but he refused to be cheered. He showed her the hospital band he'd torn off. "Maybe they can put it around your ankle," she suggested.

Nana and Boompa gave me a hug before they left. Uriah ate his hot dog and nacho fries and then got angry with his turtle drawing board. "I want to break it into a million pieces or return it!"

That's not like him.

"I want to kill myself or chop the whole room into little pieces!"

Finally he fell asleep. "Boy, I'm sure glad he's asleep," I commented to the nurse.

"Oh, decadron often causes that kind of behavior."

"It's just for nausea, isn't it? Something else should be used next time. I never want to see Uriah like that again."

I called Children's Hospital. "Four people out of seven tested in France. The person in the US didn't match," said Jan. "I'm requesting DR typing for two more people whose preliminary A and B typing match Uriah."

Sharon Repp visited while I was gone and left a note:

I stopped by. Sorry I missed you, but Uriah looks good. I will surely be praying for you. I love you and the Lord loves you.

Sharon
Psalm 121:1–5

I went to the hall and called Don. He was decisive. "I don't want Uriah to linger, but I worry about brain damage from the high liver enzymes."

"Let's get Dr. Haghighat's input, but we may as well continue treatment because they can't keep him comfortable for long—100 percent remission to 70 percent relapse in one week? Perhaps it would be more merciful for him to die from the treatment than the disease. Either way, nothing will be easy."

I tiptoed into Uriah's room. *He's still asleep—thank God—I hope it lasts a long time.*

Jerry Hanley, who owned the Rainbow Corporation, called. "I've been asked to be an apheresis donor for Uriah. Can I meet him?"

"Sure. But I must warn you, Uriah is fragile. He's not expected to have a long-term survival." I thought Jerry might change his mind, but he and his wife came to the hospital. Uriah was asleep. "Don't wake him," they whispered.

Uriah woke and talked with them, but he wasn't feeling well. After a few sentences, he seemed exhausted. "I'm sorry, I just tire so easy now."

"That's OK. We've got to be movin' on anyhow," Jerry said. He and his wife headed to the door.

"Thanks for what you've done for Uriah," I said.

Jerry paused at the door and turned toward me, as if he wanted to say something, but his jaw was rigid. He nodded his head and gently closed the door.

Years ago, on my way to the lab, I overheard a snatch of conversation from a group of people walking the opposite direction:

"Why is it only old people get cancer?" asked a woman.

"It's not only old people," a man replied. "Children get cancer too."

And you'd be surprised how many there are and how close the parent of one is to you right now, I thought.

When Uriah was diagnosed, my illusion that cancer was a disease of the old was shattered in an instant. For Jerry and his wife, I think that disillusionment occurred just now. It's hard to accept that someone so young, who's hardly begun to live, could be sentenced to an early, painful death by cancer.

I remembered the feeling of righteous indignation that engulfed me once, as I watched a couple of eleven- or twelve-year-old boys buying cigarettes from a gas station. *God, there are young people willfully killing themselves with drugs and cigarettes. They're just throwing their lives away when our children are so desperate to live. How can You allow this?* Silence. *I must let God be God.*

There are things He knows that I don't, and probably couldn't comprehend even if I did. Those things I can't understand, I must leave in the hands of a wise and loving God, knowing He'll do what's best—for all.

Eighteen

Eye of the Hurricane
(Jan.–Mar. 1991)

In the eye of the hurricane, . . .
there's a harbor safe and warm. . . .
—Phil Madeira

January 1, 1991, *CPO Family Newsletter:*

Number 1 in '91 Accept the Challenge

T HE CPO FOUNDATION IS PROUD TO BE A MAJOR CONTRIBU-
tor in the name of the Correctional Officer to the
National Bone-Marrow Donor Program. . . . Since September 1990, we have added to their registry over 2,000
potential matches for our young people. We have also
matched eight children throughout the United States. . . .[1]

The NMDP January 4:

Dear Mara,

Congratulations on your success in December! I
know that you had expected more, but each day, with
each new recruitment effort, large and small, I am amazed

at the rapid progress in which the Registry grows. The file is now 250,000 volunteers!

Sincerely yours,
Bruce Casselton
Assistant Director Community Recruitment

Thank you for your recent inquiry as to how we might encourage corporations, such as the IBM Corporation, to provide support to the National Marrow Donor Program.

I really appreciate the fact that your interest goes beyond helping your own son. You, and so many others, are helping those in need by all your work to recruit new donors to the national program!

. . . Your potential offer to use some of the money you've raised for drives for your son to do a drive at IBM has been noted. . . .

Sincerely,
Rita A. Warren
Assistant Director Corporate Recruitment

Dear First Lutheran of San Fernando Family:

Your love and support for us is incredible. We cannot thank you enough for all your hard work. We thank you for holding a bone-marrow drive—it is a gift beyond price. But you have given us even more. In December the truck broke, and we couldn't pay our bills, but we kept on trusting in God, knowing that He promised to give us everything we need. God used you to help us! Because of your hard work, we were able to fix the truck to take Uriah to the hospital, pay our bills, and even buy a couple Christmas presents. You gave us the gift of a happy Christmas! Thank you!

The Alexanders

Bruce and Mary Aartes had contacted me to organize a donor drive at the blood bank for their church. "There are ten thousand to twelve thousand members in the church," Bruce said. "I hope we can test three thousand people."

Labs can process only four hundred a day. And I don't have the one hundred fifty thousand dollars it would cost. Jean Blalock said she'd ask the City of Hope to process two hundred tests if the names could be turned in through the City of Hope.

On January 3, Noonie Fugler from the KLORD Christian radio station wrote me a letter:

> I've tried today to reach you on phone from the station. Welcome to 1991! I saw the article on Uriah in the *Press-Enterprise* Christmas Day. Great courage! It helped to stir me into action.
>
> I'd like to put together a remote broadcast on January 19 at the blood bank in San Bernardino if we could. This could coincide with Uriah's need for a match in bone marrow, the blood bank's need for publicity, National Blood Donor Month, and KLORD's need to become involved.
>
> Excuse me for not typing this—but I wanted to immediately get this into today's mail. Could you call the station Monday if you receive this in time? I've already called the blood bank, and they are game—still need to talk to the head guy—Paul Sauter. Call me ASAP and we'll see what God has in store!
>
> Much love and prayer,
> Noonie Fugler

I had listened to KLORD ever since I saw their bumper sticker on a car in Kaiser's parking lot when Uriah was diagnosed. My hands shook with excitement as I fumbled with the phone. *Plans are coinciding. God organized this one!*

The blood-bank facilities weren't available, so the Aartes got permission to use space at their church, Harvest Christian Fellowship in Riverside. With Lena Harrell's help, it was set for January 20, and KLORD planned to do a live simulcast!

After Sunday's sign-ups, I asked for 204 tests. "If there are too many people, we can send them to the other drives Lena's hoping to organize."

"My sister and I will draw the blood," Maggie Kim volunteered.

January 15

Dear Parents:

Our Parent Support Group will begin Thursday, January 31, 1991.

The primary focus of this group will be to provide an environment conducive to emotional support for families of children with serious illnesses. The last 15 minutes of the meeting will be open forum and an opportunity to share information on children's activities. . . .

Chris Baer-Arter, R.N.
Department Administrator, Pediatric Services

I was glad the Mariposas group was taken over by Lupe Friare six months later, so the children didn't lose out. But parents were not allowed to attend meetings.

Saturday, January 19
We were guests of the Showdown Band and Alan and Carrie Stroschein at their restaurant in Quartzsite

on the other side of the Colorado River. We ate dinner and listened to the band play while people danced. They dedicated a song to Uriah and gave him an autographed picture of the band.

Donations continued to arrive though we were no longer actively soliciting them:

I would like nothing better than to take a blood test for you. I have bone cancer, so I am unable to do so. [I am sending] This small offering to help a little. I will remember you in my prayers and hope you will do the same for me.

Love,
Dolona Olsen

At Harvest's fellowship hall January 20, we put up posters and arranged tables and chairs. People came to be tested before the lab technicians arrived. We scrambled to find pencils so prospective volunteers could fill out paperwork.

Candace Andrews of KLORD talked to Uriah and Joel through the window of the sound room while Debbie and I helped wherever needed. People seemed to be everywhere. Just before the end of the broadcast, I gave Noonie the tally: 289 had come to be tested.

Before 4:30 P.M. Debbie found me. "The man from the lab said he's leaving." People were waiting in line to be tested, and more were coming in the door. A long line of donors waited to give him paperwork and blood samples that had already been drawn. Because of free minority testing, funds were still available, and so were supplies.

"Are you leaving already?" I asked.

He nodded, silent and tight lipped as he continued packing.

"The drive was scheduled to last until five," I told him.

His unyielding eyes met mine. "I won't stay until five."

The crowd booed. "How can you be so heartless when a child's life is at stake?" someone shouted.

He remained adamant. *He's going to leave regardless of what I do, and if I get upset, the crowd will get more unruly.* I walked down the row of donors and collected the completed paperwork. "You'll be contacted by Lena for the next donor drive."

God, could one of these people be the one Uriah needs? Could this prevent his life from being saved? God, I'm glad You're strong enough to just make Uriah well if it's Your intention that his life go on; it's easier to forgive the lab man.

Joaquin Grijalva wasn't doing well. Robert Valdivia of Palm Springs, an eight-year old with aplastic anemia, needed a donor too. But none of the families I contacted were able to hold a donor drive. *Things are too hectic and financially impossible when your child's fighting for his life. Unless you have a lot of help, like I do, it's just not possible.*

❧ ❧ ❧

On January 21, Jan Cipkala-Gaffin, sent a Matched Unrelated Program update:

> ... international search in progress @ present 2 DRs [loci tests] are pending in US. 2 DRs are pending in France. 3 DRs pending in England.
>
> Children's Hospital of Los Angeles is currently only performing unrelated donor transplants with completely matched donors. There are institutions in the country

that are utilizing incompletely matched donors. If you require further details, please let me know.

Kaiser won't do that. And if it fails, it'll be one of the most painful ways to die. Please God, let one of the seven match— but Thy will be done.

Monday, January 21
Les Warning died suddenly from a reaction to chemotherapy. Blythe and Zion Lutheran mourned.

February 5, Matched Unrelated Program update: "There are three US donors and three in England awaiting further testing."

❧ ❧ ❧

"Don, do you think Heather is avoiding spending time with Uriah?" I worried.

His eyes blazed with fury. "You're giving up on him, aren't you?"

There are so many pressures pushing me to accept Uriah's death—my family is suffering, I'm neglecting work at church, and we need more money. I need to get a job. I feel like time is so short for our family.

Monday, February 11
Uriah was admitted to the hospital with a 50 percent relapse. Tuesday he started high-dose methotrexate; the last chemotherapy offered to put him in remission. I had to awaken him every hour for thirty hours to urinate, then every two hours for the next few days. Saturday night, he only had to get up every four hours. I was the only one he'd allow to help him, and we had to measure his urine. We were both awfully tired.

I tried to get him to eat again. He'd had fever, vomiting, and diarrhea, but he drank a little and ate a bit of banana.

During the night, his transfusion leaked all over his bed and onto the floor. Shiloh and Uriah watched it foam like billowing clouds when the nurse poured hydrogen peroxide on it.

February 14

I thought you might enjoy having a few extra copies of the February *Peacekeeper.* The cover story about Uriah is quite touching, not to mention the photos on pages 20 and 21. It just goes to show that cops really do take care of cops and their families.

We are still scheduling blood drives and will continue to go onward until we find the match that Uriah needs. I have the support of all the wardens and superintendents in California, and I am eager to take the blood drive into Washington and possibly Pennsylvania. . . .

Charleene
Office Administrator

On the cover, smiling COs in uniform filled out paperwork to be tested, and the centerfold collage showed officers being tested:

Sierra C/Os Roll Up Their Sleeves to Help Uriah
by Carolyn Conner

On Thursday, December 6, 1990, 150 concerned Sierra Conservation Center Correctional Officers, staff, and others gave blood samples as part of the ongoing effort to find a bone marrow match for young Uriah Alexander.

... At last year's CCPOA Convention in Reno ... Correctional Officer Doug Coke learned of the drive. ... Officer Coke was instrumental in organizing the effort at Sierra. ...[2]

Don requested the attorney general represent him in a lawsuit brought against him by inmate Pruitt, injured in the scuffle June 27, 1990. Don was confident he would be exonerated.

Heather wanted to buy a saxophone. She had a thriving babysitting business and wanted to secure a loan. She approached her Uncle Bob.

Dear Ms. Alexander:

I enjoyed speaking with you on February 20, 1991. I was glad to hear about your new feline friends as well as the pregnancy of your dog. Although algebra can be a tough subject, I'm sure someone as intelligent as you will have no problem with the make-up test.

Enclosed please find a check for $675.00 for the purchase of your saxophone. I'm glad you decided to continue to play, and I hope you enjoy it for years to come.

I know you are the hard-working type, but it seems to me that a girl—sorry, I mean a young woman—your age should have some money of her own, so $35.00 per month should be sufficient. If you want to pay more, that's OK; it's up to you. Well, Leah is calling me for dinner so I'd better go. Please give everyone hugs and kisses from both Leah and me. We can't wait to see you guys again. Until then—take care.

Sincerely,
Robert J. Miller
aka Guido Weirdo

We were up at Nana's cabin with Uriah February 22–24, so we dropped off the girls at Arrowhead Lutheran Camp to attend the church's snow trip with their friends, including Libby—one of Shiloh and Heather's closest friends—whose parents, Lynne and Dick Christ, were chaperons.

Saturday, February 23
Most of the MOMs had moved, and we hadn't had a meeting in a year, but when Gayle visited, we all met at Sizzler, like old times. Everyone's lost a child except me. It's good to see them and hear what they're doing.

Sunday, February 24
Lena held the last donor drive at the American Legion Hall in Riverside. Only nineteen were tested.

Don, Uriah, and I walked around Lake Gregory with Janet, Andy, Andria, and Brian later that day. Uriah's dog, Tanya, joined the Andersons' dogs, Sarge and Nakita, splashing in the lake. Andria skated past Brian and bald Uriah, who scanned the water's edge, looking for schools of catfish or prawn. We watched people flying brightly colored kites at the baseball field. Then Don and the kids fed the ducks day-old bread. *I wish we could freeze time. These are the good old days.*

Tuesday, February 26, Matched Unrelated Donor update: There were now only two donors in the United States but still three in England. "The above five potential donors were accessed for DR typing. Results pending."

The high-dose methotrexate didn't make Uriah ill. It also didn't work.

"We don't need to do a bone marrow," Dr. Haghighat said. "The 'blasts' are in his peripheral blood. It's surprising that he looks and feels well."

I'm glad Don took time off to come with us.

"There's no chance of getting him into remission?" he asked Dr. Haghighat.

"The medicine didn't work. It's the last regular chemotherapy we can use."

I shook my head. *That's it.*

Don continued to probe. "Isn't there anything new or experimental?" Immediately they opened their books and found two new treatments and then a third, more promising still. *I'm really glad Don came. I guess they couldn't offer them until we asked.*

"Jason had Ifophosfamide Mensa and UD-16, but they didn't work," Dr. Sanmarco said.

"It's used often on Ewing Sarcoma patients," Dr. Haghighat said, "but it's only been used seventeen times on leukemia patients."

Dr. Sanmarco phoned another authority to find out more. "Fifty percent of recipients went into complete remission," she reported.

Dr. Haghighat nodded. "It's not too bad to tolerate. Uriah will be in the hospital for five days, then out for a few weeks, another dose, and then a bone marrow in a few weeks."

"What do you think?" Dr. Sanmarco asked us.

Don and I turned to each other, awe etched on our faces. *Can it be we still have hope?*

"Let's try it," Don whispered.

"Are you sure?" I asked. "You'd have to take care of the girls."

He nodded emphatically.

"Thanks," we told Dr. Sanmarco. *Could this be the same doctor who wanted us to give up?*

"Thanks, Dr. Haghighat."

Uriah's room wasn't ready, so we went for dinner. Uriah ate a lot of Chinese food! He had a transfusion that night.

Wednesday, February 27, Bob was Uriah's nurse. "Uriah's count is point nine, so they won't be giving him chemotherapy, and he'll probably be sent home."

That's really different than what we planned.

He came in a little later wearing a mask and handed me one. "Uriah's count is only point forty-five. You'll have to wear a mask and change it every half hour."

A few minutes later, Dr. Tracy knocked on the door. "Here's an off-work order for Don," he said when I joined him in the hall. "How are you doing?"

"I'm a little stressed out."

"Here's something to help with stress. It won't impair your ability to think; it just helps keep your emotions in control. Use it when you need it." He handed me the prescription. "Is there anything else I can do to help?"

"I'm OK." I forced a smile. *What a good doctor.*

Later Bob brought Uriah's medicine. "Dr. Haghighat said all the white cells are blasts, so the low count doesn't matter. Uriah will get his chemotherapy as planned." Bob sat and played Trouble and Crossfire with Uriah.

Uriah dealt well with the chemo. In fact, I walked in the rain to get him more Chinese food for lunch. He ate and ate.

March 5, from the blood bank of San Bernardino and Riverside Counties:

It has indeed been a pleasure working with you. You have been a source of inspiration to me in the great spirit and dedication you have shown in securing potential bone-marrow donors.

Your whole family has shown such a positive attitude and strength during such troubling times that you have faced. I can see true empathy in your treatment of others. I want you to know that through your fathomless effort to find a donor for your son, other lives may be saved.

Through your sponsored recruitment drives 1,538 donors have joined the National Marrow Donor Program. These additional donors give hope to the many patients waiting for that miracle match to receive that "Gift of Life."

Sincerely,
Maggie Kim
Coordinator, Bone Marrow Program

Maggie's been with us from the very first bone-marrow test in Fontana. Coming from her, this means a lot.

Uriah got five days of Ifophosfamide and UD-16. The side effects were minimal, and Uriah felt well but needed platelets and red cells because the leukemia depressed his production of normal cells.

Monday, March 11

Uriah left the hospital with a white count of three hundred and strict doctor's orders to return immediately if he ran a fever because an infection could quickly become dangerous.

Tuesday, March 12

Uriah built a table while I cleaned. I put up new blinds in his room, and he placed purple pansies he bought on his windowsill. He and Shiloh helped cook spaghetti for dinner. *It's so nice to be a complete family again.* We watched *Problem Child,* and Uriah laughed until he cried.

When I got the girls up for school the next day, Uriah had a 102.5 fever.

"Get ready," I told the girls and called Don at work. "We have to take Uriah in. He's running a fever. I'll pick you up in a few minutes." I rushed to load the truck, but

Heather had already done it. "Thanks, Heather. Listen, you and Shiloh will have to walk to Theresa's after school if Daddy isn't back by then."

I waved goodbye to them at school and turned to Uriah. "How are you feeling?"

He shrugged. "I don't hurt anywhere."

We picked up Don and drove to the clinic. Uriah still felt fine but was admitted, and an antibiotic drip was started right away. We played a few hands of cards, then Don left to pick up the girls.

Uriah threw up. His fever rose to 103.9. His urine turned dark, and suddenly he looked very ill. He got blood that night. When Kathy flushed his catheter, he gasped, "My catheter's leaking!"

❧ ❧ ❧

"His catheter's fixed, but it can't be used for 48 hours. We have to start a conventional IV." Uriah screamed while several nurses made fruitless efforts. "OK. Let's call Dr. Sanmarco."

She started it in one attempt but seemed tense. "Don't touch the [IV] butterfly!" she snapped at the nurse.

"I didn't!" she protested.

Dr. Sanmarco sighed. "We have to run the IV slowly to prevent blowing the vein."

When he needs fluid and medication most! God, help him hold on until they can turn up the volume. I stayed awake praying until 3:00 A.M.

At 5:00 A.M., the nurse hung the first bag of white blood cells. "He's due for a five-day course."

I suspect his liver's in trouble because his urine is orange. "How do you feel, Uriah?"

He grinned at me and shuffled the cards, his white teeth accentuating his sallow skin. "I feel OK."

Thursday, March 14 the doctors talked to me outside Uriah's room. "There's a bar [gram] negative infection in his blood, and his liver's in trouble," Dr. Sanmarco said. "We're checking for hepatitis, maybe from the blood."

Dr. Haghighat said, "We're checking if the last chemotherapy could have caused a liver dysfunction."

"There's also a possibility the infection is causing it," Dr. Sanmarco added.

I opened a letter from Colton Joint Unified School District, which the nurse handed me: "Your child will be instructed by Mr. Nord at 11:00 A.M., Monday through Thursday."

"Mr. Nord, Uriah goes to a private school," I told him when he arrived. "He's been doing his homework on independent study because of his illness."

"That will be fine. I'll help him do that work."

He doesn't understand. Uriah may be dying. "Uriah's very ill. I don't think he can do much."

"I'll only have him do what he feels comfortable doing."

Why did they even let him in here?

The first couple times, Uriah couldn't do anything. But later he did a little. *I'm not sure which one is doing the learning. Mr. Nord seems to know very little about children like Uriah. Knowing Uriah has opened a new horizon for him. And Uriah turns everything into a game, from math to reading.*

The next day Dr. Sanmarco said, "I want to see you."

Heidi's here too. I braced myself as they led me to a conference room. Dr. Sanmarco waited until I settled in a chair. "Uriah's been having liver problems for a long time. It's worse than it's ever been. He could go really quickly. Even if he stayed the same, it would be a good sign. If it is hepatitis, there's nothing we can do, and we're already doing all we can for the kind of infection he has. Contact any family support-system you have in the area."

Huh? My family already knows we're here.

Heidi made eye contact with me. "You need to contact your family."

Oh! He's dying? I walked numbly to the private phones and started making calls. No one was home, but I got the prayer chains started.

Back at the room, I tried to interact normally with Uriah. When Don called, I tried to clue him in. "I think you and the girls need to come today and not wait until Saturday." *I hope he understands.*

At six o'clock that evening, I reached Nana. "Nana, they think Uriah's dying."

"I didn't even know he was in the hospital."

"I'm sorry. I thought Debbie told you."

Don answered the phone when I called again. *He's still home!* I explained Uriah's condition. "I hope you're not too upset to come."

"I'm OK. You remember those fifty trees we ordered for a windbreak months ago? They all came this afternoon, so we went to pick up supplies to plant them. I'll find someone to take care of the plants and animals, and we'll start packing."

Pastor called. "I'm coming out right away."

"Pastor, I don't want a stampede into his room, or he might get scared. Could you come tomorrow or Sunday?"

As I hung up, Pastor Dannenburg rapped on the door. "Is it OK if I come in and pray with you?"

After we prayed, I walked Pastor Dannenburg out to the hall. "How did you find out he was dying?"

His eyebrows shot up. "I didn't know," he said, "but God did."

Linda Pietz peeked in the door. "We just got done with Jordan's appointment. Can I pray with you before I go?"

I reached out and we clasped hands. *Wherever two or more are gathered in Your name . . .*

As Linda went out, Grandma Ruth came in. "Want to play Chameleon, Grandma?" Uriah asked.

We were still playing when Don called at nine o'clock. "We're leaving," he said.

"Are you sure you don't want to wait until tomorrow?" I asked.

"I won't sleep anyway."

At 1:30 A.M., Don scanned Uriah's sleeping form. "I'm too tired to go up to Arrowhead. We're gonna sleep in the truck in the parking lot."

"Uriah's white cells are late. I'm going to wait up for them." I was up most of the night. *I'm so worried. He looks so yellow and his breathing seems labored. His whole body vibrates with every beat of his heart. At least Don and the girls are close.*

The next day, Friday, March 15, Don and Heather stumbled in, bleary eyed, at 6:00 A.M. "How is he?"

I shrugged my shoulders. "We're just tired."

"So are we." They returned to the truck. At 9:30, Don poked his head in the room. "I'm going to get breakfast."

Dr. Sanmarco swept in and examined Uriah. "The toxins in his blood have dropped in half. . . ."

Yes! Thank You, God! I've got to let everyone know!

". . . I don't know if these lab slips are correct. It's so much less. I'm going to have the lab check again."

Debbie, Jeff, Joel, and Ellie waved to us from the sunny sidewalk outside. Jeff dumped a box of something by the window. *Snow! They must have gone to the mountains to get it!* Jeff dumped box after box, while Debbie and the kids began to build. A snowman grew outside Uriah's window. He giggled. I snapped a picture of the snowman's crooked-stick smile, pebble eyes, and leafy hands. Joel and Ellie stuck paper hearts on Uriah's window. They pelted each other with snowballs from leftover snow, then silently signed "I love you" and waved goodbye.

Now that's a long-distance hug.

Saturday, March 16. "Don, the girls aren't coming to grips with the possibility of Uriah's death," I said. "Every time he goes into the hospital, I fear it's his last stay."

He shrugged. "What can we do?"

"Uriah's as stable as he can be, under the circumstances. Let's take the girls to Rose Hills, where Lindsay is buried. Even if we don't have to use it, it would be nice to be ready."

Standing high on a ridge, we could see the city in the valley far below. "This would be a good place to see the last day and Jesus coming back to get everyone waiting for Him," I said. "Let's get one for me and you and Uriah. The girls will probably want to be with their families, when they have them."

Don nodded.

I tucked the receipts in my purse. "How do you think the girls took it?" I asked Don on the way back.

"I'm not sure."

I turned to look at them sitting in the back of the truck. Heather slid open the window to the cab. "Don't you think you're being a little melodramatic? Uriah's not really going to die. That's just an excuse so you can play favorites."

Perhaps it's better to let them keep their illusions.

Monday, March 18

Uriah was released, cheating death again. I called KLORD:

"This is Mara in Fontana. I would like you to play 'When God's People Pray' to thank the Lord for miraculously pulling my son back from the brink of death this past week, and also to thank all the people who prayed for his recovery. When God's people pray, miracles do happen!"

Matched Unrelated Donor update: only one donor in the United States and three in England accessed for DR typing.

Thursday, March 21. "My feet are itching!" Uriah complained. He scratched and scratched. "It's driving me crazy!" he yelled.

"Uriah, I can't see any rash or sores."

The doctors examined him. "There's nothing wrong with his feet."

He pointed and I daubed the itchy spots with Camphophenique. "That helped," he smiled. But only minutes later: "It's itching again," he whimpered.

Those nerves are still deadened. If it isn't physical, then it must be psychological. Is he afraid to die? I remember the terror of another boy on TV, "Please, just come and get tested to be my donor," he had sobbed. *God, he was so afraid to die. I couldn't bear it if Uriah becomes afraid to die and I can't reassure him. Please spare me that.*

"I think I have an idea," Carolyn Baschal said when I told her. "If it's all right with you, I'll give him a placebo."

"It's worth a try."

She walked to the car where Uriah sat. "I heard you're having a problem with your feet." She looked both ways to make sure no one was listening, then whispered, "I have a friend who's an old Indian medicine man. I'll ask him if he can help."

A few days later, in furtive tones, she told him, "I'm sorry it took so long. My Indian friend had to gather rare plants from a secret forest far away to make this powder for you. Now listen carefully. It must be kept in a cool, dark place. Put it on only once a day after the sun has gone down. And don't tell anyone about it, or it won't work anymore." She glanced both ways, then deposited a drawstring bag of woven cloth into his hands. "Quick, hide it in your backpack, before the sun shines on it." Uriah stuffed it in and zipped his backpack closed.

That night he disappeared into his room. As I tucked him in, he motioned me closer. "I tried that powder, and it works!" He used it for a couple weeks and then stopped. He never complained of itchy feet again, but when he was feeling stress, he would confide he had used the powder again.

"Carolyn, that powder works great. I hope your 'Indian friend' didn't have to go to much trouble."

"It's just a little scrap bag filled with browned flour."

"Thanks. It's made his life bearable again." *It wasn't the flour that soothed Uriah; it was the love of a dear friend.*

🌿 🌿 🌿

One day Mr. Johnson approached our truck in a parking lot. "Hi, Uriah. How are you?"

Uriah smiled. "I'm fine. I like your hat."

Mr. Johnson removed his baseball cap and read the inscription, "Life is what happens while you are making plans." He handed it to Uriah. "Here you go. That'll make up for the time you let me borrow your shoes."

Uriah giggled. "Thanks. I'll add it to my collection."

Friday, March 22

Uriah attended school, wearing his coonskin cap on his bald head. Mrs. Maly took pictures of the smiling class crowded around him while he told them of his adventures.

Wednesday, March 27

Dr. Haghighat wrote "No Resuscitation" on a prescription slip and held it out to me. "If Uriah dies while he's not in the hospital and someone calls 911, the emergency personnel will have to try to bring him back. Do you want that?"

Don and I looked at each other. *I hadn't even thought of that.* "If God allows Uriah to die, that's His will," I murmured.

Don looked at the floor and nodded. I took the note from Dr. Haghighat.

"All you have to do is show that to anyone responding, and they'll leave him in peace," he said softly.

I wonder if this is Dr. Haghighat's way of making sure we understand how ill Uriah is, like our taking the girls to Rose Hills to buy a plot.

March 27, the *Palo Verde Valley Times:*

Hospice helps in times of sorrow

By Robin Richards
Palo Verde Valley Times

"Helping others in their times of grief, people reach the highest point of their humanity. It's absolutely unconditional: You're there to receive nothing, but to give love."

Reverend George Cushman of Blythe's Community United Methodist Church was explaining . . . the rewards for being there for someone in their time of grief. Last May, Cushman told us about a hospice network forming in Blythe to help families of the terminally ill. . . . Their goal is to help the terminally ill and those who care for them, in the months preceding death, . . . said Cushman. "One of our goals is to allow people to stay in the home environment as long as possible, even to the point of death."[3]

I met Pastor Cushman at their meeting the following afternoon. "It's nice to know you're here if we need you."

On Saturday, March 30, we followed Nana and Boompa up to the cabin. It was spring, but the snow was up to our waists, and we had to dig our way in.

Uriah was weak, so Don carried him in and laid him on the couch. "Is there any wood for a fire?" Uriah asked.

Nana smiled. "Uriah, I know you love to see a fire in the fireplace. I ordered wood especially for you." Don and I carried armloads of wood in from the garage, and soon Uriah and Don had a cheery blaze on the hearth. *It's good to see Uriah up and active.*

Later Janet, Andy, Brian and Andria, Debbie, Jeff, Joel, and Ellie came for an Easter egg hunt in the snow. "We should have left the eggs white so they would be harder to find," Janet said. We hid them in trees and cars, buried them in the snow, and left a few in plain sight for little Ellie. Uriah put on cowboy boots and joined in the hunt. Shiloh wore sunglasses to soften the glare of sun on snow.

Soon the hunt degenerated into a snowball fight. Uriah retreated inside. Don, Andy, Janet, and the kids pelted each other with chunks of melting snow while Uriah and I watched from the living-room window. Abruptly, everyone except Don clattered into the living room, shedding coats and boots. They drifted to the window where Uriah and I gazed down on the "battlefield." Don sneaked across the side yard with an armload of snowballs. He stopped and stood up, puzzled by the emptiness of the front driveway. We all laughed at his confusion. He turned and saw us, warm and safe inside. He dropped the snowballs in disgust. The joke was on him!

After Easter dinner, Don and the kids sledded down the steep bank on the side of the cabin while I ran the camcorder from the bottom. Uriah wore the biggest smile I'd ever seen. "Whoa!" he screamed all the way down. The camera recorded the complete joy on his face.

This is how I want to remember Uriah.

I'll never forget you, Uriah!! Think of you so often— and keep in touch with your many friends and loved ones that know how you are.

Wish you could come to our house and see all the baby birds and ducks that are hatching out. So when you come home, have Mom give us a call. OK? We love you.

God's blessings,
Dave and Ruth Sheppardson

Theresa handed me the April *Peacekeeper.* "Mara, look! Pat McCullar from the academy in Galt got to be a donor!"

"Pat McCullar!" I said. She wrote us notes and did fundraising at Galt. I'm so happy for her. My only regret is, it wasn't Uriah she matched. At least someone benefited."

"Doesn't it bother you that people who partially matched Uriah are taking so long to come in for DR typing or refuse to be tested further?"

"Things change. Maybe they're pregnant or ill and can't donate. Perhaps if they tested for a particular person who died, they're not willing to donate because of grief." *God, please don't let me be like that if Uriah dies.*

❧   ❧   ❧

I thought I'd forgiven her until the day Don's ex-mistress called. "I've been tested as a donor for Uriah," she said.

"Thanks," I replied feebly. Feelings buried within me boiled to the surface. *God, You've used these donor drives to teach me about forgiveness, but this is the hardest lesson. I'm still angry. How dare she try to patch it up? I know that's wrong. God, please forgive my inability to forgive completely. At least she's thinking about someone else instead of herself now.*

"What would you do if the only person who could save your son was someone you considered your enemy?"

If it's Your will, I'd struggle to accept it. But please, don't let it be so if it would hurt my family.

Nineteen

Against the Wind
(Apr.–May 1991)

And when my heart sees no light,
help me hold on with all my might. . . .
—Michelle Wagner and Dwight Liles

Tuesday, April 2, 1991

WE ARRANGED A TEA PARTY AND INVITED JULIE MALY AND Sabrenia Baschal. Heather and Shiloh set out fancy crystal and dishes, filling them with candy and treats. When Julie arrived, they feigned putting on airs and laughed at their silliness. "Julie, I'm sure glad you're willing to come and put up with these guys," I said.

"I wouldn't miss it," she chuckled.

Monday, April 8

The NMDP sent a report of expense activity through February 28, 1991. We had raised $85,500, paid $71,700, and awaited billing for $13,200 for drives completed. We had tested 1,684 people. That left $600 in Uriah's account.

Matched Unrelated Donor update: There was one new partial match for Uriah. *I hope it's not too late.*

I called Donald Jolly. *It couldn't hurt to try their cure now.*

"We don't have any reagent available," he said. "But there's something that might help. We hope to get the doctors to cooperate. We need his medical records released and faxed to London and a synopsis of his condition, including his diagnosis, prognosis, and latest blood-work results. Then we'll treat him with a series of intramuscular shots."

"How much does it cost?"

"We don't charge for the treatment."

"That's good because we have no money left after our long search for a donor."

Wednesday, April 10

Uriah went to school again. But Julie Maly called in the middle of the day. "I'm worried about Uriah. He fell asleep in class, and I couldn't rouse him easily."

"I'm on my way."

Julie met me at the door. "I feel silly calling, but I want to be very careful."

I touched his forehead. "I'm glad you are. He's running a fever now."

The doctor admitted him.

Donald Jolly called. "Why didn't you pick up the medication April 11?"

"Uriah's in the hospital."

"I'll mail it."

Don donated blood at the blood bank April 16. "I have to donate a lot before I can become an apheresis donor."

We dropped by Maggie Kim's office. "I'm glad you're interested in becoming an apheresis donor, Don."

April 16, Don updated Warden Theo T. White on Uriah's condition:

On March 19, 1991, Uriah's doctor's informed my wife and me that all possible chemotherapies Uriah is eligible for, have been used. This included investigational and experimental chemotherapies.

We then contacted UCLA Medical Center for a second opinion, and after consultation, concurred with our doctors.

Uriah is now in 100 percent relapse, and unless we're able to find a new experimental drug or we're blessed with a miracle, Uriah will die in just a few weeks or if we're lucky a few months.

We have been briefed on what to expect as Uriah gets worse. He will be given blood infusions, antibiotics, and steroids to keep him stable. Eventually the leukemia will break down the barriers to the brain and cause seizures and eventually death; or, as the leukemic white blood cells multiply, an infection will start and may also cause death. Unfortunately his death will not be without pain.

We are hoping to keep Uriah at home as much as possible by using hospital volunteers.

Thank you again for your concern and support. It has helped us a lot in dealing with the pressures imposed by Uriah's illness and medical needs.

Respectfully submitted,
D. F. Alexander
Vocations/Industries Sgt.

Thursday, April 18

Uriah was released with a WBC count of twelve thousand. *That's the highest it's ever been. But now a high count is bad.* We helped him climb in the truck and drove for home.

Uriah watched the climbing lights of the Palm Springs tram as he had countless times on his way to and from treatments. "I sure would like to ride on that someday," he murmured.

Passing through Indio at dusk, Uriah saw hot-air balloons landing. "Could we get pictures of those balloons?" He wasn't able to walk, so Don snapped pictures and got a brochure from a balloonist.

There might not be enough time for him to go. It's just a matter of time now. Watching his WBC will give us a clue when the end is near. The doctors said his count will skyrocket because his blood will be saturated with useless cancer cells.

The following night Andy, Janet, Andria, Brian, and their dog stayed at our house. We left early the next morning for Sea World. Uriah sat at the entrance in a wheelchair with his hat and mask on. *He's not doing well. He's sleeping a lot and he's grumpy. We brought him to enjoy himself, but everything seems to bother him.*

"Janet, can Heather and Shiloh go with you?" I whispered. "Don and I are going to try to find something Uriah wants to do. I think he's frustrated because he's too weak to walk, but he might be afraid of dying."

She nodded and gave me a hug.

Seeing animals in the hospital always perked up Uriah. There's a lot of life here, but you can't touch it—except for the aquarium of dolphins!

Uriah opened his eyes and sat up when he heard their playful cries. He smiled when he found he could reach them from his chair. A dolphin stole his fish and splashed him. Uriah laughed. "You watch out, or I'll splash you back!"

It's such a relief. His whole attitude has changed.

He smiled up at me. "Mom, is it OK if I stand up to feed the dolphins?"

"Sure, if you want to," I said, holding back tears. *Thank You, God.*

The others found us and fed the dolphins before we went up the tower and looked out over Sea World. Heather pointed out the large aquariums where Shamu performed. "We want to get wet because it's so hot."

"Me too," agreed Uriah.

Don carried Uriah down to the front row to get splashed. The killer whales were visible through the clear aquarium when they swam by. No water spilled then, but their wake rose in a wave that poured over people in the first three rows. All the kids laughed and wiped their faces. When Shamu splashed the crowd with his tail, Shiloh kicked the foot of water in the aisle with her tennis shoes. "If you're not wet enough, Uriah, I'll splash you," she offered.

Monday, April 22
    The whole family went to the hospital for Uriah's appointment. Dr. Haghighat solemnly considered the lab slip. "His WBC is 169,000."
    A huge jump!
    "I'll give him a shot of vincristine to drop the WBC, but it's just a temporary measure to keep him a little more comfortable."

Mrs. Maly sent a letter home with her class: "Please pray this week for our precious Uriah—and ask for a miracle. . . ."

Sabrenia invited Julie Maly, Heather, Shiloh, and Uriah to a tea party at her house. Uriah filled his plate. He couldn't eat, but he enjoyed the games and the company of those who loved him.

April 24

. . . I know you've been in the battle a long time. But God promises to never leave you nor forsake you. He's right there with you, each and every step. Trust Him to bring to pass what is best for everyone and will give Him glory. May His grace and power be upon all of you. Especially give Uriah a big hug for me and a big hug for you all.

Margot

4/24/91

Dear Don and Myra,

We just wanted to drop a note to let you know that we are thinking of you. There are several of us who would like to help out. Can we make dinner for your family? God bless you.

Love,
Doug and Rebekah Ralston

Thursday, April 25

Uriah got a nosebleed we couldn't stop. We drove him to the hospital and he got platelets. His WBC was sixty-six hundred.

"Come back Monday for another shot of vincristine," Dr. Haghighat said.

April 26, the *Palo Verde Valley Times*:

CVSP annual picnic tomorrow at Mayflower

The staff and family of the Chuckawalla Valley State Prison (CVSP) invite everyone to attend their annual family picnic tomorrow. . . . Proceeds will be forwarded to the CVSP Games Committee . . . for . . . athletes to participate in the annual statewide summer games. . . .[1]

Don bought a family ticket. Uriah felt well but wore his mask. He stood watching the DJ. He recognized Uriah. "Do you want to help?"

Uriah grinned. "You bet!"

It's a risk being around people. But it's better to let him enjoy his last days.

Heather and her friends swam in the river. Shiloh's greyhound, Tasha, pulled Shiloh and her friend Carol in too.

Don and Heather stayed home with the flu on Monday. Shiloh and Uriah played games on the way to the hospital for his second shot of vincristine. When we arrived, I took his hand to help him out of the truck. It burned in my grasp.

"He was fine when we left home," I told Margarita, "but I think he has a fever."

"It's a 103," she confirmed, looking at the thermometer.

"Admit him," Dr. Sanmarco said. "Ten days, IV antibiotics."

"His WBC is sixty," his nurse Barbara whispered to me.

Uriah threw up blood, and it showed darkly in his stools. He took Fennergin, Tagamet, and Demerol for stomach pain. He had a cough, sore throat, and runny nose. When I took him to the bathroom, he fell and hit his head, bruising it. I called Don. "I'm coming home tomorrow to pick you up."

On Tuesday, April 30, Shiloh babysat Joel and Ellie while Debbie played with Uriah. "Thanks, Debbie. I don't want him to die alone," I whispered in the hall.

Don started to drive us back, but his arms started to shake. "Honey, I think you better take over," he sighed.

We arrived at 8:00 P.M. "Uriah's the same," Debbie whispered.

"We can give him RBCs and platelets because his counts are low. We're trying to balance his levels of calcium and electrolytes, but everything's out of whack," Dr. Sanmarco said, shaking her head.

Uriah's urine turned dark. "He's holding fluid. His urinary system is backing up," Dr. Haghighat said. "Give him Lasix," he told the nurse.

Wednesday, May 1. "I would stay if I could," Don said, "but he's recovered so many times, they don't really believe he's dying. I have to go to work."

I nodded. "I know Heather wants to get back to school too. But Shiloh wants to stay. She can keep us company," I smiled at her.

The *Palo Verde Valley Times,* May 1:

Blythe chapter named number one

Blythe's Jaycees were picked as the Chapter of the Year for . . . 17 projects in 1990.

About half of [$18,393 raised] came from a fundraiser held for bone-marrow transplant patient Uriah Alexander. The Jaycees' efforts on behalf of the local boy were also named Project of the Year. . . .[2]

Dr. Sanmarco came to Uriah's room on the morning of May 2, "Uriah's scheduled for five days of white cells because of gram-negative and gram-positive infections in his blood. I want to put him on morphine for pain. I don't know if we should continue treating him or let him go."

"Keep treating him," I said.

"I feel like there's something clogging my throat," Uriah croaked to Dr. Sanmarco.

She motioned me out of the room. "The only way to be sure is arthroscopy, and I'm afraid that would cause him to bleed because of low platelets." She paused. "We could treat him and see if he improves. Where's your husband?"

"He went back to Blythe."

She frowned. "He should stay at the hospital. Uriah's so fragile, he could go anytime."

I called Don at work and told him what Dr. Sanmarco said. "I'll go home, pack, get Heather, and come out." Don had a panic attack, so they arrived after midnight. The girls slept in the conference room. Don and I slept in Uriah's room in chairs.

Friday, May 3

Uriah's pain was excruciating to watch. His hands were horribly swollen and turned from an angry red to purple. His feet were swelling now and hurt so much he could barely hobble to the restroom. His eyes were black with bruises from his rubbing them. He had petticiae— tiny bruises from capillaries breaking—all over.

Uriah slept most of the time. Open sores in his mouth made talking painful. Occasionally he would croak, "Bathroom." He lifted his eyes toward heaven and cried when he went. He wouldn't use a bedpan, so a portable toilet was brought in so he wouldn't have to walk. He didn't play. He didn't want Renee to visit. He just wanted to sleep. *The death watch again.*

Janet and Andy and the kids, Debbie, Jeff, Joel, and Ellie visited. Nana and Boompa came later.

"We're exhausted," Don said. "Heather and I are going to the cabin to rest."

Uriah's abdomen began to bloat after they left. I phoned Don. "Honey, I know you just got there, but you've got to come back. Uriah's developed a huge swelling in his stomach."

"The X-rays were inconclusive," Dr. Sanmarco said.

"I'd like to do exploratory surgery," said one of the specialists she had called.

Dr. Sanmarco shook her head. "Low platelet count. He won't survive."

"He must be bleeding internally," another concluded. The others nodded.

If that's true, he'll bleed to death in minutes.

"There's a possibility he has internal chickenpox," Dr. Sanmarco told me. "Some of his symptoms remind me of Jeremy's. I'm going to schedule a Titer test."

Nana and Boompa sat with us until 2:00 A.M. Don and I slept in chairs. The girls slept in the conference room again.

❧   ❧   ❧

Saturday, May 4. "Mom, could I have sweet-and-sour pork?" Uriah murmured.

I moved closer. "From a restaurant?"

"No, I want you to make it."

I turned to Debbie. "I don't know if he's getting better or if it's a last request."

"I'll take Shiloh and get what you need," she said.

They carried grocery bags into the hospital and we made it in the microwave.

"Wow! You can do that in a microwave?" asked an amazed nurse.

Uriah sat up when I carried the bowl in. He took a tiny bite. Tears filled his eyes. "It hurts to eat," he said. Blood wept from sores in his mouth.

I fought back tears. *Oh, God. He's being denied his last meal.*

Don and I walked the girls to the conference room and collapsed on the couches. "What would you think . . . if we took Uriah off the medicine?" I murmured.

Heather's eyes blazed. "If you quit now," she exploded, "I would think you were murderers."

Shiloh gaped at her. "I wouldn't think you were murderers, but I would think we quit too soon."

I nodded. *Even if I can't bear to see his pain, none of these children are ready to quit.*

Sunday, May 5

A fine rash spread over Uriah's body. Large blisters appeared on his left ear. A red, raised rash filled the creases under his arms, in his elbows, and behind his knees. A skin specialist examined him. "He has two problems. One is an allergic reaction to fluconazole, the medicine for a fungal infection in his throat, which is causing the swelling in his hands and feet. The other is the rash."

Whenever Uriah requested, I put Xylocaine cream on his hands and feet for pain and wrapped them in diapers. They were so sensitive, a breath of air caused him to flinch in anguish.

Uriah watched from his window as children from the "peds" ward broke a piñata for Cinco de Mayo. Renee brought him candy and toys from the piñata. Uriah smiled. "I'll save the candy for later." He examined each toy. "Put these away for me, Mom."

That night, Don and Heather went to the cabin. Shiloh stayed with Uriah and me.

Monday, May 6

Dr. Sanmarco sighed. "I think the rash is chickenpox. It looks like the rash Jeremy had before he died."

Looking closely, I could see little blisters forming on the rash on Uriah's thighs and upper arms. It now covered his chest and stomach too.

The nurses covered Uriah's entire bed with sheets and wheeled him to the fourth floor.

The fourth-floor staff seems angry we're here.

Bob, the nurse, was sitting in the room one morning when I awoke. "I hope you don't mind. I want to stay in here in case anything happens," he said.

He's one of the few nurses who still works with Uriah. For some, it's probably just too hard to deal with the dying. Uriah's being in the hospital is harder on them—and it's harder on him. Taking him home to die would be best for everyone.

Uriah had visitors, but many left to cry after they saw his suffering and how bravely he tried to hide his pain. Jean Smith from CPOF, Brent Nelson, and Joan dropped in. Renee brought Uriah the piñata the pediatric kids had broken open. Balloon bouquets arrived from friends.

Don dropped the truck off to be worked on. "I need it back today."

Later the mechanics called. "We won't be able to get to your truck until tomorrow."

I was angry. "We wouldn't have dropped it off if we had been told that. Let me speak to your supervisor." *He knows about Uriah because of the repairs made during the Mariposas Christmas party.* "I'm sorry to bother you, but my son Uriah is dying. My husband needs to return to Blythe to get his dog, Tanya. He wants to see her one more time."

There was a long silence. "Don't you worry about a thing. Your truck will be done by five today, if I have to work on it myself."

"Thanks, I knew I could count on you."

I opened the mail.

Certificate of Appreciation from the National Marrow Donor Program

The National Marrow Donor Program gratefully acknowledges the outstanding efforts of Mara Alexander. Your work has contributed to the growing movement that offers hope and help to families around the world.

The certificate and credit really belong to the volunteers who worked hard or were tested. I'm glad so many have been tested. Even though we're losing our son, someone might get to keep theirs because of Uriah. Uriah always hoped it might help his friends, if it didn't help him.

That afternoon the doctors returned. "Although Uriah has only a fine rash on the outside," Dr. Haghighat said, "the chickenpox is attacking his internal organs, causing bleeding sores in his sinus cavities, throat, and mouth. His eyes are infected. His kidneys and liver are near failure. We can't do dialysis. The gathering fluid in his abdomen will eventually cause congestive heart failure. He has gram-negative and gram-positive infections in his blood; falling red blood cell and platelet levels; a white blood count of only

100, despite repeated transfusions; low calcium and potassium levels; and aberrant electrolyte levels."

I blinked, overwhelmed.

Dr. Sanmarco added, "We can give him one shot a day for three days of an experimental medication that will cause his body to mass-produce white blood cells, in an effort to get a response from his bone marrow."

"But you must understand," warned Dr. Haghighat, "they might be healthy cells, or they might be cancerous."

At least either reaction will speed relief of some kind to him.

Tuesday, May 7
The gram-negative and gram-positive infections in his blood disappeared. The swelling in his hands and feet began to go down, and the skin came off in a thick peel. I kept them covered with ointment and wrapped in cloth. The bruises were only red.

"His red blood and platelet count continue to fall," Dr. Haghighat said, "as well as his calcium, potassium, and electrolyte levels. We fed him intravenously, but his blood sugar got too high. We gave him insulin."

Perhaps we shouldn't treat him so his suffering will end.

"I don't want to give up," Uriah said.

The next day Dr. Sanmarco told us, "His white blood count is the same. He's dying, and there's nothing we can do about it."

I returned to Uriah's room. "How would you like to go home?"

His eyes opened wide in surprise. "Yeah!"

He's too weak to make it to Blythe. Nana and Boompa said we could take him to the cabin. I returned to the hall. "Dr. Sanmarco, we want to take Uriah home," I said. "There's nothing more you can do for him, and he wants to go home."

She looked at me like I was crazy. "Do you understand how difficult it will be?"

"He said he wants to go. We aren't worried about taking care of him. One thing does worry me, though: Heather. She won't believe us when we tell her how ill Uriah is. Would you talk to her? Perhaps she'll listen to a doctor."

Dr. Sanmarco and Heidi led Don, Heather, Shiloh, and me to a private office. Dr. Sanmarco explained Uriah's condition. "There's nothing we can do for him; he's dying. Your parents want to take him home to die." She gazed toward Shiloh and Heather. "Do you understand?" Shiloh nodded silently. Heather made no response. She avoided eye contact. "Do you understand?" Dr. Sanmarco repeated.

Heather ignored her.

"Heather, she's talking to you," I said.

"Why ask me?" snapped Heather. "I can't do anything about it!"

Dr. Sanmarco gave me a questioning glance. I turned toward Heather. "You told us you would think we were murderers if we gave up on Uriah. We just want you to know that there isn't anything left we can do."

Heather pursed her lips in mute rage and glared at me. *She feels like we're all ganging up on her. I've exposed her to the hard facts, but I feel I had no choice.* I cried. *Not only is my son suffering, but my daughters are too.*

Shiloh reached out her feet and pressed my foot between them. Our family rose and escaped from the brightly lit office into the comforting dimness of the hallway. I whispered, "Shiloh, you're the only person I know who can hug with your feet!"

Just having that settled makes me feel lighter. They're going to let us go! We can really be a family again—for a short time.

Thursday, May 9

Uriah was moved to the "peds" department to prepare for his departure. Just being in a sunshiny room where he could see outside seemed to perk him up. His WBC was 300, RBC 8.6, and platelets 9,000. Don and Heather went to Blythe for the bills and to get Tanya, then returned to the cabin.

Friday. Uriah asked, "Could you find out if Renee can play a game with me?"

I smiled and jumped up. "I'll go find her!" *He hasn't felt well enough to play for weeks!*

Rene smiled. "Sure! Tell him I'll be right there!"

Uriah tired after just a couple games, but he was happy.

Nurse after nurse dropped in. "I heard you're taking him home?" they whispered to me.

I nodded.

"Hey, Uriah," they smiled. "How ya doin'?" They hugged him.

It's probably the last time they'll see him. They're saying goodbye.

"It makes me mad that the doctors think I'm going to die," Uriah said. "I'm going to get better."

How can he be so sick and in such pain and yet still fight to live? But even this kind of life is worthwhile to Uriah. More than ever, I'm glad we allowed him to make his own choices. He deserves the dignity of being allowed to choose how he will live and where he will die. No one else should decide for him, even if he is only eight.

We wheeled Uriah out of the hospital. The nurses waved goodbye. *Dr. Sanmarco said he'll probably die by next Tuesday, May 14. At least he'll be in a familiar place with his family, his kittens, and his dog.*

May 10, Matched Unrelated Donor update: Two more potential donors. I called Jan Cipkala-Gaffin. "I don't know why the doctors haven't notified you yet. You should stop the search; it's too late. Uriah's home dying."

"I'm really sorry. I hope being home helps."

Saturday, May 11

The Rainbow

Have you ever seen a rainbow
That reaches up to the sky?
It's God's way of showing children
how to get to heaven when they die.
God reaches down His hand,
(that's the rainbow that you see)
then pulls them up to heaven
to be with Him for all eternity.

A rainbow is a sign,
a promise of God's love
to those of us on Earth
from heaven up above.
So when you see a rainbow
reaching toward the sky,
remember all the little children
and the one who had to die.

Don't think of him with sadness;
but happiness, joy, love.
Down here he was in pain and hurt,
but it's peace and joy above.
Free from pain and suffering,
free from sin and strife,
free to love forever,
and to live eternal life.

A rainbow comes and takes our young
to God's great eternal land.
We weep and cry, our sorrow's great,
but wait . . . he's in His hand.
Next time you see a rainbow,
think of all the children gone.
They're up in heaven, they laugh and play,
forever happy with each new dawn.

A rainbow is a sign,
a promise of God's love
to those of us on Earth
from heaven up above.
So when you see a rainbow
reaching toward the sky,
remember all the little children
and the One who *had* to die.[3]

—Carolyn Baschal

On Monday, May 13, a letter from Frank and Dana Matejka requested information about becoming a bone-marrow donor. I called them. "Contact Maggie Kim at the blood bank, or go to the City of Hope to be tested."

I answered a knock at the door. "Hi, I'm Pat, one of the nurses who will examine Uriah every other day." When she finished checking Uriah over, she smiled. "He looks good. He's doing great."

She doesn't know his prognosis. I followed her outside. "I guess they didn't tell you: Uriah's terminal."

She looked at me, undaunted, her bright smile undiminished. "We'll see what God has planned."

She's a nurse; how can she have hope? She knows the prognosis for a patient like Uriah. "O ye of little faith." I nodded and waved goodbye. *After all we've been through, God, I'm still walking by sight and not faith. You had to remind me again: it's not over until it's over—and if you're a Christian, it's not even over then!*

Wednesday, May 15
A book of encouraging poems arrived:
"To Dearest Mara, From Julie with warm thoughts. I love you! Julie"
We aren't forgotten, even though we're far away. Friends still care! I feel like we've let them down somehow. The entire city of Blythe took a risk by becoming involved with Uriah. They're probably bracing themselves, as we are, to deal with Uriah's death.

Friday, May 17
A courier brought more medical supplies. Uriah's lived longer than anticipated.

Saturday, May 18
"How's our boy today?" Christine, the home nurse, asked me.
"I've been able to get him to eat a little tapioca pudding and apple juice, but he looks like he's starving. His sinus infection keeps him from breathing through his nose, and I pull out the thick mucous that clogs his throat so he can breathe."
She listened to his lungs through her stethoscope. "His lungs sound better today. The fluid in his abdomen is better, his temperature is better, and his blood pressure is better too." She packed her little bag and left.
I called Julie Maly. "He's doing a little better. All his bruises and sores are healing, even his hands. But unless his body starts producing blood cells, the outcome will be the same."
He doesn't want to talk about dying. He isn't ready to accept it. Don's missed so much work, and the girls

have missed so much school—it ends in only two weeks. We're pressed between hard choices; they want to be here if something happens, but life must go on.

Uriah's on morphine, so he has no pain, but it's impossible for him to get comfortable. He sleeps most of the time. He slept more when the morphine was at ten. We turned it down, one a day, so he's only on six.

Uriah played UNO with Grandma Ruth and me today, and the day before he played with Don and me. That's better than listening to him play Monopoly with people we can't see, in a morphine dream world.

Sunday, May 19

Fred and Ruth, Debbie, Jeff, Ellie and Joel, Nana and Boompa came to visit us at the cabin. Linda Pietz, her mom, Priscilla, and Jordan also came to drop off rats for Shiloh: Pepper and Salt. Jordan said, "Here, Uriah. I brought you a real arrowhead."

Later Lena's family, Janet, Brian, and Andria came for a barbecue. "Uriah, I brought my racetrack," Brian said.

God, I'm struck by the juxtaposition of death in the midst of so much life. Uriah's dying and we all know it, but we're able to laugh and play and live around him. It's as if the shadow of death isn't so dark or terrifying when he's surrounded by friends. Death is normal, not a bizarre rarity. But the dying are often hidden away, so many people never see it. What we're doing feels more natural.

Monday, May 20

Don and Heather went to Blythe to get schoolwork, check on the animals, and get things for Uriah's memorial service.

The home nurse said Uriah's lungs were noisy today. Much worse than yesterday. He looks pale too. I'm worried about him.

When Uriah woke up, he pointed to his right lung. "Mom, it hurts here."

It's pneumonia. I knelt in front of him. "The doctors won't give you anything for this infection. If you're going to get well, it's up to you. You need to cough it up, even if it hurts, and eat and drink, even if it doesn't taste good or feel good."

He tried to cough and ate a cup of tapioca pudding. "This tastes good."

Sleepless, in the middle of the night, I gazed out at the stars shining over the mountains and sang with the radio:

It's so hard to understand,
And accept the Father's plan,
When it means my will must die.
After all those countless prayers
Can I still believe He cares,
Though I've heard no answers to my cries?

Whisper again to my heart
What I believed from the start.
Remind me Jesus answers
And when my heart sees no light,
Help me hold on with all my might,
And believe that Jesus answers.

A blaze of white tore across my view of the star-studded sky. I was so startled, I stopped singing. The radio played on:

It's true that there's one thing I need to know,
It's true my God is in control.

Hold on with all your might,
Keep trusting through the night,
Believe that Jesus answers.

Believe with all your heart.
You've known it from the start.
Believe that Jesus answers.[4]

God, that was the largest, most beautiful falling star I've ever seen. I know everything will be OK, but I'm not sure if Uriah will be with You or with us.

🌿 🌿 🌿

Charleene Corby called on Tuesday, May 21. "I'm going to be in the area, and I have something to drop off to you."

We gave her directions and she arrived in her red sports car, full of life and laughter, as always. She marched into the living room and stared at Uriah. He struggled to stay awake but couldn't keep his eyes open for long.

"He has trouble keeping awake because of his medication," I explained.

"That's OK. It's time for my appointment anyhow. Bye, Uriah."

She strolled calmly out the door, but as soon as she passed outside, her shoulders bowed, her eyes filled with tears, and she rested her head in her hands for a moment. I hugged her. *She knew when she played Monopoly with Uriah that he was terminal. I guess she thought he'd stay like that. But the child who was so robust and vibrant is now so thin and weak. . . .*

Wordlessly, she handed me the letter she'd brought:

Enclosed are money orders totaling over $300.00 raised at the Galt Academy for you and Uriah. The main person in charge of this fund-raiser/raffle is Pat McCullar. I can't begin to tell you how much we wish good health for Uriah.

With respect and warm wishes,
Glenn A. Mueller, Chairman

Dr. Sanmarco called me Friday, May 24. "What's happening?"

"All his sores have healed. He still has sinus and eye infections. He's eaten a little tapioca pudding and taken a little apple juice."

"Maybe we should examine him?"

"This is a three-day weekend. I don't think he'll make it to Tuesday," I murmured. "He looks so pale and tired."

"Let us know what's happening."

"I'll call if anything happens."

On Tuesday, May 28, Uriah was too weak to travel. Instead Pat drew some of Uriah's blood and Don took it to the doctors.

"It was the wrong type of tube," Don said when he returned. "The blood clotted. Dr. Sanmarco sent a couple new ones for tomorrow."

In the morning, Christine drew Uriah's blood into tubes. Don drove to the clinic and returned at 4:00 P.M.

"Well?" I asked.

"The doctors said there wasn't much to look at, but the white cells were all normal except one that was suspicious." He smiled. "They're coming to examine Uriah tomorrow."

"Could it be a miracle?"

Don shrugged. My eyes filled with tears.

Oh God, I'm amazed at how You're weaving our story. The roller-coaster ride isn't over yet. It's impossible to tell what will happen next; but as always, everything's in Your hands.

I called Nana. "Just pray, Mom."

I dialed Pastor. "We were just praying for you," he said.

"Well, don't stop!" I said.

"Julie Maly, I've got wonderful news for your little prayer warriors," I told her.

Dr. Haghighat called May 30. "We're on our way."

The weather was rainy and foggy, and they got lost. Don went and brought them back.

"Mom, can I have apple juice and tapioca pudding?" Uriah asked. He watched TV and seemed alert. The doctors traded surprised glances. They examined him, exchanged medical jargon, and rose. "Is there somewhere we could talk?" asked Dr. Sanmarco.

Don motioned to the dining-room table.

"His counts on the tenth of May were white blood cells 300, hemoglobin 8.6 and platelets 9,000," Dr. Sanmarco began.

"Today the white blood cells are 1,500, hemoglobin 3.6, and platelets 28,000," interjected Dr. Haghighat. "There's no sign of leukemia in his blood."

My mouth fell open.

"But the hemoglobin level is dangerously low," said Dr. Sanmarco. "His liver isn't swollen, and his spleen is OK. Could you bring him to the hospital for a bone-marrow test?"

Oh, Jesus, You really do answer! God, are You giving us a miracle? I looked at Don and saw my own awe mirrored in his face. "When?" I asked.

"It's too late today. Tomorrow morning?" Dr. Sanmarco asked.

"We'll bring him down," Don promised.

"Wait a minute," I said. "Uriah, what do you think?"

"I don't want the bone-marrow test, but I do want the medicine."

"We can give you extra morphine so it won't hurt," said Dr. Sanmarco.

"OK."

Almost anything could happen—all the way from packed marrow to remission, all the way from further treatment to nothing. I called all the prayer chains and people I could think of.

Oh, God, I'm trying not to get my hopes up, but even Uriah says he feels stronger and stronger. Boy, will the nurses be surprised when we walk back into the pediatric ward tomorrow.

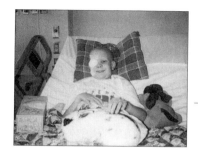

Twenty

Waiting for Dawn
(June–July 1991)

When you're lost in darkness, I will hold the light.
I will help you find your way through the night. . . .
—Steven Curtis Chapman

ON FRIDAY, MAY 31, 1991, URIAH WENT THROUGH THE BONE
marrow—without morphine. That upset him, but he
managed to use Lamaze. When we got to the ward, Nelda,
Jean, and other nurses crowded around. "Uriah, how are
you?"

"It's good to see you!"

"I get to be your nurse first," Bob said.

"I'll be right back with a game," Renee promised.

"He's in 40 percent remission," Dr. Sanmarco said.

Without any treatment! "How could that happen?"

"It may have been caused by the allergic reaction he
had to fluconazole. It must have triggered something in his
immune system to fight the cancer."

*I know it's prayer. So many people need to know! Good
news at last!*

After his first unit of blood, Uriah threw up and stopped
urinating. Dr. Sanmarco shook her head. "I've always been

sure about when to start and stop treatment, but this time I don't know how much to do." She stared at his IV pole a moment, then turned to the nurse. "Start hyperalimentation, continue giving blood to get his hemoglobin up to eleven, Tagamet for his stomach, calcium, potassium, and prednisone."

The "kitchen lady" stuck her head in Uriah's room. "I was so pleased to see his name on the dinner list with his special requests, I just had to come by and say hello!"

She's found watermelon for Uriah in the dead of winter before! God, so many good people are remembering us in their prayers!

A volunteer couple with two Chihuahua puppies opened the door. "Oh, he's asleep." They turned to go.

"Uriah, there's some puppies here," I said.

His eyes flew open and he looked around. The elderly man and woman laid the tiny, squirming, fuzzy balls on the bed. Uriah beamed and caressed them. *I hope they can see how much this rejuvenates him.*

Saturday night Uriah's breathing became labored. An oxygen mask was placed over his face. He was wired to a heart and respirator monitor, near comatose. Dr. Sanmarco looked stunned. "We don't know what to do," she said. "We fixed everything that was wrong. He should be feeling great."

Maybe that's the problem; we fixed everything.

"There's a new infection in his blood," she said. "His lungs are filling with fluid. His kidneys are in trouble. Giving him blood and raising his blood pressure may have been like putting water pressure into a weak pipe; it could leak."

She examined him again. He was sluggish and unable to speak. His pupils were barely reactive.

"We suspect either the leukemia has gone into his central nervous system [CNS], a leakage of blood in the brain, or a viral infection of the brain," she said.

Death watch, again.

I called Don at the cabin. "We have a decision to make. If they do a CAT scan, it will show if blood is leaking in his brain. The damage would already be done, but they could give him platelets to prevent more leaking. They said if they treat him for leukemia in the brain, they should treat the leukemia in his bones."

"With what?"

"I don't know. But the spinal tap to find out might make the damage worse, and if he has CNS involvement, he can't have a transplant ."

"What good could any of that do?"

"You're right. If God's going to do it, He will—without help. Everything we've done has backfired."

"I'll take Heather home today for her junior high graduation tomorrow. We'll come back Wednesday and take Uriah home to Blythe."

"That sounds wonderful. We've been away from home too long. It's far from medical help."

"I know, but I can't miss any more work."

Don's needed to be here. Uriah could have—and should have—died. That's the problem with miracles; some people don't believe he was really dying.

God, unless You intervene, we're bringing him home to die—again. God, it's so hard to get our hopes up and have them dashed. It's like a cruel joke. Why did You allow him to be in 40 percent remission and then allow such a heart-breaking blow?

All the people I told he was doing better will feel the same disappointment and hurt I feel. I hate hurting people.

Monday, June 3

The morphine was turned down another notch to only 4 ml an hour. "Don and I don't want you to treat Uriah for the infection in his blood," I told Dr. Sanmarco. "It could put more pressure on his circulatory system."

Don took Heather and Andria to Blythe for Heather's eighth-grade graduation. When Janet and Brian visited, Uriah became more alert. "Could I have some games to play with Brian?" I got out the game bag, but he was too weak to play.

He stayed up late. "Can I have fruit rolls?"

"It's too late to go out. Can I get you something from the vending machines?"

He nodded.

His breathing's irregular. I stayed up as late as I could.

In the morning sun on Tuesday, June 4, Uriah sat up. "Mom, can I watch cartoons?"

I scrambled to find them on the television. *He's awake?*

"Could I have breakfast?"

He's hungry? I set his tray on a table over his lap. *He's hard to understand, but he's talking.* He ate a few bites and drank juice and milk. *And eating! His breathing's easy, and he's coughing fluid out of his lungs.*

Uriah ate more. "Mom, could you get me something to eat from the store?"

God, what are You doing now? I raced to the store and returned. Uriah watched cartoons and ate.

Dr. Sanmarco walked into the room and froze when she saw him. She gaped and threw up her hands in disbelief. *She just can't figure out how he can keep changing so rapidly—deathly one day and surviving the next.*

Nana and Boompa trudged up the sidewalk to the pediatric ward and glanced into Uriah's room through the window. Uriah sat, eating toast and watching TV. The grim sorrow on Nana's face melted into amazement and joy. Tears of relief ran down her cheeks as Uriah waved. She stayed only minutes, but wonder glowed on her face.

God, You've granted us another miracle.

Don called from Blythe. Laughter and chatter echoed over the phone. "Heather, Andria, and Libby are getting ready for graduation. They're having a great time—Heather, your hair looks a little ragged in the back."

"Daddy!"

On the video Don made, the girls stood together like three musketeers, "All for one and one for all."

It really bothers me not to be there for her graduation, but someone has to stay with Uriah, and Don's not good at that.

Grandma Ruth sat down, awestruck by Uriah's transformation.

"Mom, you got the wrong kind of Fun Fruits," Uriah complained.

Debbie, Joel, and Ellie stopped by. Uriah seemed stronger. Renee stopped outside the sliding-glass door and waved. "I can't come in. I have a cold."

Uriah waved back enthusiastically.

Pastor Dannenburg visited and prayed with us.

"To have miracles happen, you have to be in a bad predicament in the first place," I said. I thought about the falling star in the mountains. *God is performing miracles. Not that I doubted God could perform a miracle, I just wasn't sure He would do it now.*

Wednesday, June 5, Dr. Haghighat wrote a note for Don: "This is to certify Uriah Alexander has acute lymphoblastic leukemia in relapse. Since April 29, '91, he has been in critical condition that required his parents be with him."

The prison won't believe it happened again. "What will happen with Uriah now?" I asked.

Dr. Haghighat leaned back in his chair and laughed. With a wry smile he shook his head. "I honestly don't know."

I waited impatiently for Don to call. *It's time to go.*

He called at 11:00 A.M. "I want to sleep another hour. We got home late last night."

Shiloh, Uriah, and I played games with Renee and waited.

Don called at 2:00 P.M. "I just woke up. I'll have Heather pack."

At 4:00 P.M. he called again. "I'm having trouble breathing. My asthma medication isn't working. I'll keep packing but take it easy."

I walked to the grocery store and got Polish sausages for Uriah. I made the final stitches on an afghan.

Heather crept in at 8:30 P.M.

"Finally!" I snapped. *Uh-oh. She's acting odd.* "Is Daddy OK?" I added quietly.

"He's upset. We ran into some serious idiots on the road."

I went out to the truck. Don gripped the steering wheel with both hands so tightly, his knuckles were white. "I can't calm down," he said through clenched teeth.

"You ought to see a doctor before we leave." I threw the large load of luggage I carried into the back of the truck. When I came out with another load, Don had taken everything out and was packing it in—his way.

At last Uriah climbed in the truck with his Polish sausage. He sighed. "I can't eat this." Don stopped at a Subway sandwich place. A flier about Uriah hung on the door. It was 10:00 P.M. "We're closed!" they shouted. Don pointed to the sign and then pointed to Uriah in the truck. Uriah waved. The teenage boy motioned us to wait a minute. He returned with Uriah's sandwich.

After 1:00 A.M., Don and the girls carried in bags and boxes while I set up Uriah's IV at home. "Don, I can't find the morphine cartridge."

"Heather, have you seen it?" he asked.

"Not since the cabin."

We hunted through the baggage in vain. Don sat down heavily and sighed. "I must have left all my medicine and Uriah's at Nana's cabin."

"The cartridge we're using isn't enough to make it to morning," I said.

"I guess I'll go all the way back to the cabin," Don said.

"There's no way either one of us would make it. Even if we could, it would be 10:30 tomorrow morning before we got back."

"I'm going to look in the truck again." He plodded out the door.

God, help me. What can we do? The solution flashed into my mind: *There's some left in the discarded cartridges in the sharps container!*

Don took the cartridge I found that would last until the next evening, put it on the pump, and programmed the volume. "Tomorrow morning, I'll go back and get it."

Thursday, June 6

Heather went to the last day of school, but Shiloh stayed home. I cleaned and paid bills.

The trip had taxed Uriah's energy. He slept a lot but played and ate too. If he grew stronger, he was to return for an examination Friday, June 14.

Friday, June 7

Charleene has informed me of your recent bit of good luck regarding Uriah. I can't begin to tell you how close all of us have become to this situation, and your good news is certainly well received.

. . . Meanwhile, I look forward to hearing from you again very soon, I hope with the news that Uriah is in 100 percent remission.

Sincerely,
Glenn A. Mueller, Chair

Hi, Uriah!

My name is Pat McCullar. I'm the manager of C.T.C. Rec Fund . . . at the academy in Galt. I had a yard sale last Saturday, June 1. Our academy staff and friends donated a lot of items to be sold. We sold every item. This check is a result of the sale.

I want you to know I hold you very close in my heart. Even though we've never met, I love you very, very much. Charleene Corby just phoned me. She said you are 40 percent in remission. That is so wonderful, sweetie. You keep that chin up and keep fighting.

Pat

Saturday, June 8
"Roberta, Geri, and I have taken care of Sunday school for the whole summer," Mary Watts told me.

"What a relief. Thanks!"

"You were unanimously reelected superintendent of Christian education."

"I don't know why. Everyone's doing my job for me."

Pastor visited. Later Theresa had balloons delivered, and Lori brought a decorated banner.

Sunday, June 9

"Everyone's supportive," Don said when he returned from church. "Carrie Stroschein asked if it's OK to visit. Julie sent roses and said she'll call."

Tuesday, June 11

Julie called. "Can you come for a tea party?" Uriah asked.

"Can I invite Carol too?" begged Shiloh.

Wednesday, June 12

The girls held their party in the dining room. Then they dressed up in my fancy clothes and made a silly video. Uriah and Mrs. Maly used a piano bench pulled up to the couch where Uriah lay. They didn't eat much but talked about friends and school.

God, again, I'm amazed by life and death side by side. Uriah is so ill, and the girls are so full of life. It seems like a contradiction. But it also seems the way You intended it to be. It doesn't seem to bother the girls at all. It reaffirms my belief this is the right thing to do—not just for Uriah, but for all of us. If our children live with a dying person, they understand death is not to be feared, but is a doorway to eternal life. Just like The Last Battle *by C. S. Lewis. It's not our greatest defeat; it's our greatest deliverance.*

Dearest Uriah,

It was so good to see you feeling well enough to have a tea party today. Thank you so much for having me over and sharing your smiles and your picture book with me. (But *what* are you going to do about those sisters of yours? Ha, ha!) I love you!

Mrs. Maly

Thursday, June 13

Uriah was admitted in the afternoon with a swelling under his eye half the size of a golf ball. There was no indication it would drain, but it burst after 8:00.

The next day Dr. Sanmarco informed me, "I want a bone-marrow test done today. Uriah's RBC is 9.8; his WBC 4,400; and his platelets 48,000. When he left the hospital his RBC was 6.8, WBC 1,500, and platelets 28,000."

"Have you checked the peripheral blood for blasts?" I asked.

"No."

"Perhaps the counts have gone up so quickly because of blasts."

"It's probably because of the infection."

Uriah waited until the door closed behind her. "Mom, do I have to have a bone marrow? If I do, I want Dr. Haghighat to do it."

Something's wrong.

When Dr. Haghighat came in, Uriah asked, "How is the blood?"

Dr. Haghighat paused.

"Uriah's wondering whether you checked the peripheral blood for blasts," I explained. "He's worried about having a bone marrow. Unless there's some chemo he could have, there's really no point, is there? If the bone marrow is good, it'll show soon enough."

Dr. Haghighat called back later. "I'm not going to do a bone marrow. There are 20–22 percent blasts in Uriah's blood, and his liver enzymes have gone up to 1.8. It has to be under 1.5 for him to get retinoic acid."

That's the last treatment available. At least Uriah's blood cultures have come back negative.

Don called. "Vaughn Panzer from work gave Uriah a blue Great Dane puppy."

"We were supposed to get one for Heather."

"Well if . . ."

"I know, I know," I sighed. "I've been wondering: If Uriah were miraculously healed, would people think I felt I was more deserving? Would they wonder, 'Why her son and not my child?' If he survives," I continued, "God has a job for him to do. And whatever it is, it would be harder than everything we've been through so far. Think about Moses, saved by God's intervention as a baby in the basket."

"I always thought it would be neat to have a pastor in the family," Don said.

"It might be something harder than that." Before he was born, I gave Uriah to God, just as Hannah gave Samuel to Him. *Hannah got only a little time with her son. My time may be short too. It's beginning to look bad.*

✿　✿　✿

On Saturday animals came to the ward. Uriah's count was good enough that he could touch them instead of gazing longingly from behind glass. The bunny, Misty, seemed happy to rest in the quiet gentleness of Uriah's room after the bustle of the playroom. Uriah ran his hand along her sleek back. *That's the first time I've seen Uriah smile in a long time.* Next two terriers visited. The white one, Dusty, snuggled into Uriah's lap and didn't want to leave when it was time.

Don, Heather, and Shiloh arrived at 10:25 P.M.—with a huge, gregarious puppy.

"I'll share it with Heather, but I won't give it all up," Uriah said.

"Heather can have the tail and the legs, but Uriah wants the rest," I quipped. *Uriah smiled!*

Heather and Uriah started discussing which part of the dog's anatomy the other deserved. I giggled. "I can see it now: 'I want my part of the dog to sleep with me.' 'Well, my part is going to sleep with me.'" My hands gripped each other in a mock tug of war. "*Rip!*"

Uriah laughed until he mopped tears from his eyes. *It's hard to think about going through the torture of waiting for him to die again.*

"Andy said someone from Blythe who transferred to CIM thought all the money raised for donor testing was going for our personal use," Don said. "Andy set him straight, but I wonder how many others feel like Murphy did?"

People have been very good to us, but it can't erase the agony we've felt—or that which is yet to come. "How's work?"

"So far, the job seems OK."

Uriah played games with Renee and Monopoly with Mr. Nord. "This is about math," Uriah told him.

Renee beamed at me. "Uriah's doing so well."

"I wish things were going as well on the inside," I said. Uriah's count dropped so much they gave him a pint of red cells. *I wish his breathing were more regular.*

Tuesday, June 18. Solvey took Uriah's temperature. "I'll be Uriah's nurse today. The others said he's really bad, but I know that how he is now is nothing compared to how he was before."

I remember another nurse saying, "I tried to get out of here right away yesterday because one of my patients got bad, and if something happened, I'd never get away." It's not that they lack compassion; they're trying to protect themselves. They wonder about the "what ifs" too. Perhaps they feel failure when a patient dies.

Some have told me, "Gina can't take care of those who are really sick. She always has an excuse." It's been a long time since she's been Uriah's nurse.

Jean said, "It's hard for us to keep our spirits up too." I knew a nurse who quit because she was crying all the way to work and back. At least they have a choice. Parents don't.

I'm glad Uriah wants to be home. It's a small way to say thanks to the nurses. I really appreciate the nurses who cared for Uriah when he was really sick: Bob, Rosemary, Jean, Kathy Z., Georgi-anna, Susan, and others.

Solvey turned from Uriah's IV. "You've taken such wonderful care of Uriah. You should be Mother of the Year or something."

"It wasn't me, it was God who made him do so well."

"Oh, but you really did a good job."

"I had good teachers—you nurses."

"But you did it."

She's not going to quit, is she? "Thanks." *Do the nurses and doctors think I feel self-important, holier-than-thou? I didn't have anything to do with Uriah's progress. It's God and Uriah working together—and sometimes I think we've impeded that progress. I'm so grateful God is loving and in control. It makes this nightmare more bearable.*

I jumped up in surprise when Val came in the next day. "It's so good to see you!"

"How are you? Uriah looks good."

"We're taking it a day at a time."

"I'm not working here very often now. Here's where you can contact me if you want to." She handed me a slip of paper. "Dr. Sanmarco's the one who told me how Uriah's doing. She said, 'If God's doing a miracle, He's sure doing a lousy job.'"

Uriah slept until 1:00 P.M. Don and the girls arrived at 2:30, Janet and her kids at 3:00.

"What does it take to get sprung from a place like this for lunch?" Don teased the nurse. With a hospital pass in hand, the whole crowd walked to Sizzler. Heather pushed Uriah's wheelchair while the rest of us gathered around him, laughing and joking. Uriah ordered all-you-can-eat shrimp and steak, plus the salad bar. He ate only a nibble of everything, but he ate! And he enjoyed a full share of the boisterous laughter and teasing.

Back in his room, Uriah fell asleep almost immediately. Everyone left by 7:30. Uriah woke again at 9:00 P.M. and ate a few bites of a peanut-butter-and-jelly sandwich while we played Monopoly.

The nurse double-checked his blood pressure at 10:45. "His blood pressure's 129/102. If it goes higher, I'll have to give him something to bring it down."

"He's got an itchy rash on his chest and stomach too."

"Let's change the shirt he's wearing and see if it goes away."

It was still there later, so he took Benadryl. He'd almost won the Monopoly game when we both got tired of playing. He was still awake when I got back from my midnight shower. "Would you read to me?"

I read *The Plant That Ate Dirty Socks* until my eyes were closing against my will. "Uriah, it's a quarter after one. I'm too tired to read anymore." *God, I feel so guilty. What if he dies? Will the words "Couldn't you watch with me for one hour?" echo in my mind?*

On Thursday, June 20, I washed the pus off Uriah's eye. *Today it's flat and getting a scab. I think he's about done with this eye infection.*

Dr. Haghighat examined him. "We're going to repeat Uriah's chest X-ray. His breath smells like thrush; is he using Lavoris and Nystatin?"

"I'll make sure he does."

"I'm going to give Uriah more albumin today and do a urine test."

"Why?"

"I'm trying to make sure the liver is the problem and not the kidneys."

Regardless, he won't be able to have retinoic acid. "It's God who heals, not just medicine."

Dr. Haghighat consulted Uriah's charts. "His liver enzymes are even higher today: 1.9. But his urine looks better."

I really don't know what God has planned, or why He intervened when He did. I guess I'll know when it's all over—or maybe only when we get to heaven.

Uriah slept all day June 21, but not soundly. He had bad dreams.

LaVonne and Melanie came at 2:30 P.M.

"Uriah, look. They brought you lunch and presents."

He lifted his head and smiled. "Thanks," he murmured.

At 5:00 P.M. Linda and Priscilla tapped on the door. "We left Jordan at the clinic because he might be sick." Priscilla handed me a large container.

I opened it. "Butter cookies!"

"Mark, Jordan, and Priscilla made them," Linda said. "Gotta run." She gave me a hug. "God bless you!"

I started to close the door behind them, but I spotted Dr. Sanmarco crying in the hall. "Is she all right?" I asked the nurse.

"Yeah," the nurse whispered as Dr. Sanmarco left the ward. "A little boy who was in a car accident reminded her of her grandsons."

Minutes later the PA system crackled. "Code blue, pe-diatrics, front station. Code blue, pediatrics, front station." Dr. Sanmarco ran into the ward, her coat flapping. She stopped short when she saw no bustle of activity. "It's not one of 'my' kids," she sighed in relief.

Don got memorandums instructing him that forms had to be filed at the personnel office by June 27, or we would have to pay for the time he took off while Uriah was ill.

Saturday, June 22, Dr. Haghighat sat down. "I'm afraid I'm here with bad news. Uriah's sinuses are infected."

That's no surprise.

"His fever went down."

I didn't even know he had one!

"But his white count is going up. It's 14,000 already."

Active leukemia.

"We're going to treat the infections. The CNS leukemia could cause that."

CNS leukemia! Anything is possible, but what bad news I have to share. Earlier Uriah said he felt stronger. Dr. Haghighat can give him a shot of vincristine. Maybe that will lower his liver enzymes. It's never over 'til it's over.

Uriah threw up when Dr. Haghighat examined him on Sunday, June 23. He was given Phenergan and hallucinated. Shiloh watched TV and played Nintendo. Gina was Uriah's nurse. *I know how hard this is for her; what a gift.*

Don called at 6:30 P.M. "I'm going to Tim and Lori's to work on their garage."

Jan was the night nurse. "Almost no one showed up," he apologized.

He does a good job. I wish my head would stop aching. Uriah stirred so much, I woke up every fifteen minutes. He talked in Phenergan dreams.

Monday at six Uriah tried to go to the bathroom and threw up. Kathy Z. turned to me while checking the IV and whispered, "The blood tests came back with all kinds of abnormalities."

It's nice of her to warn me, but I already know just by watching Uriah.

"Electrolytes off, potassium very low, WBC 28,000," Dr. Haghighat said solemnly.

"We still want to take him home," I said. He nodded silently.

Here we are, again. Uriah can't even have a shot of vincristine because his bowels aren't active. There's nothing the doctors can do. We're taking him home to die—again. It's in God's hands—where it's always been. Now we'll see what God intends.

God, it's hard not to try to convince You how wonderful it would be if You healed Uriah. The only one who could cure him, the only one who could receive the glory would be You. So many Christians are praying for him and so many people are watching to see what You will do. I want so much for You to heal him. I struggle to want Your will more.

I hope we can get home with Uriah. I hope God will show me how I will survive if he dies. I hope He will show me why He healed Uriah partially but not all the way. I hope I didn't mess up a miracle.

Linda called. "The kids and I are coming to visit, if that's all right."

Shiloh started a game with Priscilla and Jordan. Linda and I started to pray. Dr. Sanmarco burst in. "I need to talk to both of you!"

We stepped into the hall. "One of Uriah's tests came back positive for hepatitis. Linda and the kids have to go right away."

"I'll pray anyhow," Linda promised and clasped my hand.

Now I can't even pray with fellow Christians? We're isolated.

After she left, Kathy Z. came in. "What will you need from the Home Care Pharmacy?"

The phone rang. "How are things going?" Nana asked.

"Oh, fine." Anger and hurt roughened my voice.

"You sound . . . like you shouldn't be alone."

I struggled not to cry. "The nurse is here. I'm OK. I just found out a hepatitis test came back positive. I'll call you back later. The doctor's here." Tears trickled.

"Maybe you should go out for a while?" Dr. Sanmarco suggested.

And desert Uriah? "No, I don't think so."

"It's just that you're struggling so hard not to cry."

"That's for your benefit. Uriah's used to seeing me cry."

They drifted out into the hall, then marched back in. "Uriah needs to have an HIV test because someone in the lab contaminated themselves with his blood," Dr. Sanmarco said.

The phone rang. "I'm coming down," Janet said.

She heard the message I left this morning: "Don't wait too long. Uriah's really bad."

"Can I call you back in five minutes? The doctor's here."

"Either that or I can be on my way in five minutes."

"OK, but I have to warn you, Uriah had a positive hepatitis test, and anyone who's around him might have to get a gamma globulin shot."

"We'll take our chances. We're coming."

What a friend!

I hung up the phone and swung away from Dr. Sanmarco and Kathy. "I don't want you to make me leave."

"We wouldn't do that."

They both stepped out. *Well, if they were waiting to see me fall apart, they got what they wanted.*

Andria, Brian, and Shiloh played while Janet and I talked. "Do you want me to get dinner?" Janet asked.

"That would be great."

Janet turned at the door. "I'll take the girls to help."

Stephanie rapped on the door with two people from Victory Outreach. They didn't care about the hepatitis either. *God, even in isolation You bring people to pray with me!*

We laid hands on Uriah and prayed. In a drugged sleep, he talked without moving his lips. *It sounds like he's praying with us.* Stephanie cried. *God, this whole thing's such a struggle for her. She's just a baby Christian. You promised You won't let a wavering flame blow out.*

After Janet returned, Don and Heather arrived with the Great Dane puppy. "Don't let her knock over my IV pole," Uriah said.

"I'll take the puppy home with me so Don and the girls can stay at the hospital," Grandma Ruth offered.

"That's OK, Mom," Don said. "We really need to go to the cabin so I can pull out the carpet to dry. The puppy had an accident on the way."

Soon everyone was gone again except Shiloh, Uriah, and me.

Jan slipped in and checked Uriah's IV. "I'm the only nurse tonight."

Uriah tried to go to the bathroom at 5:30 A.M., and I had to call Jan for help. Uriah threw up.

Before Jan left, he paused. "I heard you're leaving for home. I just want you to know a lot of people are thinking about all of you and wishing you well."

I stumbled over words of thanks.

Tuesday, at last.

Dr. Sanmarco checked on us. "Do you have everything you need? What about prescriptions?"

"Can I have one for eyedrops, thrush medicine, and Tigan?"

"I'll drop off the prescriptions at the pharmacy for you."

"Thanks. That would help a lot." *She's being so nice. Maybe she feels sorry for me. Perhaps she thinks I feel betrayed by God. She doesn't understand how I view God and His ways.*

Andy pushed through the door. "Anything I can do to help?" He packed our bags until Don and Heather came. Don picked up the prescriptions, and at last, we headed for home.

Four hours later, we pushed Uriah's wheelchair into the mobile home, gave him a shot of Phenergan, and he went to sleep. I called Pastor. "I just want to let you know, we're home."

Wednesday, June 26

Uriah sat up and watched TV. "Velvet!" he called. The Great Dane puppy trotted up to him and nuzzled him with its wet nose. Uriah smiled.

Pastor called. "Can I bring communion out for you?"

"We sure need it," I said.

Thursday, June 27

"Gee, my stomach's not bothering me," Uriah said. "Maybe I'll eat something—a little later." *His eye looks better, and he's more awake.* The girls went swimming at the high school with friends, and Carol spent the night.

Uriah received a birthday a card:

. . . Our hopes and prayers for your son Uriah to find the right donor [are] still being prayed. We are hoping someday . . . to welcome Uriah into our scout troop. He will fit right in . . . he is like the boys in our troop . . . . because he is fighting this cancer with all he has in him. Uriah has help[ed] some of these boys see that life isn't as hard to them as they thought, because they look at Uriah and see him fighting cancer. So you see, Uriah has a gift. . . . Everyone Uriah came in touch with, they walk away with a smile on their face because they look at Uriah and see him facing death, and he's always smiling. Then what right have we got to feel that life is so bad? Look at Uriah; he isn't crying over the way things are for him. . . . Mrs. Alexander, you have a very special little boy, and I find it a honor . . . to have known him. We . . . are very proud to have Uriah as a honor[ary] scout of our troop.

Jack Morey

June 28

What a miracle it would be for God to completely restore Uriah's health! I continue to pray for this miracle. But I see an even greater miracle that He has already worked in your family in His love for you and the close relationship you and Uriah have with Him. I am thankful with you for that. We will continue to keep your whole family in our prayers.

Our love and best wishes,
Laurel Brann

The *Palo Verde Valley Times*, Friday, June 28:

Dear Friends:

We are so grateful that the love and concern of the people of Blythe has continued to encourage and comfort us in our struggle with Uriah's cancer. When things go wrong and death is near, many people turn away, but not the people of Blythe. . . . Please continue to pray for him and us.

With great gratitude,
Mara Lee Alexander and Family

Editor's Note:

Mara Alexander called yesterday to tell us they had brought Uriah home from the hospital. The cancer cells have shown up again and are multiplying. The pneumonia is still with him and he is very weak—but very happy to be home. . . . "His birthday is July 25," his mother said, "and he's determined to be nine years old."[1]

God, I feel a growing uneasiness. I haven't seen any more falling stars or rainbows since we've been home. I keep hearing "When You Are a Soldier" by Steven Curtis Chapman on the radio. It's about You helping us through hard times. God, I hope You're not telling me the time to part has come. You know what it's like to lose a Son.

Saturday, June 29
　　Julie Maly brought over some schoolwork. "His eye looks worse," I said, "but he's been awake most of the day."
　　Uriah stayed up late and ate two peanuts before he fell asleep.

Sunday, June 30
　　We didn't go to church. Don went to work. I cleaned and sewed. Uriah played Nintendo.
　　After Don got home from a double shift, swelling started in Uriah's cheeks and spread until his lower lip stuck out. *An allergic reaction.* I discontinued the thrush medicine. The swelling receded.

Janet called. Our conversation drifted. "It's amazing how God has worked through Uriah's life," she said.

"He can work miracles through anyone's life." *I can't believe we're talking about religion.*

"How do you become a Christian? I've felt most of my life I wanted to be a Christian, but my feelings didn't fit into religion. I always felt that to be a Christian, you had to work fast and furious to stop sinning and never sin again. Deep down inside, I've been waiting and waiting and waiting for the right time. And suddenly I feel like I've waited too long. I know what I want, I just have no idea how to ask for it."

We prayed together and she asked God into her life. "Thanks so much," she said. "I knew you were the right person to help me. You don't know how much I really love you. See you Friday!"

I wiped tears from my eyes as I hung up the phone. *God, Janet asked Jesus into her heart! But You already know that, don't You? I'm overjoyed! Her family will be coming Friday. It'll be good to see them.*

That night I was afraid Uriah would slip away. *I don't want him to be afraid.* I read him scriptures about heaven, highlighting them in blue: Philippians 1:19–23; 2 Corinthians 4:16—5:9; 2 Timothy 4:6b–8; and 1 Corinthians 15:51–55. I stayed up until 3:00 A.M. and gave him medicine for his fever.

On Monday, July 1, I woke on the couch at 9:30. Uriah was watching Heather play Nintendo. I started laundry and dishes. *Uriah's high temperature!* I trotted over and put my hand on his forehead. He felt cool to the touch. I took his temperature: it was over 103. *How could I let it get so high?* It took a long time for him to take his medicine.

His temperature rose above 104. I gave him a lukewarm sponge bath. His breathing was fast and shallow. His pulse raced.

I called Don at work. "I think you'd better come home."

Vaughn Panzer and Don clattered up the porch. Don opened the door for him. "Thanks for the ride. Come on in."

Vaughn knelt beside Uriah and spoke softly. Uriah's eyes were closed. He seemed to be concentrating on breathing, but he nodded now and then. After a few minutes, Vaughn rose and Don went out with him. Tears streamed down my face.

Don closed the front door behind him. "I hope you didn't mind me bringing Vaughn in. I wanted someone to back me up for leaving work early if there's any question about how ill Uriah is."

"That's fine."

"Girls, come out here, near Uriah." They slipped back to their room after a while. *They still don't think he'll die. I hope they're right.*

I hovered near Uriah as he tried to sleep. I tried to work on bills. Don tried to organize our video library. Uriah's temperature stabilized at 102.4. *He's had as much medicine as he can.*

"There's something in my lungs. I can't breathe," he said.

I sat him up straighter. "Did that help?"

He nodded. "I'm thirsty." I gave him small sips of water.

"My chest hurts." Don jumped to his feet and gave him a bolus of morphine. *Don's afraid Uriah will panic. God, neither of us could bear it if this brave child becomes afraid in life's final moments.* We gave Uriah three more boluses to ease the pain and open his air passageways.

"Girls, come here," I called. They crept from their room. "It's time to say goodbye." *I hope I don't have to insist with Heather.*

She gave him a hug: "I love you, Uriah." Shiloh hugged him too.

I wonder if he's as afraid of dying alone, as I am that I won't be here when the time comes. I sat beside him.

"Sit me up straighter."

I did my best.

"Water." Don held the cup to his lips. It went down the wrong pipe. Uriah didn't even cough. Don's face twisted with guilt and agony.

"It's all right. It doesn't matter," I consoled.

"I'm hungry," Shiloh said. Don went with her to make something to eat. I tried to sit Uriah up straighter. "Uriah, I'm sorry. That's the best I can do."

He gazed past my left shoulder.

"That's great. Park the car like that."

What? I looked into his eyes. His pupils completely dilated, though he continued to breathe. *He's gone!* "Don! Don! Look at his eyes!" I shouted.

Don ran from the kitchen and looked at Uriah. Confusion registered on his face. Uriah was still breathing, but his head flopped back.

"He's gone. He's gone," I lamented. "Look at his eyes."

Uriah's body ceased to breathe. After a stunned silence, I wept. I pulled Uriah's limp body into my lap and held him. *Now the long loneliness begins.*

Shiloh cried. Heather somberly watched. Don sat next to me and held him. His sobs echoed without shame.

God, did he linger until Janet became a Christian, for her benefit, or because it will be easier for me to live through the days that follow with a friend who will walk with me all the way to heaven? She and I will never have to really say goodbye. Just like Uriah.

Twenty-One

Picking Up the Pieces
(July 1–12, 1991)

*. . . The hands of time carry us from one another,
the hands of God will unite us again someday . . .*
—Morgan Cryar and Chris Harris

6:30 P.M., MONDAY, JULY 1, 1991. *What do we do now? I'm
numb, I can't think. I need to call people.* I pushed my
sorrow aside and laid Uriah's body in Don's lap. *Who first?
Grandmothers?*

"When I called this morning, I knew it would be today," Nana murmured.

I called Pastor. I called Dr. Sanmarco and made arrangements to deliver Uriah's body to the hospital. I called
Theresa, Julie, Janet, and others I could think of.

Don helped me dress Uriah in his favorite outfit. *He
wore this to the Mariposas Christmas party. He was right; it
was the last one.*

We stumbled around, trying to pack. I glanced back at
Uriah. Garfield—his marmalade, Manx kitten—was curled
up asleep in the crook of his elbow. *A Parting Gift.*

A knock at the door? Ernie Weeks, Lonn Maly, and Alan
Stroschein stood outside. "We came to help."

"May I?" Ernie nodded toward Uriah's body on the love seat. We nodded. Ernie knelt beside him and laid a hand on Uriah's head. We watched in silence. *God, will You grant the prayer of this servant?* Finally Ernie checked Uriah's pulse, gave his shoulder an affectionate squeeze, and rose to his feet with a sigh. "Would you pray with us?"

We joined hands. *Someone's missing.* I glanced around the circle. Uriah's IV pole caught my eye. *It's Uriah. God, am I always going to hurt this much?*

"We're going to do something for you," said Alan.

"It doesn't matter what, but we're going to do something," said Lonn.

I looked at Don. *We don't even know what we're supposed to be doing; what can we have them do?* "You could return some videos for us."

"Carrie and Julie said they're going to come out," said Lonn as they left.

Julie and Carrie hugged me and we cried together. "Is there anything we can do to help?"

"Pray. It's getting late, and we have a four-hour drive ahead of us. Could you help us pack?"

We threw our bags in the truck and laid Uriah's body under the shelter of the camper shell by the tailgate. We left at 9:30 P.M. The girls sat in the front with us. Not a word was spoken. No one slept. After midnight, Don and I walked into the emergency room in Fontana.

"We have our son's body in the truck," I said and held out the note from Dr. Sanmarco.

The nurse's eyes jerked up to meet mine. "What?"

I gave her the note.

Two men carried Uriah in and laid him on a bed, pulling the curtain around us. The nurse felt for his pulse. "We're just waiting for the doctor to come. Can I get you coffee or anything?"

"No, thanks." I caressed Uriah's face. Fluids had settled there, causing redness.

The doctor pushed aside the curtain. "I'm sorry. I'm required to make some observations."

"I know."

The doctor checked his eyes, listened for his heart, observed the condition of his body. "Would you like to spend some time with him?"

"Just a few minutes, please."

"I'm sorry for your loss." Sincerity was in his eyes.

"Thanks."

The curtain again divided me from the chaos of the emergency room. *Life and death.* I hugged Uriah. *I'm holding him for the last time. But he's not here. It's just an empty shell—as empty as Jesus' tomb Easter morning.*

Don and I paced back to the truck. Andy and Janet drove up. "We were waiting for you, but it got late, so we started driving to Blythe. We saw you going the other way near Cabazon."

It's so good to see friendly faces on this sad, lonely night. They followed us to Nana's cabin. As we chugged up the mountain, KLORD played, "In the eye of the hurricane, . . . there's a harbor, safe and warm."[1] And the sun rose.

Tuesday, July 2

Nana and Boompa went with us to Rose Hills. At the arrangements office, we were introduced to Brooke Ortiz. My mind felt blank and numb. Brooke gently guided us through the things we needed to do: have Uriah's body released, choose a casket and a date for the services, order death certificates, and arrange for pallbearers.

The day after Uriah's death, I heard my voice come over KLORD: "Hi. This is Mara. I'd like to request the song, 'Home Free' by Wayne Watson and dedicate it to all the people who prayed for Uriah, who is now truly home free. . . ."

July 3, 1991, the *Palo Verde Valley Times:*

Where did the rainbow go?

By Dona James

Eight-year-old Uriah Alexander, a leukemia victim who won the heart of Blythe, died at his home Monday evening. . . .

"He was very weak and was having difficulty breathing," his mother said. "He wasn't in pain, he just couldn't get the air he needed into his lungs."

. . . The community of Blythe . . . raised in excess of $50,000 to pay for bone-marrow testing. Although no donor match was found for Uriah, several other children needing transplants did find matches.

And Uriah, because of the child that he was, was happy about that. He was grateful, as were his parents, that someone was being helped.

Uriah's faith was deep and his acceptance as to God's will was very solid. But, along with the acceptance, he also had a strong will to live. . . .

Rainbows held a special meaning for Uriah. They were a promise for him and a promise for his family.

". . . *Rainbows are a lot like me, aren't they," Uriah said. "I may be gone but, after a while, you're going to see me again."*[2]

Below the article was a poem I'd written years before:

. . . Our freedoms will be vastly more,
As we step out on life's opposite shore;
No more struggle with sin, pain, or sickness,

No suffering, hunger, thirst, death, or sadness.
For as our worn-out physical selves
Are cast away like fragile, empty shells
Perfect, like Him, we will arise
To a perfect world beyond earthly skies.
With our perfect Creator we will be,
For "the truth will make you truly free!"[3]

More than a hundred sympathy cards from young and old arrived.

July 3, 1991
The Word, sent to CVSP employees:

. . . Uriah was an inspiration to us all. He taught us the true meaning of courage in the eyes of his own personal fate. Although he will be sorely missed, he left a mark on this world that will never be forgotten.

The Alexander family expresses their love and heartfelt thanks to everyone who gave assistance and displayed their support throughout this ordeal.

Theo White, Warden (A)

The Fontana *Sun,* July 4, 1991:

Fontana boy with leukemia dies; search for marrow donor futile

By Tommy Li
The Sun's Fontana Bureau

Uriah Alexander fulfilled most of his wishes in eight short years—from fishing to riding in a helicopter.

. . . On Monday night, the former Fontana boy died in his Blythe home after a valiant fight against leukemia. He was just shy of his ninth birthday.

. . . Over the past year, the Alexanders had hoped to save Uriah by finding a compatible bone-marrow donor. . . .

The efforts attracted widespread media attention. A total of 4,384 people were tested, but no match was found.

Despite her son's death, Alexander knows the effort to find a bone-marrow donor wasn't in vain. It helped save the lives of 17 other cancer patients because matches were found for them.

"It's almost a living memorial that he left behind," she said. . . .[4]

Friday, July 5

This is the day I have wondered about for so long. It doesn't seem quite real, rather, like a dream. Perhaps that's how You get us through these things, God. I put Ripples, Uriah's toy dog, in the casket; his special pillow and blanket; and a deck of UNO cards. *He doesn't quite look like himself without his bright smile. It makes it easier to know Uriah isn't in that empty shell.*

A long procession crept to the little plot high on the hillside. We picked our way across the graveyard to a line of folding chairs. The white hearse arrived. Boompa, Tim Ray, Steve Shay, Jack Neece, Alan Stroschein, Kenny Alexander, Brian Jordan, and Andy Anderson hoisted the coffin onto the stand. It was draped with the rainbow banner. Flowers were placed over and around it.

Pastor moved to the front of the gathering:

". . . 'In my Father's house are many rooms.' I can just picture Uriah's room. I bet you can too. Just think about it . . . he's there. Be comforted knowing it's farewell and not goodbye.

"Gracious heavenly Father, we commend to Your loving care little Uriah, whose face was such a shining light in so many people's lives, whose smile brought hope and encouragement to many. His rainbow of hope, one that we all need to cherish. Touch . . . all who especially mourn his loss, . . . help them even in this sad time, bring some good from it. . . ."

It's so strange to walk away and leave part of yourself there in a little box to be placed under the dirt. I felt empty yet lighter as we drove to the reception. *It's time to focus on positive things I can do. I'll be able to spend more time with the girls, and Don can advance in his career. It's hard not to feel guilty about looking forward to good things.*

❦ ❦ ❦

"This card is to Joshua's family," I teased Rick Andrews, a counselor at Cucamonga Junior High.

"I knew it was one of those Old Testament, Bible names," he sighed.

"You work with so many kids a day, it's no wonder you can't remember!" *It's such a relief to joke about things.* Like the apple juice in the urine specimen container in Irma Bombeck's book, *I Want to Grow Hair, I Want to Grow Up, I Want to Go to Boise.* When I read it, I laughed until I cried, and I felt so much better.

Dear Mara,

I'm very sorry to hear about your loss. When you called me the other night, it was just like reliving Joaquin's death. The way you talked about it made me so proud of you. I am so glad I had a chance to meet you (on the phone). I know Uriah and Joaquin are safe now with God, and that means leukemia cannot hurt them anymore. You really helped and supported me, Mara. I really am thankful for being able to talk with you.

Thanks for being there for me, Mara.

Love,
Pennie

Saturday, July 6

Pastor Dannenberg and Pastor Hoemann did the memorial service for Uriah at First Lutheran Church in Fontana.

As I approached the podium, my eyes passed over the small gathering. Memories of times they spent with Uriah ran through my mind. *God, they each know part of the wonderful story You've woven with Uriah's short life.*

". . . As Uriah grew, it became apparent he saw the world from a very different perspective than other children. . . . Many people said he had such a grown-up sense of humor for his age and was so happy in spite of his illness.

"Although over $85,853 was raised and 4,384 people were tested to be donors, we never found a match for Uriah. But 19 other people did find a match. And people will continue to benefit for the next ten years.

"Uriah knew that people's earthly bodies always die, but he had a hope that went beyond that. A hope for a new life without pain, sickness, or chemotherapy. A life where our joy is complete and our dearest hope is fulfilled. Uriah is still alive—he has only relocated to a better place.

"We will never have to worry about Uriah again, for he is truly free, at home with Jesus; he has received the ultimate healing. Those of us who belong to the Lord will see Uriah again.

"'Home Free' was written by Wayne Watson and dedicated to his best friend's wife, Sandra, who died of cancer. The following dedication and song sum up our feelings about Uriah and God."

We prayed for Sandra and enlisted the prayers of those who never had the pleasure of knowing her. We believed Sandra would walk away from that hospital bed. . . . believed it and prayed for it. We knew one day she'd be home. God answered our prayer, not like we had hoped, but still, He answered. The best thing we learned . . . was to let God be God! Even when it makes no sense. . . .[5]

Out in the corridors we pray for life,
A mother for her baby, a husband for his wife.
Sometimes the good die young, it's sad but true.
And while we pray for one more heartbeat,
The real comfort is in You.

I know, every prayer gets answered,
But the hardest one to pray, is Lord above,
Oh, Lord, not mine, but Your will be done.
Oh, let it be. I know your goin' home. . . .
Home free. . . .[6]

We comforted, and were comforted by, those who had come. *Life will never be the same, but will it be tolerable?*

We stayed at Nana's cabin for a couple days. Once home, our family of four hauled boxes of cards, letters, paper cranes, and mementos people had given Uriah to Zion Lutheran Church. We attached them to the parish hall walls with hospital paper tape. Colorful drawings, letters, and cards covered the walls. Strings of origami cranes hung from the ceiling.

Pastor surveyed our handiwork with approval. He paused. "Mara, would you consider becoming the church secretary?"

"What do you think?" I asked Don.

"Seems like a good idea."

I turned to Pastor. "Can I start in August? I need a little time—to get organized."

"Sure!"

July 8, 1991

Julie Maly sent the card "The Plan of the Master Weaver":

"Uriah has seen the canvas—Glory be to God! We love you!"

The mourners filled a book and signed a second. Rainbow flower arrangements and balloon bouquets nestled around a table with a picture of Uriah below the altar. Our family sat in the front row.

Pastor Hoemann welcomed us to ". . . a time of reflection and remembrance of the contributions, the smiles, the influence that a little boy had on so many people. That little boy, Uriah, certainly touched the hearts of many, many people. . . .

"We think of the people who rallied to do all that was humanly possible to save his life. We know that inside he had a far greater gift, the gift that was beyond the price of any dollars or cents or anything else . . . the gift of faith, the gift of life. . . ."

Heather giggled when I told about the water fight in the hospital, and everyone laughed when I held up Chemo Punk. My voice broke as I read the dedication Wayne Watson made to Sandra. I returned to my seat, wiping my eyes. Don patted my back.

Soon everyone was in the parish hall, holding refreshments and looking at the artwork on the walls. Uriah's friends hunted their handiwork. Shouts of "Here's one I did!" rang through the hall as parents were tugged over to survey the masterpiece.

I pulled bags out of the truck. Uriah would want his treasures to be enjoyed by others instead of lying in a box to gather dust. The children smiled and grasped with reverence their parting gifts from Uriah.

We got cards from Uriah's classmates, organizations that helped us raise funds for testing, and the blood bank. Mary Baschal put together a booklet about Uriah to share with the children in San Fernando when they returned to school.

Someone Don worked with gave us an old "45" phonograph record with the song "Families Are Forever" written by Scott Strong. The lyrics described a mother's conversation with her eight-year-old son just before she dies. She tells him, "Families are forever."

"How will I know you're there if I can't see you?" he asked her.

She replied, "I'll build you a rainbow . . ."

July 10, 1991

. . . I'll always cherish the memory of the first time I met Uriah at Kmart. Such a delightful lad, and I know he is still smiling down on us, telling us, "See you later—be happy and take care."

> Love and God's blessings,
> Dave and Ruth Sheppardson

July 11, 1991
    Don's memo to CVSP staff:

. . . With the help of CCPOA, Correctional Peace Officer's Foundation, the city of Blythe and yourselves, enough money was raised to test over 4,400 people. So far, 17

435

people, of which 16 work C.D.C., have matched patients who would have soon died without a bone-marrow transplant. This makes my son's death easier to bear and gives meaning to his struggle.

July 12, 1991

Dear Don and Mara and Family,

. . . We want you to know that we will never forget how inspiring it was for us that Uriah would come and help pass out our fliers detailing his plight. It made it really difficult for the employees to fabricate excuses to avoid distributing fliers. . . . Uriah left a legacy to the town of Blythe in his bravery and his desire to hold onto life when the odds always seemed to hover against him. He brought this town together more than any other single event. . . . Maybe part of Uriah's mission on earth was to get the rest of us to pull together instead of coming apart. . . . We know God has a special place for Uriah in heaven, . . . the whole Alexander family is special to God . . . you were given the gift of sharing in and learning from this special child's triumphs and tragedies.

Mike and Robin Madrigal and the crew
Domino's Pizza, Blythe

Twenty-Two

Dreams of Desperation
(July 13–Oct. 1, 1991)

*She pointed to a smiling figure—above the angels,
surrounded by balloons and flowers, under the cross—
with a catheter in his chest.*

M Y NIGHTS WERE FILLED WITH DARK, DREAMLESS SLEEP. OFTEN
I would awaken at 2:00 A.M., but Uriah's catheter no
longer needed care. Instead I would stumble to the girls'
room and check on them.

One morning I awoke with pleasure. I had dreamed of
Uriah! *I know he's not here, but it's like I saw him and we
played a game.* It was easier to face the night after that.

Sunday, July 13
    Donald Jolly called: "We have some reagent for
Uriah."
    I almost dropped the phone. "It's too late. We al-
ready buried him."
    "This new compound is really wonderful."
    Doesn't he understand? "Unless it can raise the dead,
it's no good to us now."
    The dial tone buzzed over the phone.

I left messages at his office when Uriah was dying and pleaded for him to send some before it was too late. He never returned those desperate calls.

Tuesday, July 16

A dedication on KJMB radio, Blythe: "To the Alexander family of Blythe. They lost their very courageous eight-year-old son earlier this month to leukemia. And T. Crumdy, correctional officer at Chuckawalla Valley State Prison, sings this song he recorded himself, and the name of the song is 'The Way We Were.'"

Maggie Kim called. "I would like to write an article about Uriah for our newsletter if it's OK." We dropped off a picture of Uriah and the speech from the memorial service.

Saturday, July 20

Diana's daughter, Jenny, had part of one leg removed because of bone cancer:

. . . Jenny wrote Dave Drevecky, the baseball player, a letter. She told him that nothing can come upon a child of God that hasn't first gone through the sovereign hand of God. Then she told him that he was a conqueror because he never lost the faith and determination that God had given him. . . .

Thursday, July 25

Uriah would have been nine today. Don arranged a swap and went to a doctor's appointment instead of work. Keeping busy makes the time pass quicker.

Tuesday, July 30

Don came home from work and pressed a tape into my hand. "Someone at work returned this today."

"Mike Warnke? We don't own a Mike Warnke tape."

Don shrugged.

A Christian comedian? I popped the tape into the stereo out of curiosity. I was amazed when he compared death to driving a car that breaks down. When you get out and walk, you don't cease to exist, you just enter a realm your senses were unable to perceive before.

God, You sent this tape to us! I was troubled by Uriah's last words. I thought he didn't know what was happening when he died. Now I understand. Uriah wasn't talking to me. Jesus was standing there saying, "Uriah, how would you like to leave that old, worn out body behind and join Me in Paradise today?" And Uriah replied, "That's great! Park the car like that!"

Tina trained me as Zion's secretary in early August. Flipping through the church card file, I saw our family address card and froze. *Uriah's name is crossed out!* I blinked back tears. *It's necessary, I guess.* I picked up a stack of inactive files. *Tina said to put these in the "dead files."* When I reached the storage boxes, a few more files lay there. Uriah's was on top. *That gives a new meaning to the term dead files!* But the ache in my heart gave way to wonder when I read Tina's note on the front: "Transferred to heaven 7-1-91."

Dona James asked me to work as a reporter for the *Palo Verde Valley Times.* When I interviewed Dave Distel, principal of Twin Palms, we talked briefly about Uriah. "Uriah's not really gone," I said.

"Sort of like Dave Drevecky? It's gone, but it feels like it's still there."

"Not exactly. I'm a Christian." *God, You've placed me here for a purpose. I'm seeing and hearing things about Uriah I would have missed otherwise. The unexpected things always jolt me. They hurt, but it's bittersweet; the twinge of sorrow is balanced by the pleasure of discovering another piece of his story.*

August 12

Thank you so much for letting us use Uriah's picture and the story from the memorial service! As soon as the article comes out in our paper, *The HemoGlobe,* I will send you a copy. Jeff has matched a patient with his tissue type—I am doing the blood specimen for the third test today. Hopefully he will match and be able to donate to save another patient's life!

Sincerely,
Maggie Kim

Dear Mara-

We just found a roll of film. When we got it developed, we had these pictures of the Christmas party. We thought that you might like them. Mara, thank you for being my mentor in the clinic. You always helped me sort things out, and I appreciate it. Hope things are going better for you all.

Affectionately,
Terri, Sam, and Sami

I flipped through the pictures eagerly, the pangs of grief dulled by the joy of reminiscence. *God, this mix of pleasure and pain every time an unexpected remembrance of Uriah comes to light is so odd. Uriah's superballs lying in some forgotten corner are like little emotional land mines. I never know when I'll find one and feel sorrow slash my heart. Yet I treasure these tokens of his existence.*

August 30, the *Palo Verde Valley Times:*

Four-year old stricken

By Mara Alexander

Last Saturday a cheerful little boy from Blythe celebrated his fourth birthday. There was a Mickey and Minnie Mouse cake, ice cream, and lots of presents to open—especially his favorite toys, Barbies!

. . . Although Andrew DeLeon seems like a healthy four-year old, he suffers from acute myelocytic leukemia (AML), a rare disorder that usually afflicts young adults over the age of 25. He has been in protective isolation since July 26, undergoing chemotherapy. They won't know if the treatment has been effective until he has another bone-marrow test in a few days. . . .[1]

My role has changed. Now I write the articles and pray Andrew will fare better than Uriah.

September 3, Heather wrote to her friend Scarlett from Bear Gulch:

So how are you? I'm fine. I can't believe we're in high school now. I made the Honors English class too. I'm in cross-country and flag football, and I'm doing OK.

In cross-country yesterday we ran three miles all around a canal. It was about 105 degrees out, so when I was done, I jumped into the canal.

I'm going up to Arrowhead this weekend to see Andie and have a surprise birthday party for my mom.

I can't wait till Halloween. I'm planning a big party, probably in Arrowhead. Arrowhead isn't that far from Rialto, so if you can come, consider yourself invited.

Heather

Friday, September 6

"We're going to Arrowhead tonight," Don said.

"What?" I gasped. "That means I've got to get the church bulletin done early and put off one of my stories for the paper."

He sighed. "It was supposed to be a surprise. I'm taking you on a double date with Andy and Janet for your birthday."

Saturday the four of us drove to the clothing district in Los Angeles. Janet and I modeled beautiful, impractical outfits, then chose a dress each and wore them to a fancy restaurant. "This was a lot of fun," I said.

Janet nodded. "We need to do it again sometime."

Wednesday, September 11

Don and I returned to San Fernando for First Lutheran School's memorial service. When principal Earl Reynolds introduced us, I came forward to share Uriah's story. The kids giggled when I told them about Uriah's squirting nurses with syringes and passed around the pictures we brought of Uriah.

". . . I think it's important to have fun no matter where God puts you," I said. "It's easy to feel down if something that doesn't seem good is happening to you, but you gotta look around and find a good thing in it.

"We took those pictures you sent Uriah and put them up all over the walls. When the nurses came in, they saw all your faith. You touched more people than just Uriah. Everyone who walked into Uriah's room saw the wonderful things that you did, and it was a blessing to them. I know it was a blessing to us. . . . I want to thank you for being such an important part of Uriah's life.

". . . He's up there in heaven right now. When we get up there, you are going to get to meet him, and he'll tell you about all this himself."

We followed Earl to the high school, and I gave another speech.

The children of First Lutheran sent us rainbow pictures:

Hello:

I just wanted to let you know that Uriah is in my thoughts. Someday like he says the rainbow's gone for a while but we'll see it again soon. I'll get to meet Uriah. Believe me, I know [how] it is to have a family member have cancer. My mom had cancer two years ago and thankfully the loving Lord healed her.

Elizabeth Mitzenmacher

I'm very sorry Uriah died. I was hoping he wouldn't. I'm happy for him anyway because I know he's in heaven. It was kind of how you said this morning during chapel. I didn't know him, but I felt like I did. I admire you for being so strong and going to every extent to try [to] let Uriah live, but I guess there's no changing God's will.

Yolanda M. Regla

As you know God's love is very special. I can understand what you're going through. I have had quite a few people in my family die one was my uncle. He was killed in a car accident it was very hard on my family, but at the same time I was glad because I knew he was in heaven.

Uriah was very special to all of us.

Rochelle Courtney, sixth grade

The rainbow on Rochelle's picture curved over two little houses. One said "Mr. Uriah Alexander," the other "my uncle Mr. Ron Courtney."

When they had that blood testing my mother and sister went down. I think that is the only time that my sister ever has or ever will willingly give blood. Usually we have to practically strap her down to do it. That's how much Uriah effected us with his happiness.

Leah C. Blose

One day Nadine Evens handed me a picture her five-year old had drawn of a church. "Joey told me the people at the bottom are in church, the ones floating near the ceiling are angels, and he said that's Uriah." She pointed to a smiling figure above the angels, surrounded by balloons and flowers, under the cross with a catheter in his chest. My eyes filled with tears. *To think someone so young could understand! No wonder You say we must come with the faith of a child.*

Heather moved into Uriah's room and hung up posters, necklaces, and keepsakes.

"How's it coming?" I asked, peeking in. *She left Uriah's posters and drawings up? That's not like her.*

One morning we passed boys walking toward the bus stop. Heather murmured, "Why does everyone look like Uriah?"

I turned in surprise. *She's serious.* "I know what you mean. I've done a few double takes because someone looks like Uriah. I seem to compare everyone to Uriah: 'His hair looks like Uriah's'; 'They said that like Uriah.'" *She's missing him too.*

"I didn't really believe Uriah would die," Shiloh said. "I didn't believe it when we told him goodbye. Not even when

444

he stopped breathing. Not until we started driving back to Kaiser did I believe."

We got the copy of the *HemoGlobe* Maggie Kim promised. Uriah smiled above the words, "Rainbows are a lot like me . . . I may be gone, but after a while you're going to see me again."

Young boy's struggle for life helps others

. . . Uriah Elijah Jeremiah Israel Alexander quietly passed away July 1, 1991 while waiting for a match for a bone-marrow transplant. . . . Through the efforts of Uriah's family, friends, community members, the NMDP, the blood center and others, $85,853 were raised and 4,384 people were tested and added to the NMDP Registry. . . . In July, a patient received a bone-marrow transplant from a donor who volunteered at a blood center recruitment drive held by Uriah's family. . . .[2]

September 20, the *Palo Verde Valley Times:*

Bake sale to benefit young leukemia victim, Saturday

By Mara Alexander

Although Andrew DeLeon is doing better, his leukemia didn't respond to his second course of chemotherapy as well as doctors had hoped. . . .

Andrew doesn't have just one type of leukemia, he has two. Previously, the predominant type was acute myelocytic leukemia (AML), but now the other type, acute lymphocytic leukemia (ALL) is more prevalent.

. . . The Los Amigos Golf Tournament, held last September 8, generated $2,000 in funds to benefit Andrew and Michelle Contreras, another child from Blythe who suffers from cancer. . . .

"Andrew really likes getting mail. He always asks, 'Is that for me?'" said Jeannie. "We want to thank everyone for their help."[3]

Rain splattered in the headlights. Brakes screamed. There was twisted metal, shattered glass, blanket-draped bodies. "I'm sorry," the man in uniform said. "They're all dead."

I leaped up with such violence into the quiet darkness that I almost fell out of bed. Don's steady, calm breathing reassured me. *It's only a dream.*

God, I couldn't go on alone. I need someone—at least Shiloh, or I couldn't do it.

The dream returned for three weeks.

God, why am I having these dreams? Is it a reaction to Uriah's death? Please make them go away.

They stopped abruptly.

Thanks, God.

※ ※ ※

"Look, Mom." Heather handed me some sketches. "These are the outfits my band will wear on *Star Search* when we play my songs."

"I'll help sew them," I offered. *She'll get there someday. She's already written the songs and a letter to* Star Search *about "Bad Attitude."*

※ ※ ※

"Daddy got that new Bill Cosby movie," Heather announced and plopped down on the couch.

"What's that movie supposed to mean?" Shiloh asked afterward.

"Your family's more important than your work," Don said simply.

❧　❧　❧

"Come on, we're going to Pomona," Don told us. "My uncle's here from Boise."

The family gathered in Grandma Ruth's living room and bantered about family news.

"Recently your mom and I accepted Christ," Aunt Pam told us.

Don's mouth dropped open. He turned to Grandma Ruth. She smiled.

The stars were bright on the way home. "Honey, I'm so glad," I said.

"Now I don't have to worry about them anymore," he sighed with relief.

❧　❧　❧

Our old truck was worn out. Don returned from San Bernardino with a Nissan Pathfinder.

"It's pretty," I said, "but is it big enough?"

"They still have to put the tire bracket on the back; then we'll have more room," Don said. "I need a physical to finish the paperwork for the sheriff's reserves too."

"Heather needs a physical so she can be on the cross-country team."

"A doctor in town can do her physical," Don said.

"But Kaiser has her medical records. Remember her problems with her knee?" I asked. "I don't want anything to happen to her, and you're going anyway."

He nodded.

❧ ❧ ❧

It was still dark when Don bent to kiss me goodbye. "Hey, sleepyhead. It's five, we gotta go."

I blinked, trying to wake up. "OK, honey. Be careful. Did Heather get her homework?"

"Yeah. We'll see you tonight."

"All right. I love you."

"Love you too. Bye." He shut the door gently.

We expected to be together that night—and for years to come—but it was not so.

Twenty-Three

House of Cards
(Oct. 2–Oct. 9, 1991)

Jesus keep my longing heart from breaking clean in two.
Oh, stand by me Lord and help me see this through,
A Father knows how bad it feels to lose someone like you. . . .
—Bryan Duncan and Randy Lee

T HE ROP STUDENT LOOKED STARTLED WHEN I HURRIED INTO
the office that morning, October 2, 1991.

"I'm sorry," she stammered.

She must be talking about Uriah. "It's OK now."

Mr. Maly followed Shiloh into the office. "What have you heard?" he asked me.

"About what?" *What could Shiloh have done? Lonn's eyes look strange.*

He closed his office door behind Shiloh and motioned me toward Pastor's empty office. He sat on the edge of his seat, tense as a spring.

Whatever it is, it's important. I closed the door and sank into the closest chair. He stared at the floor a moment. *His eyes are rimmed with red.* My eyes dropped to the floor.

He took a deep breath, "I heard that there's been an accident. . . ."

449

My eyes snapped up to meet his. *The dreams! Are they alive?*

". . . I heard Don's dead."

"What about Heather?"

His eyes widened. "She was with him?" his voice shrilled.

I need to be with her if she's alive. I turned to the phone and dialed the highway patrol.

"I'm sorry, but we are unable to release any information at this time."

I slapped the phone down and spun toward Lonn. "How did you find out about Don?"

"Vaughn called Pastor from the prison. They went to find you at your house."

"We rode down with Linda Mendez." I dialed the prison.

"Chuckawalla Valley State Prison, Lt. Burke."

"Hi, Lt. Burke. This is Mara Alexander. Don told me if I ever needed help, you were someone I could count on. I need help now. The highway patrol won't tell me if Don and Heather are dead or alive."

He cleared his throat. "I—I don't want to tell you."

"Please," I begged. "I need to know."

"It's unconfirmed," his voice cracked, "but I heard three people were dead at the scene."

Oh, God! Why are You taking everyone away from me? If I'd asked for Heather's life too, would she be alive now? I sobbed into the phone. "I'm sorry I'm crying. I'm glad you told me. I needed to know."

"It's OK. It's me too," he said thickly.

Shiloh's waiting in the principal's office. God, how can I tell her without destroying her? There is no gentle way to break this news to her. I went in Lonn's office and closed the door. *We only have each other now. My whole living family is just Shiloh and me, in this tiny room.* I gasped.

Shiloh spun toward me. "What did I do wrong?"

I gave her a hug. "You didn't do anything." *Here we go, God. Give me the right words.* "I have some bad news. Daddy and Heather were killed in a traffic accident this morning."

She searched my eyes. Her own filled with tears that spilled down her cheeks. "Why is all this happening to us?" she demanded. "Daddy's a careful driver!"

"I don't know why, but God has a reason. It was an accident. Maybe someone else made a mistake, or something went wrong with the new car."

She paused, then murmured, "How come we didn't get to go?"

God, it isn't death she fears; it's being left behind. The phone rang and our time alone was gone. Dozens of people came to comfort us when they heard the news.

I need to tell relatives. I'll call the strongest first, so those who will be hurt most will be told by someone they can lean on. Don's mom needs to be told first. Aunt Pam and Sherman live next door. I punched the number.

Pam bubbled, as always. "Well, hi, Mara! How are you doing?"

"Listen, Pam, is Sherman there?"

"He's just leaving—"

"This is important. Hurry and catch him if you can."

The phone clattered, and moments later I heard shuffling sounds. "I just caught him," she puffed.

"Are you sitting down?"

Rustling. "Yes. OK."

"Don and Heather were killed in a traffic accident this morning."

"No," she stated. "No, no, no, no, no!" as if emphatic denial could reverse what she'd been told. "Oh, God, no!" she cried. Her voice muffled.

Sherman's holding her, consoling her without knowing what's happened. Thank You, God, for Sherman.

After a while Pam's voice sobbed, "Is there anything we can do?"

"I'm sorry. I didn't know who else to call. Ruth needs to be told, but I want someone there to make sure she's all right."

"We'll take care of it. We'll pick her up from work and go to Marilyn's. But what about you?"

"We've got a lot of friends helping us. We'll come as soon as we can."

❦ ❦ ❦

Don's brother called, devastated. "I'm the black sheep of the family," Kenny lamented. "It should have been me!"

"No one would have wanted that," I said. "You're hardly what I would call a black sheep. But if you're feeling remorse for things you've done, it's not too late to change. Your mom really needs you now."

❦ ❦ ❦

Who do I contact on my side of the family? Boompa was at work when I called. "I'll go get Nana at work and we'll tell Debbie," he said.

A reporter from the *Press-Enterprise* called. I gave her my limited information. "That's all I know; is there anything you could tell me?"

"No. I'll get my information from the police reports," she dodged.

Editor Dona James rapped on Lonn's open office door. "I was about to call and let you know why I hadn't come in," I apologized.

452

"Don't worry about it. I've got your paycheck waiting at the office."

"I'll come by before I leave town."

🌿 🌿 🌿

Libby! She and Heather are so close. I dialed her home number. "Dick, I'm so glad you're home! Heather was killed in a traffic accident this morning, and I'm worried how Libby will do if she finds out at school."

"I'll pick her up."

🌿 🌿 🌿

Pastor canceled his morning schedule and drove us to the *Times* office. My coworkers turned away and busily peered into their desk drawers and computers. *They don't know how to react.*

"I'd like to come out to the house later this afternoon for more information," Dona said. "Can I bring a gift for Shiloh? A dress or something?"

"Sure, but we've got to leave this evening."

As I walked to Pastor's truck, Dick pulled into the parking lot with Libby. She, Shiloh, and I held onto each other and cried. *They've lost their best friend, and I've lost a part of myself.*

Courtney, Libby's sister, drove up. "If you ever need a big sister, Shiloh, I'd be glad to be one." She joined our tearful circle of grief.

Pastor drove to McDonald's. *Lunch time already?* Shiloh got a happy meal. *At least some things don't change.*

At our mobile home on the edge of the desert, far from town, Pastor read aloud from Revelation as I tried to pack for another funeral. *That mind-numbing feeling is back. This time I'll have to do everything myself. It'll always be that way now.*

The phone rang. "Hello?" I asked.

"This is Dr. Sanguesa. I . . . I heard you and your husband had been killed, and I was calling to check on Shiloh and Heather."

"Heather died in the accident. Shiloh's here with me."

"Come by the office when you can. I'll call in a prescription for something to help you sleep."

"Dr. Sanguesa, how did you find out?"

"Dr. Sanmarco told me."

News about Don and Heather's deaths must have traveled the same communication lines information about Uriah did. It must have been relayed from one California prison to the next. Most of California probably knew before we did. Don's friend Henry works at CIM, and his son is Dr. Sanmarco's patient. I bet he told her.

The phone rang again. "Hello?"

"Mara, this is Heidi Walker from Kaiser. Rumors are flying around . . ."

"My husband and daughter were killed this morning in a car accident," I said.

Silence.

"Would you let the nurses know so they can come to the services?"

"Certainly."

❧ ❧ ❧

People began to stop by. Theresa Kelm and Vaughn Panzer tapped on the door. "The prison would like to retire Don's badge. Do you have a picture of him in uniform?"

We pored over photo albums. "There are hardly any photos of Don," I sighed. "He's the one who took the pictures."

"We'll just use your family picture taken at church a year ago."

Lord, I feel like I've been climbing a staircase; every step is more difficult, each has a lesson to be learned before the next step can be taken. At every step I find myself saying, "I hope this is the hardest thing I ever have to do." God, You refine those whom You love. "Behold, I have refined you, but not like silver. I have tried you in the furnace of affliction" (Isa. 48:10). Does that mean those who try to be faithful will face more trials than those who don't? And the harder I try, the more extreme my trials will become? Is that fair? . . . I can't change. I have to do what's right. The alternative is unacceptable. As Peter said, "Lord, to whom shall we go? You have the words of eternal life."

Job said, "Lord, who can resist You?" You have complete control over my life and love me more than I can ever know. We don't have to worry about money because it's just after payday, and Don took care of the new auto insurance yesterday. When I see how carefully You've planned things, I don't doubt Your existence or Your love. I don't understand why it happened, but just as with Uriah, I believe You've done the best thing for everyone. Don, Heather, and Uriah are up there partying—it's Shiloh I worry about now. But thanks for leaving her here with me, God. You know how much I need her. God, I want to learn whatever I'm supposed to the first time; I don't want to repeat this lesson!

The Andersons arrived. Brian and Andria raced to Shiloh's room. "Could you help Shiloh choose an outfit for Heather to wear?" I called after them.

I phoned the coroner. "How do I pick up Don's personal effects? I want his wedding ring for the funeral."

"We'll make special arrangements so you can pick them up from Sgt. Soto after hours at the sheriff's station in Indio."

"Thanks so much."

The *Zion Times,* October 2:

WE SAY GOODBYE, FOR NOW, to one of our graduates, HEATHER ALEXANDER and her father DON ALEXANDER. God, in His Almighty wisdom, chose today for them to go home to heaven. . . . We're sure Uriah was awaiting their arrival.[1]

At 5:00 P.M. Brian, Shiloh, Andria, and I squeezed into the back of the Andersons' truck. As we drove, I scanned the highway near Red Cloud Road for the accident scene but saw nothing. In Indio I filled out the forms Sgt. Soto handed me. He returned with Don's briefcase, split open but still latched. As he pulled Don's wallet and ring from a manila envelope, all denial passed away.

At 10:00 P.M. we scurried out of the frosty air into Nana's brightly lit cabin. Nana, Boompa, Debbie, Jeff, and the kids were there. Shiloh and I dropped our bags in the blue room. *I'm awfully tired, but there are phone calls that have to be returned.*

"With your permission, the prison would like to bury Don with full police honors," Lori Shay said.

"Don would have loved that," Nana said.

Ruth agreed.

I snuggled into the trundle bed next to Shiloh's and tuned the radio to KLORD. *This first night alone will be the hardest. I want Christian music playing if I wake up.* A Michael W. Smith and Wayne Kirkpatrick song I'd never heard drifted through the night:

Seems like it was only yesterday,
She was living here. Yeah, she was living here.
Lord knows why He's taken her away,
It isn't very clear, no, it isn't very clear. . . .

I hear Leesha, singing in heaven tonight
And in between the sadness, I hear Leesha
Telling me that she's alright. . . .[2]

I woke at six. *The radio's playing. Where am I? Don! Heather!* I rolled over. *Shiloh's still here. . . . We need to pick some dreams, something to look forward to, to keep us going through the pain.*

The radio announced, "We're giving away Bryan Duncan concert tickets to the first person who can tell me how many left-handed presidents the United States has had."

A Bryan Duncan concert! I got on the phone. "Seven," I guessed.

"Too high. Call again."

I got through again! "Three."

"Too low."

I punched the buttons again. "Four."

"That's correct! We're sending tickets for two."

God, it's just what we need—and You knew it! Thanks!

Funerals are important but must be put together in just days, while one is still struggling with loss. *I need pictures of them, but how?* I picked up the phone and dialed Palo

Verde Valley High School. "Could I get a copy of Heather's ASB picture? She took it only days ago, but . . ."

"Tomorrow morning the company in Anaheim will call and tell you where to pick it up."

I called the *Daily Bulletin*. "Peggy, can I get a copy of the picture your photographer took of Don holding Uriah last year?"

"Sure," she said.

Thanks, God!

Thursday, October 3

Andy returned from the Chino prison with two envelopes of money. "There's two more circulating."

Nana, Boompa, Debbie, Grandma Ruth, Marilyn, and I crowded into Brooke Ortiz's office at the mortuary to make arrangements. "I'd hoped not to see you here again for a long time," she told me. "The coroner still isn't done with the bodies, so the funeral can't be held until Monday."

Shiloh and I chose coffins and gave Brooke the uniform Don would wear, Heather's graduation dress, and pictures of how they once looked.

I phoned Chuckawalla prison. "This is Mara Alexander. I'd like to talk to someone about Don's coworkers who will be pallbearers. I hope they'll be able to have the day off."

"We might not be able to do that."

I'm being selfish. After all, just because my world's changed completely doesn't mean the rest of the planet has.

"Other people might be able to be the pallbearers."

"I'm sorry to cause trouble. If Don's friends can't be pallbearers, he would probably have wanted family members to do it instead."

Fortunately his coworkers were all able to attend.

The first of an avalanche of cards arrived October 3 from a kaleidoscope of people. Envelopes of donations signed on both sides by countless officers from RC West, CIM, and distant Chuckawalla were delivered to the cabin.

October 4, 1991:

Two claimed in crash
by Dona James, Editor
Palo Verde Valley Times

Don, Mara, Heather, Shiloh, and Uriah . . . they were a close-knit family. They fished and camped together, worshiped together, and laughed together.

And they loved.

Don and Mara were high-school sweethearts, and with their three children, were a solid American family.

The five of them were together through everything. Now they are a family of two.

The community of Blythe and the entire valley rallied around the Alexanders as eight-year-old Uriah battled leukemia and lost to the disease in July.

Now, just three months later, friends and neighbors are offering their support again.

News of the tragic deaths of Don and Heather on Wednesday morning has shaken the community, leaving the town's people in shock.

What started as a routine trip to Riverside—an appointment for Don and a track physical for Heather—turned into another tragedy and the shattering of a family.

Don, a sergeant at Chuckawalla Valley State Prison, and Heather, a freshman at Palo Verde Valley High School, left home around 5:00 A.M. Their lives were ended in a bizarre chain of events and head-on collision on Interstate 10, west of Desert Center (see inset).[3]

Tears filled my eyes. I brushed them away, anxious to know more.

> Why did Don and Heather Alexander have to die?
> . . . Here is what is known so far:
> Don and Heather were traveling west on Interstate 10, about three miles east of Red Cloud. It was around 6:30 A.M. Just about sunup.
> A few miles ahead of them, a red 1988 Toyota pickup was also traveling west. Suddenly the pickup made a U-turn, heading back to the east in the fast lane of the west-bound freeway.
> An eyewitness, a truck driver, kept pace with the errant vehicle in the east-bound lane. The Toyota accelerated to around 60 mph.
> Blowing his air horn to get the driver's attention, the trucker reported the driver looked over at him, then back at the oncoming traffic. Then he sped up. Driving directly into Don's Nissan Pathfinder. Head-on.
> On impact, Don's vehicle flipped completely over onto its top. The Toyota burst into flames, the driver, pinned in the vehicle, was burned beyond recognition. He remains unidentified. . . .
> Even the seatbelts Don and Heather wore couldn't save them. Don was dead in the vehicle. Heather, pulled from the car by a passing motorist, died at the scene a few moments later.[4]

Bob and Leah had only just arrived at Nana's cabin when he got a call. "My mom's at the hospital. They think it's her heart." Bob and Leah headed for the door.

"I'm going too, Mom," Shiloh said.

"Not without me." I grabbed my coat.

"Bob's mom had a heart attack," Leah said in the hospital hallway, "but she's OK now."

"Can I see if Jean is working in peds?" Shiloh begged.

I nodded and she dashed off. She returned moments later.

"Not there?" I asked.

She avoided my eyes. "Dr. Sanmarco's coming."

Almost at once I heard her voice. "Are you all right? Why are you here?"

"We're fine. My brother-in-law's mother had a heart attack."

She searched my face a moment, gauging my stability. "If there's anything we can do to help, just call." She turned back to the world of the ward.

🙠 🙠 🙠

"I haven't written a eulogy yet," I thought aloud.

Nana looked up with dismay. "I don't think we could take it."

All this doesn't affect just me. My family feels the strain too. They're protective of me and jealous of my time. They want to help but resent people outside the family complicating things with attempts to help. At least one person thought they weren't wanted at the funeral. I feel like the rope in a tug of war. People trying to help are tearing me apart unintentionally.

🙠 🙠 🙠

None of us had ever seen the picture of Heather that Jeff carried into the house. He peeled off the brown paper and leaned it against the hearth. Red curls floated above her forehead and flowed over her shoulders. Her brown eyes glowed with warmth. *The perfect Mona Lisa smile. She's beautiful; no longer a child but a young woman.* No one spoke a word; sorrow hung in our silence. *She should be just beginning her life, not being buried. It's so senseless.* All the men turned and slipped away to be alone. *I've never seen anything like that before—I hope I never do again.*

※⁓ ※⁓ ※⁓

The delivery truck rattled up the hill with another bright bouquet. I read the small white tag, "Heather Kelm?" A stab of pain and regret throbbed to the surface. I thought with jealousy of the times Theresa had been there for Heather when I couldn't, such as her graduation. *It was good for Heather; I wanted someone to be there. I wish it could have been me! But I didn't want Uriah to die alone. I told myself his need was greater: 'Uriah won't be with us long. Heather and I have a whole lifetime to spend together. I missed her junior high graduation, but I'll be there for her high school graduation.' How could I know I had only three months more to spend with her? But even if I had known, could I have left Uriah alone in his agony? It was a bitter choice. Now I feel unspeakable anguish. Regret is a deep, unseen wound in the soul.*

Things were left unsaid between Heather and me. The last thing she wanted was to be like me. Yet, of all my children, Heather was most like me. Losing her was like losing a large part of myself. She had been openly contemptuous of me for years. Only after Uriah's death did the beautiful adult she would become begin to shine through now and then, like the sun breaking through the clouds. The stormy, turbulent emotions of adolescence were passing away, and soon she would have been not only my daughter but also my friend. I was looking forward to that day with great expectation. *Now it will never come.*

I must console myself with the thought that one day I'll be able to spend all the time I want with her. Not in fleeting hours and minutes but in a timeless place that will allow all the un-said things to be said and all the unhealed wounds, caused by her being ripped away, to be soothed and mended.

I gathered mementos for the eulogy. I picked up a card Uriah had made in Sunday school one year; it was shaped like a shirt with an orange tie. "Daddy, I love you because you bought me a kite." Shiloh's seven-year-old scrawl declared, "To the best Dad in the world! You're always there to give a hug, and always there to smash a bug! HAPPY FATHER'S DAY!"

I found Heather's "personality album":

If I could be any popular star, I'd want to be myself because I don't really want to be anybody but me. . . . I'd make my first million by being a singer. . . . The two best gifts anyone could give me would be a spiral perm and pale green contacts. . . . In ten years I expect to be a vet[erinarian] and adopt four kids. . . . The three most important words in the English language are *Yes, No,* and *Aaaaaah!*

I chuckled. "Yep! That's Heather."

On Sunday, October 6, the crisp autumn air assailed us as Nana and Boompa, Debbie and her family, Janet Anderson, Theresa Kelm, and I huddled together with the faithful at Mt. Calvary Lutheran Church in Lake Arrowhead. "There's no place like home, because the treasure of our family is there," Pastor Courson's sermon concluded.

Theresa and I carried steaming cups to the Sunday-school circle at the back of the sanctuary. In the midst of our study, a troubled woman lamented, "So many bad things are happening in the world, I can't see how God can be in control."

Pastor Courson opened his mouth to answer, but I blurted out, "I'd like to respond to that if it's OK." *Is this how Jeremiah felt?* ". . . There is in my heart as it were a burning fire shut up in my bones, and I am weary with holding it in, and I cannot" (Jer. 20:9). I turned to her and the words burst forth. "I just lost my husband and daughter, and three months ago, Uriah. If I didn't believe God was in control, I wouldn't be able to go on living. The pain would be too incredible.

"It must have seemed like God had lost control to the disciples when they watched Jesus die on the cross. 'How could God let that happen? He was the Promised One, and God let Him die.' They didn't understand God had a plan they couldn't see. It was through Jesus' death that God blessed the entire world. Everyone has the opportunity to go to heaven because of Jesus' sacrifice. But on that awful, dark day it looked like the final defeat.

"Satan would like us to think he's in control. He makes it seem huge waves of evil will engulf us, like the Sea of Galilee when Peter walked its stormy surface to Jesus, but with a single word Jesus calmed the sea, and He rose again, so we know who's in control.

"Faith is trusting that God is loving and knows what He's doing. We're looking at the tapestry of life from the back side, and God's workings can seem like tangled threads, but one day we'll see the exquisite way God has woven our lives together. Don and Heather's deaths weren't just an accident. I don't know why, but God had a reason for taking them when He did, and they're with Him now. My daughter and I have been left here, and though it's hard, I know that's not an accident either. God has a purpose for everything He allows. He still has something for me to do. Something good lies ahead. I just don't know what it is—yet!"

She removed her glasses and wiped tears away. "You're right," she sighed.

Monday, October 7

I watched from the second floor as people made their way toward us. They loitered outside the viewing room and spoke in hushed tones. At last the funeral director stuck his head out the door and beckoned to me. Shiloh and I clasped hands as the door clicked shut behind us. We slipped silent as the shadows to the front of the dark, cold room where Don and Heather lay in caskets. I held my breath and peered in. *It's Don, but he doesn't look like himself.* I paced to the next wooden box. *She's pretty, but it's not quite Heather. It's strange, but until I saw them lying there, part of me still denied it was true. At last it's real.* Shiloh and I clung together. *We're all that's left.*

Family and friends paid their respects and comforted us with words and hugs. "I don't know how long it will be before I can come back to work," I whispered to Lonn and Julie Maly.

They exchanged surprised glances. "We thought you'd want to move closer to your family," Julie explained.

"There have been too many changes in our lives already. It would be best to stay put, at least until Shiloh graduates from eighth grade."

They smiled and hugged me.

The long line of cars inched up the hill to open graves next to Uriah's. Shiloh and I sat in the front row under the canopy between Nana and Grandma Ruth. The pinwheel Joel held for Heather's grave spun and glittered in the breeze. The air was perfumed by mounds of flowers. Shiloh clutched a dozen long-stem roses, like the bouquet Grandma Ruth cradled, from CVSP in memory of Heather and Don.

Brian, Jack, Kenny, Jeff, Bob, and Mark hoisted Heather's casket from the first hearse. Don's flag-draped coffin was borne by his uniformed fellow officers—and friends: Tim Ray, Steve Shay, Andy Anderson, Darren King, Sgt. John McDonald, Vaughn Panzer, Dave Long, Mark Kelm, and Henry Proventure. The color guard honored their fallen sergeant. The thunder of the twenty-one gun salute made me jump as a cloud of acrid smoke dimmed the sunshine. Lt. Jeff Burke pressed into my hands the ceremoniously folded flag from Don's coffin. The lonely sound of bagpipes drifted across the cut, green grass to silent mourners. After Spock's funeral on a *Star Trek* movie, Don had commented, "When I die, I want it played that way at my funeral." *I never thought I'd hear it played for him—and certainly not so soon.*

Tim Ray touched my shoulder, "Did you see the deer?"

"What?"

"A deer came out of the trees and stared at us. Don always told me he wanted to hunt deer, but he never had time. It must have been sent for his service."

Again, there was an outpouring of cards from those who helped us search for Uriah's donor and from correctional officers throughout the state of California. Cards from CVSP and the honor guard had over five hundred signatures. *Lord, this outpouring of support is tremendous. I'm amazed by the number of people who care.*

October 9, *Palo Verde Valley Times*:

Alexanders' killer identified

The man who killed Don and Heather Alexander in a head-on crash, last Wednesday, has been identified.

According to the California Highway Patrol in Indio, the driver, burned beyond recognition in the crash . . . turned his vehicle around and started traveling back down the freeway in the wrong lane. Before striking the

Alexander vehicle, police report that he had accelerated to more than 80 mph.

"Had he lived, he probably would have been charged with murder," said the CHP. "Considering he willfully, deliberately premeditated his action. . . ."

A toxicology report, revealing the presence of alcohol or other substances, is being attempted by the coroner's office. . . . [His] record, said the patrol, indicates he received a drunken driving conviction in 1983, was convicted of driving on a suspended license in 1986, and had received convictions for infractions in 1990.[5]

Zion Times, October 9:

ALEXANDER MEMORIAL SERVICE—will be held tomorrow evening, October 10, at 7:00 P.M. in the Zion Lutheran Church sanctuary.[6]

The mourners rustled down the aisle toward pictures of Don and Heather. A flood of memories of our family, whole and together, passed through my mind. *It will be that way again, but not in this world. How will life be now? I feel like half a person sitting here, with most of my family gone. God, You have to see us through, because I can't do it on my own. But You know that.*

The choir sang. Pastor gave a message and read remembrances of Don and Heather. We held hands and prayed the Lord's Prayer. The sound of bagpipes floated out of the sanctuary, while Shiloh chatted with friends and I stood in the long reception line. *Well, here I am, again. But this time, I'm by myself. So many people from the prison and church. Even Mayor Doris Morgan. I'm glad to see each of them, but I feel so tired and "washed out." I'll be glad to go home—though it no longer seems like home.*

Twenty-Four

Cloud Castles
(Oct. 10–Dec. 1991)

Someday I will be by her side,
And we can explore the heavens with an everlasting stride.
—Libby Christ

I HOPE WE DIDN'T CAUSE ANY HURT FEELINGS," LORI RAY SAID. "They wanted to buy you new furniture while you were gone."

"I'm glad I left you in charge," I replied. "I know people just want to help, but I need to be the one to decide when to get rid of the couch where Uriah died."

"They said it could only hold awful memories for you."

"Actually, it's familiar and comforting."

October 5

You don't know me, but we have a bond in the Lord. I teach at First Lutheran High in Sylmar and so I was there when you and your husband came to our campus recently and you spoke so bravely to us about your son, Uriah's, joyful life. I admired your courage, patience, and hope. I can't even let myself imagine how I would cope with losing my husband and daughter also. It must seem to you terribly unfair that God would allow this to happen! Even remembering that they are now in heaven with Uriah rejoicing, how do you adjust to your life without them? I pray that you have a good support system there with family, church, and friends, and I understand that you have another daughter to care for and love. She must be a great comfort to you. I want you to know that we teachers prayed for you with our students in all our classes the day we heard your news. I do so wish there were something I could do to help you get through this time, but I fear that your pain must be too great for earthly efforts alone to ease. This is definitely a job for the Lord.

I hope you will let us know if there is something we could do.

May God bless you and give you peace.

Miriam

CPOF announced plans for a donor drive in Washington, with hopes that testing of correctional officers nationwide would follow.

We agonized with you through the painful loss of Uriah—now words can't express our feelings over your new loss. But please know that many like us hurt for you and want to surround you with the shield of Christian love.

May you find comfort in the never-ending love of Jesus Christ, who knows your pain and can heal you with His love even though it may not seem possible at first. Our prayers will continue for you.

God bless,
Linda and Jerry Hoffort

A card signed by ten of Heather's friends contained a message from her teacher:

> I had Heather a year ago in my science class. She was a delight and a very good student—one of those that teachers always remember. Heather was mature for her age. I remember her as a hard worker and very sweet. Nothing can take the hurt from losing a loved one—but we have that blessed hope of seeing them again one day. Heather is well where she's at—I trust you will be too.
>
> All my love and prayers,
> Mrs. Sharron Maurice
> Blythe Middle School

> The Lord must have something absolutely wonderful for you to test you this hard. I've never known of something this extreme to happen to one lovely individual. Be sure and at least get up every morning no matter how hard it is.
>
> Love,
> Caron [Almquist] and family

> Several years ago I had Heather in kindergarten at Valle Vista and then in first grade at Bear Gulch. I have so many good memories of her. She was such a sweet and gentle child and the only child in my 21 years of teaching that I recommended skipping a grade. If I had to pick one word to describe Heather, it would be that she was a very "loving" child. I'm sure she has touched the lives of others as she touched mine. May God give you comfort at this time.
>
> Sincerely,
> Linda Cook

The children of First Lutheran School of San Fernando wrote essays about rainbows and sent them to me. I cried as I read the wisdom of the children of God:

At school when Mrs. Bashel got the phone call the hole class was talking. Then Mrs. Reynolds came in and told us what happend the hole intire class was quite all avussuden. Then we prayed but we were sad and happy cause even though they died we new he was going to heaven.

from Ernie

It's hard to say goodbye,
To someone you luv.
It makes you want to cry,
Even thou,
You know,
There in Heaven above.
You ask God, "Without them how will I survive?"
But you realize, sooner or later you must go on with your lives.

Remember you will soon,
Be united to them again.
But until then you cant stop your lives,
Even without them, you must again begin.

Luv and sympathy,
Yolanda M.

When me and my class herd on 10-3-91 I know just like me the class was very sad. How could this happen? I thought. And I thought it over. I figured that God wanted Uriah, Heather, and Mr. Alexander with him.

When I told the news to my father and Grandparents who go to the church and I think they had the blood test I could till they were sad and devistated. My mother is one of the 1st grade teachers at the school Mrs. Courtney. When you came to the school I was delighted to finaly see and meet you. I can understand why you are sad but cheer up!!! Theyre in heavenly bodys and all. If you ever wish to, write me.

We all love you lots,
Rochelle Courtney

God's love
by Heidi

God's love is the most powerful thing on earth. And we should love God like He loves us and like Uriah loves God. Uriah's love for God brought many peopole to God. And I think our love for God should bring others to God like Uriah did.

Rainbows
by Leah

I love rainbows are a beautiful part of rain. Its like magic one minute its dark and stormy and you think this horrible, but the next minute the sun is shining everything looks clean and new and you have got one rainbow. I know I'm starting to sound like one of those crazy handbooks, but I'll finish it anyway. Your life is dark and gloomy now but in awhile it will straiten up and the rain would have stopped and you'll have to start all over. You have memories of Don, Heather, and Uriah. But its good to be able to make memories whith someone else.

Rainbows are beutiful they have so many different colors. God said that he gave us the rainbow as a promise that he wouldn't flood our earth again. And he kept his promise. When I see rainbows I think of Uriah, Don, and Heather.

[by] Vanessa

Rainbows rainbows [Uriah] loved rainbows. I know why, they are beatiful just like your family was. [Uriah] and your family were great people because of their love to Jesus. Now they are internal life. Rainbows have all kinds of wonderful color and are bright and everyone loves them.

[by] Kiki

I think Uriah's thoughts about seeing the other side of the rainbow was a very smart thing. Whenever I see a rainbow, I sort of get a happy feeling inside and think it's hard to believe heaven can be hundreds [of] times prettier.

[by] Elizabeth

Monday, October 14

I returned to work. Don's birthday. I need the money, and it'll do me good to do something.

"Can you come to the Courtesy Coffee Shop?" a woman on the phone asked. "We held a drawing and raised some money for Shiloh and you."

"Thanks, we need it."

I decided not to pursue litigation. *I feel sorry for that man's wife. She has no auto insurance and can't collect life insurance. God's taken care of me so far, and I know He will in the future. If anyone's wronged me, God will punish them.*

Shiloh and I attended the Bryan Duncan concert that night. *God, it's clever of You to arrange this on Don's birthday so I won't have too much time to think. Don, Heather, and Uriah are never far from my mind.*

October 15

The newspaper account of your loss of husband and daughter caused me to break into tears. Out came the "Why, Lord?" and "It's not fair, it's too much for them to bear." Then I remembered the new song I had acquired and later I read in Ruth Graham's book the entry I sent you.

As one sister in Christ's family to another—I hope each of these has a comforting and strengthening effect on you and Shiloh. You're in my prayers.

Love,
Claire John

Shiloh's chapter-one teacher sent this note home:

It's a bit soon to evaluate Shiloh's work at this time, but she seems calm enough and is working well. I have great faith in Shiloh. I'm sure she will make progress as the year goes on. I'll keep in touch with you.

Sincerely,
Floe Lloyd

October 16, 1991

Call if you need to talk. It's hard when your family and friends don't feel like talking to you about the ones who have "gone home."

Margot

Sometimes it does seem like people are uneasy when I talk about Don, Heather, and Uriah. Yet it's impossible not to talk about them. They aren't dead to me. They're just living elsewhere.

The enclosed check is from the students at First Lutheran High School in memory of Uriah, donated at our weekly chapel service. We are also aware of the recent loss of your husband and daughter. May the Lord grant you strength and comfort.

Yours in Christ,
William Stark, Principal

October 17, 1991

I wanted to take a moment to let you know how sorry I am to hear of the loss of your husband and daughter. I so admired the witness you all were during the times at the hospital with Uriah. I'm sure the three of them are personally asking Jesus to sustain and guide you at this time. You are both in my prayers often.

Ruth Vandergoot

October 18, 1991

I was thinking of you and how much I admire the strength God has provided in times of need and crisis—

and you display perfect faith in the heavenly Father. My life is richer for knowing you. Thank you—

Teena
[Principal,
Margaret White Elementary School]

God, people like Teena quietly shape others' lives with their encouragement, as Barnabas did.

October 21

I fingered the envelope from the Highway Patrol. *The accident report!* Phrases stuck in my mind as I skimmed the 20-page report:

DR-1 [Driver 1] . . . was burned over the entire body and charred black and very obviously deceased. . . . DR-2 [Driver 2] (Alexander) was obviously deceased. . . . Heather Alexander . . . was covered with a yellow blanket and apparently received fatal injury. . . . No skids were at the scene. . . . Driver #2 was not in a fastened position, however the strap did show twist and stretch signs and was severed. . . . A pocket knife with a long open blade was lying on the roadway, alongside the driver's door. . . .

. . . Kenneth Rataezyk, a truck driver . . . Related he was driving eastbound on I.S. 10. . . . He observed V-1 eastbound in the W-1 lane, at what Ken estimated to be 80 mph. . . . Ken said he saw several vehicles swerve to the right to a avoid a head-on collision with V-1. Suddenly, he saw V-2 . . . in a clear head-on course with the wrong way direction of V-1. . . . Ken did assist witness #3 in the removal of burning V-1 from contact with V-2.

Wit #5 said that he was traveling with another truck driver [eastbound]. They blew their air horns

. . . the driver of the red Toyota look[ed] over at him
. . . the more cars the red Toyota met, the faster he
would drive. . . . [V-2] had changed to W-1 lane to
pass big rig truck . . . flipped over on impact, when
he went by the accident site he saw a person hanging upside down in the seat belt. . . .

Cause: . . . Driver #1 with his willful, deliberate,
and premeditated actions and final results, did mani-
fest with intention and malice, both expressed and
implied, to take away the life of a fellow creature and
did so to the occupants of V-2. In this instance DR-1
committed 187 P.C. Murder of the First Degree.

Later it was determined the Toyota driver had alcohol
in his blood.

October 23

I can't begin to tell you how sorry I was to hear of the
tragedy you have had to endure this year. My father was
a pentecost preacher back in the hills of Kentucky where
I was born and raised. The song I have enclosed was his
favorite hymn. The words of this song say a lot, and I
have drawn a lot of comfort from them through the years.
I hope you will also.

Love and prayers,
Judy Mulvaney [maker of the rainbow clown]

Death is an angel sent down from above,
Sent for the buds and the flowers we love;
Truly 'tis so, for in heaven's own way
Each soul is a flow'r in the Master's bouquet.

Let us be faithful till life's work is done,
Blooming with love till the reaper shall come;

> Then we'll be gathered together for aye,
> Transplanted to bloom in the Master's bouquet.

October 28, 1991

Distant Friendship

Sometimes I look at my reflection
    and hope to see hers.
I hope that there may be a connection
    between my world and hers.
But those are only hopes.

Sometimes I lay awake at night
    wondering what she is doing.
Hoping she can spare some time
    to watch over me as I'm growing.
Maybe she is, maybe she is not.
    But all the same it is a nice thought.

Maybe she is beside me holding my hand.
    Or maybe she is busy in her glorious land.
Someday I will be by her side,
    And we can explore the heavens
    with an everlasting stride.

But until then I will yearn for her company.
    Even though I know in my heart she is always with me.

—By Libby Christ, for Heather

Tuesday, October 29
    Over 100 cards were sent. The encouragement was great and the wise words many. *Once again, I'm in debt to so many who give so much of themselves.*

October 30, 1991

On behalf of Loma Linda Eye and Tissue Bank, I wanted to express my deepest sympathy on the death of your husband Donald and your daughter Heather.

Through your caring decision there are now four people who have had their sight restored through corneal transplantation surgery. . . . One from Compre, Los Angeles, San Bernardino, and San Gabriel, California. On behalf of these recipients, please accept our profound gratitude for this miracle.

> Sincerely,
> Betsy A. Crowl
> Executive Director

Thursday, October 31

Lynette Panzer got a huge donation of pumpkins from Albertson's for the church All Saints party Christian pumpkin carving contest. She and Theresa helped me with the Bible character costume contest.

I didn't realize most insurance policies and wills require you to survive the decedent by thirty days. We've got to get by for a month without income!

When the insurance representative finally came, he'd heard strange rumors about Don's death. "I heard that you and your husband had a dream about the accident and woke up and told each other."

"I'm the only one who had a dream, and I didn't think anything about it at the time. Don never knew I had it."

"I heard you just took out an insurance policy too."

"We just adjusted our *car* insurance to cover our new car." *He can't think we set this up. Could he?* "We've been paying for Don's life insurance for years."

"I heard you had to go into debt because of Uriah's illness."

Suddenly I was angry. *He thinks this was a plot to collect insurance money?* "We had excellent medical insurance, and only a manageable debt from Uriah's illness is left." *Does he think I would sacrifice my husband and daughter for money? They're looking for an excuse not to pay their debt. I guess I won't be able to count on them.*

I talked to Pastor and he contacted the insurance company. They straightened things out immediately, which was a relief. *With the insurance settlement and my two jobs, I'll be able to pay for the funerals and keep a roof over our heads. Until then, things will be tight.* Gifts from well-wishers helped. Tim Ray helped me sell Don's guns. *I never appreciated them before, but those guns are sustaining us now.*

I used Don's camera to snap photos for the paper on the sidelines of the high school football game. *What would Don think if he could see me now? I'm using your camera, honey! It's amazing how God's provided for us in ways I couldn't have planned. He's had Don leave behind the tools I need.*

Sunday, November 9

During a circle prayer in Sunday school with students and teachers, everyone held hands and thanked God for something. We were thankful for sunshine, families, sisters, brothers, and pets. Teacher Geri Allen's prayer caught me by surprise. "I'm thankful for Mara and her faith in God. It's wonderful she can be so certain they're in heaven."

I'm thankful for that too, God. I know where they are. If they hadn't been Christians or I was unsure of their faith, I would wonder if I'd see them again.

November 13, 1991

It is difficult to tell you how deeply I and the employees of the California Rehabilitation Center feel about the recent tragic losses that have occurred to both you and your family.

Some of the employees of CRC directly knew Donald, while many others have come to know you and your family through their courageous strengths and inspirational efforts during these difficult times. . . .

Ms. Alexander, our thoughts are with you, and we extend our deepest sympathy. I hope that the enclosed contributions from our caring employees will in some manner assist you in defraying the personal costs often associated with these tragic occurrences.

If I or any of our staff at CRC can do anything within our power to provide you with further assistance, as a member of our extended family, please feel free to call me directly.

Sincerely,
Art Calderon, Warden

On Shiloh's twelfth birthday I gave her a gift from her father. He'd bought the .22 rifle September 14 and hid it on top of the canopy over our bed. He'd grinned. "I can't wait to see her face when she opens it."

She cradled the last gift from her dad. "I'm glad he picked something special."

It would have been so much better if he could have given it to her himself.

Shiloh's friend Jenny Miller had the same birthday: November 11. Her mom suggested we throw a pizza party together. *It's so important to keep Shiloh involved with friends. Sometimes her grief is so hard to bear. I can tell she's terribly lonely, especially with me working long hours.*

On Thursday, November 14, Judy Sullivan, a representative for California Casualty auto insurance called. She was very helpful. On one of our many phone conversations she mentioned she too had been widowed at a young age. *That explains how she knows exactly what I'm going through!* "Judy, can I ask you a personal question? It's something I've been wondering ever since Don's death. Is it possible to start over? Or should I just expect to spend the rest of my life alone?"

"I've remarried."

"How is it?"

"It's wonderful! I was young when I married the first time, and though I loved my first husband dearly, the second time I knew exactly what qualities I was looking for in a man."

"Maybe someday God will bless me like that too."

Judy and I talked on the phone about business a lot, unfortunately. She'd sent the insurance check to the Nissan Corporation, and it was returned as undeliverable. Nissan Corporation called me about our delinquent car payment. "It was totaled in a car accident October 2, but we were insured," I said. I gave them Judy's phone number. They never called her. Every couple weeks they called me. At first the calls were reminders, but soon the calls became surly. One woman demanded, "Do you want to keep the Pathfinder or should we just come and get it?" Every time I explained, their attitude changed and they promised to put a note on my file. But it never helped. The calls continued though my insurance company issued another check.

November 19, 1991

I think of you so often and continually remember you in my prayers. I pray God is keeping His grace on you. As the holidays come upon us, I pray God will give you loving, precious memories and grant you His joy in making new memories with friends and loved ones. May His peace soothe your hearts and minds as you continue to trust in Him. God bless you!

Love in Christ,
Margot

On December 2, I found a plain, white envelope with no return address in my PO box. Inside was sixty dollars wrapped in paper with a little card, "PASS IT ON. You are loved." What a wonderful Christmas present!

Thursday, December 3
Nana called. "Aunt Elaine is worried because a check they sent wasn't cashed."

I looked through the bin of cards. *I didn't remember how many there were!* I found one with $113 cash in it. There was another $300 of checks there. *I didn't realize how fogged I must have been until tonight.* [The card from Aunt Elaine showed up years later in a book in Shiloh's room, with the check still in it.]

Saturday, December 7
I cried as I typed the church bulletin for December 8. *Heather's birthday.*

I took a picture for the paper of Dr. Thomas—principal of Blythe Middle School—accepting a check for the Lion's Quest program. "How are you?" he asked.

"It's kind of bumpy going into the holidays."

The secretary talked to me about my losses. Cindy Lofton talked about Uriah. *People really care how we are.*

Sunday, December 8
Nana and Boompa came at eight this morning. Shiloh and I took them for a tour of Blythe and Christmas shop-

ping in Quartzsite. They left at four o'clock, and we went to the Blythe Christmas parade. I photographed the parade for the paper while Shiloh rode on Zion's float.

It was hard to sleep at night. I dreamed Don was just away at work. In the early hours, I awakened with a start as the sound of his motorcycle approached from the freeway. I sat up. *I'm not dreaming.* It stopped at the corner, then drove down the street toward our house, but then it faded away. I felt sweaty and shaky. *I hope I'm not cracking under the pressure.*

I called the friend who had Don's motorcycle at his house. "We sold it to a relative in San Bernardino, and he hasn't paid for it yet," the friend's wife told me.

(In the summer of 1995, I confronted Don's friend. "We sold it to an officer who lived half a block from you," he said. "Didn't my wife pay you?" *I didn't imagine it! It really was Don's motorcycle.*)

Sunday, December 15
    Nana and Joel picked up a copy of the picture taken of Don and Uriah by the *Daily Bulletin* just before Christmas. The photographer pulled the picture out of the envelope to make sure it was the right one. Joel started to cry. "I guess that's it," he said sheepishly.

December 18

Mara, I am enclosing here the letter we are sending to all our members. . . . It's amazing to me that the Foundation has indeed grown into what it actually envisioned . . . four years ago—an organization that really does assist and help take care of our own.

With love and respect,
Charleene, Administrator

The letter had a paragraph about our family:

> . . . Of course everyone remembers young Uriah Alexander, for whom we tried to find the bone marrow match and donor that might have saved his life; but Uriah succumbed to his leukemia on July 1. Three months later, almost to the day, Uriah's father Don and older sister Heather Sunshine were killed in a head-on collision. In so short a time, a family that once numbered five was reduced to a family of two. . . . Though we did not find a match for Uriah Alexander, . . . a correctional officer from Pelican Bay State Prison . . . matched . . . a patient listed with the National Bone Marrow Registry. . . . I would like to give credit, and thanks, to Officer Dona Burke for giving part of herself to save the life of another young person. . . .[1]

There were lots of Christmas cards that year. *People continue to pray for us, God. I feel like we're getting a crash course in grief: Don's birthday, Thanksgiving, Heather's birthday, and Christmas already.*

Shiloh and I were so busy, we were never home except to sleep. We rose at five and returned home after ten. Weekends were spent trying to catch up on home maintenance and cleaning—without Don's help.

Crazy little things got me the most. I no longer had anyone to open difficult jars. The sprinklers stopped working until I found the special wrench needed to open the filter and replace the cartridge.

That night I sat on the porch swing Don had helped me build and looked up at the bright stars. "Hi, honey! How am I doin'?" *I miss you so much. It's hard to become self-sufficient. I'm worried about Shiloh. She always wears black and buries herself in books. I'm going to quit writing for the paper so I can spend more time with her. After all, she's more important than work. Right, Ghost Dad?*

Twenty-Five

Beyond the Rainbow
(1992)

*The God who could turn His Son's torture
and death into a victory
can do the same with the tragedies in my life.*

Wednesday, January 1, 1992

SHILOH AND I LEFT BLYTHE FOR A VISIT WITH JOANNA IN OR-egon. We stopped at Nana's cabin on the way. "Yesterday was my last day of work at the paper," I told Nana. "I'll still be a stringer for photography and stories. I must start writing that book. It seems like such a huge feat to accomplish, I guess that's why I'm dragging my feet.

"There's a scholarship fund at the high school in Heather's name, a refurbishing of the fellowship hall at Zion Lutheran Church dedicated to all the Alexanders, and a fund for a play structure at Zion Lutheran School in memory of Uriah."

I looked out the window at Shiloh trying to play in the snow alone. "She looks so lonely in the snow. She really needs her daddy or Heather for a snow fight and sledding. Sometimes I worry about trying to raise her on my own. I'd like to marry again and maybe have more children, but the problem is finding someone worthwhile to spend my life with."

Driving to Oregon gave me a lot of time to think. *I've cried more about Heather than Don. There was a good possibility Don would die because of his line of work, but I expected Heather to live a long life. It turned out Heather was right: she never got married or had children, and she's living in a mansion with her friends—when they get there.*

I don't know what I'm supposed to be doing, God. I know You have something You want me to do, but what? I don't feel like I'm doing a good job of anything.

❦ ❦ ❦

Nissan Corporation continued to call and demand money for the car. Shiloh got a call while I was at work. "May we speak with Don Alexander?" they asked her.

"He's dead," she murmured.

"Well, where can we reach him?"

What could Shiloh say? Six feet under at Rose Hills? Shiloh called me, "Mom, you won't believe what they said to me!"

I called them back. "I need to speak to your superior."

"I can put a note on your file so no one will call for seven days."

"This needs to be resolved, not delayed."

After a few minutes, a man with a deep voice picked up the phone. "Yes?" He listened to my explanation. "I can't understand why the account wasn't put in our insurance settlement file so we would call the insurance company instead of you," he said. "It should have been done on the first phone contact."

"I can't understand either."

Sunday, January 12

"Twenty-seven people joined the church in October," Pastor told me. "A lot of it is because of Shiloh and you and how you're dealing with the situation."

God, I'm weak and I know it. Help me keep pointing them to You. You're the one who's strong. I'm so naive and I've never been so aware of it. It's a big world and, without You, I'd be facing it alone.

Thursday, January 16

The NMDP status report showed we had raised almost $86,000: 1,684 donors had been tested, $71,496 had been paid, and $13,350 was billed for drives conducted. There was $1,100 left for new drives.

I cleaned out the shed and found pictures Don and I took in college. I didn't cry, but I felt washed out. I was glad Janet called.

I called Mrs. McHargue about the book. "I want to write the parts I know, but the town's response is a side of the story I wasn't around to see. Could you write a synopsis and outline for the book while I work on organizing the boxes of material I have?"

"We can give it a try, but we're planning to move."

"There's always the mail."

Monday, January 20

I checked my list of things to be done before Shiloh and I left for New York to visit Leah and Bob. *I won't be back before the donor drive for Andrew DeLeon!* I wrote an article and got out materials from our earlier drives.

Tuesday, January 21

We got up at 5:30 so I could type the article at the paper before I went to work at church. At lunch, a friend and I talked about her marriage that was in danger of breaking up. *Such fragile relationships all around. Do I dare get involved with someone new?*

Johnny Tellez picked up the supplies for the donor drive. "I may not be there either," he said.

"Here's a number where I can be reached. Theresa's done lots of them," I said.

Wednesday, January 22

Since Don and Heather died, I keep hoping God will show me what to do, but maybe He wants me to discover it on my own. There are so many directions I could go. Perhaps it's more freedom than I'm prepared to deal with. So many people and experiences lie ahead.

It's hard to see families growing around me when my family keeps getting smaller. Sometimes I think it would be nice to start another, and sometimes I feel that's not what God has in mind. He'll lead me the right way. It's a good thing I don't know what lies ahead or I probably couldn't face it. Life a day at a time is hard enough, just like Jesus said.

Friday, February 14

Shiloh gave me a puzzle postcard of a stamp that said "LOVE." On the back, "Happy Valentine's Day, Mommy." My valentine appeared in the *Palo Verde Valley Times*. A kitten held a heart that said, "To Shiloh, the sweetest girl I know."

I called the prison, "Who do I need to contact about a lawsuit an inmate filed against Don?"

"Don't worry about it. It's all taken care of."

I'd better look into it. Everything that should be "no problem" is always a problem for me. Steve and Lori Shay found the Pathfinder in a junkyard after the crash and gathered Don's scattered papers. Thanks to them, I have the papers from the case.

I tried to contact the attorney general's office, but it had moved, and I spent hours being transferred from one person to another without contacting anyone who could tell me the status of the case or a number where I could reach those representing Don.

Then they sent me a letter. Mervyn Lazarus, an attorney, was attempting to name me as a defendant in the lawsuit in Don's place. Felix Leatherwood, deputy attorney general, had represented Don in the case. "We'll represent you if you complete the paperwork I send and return it immediately. You can't be named in the lawsuit because punitive damages are cut off when a plaintiff passes away. Don't talk to Pruitt's attorney. If he contacts you, call Lydia Anderson at Chuckawalla Valley State Prison."

On March 2, I received a press release from the NMDP. *There's more than half a million donors in the registry!*

Thursday, March 19
    Shiloh's teacher, Mrs. Fisher, came into the office at lunchtime. "I'm worried about Shiloh. She keeps talking about Don, Heather, and Uriah in the present tense. She gave Michael, a new student, the impression they're still alive."
    I talked to Shiloh. "No, I didn't," she said. "Mrs. Fisher's acting strange."
    God, help me know what to do.

My NMDP report of March 20 showed there was still $1,100.78 in the account. *I could release the money to the NMDP to use for testing, but I want to use that money for donor drives in Uriah's memory. People donated the money for us to locate donors, and that's what Uriah would have wanted. But time to organize them is difficult to find.*

Tuesday, March 24

Michael said Shiloh didn't tell him Don, Heather, and Uriah were dead. I'm really worried about her. Pastor said he would talk to her.

Saturday, April 9

Today is gearing up to be a killer. Especially since we're leaving tomorrow for a trip to the Sequoias. Suddenly there's a Quince Años to attend, rainbow suckers to buy, a banner to make, a bulletin to finish, packing and grocery shopping, and a singles' barbecue to attend. Not to mention I just covered the prison's Gong Show and had dinner with the Baschals last night.

But Shiloh and I even managed a short swim at the river with friends from church that afternoon.

Shiloh danced at the Quince Años with friends until ten o'clock. "Please, Mom. Can I stay a bit longer?"

"We can stay until your friends leave." *I'll just sit and watch for half an hour.*

"I'm Victor, from 'Huma'," a young man said. "You want to dance?"

I turned to see who he was talking to behind me, but no one was there. *Me?* "I don't know how."

"I'll teach you."

I was nervous as he led me to the dance floor. He started whirling around the floor. All I had to do was pick up my feet and let them fall. We twirled across the floor with fancy flourishes.

We took a break and tried to bridge the language barrier. He put his arm around me and held my hand. *Uh-oh. He's been drinking—or something.*

"I'm not a user," he said with a thick accent. "I believe in God."

How am I going to get out of this? It's definitely time to go home—alone! I saw Shiloh dancing with a man who looked my age. I jumped to my feet and threaded my way to her. I shouted in her ear over the loud music, "It's time to go!"

She headed for the door followed by her "partner." He turned back to the party when he realized Shiloh and I were together, but Victor followed us all the way to the truck. He looked forlorn, standing alone as I climbed in. "I'll never forget you," he said.

I hugged him. "Thanks for teaching me to dance. I'll never forget you either." Shiloh and I drove back to the safety of our home. *What an education! I didn't like the singles scene the first time. I'm even less ready for it now!*

Sunday, April 13

The kids did a great job on the Easter Sunday-school play. I had trouble getting pictures of Shiloh being confirmed because she was on the other side of the church. After the service, we had a Sunday-school cast party and passed out rainbow suckers and Christian T-shirts. I folded the confirmation robes and took off the boutonnieres. Shiloh and I went to Sizzler for lunch, then to the river with friends.

Tuesday, April 14

Rick Avery and Diana, Doug Clendaniels, Steve Hagar, and Lori and Tim Ray will work on the roof Wednesday. I'm glad people are still willing to help.

Wednesday, April 15

I received the paperwork from the attorney general's office and filled it out. I hope they're right and I can't be named in this lawsuit. I'd like this nightmare to end. If I have to pay for something Don didn't do, how will I make ends meet? We'll know after the hearing May 11.

Old photos of Disneyland showed up double-exposed. In the background of shots of Shiloh dressed for the '50s dance were pictures of Uriah and her at the petting zoo. On a shot of our dogs lying in the yard in the setting sun, Uriah appears in their midst in a wheelchair munching on a churro with Grandma Ruth and me. On photos of friends at a swimming pool, we waited in line for a ride while Heather laughed with glee.

I tried to sleep. *I'm hurting inside more than ever. I miss Don so much. I'll never be able to find someone who loves me as much as he did.*

Friday, April 24

God knows what I need and will supply it. I want more children; but is that what God knows is right for me? Shiloh said, "I like it better when it's crowded," but God will provide what she needs too.

May 7

I have heard such good reports about what a beaming light you are! Praise God!

Sure, we all know you mourn and have very hard days of "longing." What a heavy burden has been set before you. But the devil, our adversary, has not robbed you of your JOY IN THE LORD! You have been wounded but [are] still marching in the ARMY. It brings me so much joy to hear how you have decided to go on to glory! Of course our strength comes from the Lord—and I know that that is what you will tell me, but we still have the choice—whether or not to allow God to take control of our lives. May God continue to give His strength and fill your heart with joy.

Love,
Diana [MOMs group]

May 26, 1992

It is so great that you are working at your church. Keeping in close touch with your Lord is how I'm doing it too. . . . It has been a year since Uncle Henry went to heaven. I do miss him. He had so many things wrong with him that it is a blessing to have him with his Savior. I pray for you each day, committing you and Shiloh in His keeping,

Aunt Alice E

"My name's Gloria Garcia," said a young voice on the phone. "I'm a student at Palo Verde Valley High School on the yearbook staff. I've been assigned to do a page about Heather. I need pictures of her and anything else you think might belong there."

Along with silly and beautiful pictures of Heather was a song she was writing at the time of her death:

Best Friends

Friends . . . friends forever,
never to part,
but always to share.
Friends . . . real, good and true friends.
Friends like . . . you and me.
Best friends.

And friends are friends forever,
That's just the way it is;
And if you are a true friend,
Then your friendship will not end.
Moving forces us to part,
But not really in heart,
Because in heart we're together . . .
Forever . . .

"Would you sign this?" I asked Gloria when I picked up Heather's yearbook:

"I hope you enjoy the memories this paragraph brings to you. Always, Gloria"

Friday, June 5
I covered the high school graduation for the *Times*. Austin Sorenson was valedictorian:
"I would . . . like to remember some members of our class that are unable to be here tonight. Summer Seeley is one. I didn't really know her well, but I do remember she was always smiling.
"The other is Heather Alexander. She was involved in track. The day she was killed, she was on her way to get a physical for track. We dedicated our next track meet to Heather, and it must have worked, because it was the only one we won."

God, only You could bring me here to hear this. I could have missed this precious memory so easily. You drop them into my life like jewels that I treasure in my heart. Afterward I thanked Austin. "Heather would have loved it!"

Thursday, June 25
Don received a questionnaire from a group asking for information about the Pathfinder. I wonder if we will

ever be done with that Pathfinder. I'll keep the key on my key chain; a reminder of how quickly life can change.

Tuesday, July 7

A package arrived at Zion Lutheran School from the Malys vacationing in Iowa. A rainbow blazed across the cover of the book inside, *There Is A Rainbow Behind Every Dark Cloud,* printed by Celestial Arts, "written for children like us who have gotten sick with cancer, leukemia, and other sicknesses where you think you might die. We find as we help each other, we help ourselves."

Inside Julie had written:

For Mara, with warm, full-of-love memories of our Uriah. Saw this book and had to get it for you— especially since I know your desire to put Uriah's story in book form. And our spirits are with yours, Mara, because we came across this treasure the anniversary week of Uriah's "triumphant entry" into God's heavenly kingdom. Please know that he lives on through us who loved him so much.

Hugs,
Jules and Lonn

Wednesday, July 8

I opened a letter from TLC ministries to "the parents of Heather Alexander." The newsletter was written by a bereaved couple to "minister comfort and encouragement to bereaved parents and their surviving children . . . through the counsel . . . of God's Word." What a wonderful ministry those parents have begun! They've turned a devastating loss into a positive thing. That's what I'd like to do. I just need to find the ministry God intended.

Saturday, July 11

Chad Comstock was the third graduate of Zion Lutheran School killed in a tragic traffic accident. Lonn returned from his vacation to the dismal news. Since Pastor was on vacation, Lonn officiated the memorial service July 15. He's troubled by these deaths. He's a teacher, training children to shape a future for themselves, and three of them lost their futures so young and needlessly. *God, what purpose do You have for allowing this?*

Sunday, July 19

I put flowers on the altar in memory of Don, Heather, and Uriah. Shiloh and I sat with Ernie Weeks and Lt. Burke. Theresa Kelm and Debbie Swanson became the directors of Christian education. I see God drawing my time in Blythe to a close.

Sunday, July 26

I think Danny's serious. He showed up in church and comes to see me in the office. It's what I've prayed and dreamed about, but now I'm afraid. What if he just wants a fling? What if things don't work out and I get hurt? I want to run away. My vacation is only a week and a half away. If this isn't God's plan, Danny will find someone new by the time I return.

Carrie always left encouraging little notes on my desk. "Have a nice, safe trip. See ya when you get back! Smiles, Carrie." Under it was a little hardbound book: *Look for the Rainbow.*

On the way to Oregon, Shiloh and I stopped to visit the nurses in the pediatric ward. Someone I hadn't seen in a long time smiled and gave me a hug. "How's Uriah doing?"

The lively chatter of the nurses ceased. "I need to check something," one murmured in the sudden silence. They scattered and disappeared through various doors. My friend blinked after them. It seemed like I was back in that room with Shiloh all those miles and minutes from where I now stood. "I'm sorry," I said softly, looking into her eyes. "Uriah died last July."

A look of horror and embarrassment crossed her face. "I'm—I'm sorry."

"It's OK. He died at home without fear or pain with all of us around him. He even played with his toys the day he died."

She left quickly.

I wonder how much longer these things will happen?

Shiloh and I visited Joanna's family, took a mail-boat trip up the Rogue River, hiked on the beach, flew in a light plane, rode horses on the beach, camped in Idaho, visited Don's relatives in Boise, and rafted on their river. We returned through Utah; *Heather would have loved it here.*

Throughout the trip, I thought about Danny and what could happen. When I got home, there were seven messages from him on the answering machine. *I guess he isn't going to go away.*

He offered to fix some broken windows. And he did. I asked him to stay for dinner.

Thursday, August 27
I was a volunteer at the CPOF booth in Reno at the CCPOA conference. I wrote a speech in case I had to address the assembly. It was a good thing I did:

Thank You, CPOF

The following is the text of an address to the over 400 delegates and guests at the annual convention of the California Correctional Peace Officers Association (CCPOA) on August 27, 1992, by Mara Alexander.

The only thing certain about life is change. Sometimes it can be sudden and drastic, such as the deaths of Don and Heather. . . . Sometimes it is slow and painful, and we struggle against it, like Uriah's eight-year fight against leukemia. A tremendous change in our lives can leave us reeling and unable to cope.

Without a doubt, when we clasp hands and face the future together, we are much stronger than if we stumble on alone. That is what CPOF and CCPOA are for: they unite and support us when we are most in need of help.

The CPO Foundation supported us in our search for a donor for Uriah. I am grateful for this opportunity to thank those of you who were tested for Uriah and whose facilities held donor drives. I hope you will carry that thanks back to your institutions when you return. Because of those drives, three people have had their transplants and 19 people have found their donors. CPOF is still doing testing, and I would encourage you to be tested if you haven't already done so. It costs you nothing, and it can give someone a whole new life. . . .

I encourage all of you to support these groups in any way you can; when we stand together, we are strong.[1]

Sunday, August 30

At the Sunday-school picnic, they dedicated the refurbished fellowship hall to the memory of Don, Heather, and Uriah.

I received a letter from Felix Leatherwood dated September 28: "As you know the United States District Court substituted the estate of your late husband in the above entitled matter."

What! No, I didn't know. To prevent a conflict of interest, they couldn't represent me. I was encouraged to "immediately contact Mr. Longyear," whom they had retained to represent me.

"I'm very glad you called," Mr. Longyear said. "I have only an address for you and no phone number. The depositions begin October 9, and I need substitution papers signed and returned immediately. I haven't received written reports on the investigation, and I was told none were written."

"I have them. I'll mail copies to you. Does this inmate know where I am? Do I need a restraining order? Can he take away the little I have to support my daughter and me?"

"He probably won't seek you out as long as he hopes to profit from the lawsuit. The rest can only be determined by the court during the trial in December. Pruitt's lawyer will be contacting you to arrange for papers to be served. Don't discuss the case with him. Just set up a place and time where you can be given the papers by an impartial party."

Lawyer Lazarus called. "I'm sorry you lost your husband. I heard he left you something."

Seething anger tried to erupt. *So many rumors fly around the prison. Pruitt probably heard something like that. Don left me a lot of bills. You want to ask your client if he'd like to help me pay them?* I choked back the words. *It won't do any good to let him know he can provoke me.* "Do you have some papers to give me?" I replied evenly.

"Where can we find you?"

"Deliver them to the church office, my place of employment." *At least there I'll be surrounded by people.*

They came on the anniversary of Don and Heather's deaths. *It's a bad day anyhow.*

After the depositions, Van Longyear contacted me. "I'm recommending the state settle out of court. I don't think the case can be won in the wake of other court cases involving blacks and police groups."

Don wasn't prejudiced! He told me the district attorney's office was certain they could win when he was alive—but he's not alive now. "Isn't there anything I can do to defend the honor of the man I loved? He'll be assumed guilty of a crime he didn't commit."

"Probably not."

The state settled the case out of court October 19.

When the playground structures purchased with Uriah's memorial fund were dedicated, the school children gathered around the equipment they had painted rainbow colors. As Lonn read Psalm 100, tears trickled down Julie Maly's cheeks. I put my arm around her and cried with her. Lori Ray patted us on the back. Carrie Stroschein whispered, "I think you two need to look over there."

Instead of the usual hot, dry Blythe weather, clouds encircled the bright blue sky but didn't block the sun. We looked where Carrie pointed and saw a rainbow. Julie began to laugh and cry. "That Uriah. He's up there smiling down at us."

Thursday, October 22

The NMDP report informed me there was still $2,685.78 in the account.

Bob Jensen, a teacher and member of Zion Lutheran Church, came into the office. He handed me a copy of an essay Amanda Miller had written for US history. "The assignment was to write about a leader in their life."

Why is he giving this to me?

Leader in Your Life

There are many famous leaders in our nation. I choose to recognize a person who isn't famous, but someone who I admire. This person is a local resident in Blythe, her name is Mara Alexander. I feel that she is a great leader of life. She has been through much pain in life, yet she still lives on and helps other people through life. She lost her husband and daughter to a car accident and her son to cancer. She is one strong woman. She works at the local newspaper, helps out the Lutheran Church, which she attends, helps within the school, and does her best to support her other daughter, who is all the family she has left. Even through all her losses and trouble she remains loyal and faithful to God and her friends. That's why I believe she is one of the greatest leaders and I admire her.

I don't think that I share too many qualities with her. I feel that if I was to go through everything that she has gone through, I wouldn't be able to survive and go on with my life. I would probably hate life and I wouldn't be a very pleasant person. All though I do feel in certain situations I would make a good leader. I am always willing to listen and try and help when I can. I also believe in standing up for what you believe in, and I think that to be a leader of a cause or anything you have to be willing to stand up for what you believe in.

I'm flabbergasted. You can never tell who's watching you! I wrote her a letter:

Thank you so for sharing your leadership essay with me. I never thought of myself as a leader, and I didn't realize anyone noticed what I do. It just goes to show that everything we do affects someone.

Although you feel you don't have much in common with me, I think you have many qualities that will make you able to overcome the obstacles that we all face in life. Being willing and able to listen, always being willing to try, focusing on helping others instead of yourself, being willing to stand up for what you believe is right—even if you stand alone—those truly are the qualities of a real leader. Your ability to empathize with someone else who has experienced something you never have is a valuable asset and is unusual in one so young. May it serve you well in the future.

I really am not strong; I am very weak and I know it. So instead of relying on my strength, I let go and let God. He is my strength and my shield. Although a lot of tragic things have happened to my family, I know that "all things work together for good for those who love the Lord." The same God who could turn His Son's torture and death into a victory can do the same with all the tragedies in my life. I know that God has a plan for Shiloh and [me]. I may not be able to see it now—it's like looking at the wrong side of a tapestry—but someday I will see the right side, and I will rejoice in that bright kingdom with those I miss now.

God bless you, Amanda. You are special—don't ever forget that.

Love in Christ,
Mara

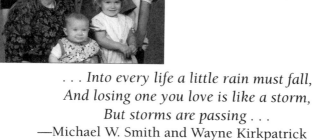

Twenty-Six

Storms Passing
(1993–Present)

> *. . . Into every life a little rain must fall,*
> *And losing one you love is like a storm,*
> *But storms are passing . . .*
> —Michael W. Smith and Wayne Kirkpatrick

D ANNY CONTINUED TO COURT ME. HE'D COME FROM SAN DIego to Blythe for the weekend on business but arranged to continue working in Blythe after he met me. The more I got to know him, the more I fell in love.

Palo Verde Valley Times, November 11, 1992:

Alexander, Azlin to Wed

A January 9, 1993 wedding is set uniting Mara Lee Alexander . . . to Danny Ray Azlin. . . . The bride-to-be is a secretary at Zion Lutheran School and has been in Blythe three years. The groom-elect is a building inspector from San Diego, currently working on the new prison.[1]

February 22, 1993

Hi! Mr. and Mrs. Danny Azlin—Thought you might need an extra copy—Lovely picture—wish you years of happiness—God's blessings.

Sincerely,
Dave and Ruth Sheppardson

Only months later, she joined Uriah.

Friday, April 2. *A sympathy card from Debbie DeForge to Mara Alexander? But why?*

Dear Mara,

I'm sorry I don't remember your new married name. I was real hesitant in writing this to you. I just found out about the tragedy in your family.

I was at Kaiser in a support group that they have gotten together. I just cried when I heard [your husband and daughter were killed three months after Uriah's death], I couldn't believe it. I'm so sorry, I don't even know what to say. They told me that you have had your church and God to help you through this, and of course your new husband and your daughter. I'm glad to hear you are still letting God in your life, sometimes people don't and they blame Him for the tragedies. The ladies at the group told me that your daughter wasn't doing too good. I hope she has improved and I will pray for her. She has been through so much; you all have. My thoughts and prayers are with you.

Love,
Debbie DeForge

Memorial Day, 1993

Debbie's family, Andria, Brian, and Shiloh placed flowers by the gravestones Shiloh and I had designed. Danny and I took pictures while they knelt by Don's black stone etched with a fishing pole and tackle box, gun, and target. BELOVED HUSBAND, FATHER, SON, FRIEND. I WILL REMEMBER YOU.

Joel stuck a pinwheel next to Heather's shiny blue stone, which sparkled in the sun. A scroll with roses and a prancing unicorn bordered the inscription: AWAY WITH FRIENDS IN HER MANSION FOREVER.

A pinwheel spun beside Uriah's rainbow stone, engraved with clouds and a rainbow above mountains. Trees surrounded the inscription: THERE'S A RAINBOW BE-HIND THE CLOUDS.

It's time to move on. Shiloh's graduated. Danny's completed his work on the new prison and needs to return to the San Diego area.

Monday, August 16

We moved to a rental home in San Marcos, California. Shiloh was homesick, but we needed a home close enough to Danny's work and his boys.

Tuesday, September 7

The baby's kicking hard enough that I can feel it with my hand.

October 2, 1993, 2:30 A.M.

This letter is to you, Shiloh, my fair, sweet child.

I dreamed you were younger—one of those angelic, smiling faces that I put into the photo album today. You brought me a drawing you'd made of an intricate cross, its top encircled in a halo shaped like a thunderous cloud. "It's wonderful," I told you. "But it could have been better if you'd added a little shading here and there." You kept smiling, and I could feel how much you loved me. I felt stupid for missing the whole point.

I awoke and thought of the times you brought me little pictures and loving notes. I enjoyed them, yet, I missed the point; I never realized how much those pictures meant to me or how I'd miss them when they no longer came.

When you and I slept in the same room after they all died, you used to ask me to read to you. I tried to spend more time with you and cut down on the hours I worked, but I wasn't quick enough, and my little girl grew into a young woman while I was in the midst of my grief.

I'm so thankful for this baby; when you are no longer here to hug me, there will be a small person to hold. I wonder, how was Nana able to let us go? It's hard for me to watch you grow up and let you go. It's probably the hardest part of being a parent.

I'll treasure every wonderful moment before you move out and I see you only a few weekends a year. Our life together will be forever at an end—until this world passes.

P.S. No, this does not mean you don't have to do chores anymore! (Ha, ha!)

October 16, 1993

It was so odd how I ran across these today. A bunch of pictures from a 1987 bake sale! God must have wanted me to find them. Yesterday was Jason's birthday. He would have been 22. Those were some of the happier

moments. It's nice to smile and remember in the midst
of our busy lives.

All my love,
Margot

There sat five-year-old Uriah stuffing a cupcake into his
mouth. I held grinning Uriah in his purple, Garfield "Cat-
Lover" shirt. Joel, Heather, Uriah, and Shiloh munched chocolate cupcakes. *Someone once told me grief never goes away, it
just changes. I have to agree. Earlier those pictures would have
caused a flood of tears and a stab of pain, but now they cause
warmth to fill my heart and mind, like the glow of a beautiful
sunset in the distant past. I can't make new memories of those
who have gone from my life, but every now and then God re-
veals a glimpse of them I never saw before. What a wonderful
gift! Thanks, God! Thanks, Margot.*

November 1993

"Diana Leach . . . plans to participate in the 1994 LA
Marathon on March 6 in memory of Larry Miller's grand-
son Uriah who died in 1991 . . . after a long and brave
battle with leukemia. All proceeds benefit the local Leukemia Society of America. . . ."
Mara—Thought you would want to see the fliers
using the materials you sent. Thank you.

Sincerely,
Diana Leach

Thursday, January 13, 1994
I smiled and handed pencils and stickers to donors
who beamed as they pulled sleeves down over their

bandages. Hazel Sayers of the San Diego Blood Bank drifted over to me. "There's Paul," she nodded toward a blond, robust eight-year old with prednisone cheeks.

"Thanks for arranging this drive," I said. "It's important that all the money in Uriah's account be used."

"Well, this ought to do it. We're having a pretty good turnout," she said.

"I hope Paul finds someone."

"The odds are better every time we hold a test."

February 5, 1994

As I snuggled under the covers, I gazed out at the stars over Valley Center. "Boy, Danny, I'm really tired even though I didn't help much."

"I hope you didn't do too much. Isn't this a great house?"

"Yep. I'm glad we're all moved in since the baby is due any day." I stiffened as a sudden sensation like a sitz bath washed over me. "Honey! Quick! Get a towel!"

Danny rushed off while I struggled to my feet. He returned with a hand towel. I giggled at the absurdity of his minuscule offering. "No, honey. A big towel!"

Hours later, Kaylynn greeted the dawn with tears of surprise.

Memorial Day, 1994

Shiloh and her boyfriend Bill carried flowers across the cemetery, while I followed with Kaylynn. I overheard her tell Bill, "I understand now that life is like a book. When you finish one chapter, you open the next one and go on."

She's finally able to go on with her life!

A few days later she showed me a picture she'd drawn. A little heart-shaped butterfly flew from a dark room through an open window into the beautiful world outside. *For years she's drawn pictures of a heart pierced by a dagger, dripping with blood. My prayers have been answered! God, I'm so glad she's escaped her pain at last!*

Friday, April 29.

"I'm calling about my son's NMDP account."

"Account number?" the clerk asked.

I looked at the old statement I held. "Account number two?"

"Two?" he repeated doubtfully.

"It's been open for a long time."

"Uriah Alexander?"

"That's right." *I never realized how early we came into the NMDP program. If Uriah had needed them earlier, they wouldn't have been there.*

"The account is closed now. I'll send you a copy for your records."

Eighteen hundred thirty-seven people were tested at a cost of $91,496. *God, that's so much more than the 100 donors I dreamed of in the beginning. Thank You! You take my small dreams and make them more than I hope for, if I let You. Just like loaves and fishes. Added to CPOF's testing that's over four thousand, and only You know how many more were tested for Uriah at the City of Hope and the blood bank.*

Friday, May 12, 1995

I caressed the face of the tiny, sleeping, baby boy nestled in the crook of my arm. *God, You are so kind to give me a son and daughter again.* "The Lord giveth and the Lord taketh away," *and as Job found, You give again.*

August 1995

God, it's hard for me to understand why some people who gave me lots of support during Uriah's illness have themselves been visited with tragedy. Terri Tam's daughter has leukemia. Tracy Sudyka's daughter, Haley, was diagnosed with leukemia. John Mullion's mother remains in an inexplicable coma. Jeri Allen's daughter died too. At least they all have You in their lives.

The dark-haired cashier in Blythe's Kmart looked at me closely. "I know you don't know me, but you're Mara, aren't you?"

I nodded in mute surprise.

"Jeannie's my aunt," she gushed. "I just had to tell you, Andrew's getting off of his chemotherapy next week! We're so happy. It looks like he's going to be OK!"

Wow! Andrew DeLeon found a donor, but he's doing so well he won't need one. Uriah would be pleased. And somehow, I think he knows.

$$\approx\quad\approx\quad\approx$$

On Tuesday, April 23, 1996, I turned from my computer and picked up the ringing phone. "Hello?"

"Mara? This is Maggie Kim. I have a surprise for you. I've been meaning to call you about a bone-marrow donor who's sitting in my office. He's a CHP who tested to be a donor at one of Uriah's drives. He gave Uriah a cap."

"I know who it is: Carlos Castro!"

"Yes! He matched a twelve-year-old boy and gave the transplant April nineteenth. He'd like to talk to you if that's OK?"

"Sure!"

Carlos cleared his throat. "I've felt guilty for years that I wasn't able to return to visit Uriah again. I hope I've redeemed myself a little by being a donor."

"Are you kidding? That's exactly what Uriah wanted—that someone might live, even if he couldn't. I'm sure Uriah's smiling down on you. You're an answer to prayer. Can I share this information in my book?

"Sure. My wife can't wait until she matches!"

All of this seems to come out of the blue. How like You, God. Your timing is so perfect! And You don't leave loose ends. Even though You've so often provided in miraculous ways, it still amazes me when You step in and touch my life again. Just as Jesus' disciples were astounded when He fed five thousand with a boy's lunch, I'm astonished at the incredible impact Uriah's eight short years of life made when placed in Your hands.

Tuesday, September 17, 1996

Danny and I attended a marrow donor's dinner at the San Bernardino Blood Bank. Maggie Kim, Tami Brown, and others from our search for Uriah's donor were there. "I think of her as one of our 'founding fathers,'" Maggie said before she handed me the polished walnut Founder's Award. "She was there when the NMDP first started helping host donor drives."

They've come a long way: May 1, 1995, their registered donors number 1.6 million with 3,380 transplants completed.[2]

On vacation in the summer of 1995, we stopped at Morro Bay. As I hiked through the sandy dunes toward the pounding surf, I spied a lone sign surrounded by flowers. The words were faded by years but still legible:

In memory of our sons who died February 19, 1989: Steven Doody : Christopher Cabral

May you always walk in sunshine,
And God's love around you flow.

For the happiness you gave us,
No one will ever know.
It broke our hearts to lose you,
But you did not go alone;
A part of us went with you,
The day God called you home.
A million times we've needed you,
A million times we've cried.
If love could only have saved you,
You never would have died.

I stumbled away with tears in my eyes and scanned the liquid, blue horizon that swelled and crashed into white foam where the sand ended. *How true that was of Uriah. So many people praying and helping, yet it wasn't God's wish that he remain here with us.*

I still think about Don, Heather, and Uriah every day. Just because they're gone doesn't mean they're forgotten. *Thanks, God, for giving me such a patient, understanding husband. Danny doesn't resent the pictures of my first family across from the pictures of our family, or the time I've spent writing. He's encouraged me.*

God, it would be easy to remain in the past and dwell in old, happy memories, but You have new adventures for me. I'm still climbing that staircase—I hope being a stepparent is the hardest thing I ever have to do. The kids are great, God, I just wish I had more wisdom to handle every unusual dilemma. Five kids are definitely my limit!

The sun turned the clouds to bright orange as it kissed the horizon. I watched Shiloh, Daniel, Zack, and Kaylynn looking for shells while Danny carried Justin. *My family is getting so big, God! Someday we'll all be together in Your kingdom on the other side of life. What a reunion that will be!*

Notes

Cover Photo

Original photo by Nick Souza, copyright © 1990 by the Press-Enterprise. Reprinted with permission.

Chapter One

1. B. R. Birkiner, M.D. and G. Hoffman, M.D. *The Blood Handbook* (Vancouver and Point Roberts: Hartley and Marks, Inc., 1992), 172.

Chapter Two

1. Heavilin, Marilyn Willett, *December's Song* (San Bernardino: Here's Life Publishers, Inc., 1988), 21.

Chapter Three

1. Newton, "Our Dear Sweet Aaron," *Inland Empire Chapter of Candlelighters Newsletter,* vol. 3, no. 3, June 1984, 6.

Chapter Seven

1. Frances F. Sharkey, M. D., *A Parting Gift*, 44. Copyright © 1982 by Frances Sharkey, M.D. Reprinted by permission of Frances Sharkey, M.D. All rights are reserved by the author.
2. Ibid., 147.
3. Ibid., 152.
4. Ibid., 167.
5. T. B. Walington, "Cytomegalovirus and Transfusion," John D. Cash, ed., *Progress in Transfusion Medicine*, vol. 2, (Edingburgh and New York, Churchill Livingstone, 1987), 27, 31, 35.

Chapter Nine

1. Lonn Maly, ed., "Good-bye Mrs. Owens," *Zion Times*, 6 September 1989, vol. 9, no. 2, 1. Used with Permission.

Chapter Thirteen

1. Louise Skura, "Uriah has hope for donor," *Fontana Herald-News*, 1 August 1990, A1. © 1990, The *Fontana Herald-News*. Reprinted with permission.
2. Dona James, "There's a rainbow behind the clouds," *Palo Verde Valley Times*, 8 August 1990, 1. © 1990, The *Palo Verde Valley Times*. Reprinted with permission.
3. "Warden urges support," *Palo Verde Valley Times*, 8 August 1990, 1. © 1990, The *Palo Verde Valey Times*. Reprinted with permission.
4. "Community of Blythe united in projects," *Palo Verde Valley Times*, 10 August 1990, 1. © 1990, The *Palo Verde Valley Times*. Reprinted with permission.
5. Ibid.
6. Peggy Olsen, "8-year-old Uriah looking for the perfect match," *Inland Valley Daily Bulletin*, 16 August 1990, F1. © 1990, The *Inland Valley Daily Bulletin*. Reprinted with permission.
7. Ibid.
8. "Some pain in saving stranger," *Inland Valley Daily Bulletin*, 16 August 1990, F1. © 1990, The *Inland Valley Daily Bulletin*. Reprinted with permission.
9. "Keep the love and prayers flowing," *Palo Verde Valley Times*, 17 August 1990, 1. © 1990, The *Palo Verde Valley Times*. Reprinted with permission.
10. Ibid.
11. Tommy Li, "Leukemia victim, 8, tries to pack full life into time remaining," *San Bernardino County Sun*, B1. © 1990, The *San Bernardino County Sun*. Reprinted with permission.
12. "Donor testing dates draw near for Uriah," *Palo Verde Valley Times*, 22 August 1990, 1. © 1990, The *Palo Verde Valley Times*. Reprinted with permission.
13. Ibid.
14. Copyright © 1990 by KECY TV. Reprinted with permission.
15. "123 test as marrow donors for Uriah," *Palo Verde Valley Times*, 29 August 1990, 1. © 1990, The *Palo Verde Valley Times*. Reprinted with permission.

Chapter Fourteen

1. "Take me out to the ball game," *Palo Verde Valley Times,* 29 August 1990, 11. © 1990, The *Palo Verde Valley Times.* Reprinted with permission.

2. "Uriah back in hospital," *Palo Verde Valley Times,* 5 September 1990, 1. © 1990, The *Palo Verde Valley Times.* Reprinted with permission.

3. "Ice-sitting contest planned," *Palo Verde Valley Times,* 5 September 1990, 2. © 1990, The *Palo Verde Valley Times.* Reprinted with permission.

4. "Bone-Marrow Donor Needed," Mt. Calvary Lutheran Church, Lake Arrowhead, September 1990 newsletter. Reprinted with permission.

5. "Blood drive set next Friday for Uriah," *Palo Verde Valley Times,* 7 September 1990, 1. © 1990, The *Palo Verde Valley Times.* Reprinted with permission.

6. © 1990, the *Inland Valley Daily Bulletin.* Reprinted with permission.

7. Copyright © 1990 by Sarkes Tarzian, Inc. Used with permission.

8. "Uriah: Blood drive today, golf and dinner this weekend," *Palo Verde Valley Times,* 14 September 1990, 1. © 1990, The *Palo Verde Valley Times.* Reprinted with permission.

9. Ibid.

10. Michel Nolan, "Fate of 8-year old hangs on transplant from some stranger," *San Bernardino County Sun,* 16 September 1990, B1. © 1990, *The San Bernardino County Sun.* Reprinted with permission.

11. "Dinner-dance for Uriah pays off," *Palo Verde Valley Times,* 16 September 1990, 1. © 1990, The *Palo Verde Valley Times.* Reprinted with permission.

12. Peggy Olsen, "Group to hold fund-raiser to help boy with leukemia," *Inland Valley Daily Bulletin,* 18 September 1990, B3. © 1990, The *Inland Valley Daily Bulletin.* Reprinted with permission.

13. Copyright © 1990 by KCBS TV. Reprinted with permission.

14. "Battle for Uriah continues," *Palo Verde Valley Times,* 19 September 1990, 1. © 1990, The *Palo Verde Valley Times.* Reprinted with permission.

15. For Better or for Worse. © Lynn Johnson Productions, Inc./Dist. by United Features Syndicate, Inc. Reprinted with permission.

16. Copyright © 1990 by KABC TV. Reprinted with permission.

17. Tommy Li, "Volunteers brave needles for boy with leukemia," *San Bernardino County Sun,* 27 September 1990, B1. © 1990, *The San Bernardino County Sun.* Reprinted with permission.

18. Sharon Greengold, "Donors give to help little boy live," *Inland Valley Daily Bulletin,* 27 September 1990. © 1990, The *Inland Valley Daily Bulletin.* Reprinted with permission.

Chapter Fifteen

1. *Courier,* Rialto Community Baptist Church, October 1990. Reprinted with permission.

2. Paul Hughes, "Educators seek donors for stricken child," *Inland Valley Daily Bulletin,* 6 October 1990, B3. © 1990, The *Inland Valley Daily Bulletin.* Reprinted with permission.

3. "Firemen help," *Palo Verde Valley Times,* 10 October 1990, 8. © 1990, The *Palo Verde Valley Times.* Reprinted with permission.

4. "Remembering," Palo Verde Valley Times, 10 October 1990, 8. © 1990, The *Palo Verde Valley Times.* Reprinted with permission.

5. Jeremiah 28:9.

6. "Successful party," *Palo Verde Valley Times,* 17 October 1990, 2. © 1990, The *Palo Verde Valley Times.* Reprinted with permission.

7. "Students make cranes," *Palo Verde Valley Times,* 24 October 1990, 3. © 1990, The *Palo Verde Valley Times.* Reprinted with permission.

8. "Chicano Correctional Workers Association," *Chuckawalla Chatter,* July 1991, 2. Reprinted with permission.

Chapter Sixteen

1. Peggy Olsen, "Bone-marrow donor recounts emotional bond with recipient," *Inland Valley Daily Bulletin,* 5 November 1990, B3. © 1990, The *Inland Valley Daily Bulletin.* Reprinted with permission.

2. Peggy Olsen, "Young leukemia victim is living on borrowed time," *Inland Valley Daily Bulletin,* 5 November 1990, B3. © 1990, The *Inland Valley Daily Bulletin.* Reprinted with permission.

3. "No match for Uriah so far," *Palo Verde Valley Times.* © 1990, The *Palo Verde Valley Times.* Reprinted with permission.

4. "Uriah . . ." *Palo Verde Valley Times,* 16 November 1990, 3. © 1990, The *Palo Verde Valley Times.* Reprinted with permission.

5. Tommy Li, "Leukemia patient suffers fourth relapse," *The San Bernardino County Sun,* 21 November 1990, B1. © 1990, *The San Bernardino County Sun.* Reprinted with permission.

6. "Uriah needs your prayers," *Palo Verde Valley Times*, 21 November 1990, 1. © 1990, The *Palo Verde Valley Times*. Reprinted with permission.

7. Ibid.

8. George Cushman, "Recognize the specialness," *Palo Verde Valley Times*, 23 November 1990, 2. © 1990, The *Palo Verde Valley Times*. Reprinted with permission.

9. Peggy Olsen, "Victim hopes for a miracle," *Inland Valley Daily Bulletin*, 29 November 1990. © 1990, The *Inland Valley Daily Bulletin*. Reprinted with permission.

Chapter Seventeen

1. Copyright © 1990, Correctional Peace Officers Foundation, Inc. Reprinted with permission.

2. Theresa Kelm, "Thanks to Blythe," *Palo Verde Valley Times*, 21 December 1990, 4. © 1990, The *Palo Verde Valley Times*. Reprinted with permission.

3. Janet Gilmore, "Boy's wish: the right donor," the *Press-Enterprise*, 25, December 1990, B1. Reprinted with permission from the *Press-Enterprise*.

4. "Blythe is special," *Palo Verde Valley Times*, 28 December 1990, 4. © 1990, The *Palo Verde Valley Times*. Reprinted with permission.

Chapter Eighteen

1. Glenn Mueller, "Number 1 in '91, Accept the Challenge," *CPO Family Newsletter*, 1 January 1991, vol. 2 no 1, 3. © 1991, Correctional Peace Officers Foundation, Inc. Reprinted with permission.

2. Carolyn Conner, "Sierra C/Os Roll Up Their Sleeves to Help Uriah," *Peacekeeper*, February 1991, vol. 9, no. 2, 3. © 1991, *Peacekeeper Magazine*, California Correctional Peace Officers Association. Reprinted with permission.

3. Robin Richards, "Hospice helps in times of sorrow," *Palo Verde Valley Times*, 27 March 1991, B1. © 1991, The *Palo Verde Valley Times*. Reprinted with permission.

Chapter Nineteen

1. "CVSP annual picnic tomorrow at Mayflower," *Palo Verde Valley Times*, 26 September 1991. © 1991, The *Palo Verde Valley Times*. Reprinted with permission.

2. "Blythe chapter named number one," *Palo Verde Valley Times*, 1 May 1991, 1. © 1991, The *Palo Verde Valley Times*. Reprinted with permission.
3. Carolyn Baschal, "The Rainbow," reprinted with permission.
4. "Jesus Answers," Words and Music by Michelle Wagner and Dwight Liles, Copyright © 1991, Ariose/Paragon Music Corp./ASCAP. All rights reserved. Reprinted by special permission of Brentwood-Benson Music Publishing, Inc. and Ariose Music.

Chapter Twenty

1. Mara Alexander, "Keep the prayers coming for Uriah," *Palo Verde Valley Times*, 28 June 1991, 1. © 1991, The *Palo Verde Valley Times*. Reprinted with permission.

Chapter Twenty-One

1. "Eye of the Hurricane," Words and Music by Phil Madiera. Copyright © 1989 by Little Dude Music/ASCAP.
2. Dona James, "Where did the rainbow go?", *Palo Verde Valley Times*, 3 July 1991, 1. © 1991, The *Palo Verde Valley Times*. Reprinted with permission.
3. Mara Alexander, "The Shadow of Freedom," *Palo Verde Valley Times*, 3 July 1991, 1. © 1991, The *Palo Verde Valley Times*. Reprinted with permission.
4. Tommy Li, "Fontana boy with leukemia dies; search for marrow donor futile," *San Bernardino County Sun,* 4 July 1991, B1. © 1991, *The San Bernardino County Sun*. Reprinted with permission.
5. Dedication to Sandra by Wayne Watson, Copyright © 1990 Word Music, Inc. (ASCAP), 65 Music Square West, Nashville, TN 37203/ Material Music, Inc. (Admin. By Word Music, Inc.) (ASCAP) 65 Music Square West, Nashville, TN 37203. All Rights Reserved. Made in the U.S.A. International Copyright Secured. USED BY PERMISSION.
6. "Home Free" Words and Music by Wayne Watson, Copyright © 1990 Word Music, Inc. (ASCAP), 65 Music Square West, Nashville, TN 37203/ Material Music, Inc. (Admin. By Word Music, Inc.) (ASCAP) 65 Music Square West, Nashville, TN 37203. All Rights Reserved. Made in the U.S.A. International Copyright Secured. USED BY PERMISSION.

Chapter Twenty-Two

1. Mara Alexander, "Four-year old stricken," *Palo Verde Valley Times,* 30 August 1991, 1. © 1991, The *Palo Verde Valley Times.* Reprinted with permission.
2. Leslie G. Stant, ed. "Young Boy's Struggle for Life Helps Others," *HemoGlobe,* Fall 1991, 4. © 1991, Blood Bank of San Bernardino and Riverside Counties. Reprinted with permission.
3. Mara Alexander, "Bake sale to benefit young leukemia victim, Saturday," *Palo Verde Valley Times,* 20 September 1991. © 1991, The *Palo Verde Valley Times.* Reprinted with permission.

Chapter Twenty-Three

1. Lonn Maly, ed. *Zion Times,* 9 October 1991, vol. 11, no. 7, 1. Reprinted with permission.
2. **"I Hear Leesha,"** Words and Music by Michael W. Smith and Wayne Kirkpatirck. Copyright © 1988 by Milene Music, Inc. and Careers-BMG Music Publishing, Inc. All Rights Reserved. Used by permission.
3. Dona James, "Two claimed in crash," *Palo Verde Valley Times,* 4 October 1991, 1. © 1991, The *Palo Verde Valley Times.* Reprinted with permission.
4. Ibid.
5. "Alexanders' killer identified," *Palo Verde Valley Times,* 9 October 1991, 1. © 1991, The *Palo Verde Valley Times.* Reprinted with permission.
6. Lonn Maly, ed. "Alexander Memorial Service," *Zion Times,* vol. 11, no. 8, 1. Reprinted with permission.

Chapter Twenty-Four

1. Copyright © 1991, Correctional Peace Officers Foundation, Inc. Reprinted with permission.

Chapter Twenty-Five

1. Mara Alexander, "Thank You, CPOF," *CPO Family,* Fourth Quarter 1992, vol. 2, no. 6, 12. © 1992, Correctional Peace Officers Foundation, Inc. Reprinted with permission.

Chapter Twenty-Six

1. "Alexander, Azlin to Wed," *Palo Verde Valley Times*, 11 November 1992, 12. © 1992, The *Palo Verde Valley Times*. Reprinted with permission.

2. "International network expands to 1.6 million volunteers," *Marrow Messenger*, 1995, vol. 5, 2.

To order additional copies of

Beyond The
RAINBOW

Have your credit card ready and call

(877) 421-READ (7323)

or send $22.95 each plus $3.95* S&H to

WinePress Publishing
PO Box 428
Enumclaw, WA 98022

* add $1.00 S&H for each additional book ordered